Erik J. Zürcher is Professor of Turkish Studies at the University of Leiden and Director of the International Institute of Social History at Amsterdam. He is the author of numerous books on Turkey, including Turkey: *A Modern History* (I.B.Tauris), which has been translated into seven languages; *Arming the State: Military Conscription in the Middle East and Central Asia, 1775–1925; Identity Politics in Central Asia and the Muslim World; and Men of Order: Authoritarian Modernization under Atatürk and Reza Shah* (all I.B.Tauris).

GW00646510

The
YOUNG TURK LEGACY

AND NATION BUILDING

From the Ottoman Empire to Atatürk's Turkey

ERIK J. ZÜRCHER

I.B. TAURIS

LONDON · NEW YORK

In memory of Erik Zürcher
1928–2008

First published in 2010 by I.B.Tauris & Co Ltd. Reprinted 2012, 2014
6 Salem Road, London W2 4BU
175 Fifth Avenue, New York NY 10010
www.ibtauris.com

Distributed in the United States and Canada Exclusively by Palgrave Macmillan
175 Fifth Avenue, New York NY 10010

Library of Modern Middle East Studies: 87

ISBN: 978 1 84885 271 6 (HB)
      978 1 84885 272 3 (PB)

A full CIP record for this book is available from the British Library
A full CIP record is available from the Library of Congress

Library of Congress Catalog Card Number: available

Printed and bound CPI Group (UK) Ltd, Croydon, CR0 4YY

Contents

Preface: Thirty Years of Turkish History

The year 1977 was a year of beginnings and ends. It was the year that Punk and New Wave music made their major breakthrough (with albums by The Clash, The Ramones and The Talking Heads among others) and in which Liverpool FC won its first of many European cups. It was the last year the Orient Express, by then a slow and rather dirty shadow of its former self, ran between Paris and Istanbul. It was also the year in which a 24-year-old student of Turkology (to use the quaint terminology of European oriental studies) at Leiden University, who incidentally had been on the Orient Express four times in the preceding years, took a stab at his first attempt at historical research on early twentieth-century Turkey. I was that student, and the product of my attempt was my MA thesis on the Izmir conspiracy of 1926 and the subsequent political trials.

Over the years many people have asked me, as undoubtedly they have asked every single one of my colleagues, what it was that first brought me to Turkish studies. As one does on such occasions, I have come up with many reasonable and plausible answers, but the only honest one would be: 'I really don't know.' Having a father who for many years held the chair of East Asian history at Leiden, obviously rendered thinking about oriental studies an option. If one can make a living studying Chinese or Sanskrit, anything is possible. Around age 12 I became fascinated with the classic adventure books of the German author Karl May, not the better known ones about a hero implausibly called Old Shatterhand among the North American Indians, but the ones about the equally implausible protagonist called Kara Ben Nemsi, a German traveller in the Ottoman Middle East of the late nineteenth century. In spite of the rather strong anti-Turkish bias in these books (which romanticized 'noble savages' like the Arab Bedouins and Albanian and Kurdish tribesmen) they produced in me a lasting fascination for the Ottoman Empire. I wrote term papers and did assignments on the Ottomans in high school. To find true faith of course one first has to be tempted and I was, playing seriously with the idea of studying Japanese before enrolling in the Middle East Studies programme of Leiden University. Once there, I opted for Arabic as my first language, but after a dismal first year, in which I failed nearly every exam, changed to Turkish. That choice had as much to do with the teachers as with the subjects taught. Having achieved my 'candidacy' (the equivalent of the modern BA), I concentrated on Ottoman and Turkish history in my MA years, guided by an inspirational and erudite teacher, Dr Alexander de Groot. As for the last two years of my studies I was the only student in the class, it was just as well that I hit upon such a good teacher. The alternative does not bear thinking about. I myself must have been less inspiring, at least that is what I concluded when on one occasion I looked up from my reading of a seventeenth-century Ottoman chronicle to find my teacher sound asleep.

My MA thesis, though flawed in many respects, determined the direction my research in the next decades would take. It was based on a hunch, an idea that there was something very strange about the way the conspiracy and the trials of 1926 were depicted in Turkish and Western historiography. After all, in that historiography, the creation of modern Turkey was portrayed as the work of one man, Mustafa Kemal Atatürk, and a small circle of supporters. It was also depicted as having started in 1919 after the demise of the empire and disappearance of the Young Turks. Yet, in this historiography the 1926 purges were a way for the new, Kemalist, regime to deal with a threat from the outside, i.e. that of the former Unionists. But why was there a need, seven years after the end of the Unionist regime and three years after the establishment of the republic to purge the remaining leaders of the former regime as well as most of Mustafa Kemal's co-leaders of the national independence movement after World War I if the Kemalists had already successfully supplanted them? My conclusion was that the trials were political purges and that Mustafa Kemal felt the need for these because his movement in 1919 had been started by the former Unionists and he had only gradually taken control of it. The movement and the republic that came out of it were built on a foundation formed by the former Committee of Union and Progress (CUP), and its former leaders could therefore conceivably challenge Mustafa Kemal as its leader. The other group to be purged, Mustafa Kemal's co-leaders, were also former Unionists but had the added prestige of being national heroes of the independence war. They, too, could challenge his leadership and indeed had done so two years before, when they had started an opposition party, the Progressive Republican Party. In short, the independence movement and the republic were started and led by Unionists and built on the remnants of the CUP. Far from being a reckoning with Unionist outsiders by Kemalist insiders as the accepted historiography would have it, the 1926 trials were a way for one group of former Unionists (that around Kemal) to ward off the challenges from within of other former Unionists who could contest Kemal's leadership because, like him, they had a credible claim on the loyalty of the political élite.

After completing the MA degree, and facing a second temptation (this time to enter the diplomatic service, which had always taken its share of Leiden orientalists), I started teaching in Nijmegen University and over the next 15 years produced two books that were the logical extension of the MA thesis. One of them was my Ph.D. thesis, defended in Leiden in 1984 and published as *The Unionist Factor. The Role of the Committee of Union and Progress in the Turkish National Movement (1905–1926).* This study emphasized the continuity between the Young Turk period in late Ottoman history and the early republic. It investigated Mustafa Kemal's place within the Committee and the Committee's role in the independence movement led by Kemal. My conclusion was far-reaching and ran counter to everything that was and is sacred in the official historiography of the Turkish republic. I attempted to show that the national resistance movement after World War I was not only built on the remnants of the CUP, but that the CUP leadership actually planned and organized the resistance and launched Mustafa Kemal as its leader. I described his struggle to become the unchallenged leader of the movement and explained the 1926 crackdown from the sense of vulnerability this left him with. The second book came out in 1991. It was entitled *Political Opposition in the Early Turkish Republic. The Progressive Republican Party (1924–5)* and it dealt with the background of the second group to be purged in 1926, the former co-leaders of the national resistance, who had broken with Kemal in 1924. The study tried to show that the Progressive Republicans had not been a conservative or even reactionary movement, but in fact part of the secularist and nationalist mainstream of the Young Turk movement. Where it differed from Kemal's wing was in its emphasis on separation of powers and economic liberalism. Both books had a fair degree of impact, especially after they had been published in Turkish translation.

My work on the embryonic phase of the Turkish republic naturally brought with it a confrontation with the established historiography and thus also a critique of the sources and of the generally accepted periodization. I strongly argued in favour of continuity between the late Ottoman Empire and the early republic, something that was perhaps best expressed in the textbook *Turkey. A Modern History* that appeared in 1993 and saw many editions and translations over the next 15 years. The second section of the textbook was called *The Young Turk Period 1908–1950*, a very controversial statement at the time although more widely accepted nowadays.

In the 1990s my interest gradually switched from the political intrigues of the élite to the social history of the period, as I came to see the period of World War I, the era least explored in the literature, as the most traumatic but also the most formative and important period in modern Turkish history. I became particularly interested in the history of conscription and the fate of the conscripted soldiery, but also came to realize that one cannot understand modern Turkey adequately without taking into account both the mass migration (and deportation) of Muslims from the Balkans and the Caucasus, the Armenian genocide of 1915 and the expulsion of the Greek orthodox. Together these processes produced the Anatolia that we know today.

Biography, and in particular the collective biography (or prosopography) of the Young Turk generation has remained a strong interest throughout as I have always felt very strongly that we need to get at the personal histories of the Young Turks and Kemalists if we want to understand their ideas and their political choices.

Early in 2008 I was tempted a third time to leave the field of Turkish studies and this time I succumbed, at least in part, when I accepted to become the general director of the International Institute of Social History in Amsterdam for four days a week, remaining for one day a week in Leiden University. This change seemed to be an excellent occasion to organize a small retrospective of my work of the past 30 years by bringing together the texts of some of the more interesting articles written during that period. Most of the chapters in this volume were published before, but quite a few may now be difficult to trace. Others were only published in Dutch or in Turkish.

The articles presented here have all been revised, some lightly and some quite thoroughly. Overlaps between different articles have been taken out as much as possible and in some cases several articles have been collapsed into a single new text. In the way the chapters have been arranged in the volume, I have tried to achieve at the same time a certain thematic unity and a logical chronological sequence. I am very grateful to Rachel Prager for the copy editing and correction of the English, and to Kim van der Zouw for the final editing. I thank Lester Crook, commissioning editor at I.B. Tauris, for his patience and encouragement.

Erik J. Zürcher
Leiden/Amsterdam.

I. SOURCES AND LITERATURE

Introduction

In the late 1970s and the 1980s, when I was just starting out in the field, Turkish state archives were still very inaccessible. This was especially true in the years after the military takeover of September 1980, precisely when I was working on my Ph.D. thesis. As a consequence, my efforts to present a version of early twentieth-century Turkish history that differed substantially from the generally accepted one had to be based largely on eyewitness accounts. These had been published in quite large numbers in the 1950s and 1960s, when the introduction of democracy and the lifting of censorship made it possible to do so. While many of these memoirs and autobiographies of protagonists of the constitutional revolution and the national independence struggle sold quite well in their day, their impact on the established version of 'the history of the Turkish revolution' (as the subject was and is officially called) remained negligible. History teaching at all levels remained true to the version propounded by Mustafa Kemal Atatürk in the years 1922–7 and elaborated on by his followers.

In this first part of the volume we encounter discrepancies between this official history, and a competing counter-history, written by Atatürk's contemporary, brother-in-arms and then adversary, General Kâzım Karabekir. His is but one of many memoirs, but it is especially interesting for two reasons: Karabekir took part in all the important events that marked Atatürk's life, so theirs can be seen as parallel lives; and the book Karabekir wrote (among many others, all of them published posthumously) adheres to the same format as *Nutuk*, Atatürk's great speech of 1927. It covers the same period, is long and detailed, and is supported by many documents.

Of course, when comparing different memoirs and even more so when we decide to use one set of memoirs to discount the version presented in another, the question of credibility comes into play. If we argue that Atatürk took liberties with the truth, why should Karabekir's account be viewed as any more truthful? I was very much aware of this problem when working with memoirs for my *Unionist Factor* (1984), and sought to tackle it the best I could by evaluating accounts on the basis of four criteria: consistency, inner logic, chronology and accumulation. The preferred version had to be consistent with what the author is saying elsewhere and to display a certain logic in the argument, it had to fit in with known chronological data and, preferably, it had to be confirmed in other, similar, accounts by other authors. Obviously the source gains in credibility whenever supporting documents are presented, in the original Ottoman even if not in facsimile. As I argue in the chapter on Karabekir, the reliability of the memoirs is often greatest, when the subject is furthest removed from the aim of the author. In other words and to give but one example: Whereas we do not necessarily have to believe every Young Turk who describes how he saved the fatherland almost single-handedly, there is good cause to believe him when he describes the initiation rites of the Committee for Union and Progress (CUP) in a way that is consistent with the descriptions presented in two or three other memoirs.

Recently, I have returned to the use of memoirs as a historical source when preparing for the chapter that follows on the historiography of the constitutional revolution and once again I have been surprised by the opportunities that close – and parallel – reading of these sources affords the historian, not instead of but in conjunction with archival sources. It is exactly in the similarities between memoirs of, for instance, Niyazi and Enver, that the pattern in the preparation of the revolution is revealed.

Efforts to undermine a hegemonic discourse like the Kemalist one on the basis of alternative sources almost inevitably lead to a discussion on the periodization that underlies the hegemonic version. Atatürk's speech and the whole historiography built on it, imposes a periodization that sharply separates the national struggle period after World War I from the preceding second constitutional period, and at the same time constructs continuity between this national struggle period and the following republican era. In the chapter on Atatürk's speech I argue that a diametrically opposed periodization, which emphasizes the continuities between the second constitutional period and the national struggle on the one hand and sees the imposition of the secularist republican regime in 1923 as a clear break with the immediate past makes more sense. As I have argued elsewhere,[1] it is also possible and interesting to attempt a further periodization within both the Young Turk period and the Kemalist one. In each of these periods we can discern three stages, one in which the movement can be characterized as a liberation movement (1906–08 in the case of the

CUP, 1918–22 in the case of the Kemalists), one in which victory has been achieved and democratic pluralism (including a free press and multi-party politics) gets a chance (1908–13 and 1922–5) and finally one in which an authoritarian regime is established during which the ruling party uses its monopoly on power to execute far-reaching reforms that probably would not have been possible under a democratic system (1913–18 and 1925–45 respectively).

One of the characteristics of the Kemalist view of history is that it is based on a strict black-and-white opposition between the forces of progress (identified as the *Tanzimat* reformers of the mid-nineteenth century, the Young Turks and of course the Kemalist republic itself) and the forces of reaction that try to reverse the process of modernization, to halt Turkey's progress on the 'road to contemporary civilization' (to use Atatürk's own phrase). As Andrew Davison has remarked,[2] the Kemalist interpretation fits very snugly in the modernization paradigm that became dominant in Middle Eastern Studies in the 1950s after the publication of Daniel Lerner's *Passing of Traditional Society in the Middle East*. It is only fitting therefore that a critique of one of the two most important books on Turkish history to come out of the modernization school, Bernard Lewis's *Emergence of Modern Turkey*, a book that dominated the field for a generation, should also be included in this part on sources and literature.

1. The Politician as Historian, Historians in Politics: On the *Nutuk* (Speech) of Mustafa Kemal Pasha*

In October 1927 Mustafa Kemal Pasha, the later Atatürk, delivered a speech to the congress of the Republican People's Party (RPP). All in all his speech at the congress, known in Turkish historiography simply as *Nutuk* (Speech), would take 36 hours and 33 minutes, spread out over six days.

In this chapter I analyse the character of this speech and its role in the modern history and historiography of Turkey. It is a subject that has been significant for me personally, for my first foray into the field (my research of the years 1978–84 into the role of the CUP in the Turkish independence struggle and that of the years 1985–9 into the first opposition party of the republic) often involved a direct confrontation with the version of the history of the period 1919–27 left to us by Atatürk.

In the spring of 1927 Atatürk began preparations for the great speech he was to deliver in the autumn. He had at his disposal in his presidential villa in Çankaya both his own correspondence files and the most important dossiers from the archives of the republic. His method of working was as follows: first he would seek out the most important documents, then he would take notes, and from these notes he would then dictate for several hours on end to secretaries who would be regularly relieved. The production of the day would often be tried out on his circle of trusted friends and collaborators, who were invited almost every night to the presidential villa to eat, drink and talk. It therefore comes as no big surprise that it was common knowledge in Ankara in 1927 that the president was preparing a detailed survey of the events since 1919.[1]

In the night of 22–23 May Atatürk for the second time in four years suffered a mild heart attack,[2] which temporarily interrupted the writing of the speech. After resting for two weeks, he then travelled to Istanbul for further recovery at the end of June. This was actually the first time he set foot in the old capital since he had left it in May 1919. He settled himself in the old sultan's palace of Dolmabahçe on the shore of the Bosphorus and there he continued to work on the text.

His efforts ultimately resulted in the six-day speech at the first party congress of the RPP, the party that had been founded by Atatürk himself in 1923 and that was the only legal party in Turkey at the time. Atatürk spoke every day for about three hours in the morning and again for three hours in the afternoon, from 15 to 20 October. The newspapers, which since the spring of 1925 had been under tight government control, published summaries of the president's words every day.

Officially, the subject matter of the speech was the history of the emergence of the new Turkey, from the start of the national resistance movement in 1919 until the year 1927. In reality, the story ends roughly at the end of 1924, with the events in the years 1925–7, comprising 30 per cent of the period discussed, covered in only about 1.5 per cent of the total text. It is possible that this last period would have received more attention had Atatürk been able to continue his work during the summer, but I don't think that was the case. The lack of attention to the most recent years can be adequately explained in light of the real purpose of the speech, to which I will return later.

Publication history

Shortly after the party congress the speech became available in print under the auspices of the *Türk Tayyare Cemiyeti* (Turkish Aeroplane Society).[3] There were two editions: a luxury edition in two volumes, the text of which had been printed in Istanbul with maps and illustrations printed in Vienna; and a popular edition, also in two volumes, on cheaper paper. Of the popular edition the Ministry of Education printed and distributed 50,000 copies. To put this number into perspective, Turkey at the time had about 13.5 million inhabitants, and only about 1.4 million of those inhabitants were literate.[4] A first edition of 50,000 is enormous when set off against this number (the equivalent of a print run of about 10.7 million copies in the contemporary USA) and indicates the importance attached to the text by the leadership of the Turkish republic right from the start.

In later years there were three more editions of the original text, all of them in the new Latin alphabet that had been introduced from January 1929. Those of 1934 and 1938 were published by the Ministry of Culture, that of 1952–9 by the Institute for the Study of the Turkish Revolution (*Türk Devrim Tarihi Enstitüsü*) for the Ministry of Education. This last-named edition was reprinted 14 times until 1981.[5] With the exception of the cheap and heavily subsidized edition of 1938, all editions in the new alphabet consisted of three volumes, two of them containing text and one with supporting documents.

Apart from these editions of the original text, which in linguistic terms can only be termed Ottoman source documents, the Turkish Linguistic Society (*Türk Dil Kurumu*) beginning in 1963 issued at least six printings of a version called *Söylev*. 'Söylev', a neologism, is synonymous to 'nutuk' and is used to designate a version of the text that has been converted, or translated, into 'pure' Turkish by replacing most of the originally Arabic and Persian vocabulary with Turkish words, many of which had been newly created by the society. In 1973–5 yet another, different, modernized version appeared at Ankara University Press, this time in two volumes and without the supporting documents.[6] This edition was a reaction to the one published by the Turkish Linguistic Society a decade earlier that had been judged artificial and purist by many. This time there was an attempt to write in a more natural Turkish, closer to the everyday usage of the 1970s. Finally, the committee in charge of the celebration of Atatürk's 100th anniversary in 1981 decided to make one more attempt to render the Ottoman of the 1927 version into modern Turkish in a manner that would have made the text accessible and, it was hoped, enjoyable to read. The commission was given to Professor Zeynep Korkmaz and she produced the book in a single volume in 1991.[7] It was published by the Atatürk Research Institute in Ankara and it is probably the most successful of the conversions. It goes without saying that in their efforts to modernize the text each of the editors had to make choices in which a great deal of interpretation was involved.

The reason that these editions in contemporary (or supposedly modern) Turkish appeared was that the generations that could read and understand Atatürk's text were starting to die out. Atatürk's language is late Ottoman. He modelled his style on that of the great mid-nineteenth century writer and politician Namık Kemal, with whose work he became familiar through his schoolmate, the Young Turk poet and orator Ömer Naci.[8] Although Namık Kemal's style was considered refreshingly direct and modern in the 1860s and 1870s, his language is full of vocabulary and syntactical elements borrowed from Arabic and Persian. The same is true for Atatürk' usage in the *Nutuk*. Of the vocabulary roughly 85 per cent is derived from these languages. The language reform that Turkey has undergone from the 1930s has had such a great cumulative effect that modern-day Turks cannot read the text without special training.

The conversion of the text into modern Turkish is called 'simplification' (*sadeleştirme*) or 'purification' (*özleştirme*) in the different editions themselves. Nowadays the process is usually called 'translation into Turkish' (*Türkçeye çevrilme*), a term that seems to indicate that for modern Turks Ottoman is no longer seen as part of their own language. It is ironic that this is true even for the language of the founder of modern Turkey.

A really simplified version also exists in the shape of a kind of 'children's bible' published by the newspaper *Milliyet,* and over the years the *Nutuk* has also been the subject matter of several (very serious) comic books.

The *Nutuk* was translated into French, German and English immediately after its first appearance. All of these translations were published by Koehler's publishing house in Leipzig, Germany. The German translation by Dr Paul Roth[9] is excellent, but the two other versions that were translated from the German, are unreliable. Nevertheless, the English translation[10] has been reprinted by the Turkish Ministry of Education twice, in 1962 and 1973. A Russian translation in four volumes appeared in Moscow in the years 1929–34.

Given the attention the text has received and the dominance it has acquired as the master narrative for the history of Turkey in the years 1919–27, it is surprising that there still does not exist a truly scholarly, critical edition of the *Nutuk*. The manuscript, including corrections made by Atatürk himself on the typescripts produced by his secretaries, was kept in the presidential palace during his lifetime and then deposited in the safe of the Agricultural Bank in Ankara. Later it was moved to the archives of the War History Department of the Turkish General Staff (ATASE), which is perhaps the most inaccessible of all Turkish archives. To the best of our knowledge that is still where it remains. A critical edition based on the manuscript, the existing archives and the accounts of Atatürk's contemporaries undoubtedly would fill an important void. Very recently, in the spring of 2008, a team of leading Turkish historians (Ahmet Kuyaş, Cemil Koçak, Mete Tunçay and Zafer Toprak) announced their intention to publish a critical edition, in which they will collate the text with evidence from Atatürk's contemporaries.[11] Its publication will be a significant step forward, but the project is based on the published version of 1927, not on the manuscript.

The influence of the *Nutuk* on Turkish historiography

The *Nutuk* has exerted immense influence on the historiography of the national resistance movement and the emergence of the republic, both inside Turkey and outside the country. Turkish history textbooks for school and university paraphrase the *Nutuk* or include whole sections. In the popular writing on Turkey, as well as in most of the academic literature, the version of events presented in the *Nutuk* is preserved in its essential points. This is true both for publications from Turkey and for those from abroad.

Undoubtedly, Atatürk's unassailable position as the liberator and founder of modern Turkey partly explains the acceptance of his words as objective truth. The existence of a law banning defamation of Atatürk in Turkey also plays a role, but beyond that, it also has to do with the degree to which we have at our disposal independent sources to verify Atatürk's account. Here the situation is still far from satisfactory. For many years the restrictive archival regime in Turkey was criticized by historians both inside the country and out, and rightly so, but since 1989 both access to, and cataloguing of, the main collections in the state archives (the Ottoman and Republican Archives of the Prime Ministerial Archives, *Başbakanlık Arşivi*) has vastly improved. With some exceptions, the material older than 50 years that has been catalogued is now also freely accessible to historians.

Where research on the *Nutuk* is concerned, however, this does not solve all the problems. For the history of the national independence movement and the birth of the republic, the main subjects of the *Nutuk*, the ATASE, the collections of the Institute for the Study of the Turkish Revolution and the presidential archives (which hold the 'Atatürk Archive') are the most important archival resources and they are far less accessible. Because of this prevailing situation, not only foreign historians, but also Turkish ones, have recourse to the archival records of Britain, the United States, France, Germany and Russia. They, however, can only very partially replace the Turkish materials and they are of very little use where the real subject of *Nutuk* is concerned (of which more below).

No systematic publication of documents on the Turkish independence movement has ever been undertaken, in spite of the importance attached to the 'history of the Turkish revolution and principles of Atatürk', a required subject in secondary and higher education in Turkey. The Turkish press is very useful source for the period up to March 1925, when very strict censorship was introduced under the Law on the Maintenance of Order (*Takrir-i Sükûn Kanunu*). Before that, the press, which had grown into a mature medium in the second constitutional period, was quite active and critical.

Finally, we have at our disposal the accounts of Atatürk's contemporaries and colleagues. Many of them have published their reminiscences, but almost without exception they did so starting in the 1950s, when the liberalization of the Turkish political system and the softening of censorship created a climate in which this was possible. Where the Turkish-speaking public was concerned, therefore, the *Nutuk* held sway as the unchallenged truth for about 25 years, long enough for it to completely dominate historiography as it evolved in the republic. When, from the 1950s onwards, increasing numbers of memoirs appeared that differed from the version given in the *Nutuk*, even if they did not openly challenge it, it was too late for them to have any serious influence on the established, official historiography that was being taught in schools and universities. The official version, based on Atatürk's testimony, was perpetuated in textbooks and primers. With the increase of ideological challenges to Kemalism in Turkey from the 1960s onwards, the correct teaching of 'history of the Turkish revolution and the principles of Atatürk' gained added importance as an antidote in the eyes of the Kemalist state, which promoted Ataturkism in general, but with even more emphasis in the context of the celebrations of 50 years of republic (1973, at the end of the army-backed tutelary regime of 1971–3), the centenary of Atatürk (1981, a year after the military takeover led by general Kenan Evren) and the 75th anniversary of the republic (1998, a year after the ousting of the Islamist government of Necmettin Erbakan by the military).

What is the *Nutuk* about?

In Atatürk's own words he intended to 'explain how a great nation, which was thought to have come to the end of its national existence, had gained its independence and had founded a national and modern state based on the latest principles of science and technology'. He would be happy if he 'had been able to clear up some points that would be able to make my nation and our future children attentive and wakeful'.[12]

Generally, his claim that the *Nutuk* is essentially concerned with writing the history of the independence struggle and the founding of the republic has been accepted both in Turkey and abroad. Beginning in the 1970s, there has been some discussion in Turkey on the questions of whether the text should be seen as straight history or as a source for historiography, and whether it was right for a politician like Atatürk to write history himself, rather than leaving that task to later generations.[13] Some commentaries appear to recognize that the speech is also a political document, with their characterization of the *Nutuk* as a manifesto with which Atatürk symbolically closes one period and points the way to the future. After all, he emphasizes that 'this is the story of a period that has finally come to an end'. This aspect receives scant attention in the discussion, however, and anyway is not seen as something that undermines the essential truthfulness and reliability of the account. In the eyes of Turkish historians the reliability of the *Nutuk* is demonstrated by the inclusion of a large number of original documents. The fact that these were selected by Atatürk himself is not seen as a problem.

In my view this approach fundamentally fails to appreciate what the *Nutuk* is about and why it was written. To understand its true function, we have to set the speech in the time and context in which it was conceived.

The years immediately preceding the giving of the speech in October 1927 were not only a period of far-reaching, radical reform; they were also the period in which all forms of political opposition were suppressed. The tensions within the People's Party between proponents of an authoritarian regime and radical reform on the one hand and moderate liberals on the other had resulted in late 1924 in a split in the party and the founding of an official opposition party, the Progressive Republican Party (*Terakkiperver Cumhuriyet Fırkası*) (PRP) by a number of leading figures in the national resistance movement. With the exception of Fevzi Çakmak and İsmet İnönü (who, in 1924, were chief of the general staff and prime minister, respectively), all the top military leaders of the liberation war (i.e. Kâzım Karabekir, Refet Bele, Ali Fuat [Cebesoy],[14] Cafer Tayyar [Eğilmez], Hüseyin Rauf [Orbay]) joined the opposition. At first the opposition was tolerated, but when a Kurdish rebellion broke out in the southeast in February 1925, the radicals in the RPP used it to proclaim martial law, push through the Law on the Maintenance of Order (*Takrir-i Sükûn Kanunu*) and institute 'Independence Tribunals', which dealt summarily with opponents of the regime. The Kurdish rebellion was suppressed, but so too were the opposition party and the independent press.

In the summer of 1926 the discovery of a plot to assassinate the president was used to eliminate all potential rivals to Atatürk and his party. In two show trials, one in Izmir and one in Ankara, the remaining former leaders of the CUP and the top ranks of the PRP were accused of complicity. Most of the former Unionist leaders, people like Cavit and Dr Nâzım, were given a death sentence and hanged, but the former PRP leaders, as heroes of the liberation war, possessed enormous prestige among the population and especially within the army, rendering similar treatment for them too risky. The only PRP leader who was convicted was Hüseyin Rauf [Orbay]. This former naval captain had become a national hero due to his exploits with the cruiser *Hamidiye* during the Balkan War, and he had been the resistance movement's second most important figure until his arrest by the British in March 1920. After nearly two years of internment on Malta, he had returned to serve as prime minister of the national resistance movement in 1922–3. After falling out with Atatürk in 1923, he had become the leader of the PRP in 1924. Following the suppression of the opposition party he had left the country and settled in London. The Izmir independence tribunal convicted him *in absentia* to ten years imprisonment with hard labour in July 1926, but Rauf defended himself in two open letters, addressed to the president of the Turkish national assembly. In these letters he characterized the behaviour of the government and the independence tribunal as unlawful, pointing out that many of the accused were parliamentarians who were entitled to inviolability under the constitution. Copies of the letters were sent to the editorial offices of all major Turkish newspapers.

When Atatürk first started to write his great speech these events lay only a few months in the past, and the position of the generals and the way they had been treated in the tribunals were still debated among the public. I am convinced that the *Nutuk* has to be seen, and read, primarily as an attempt by Atatürk to vindicate the political purges six months earlier. Criticism of the leaders of the opposition and systematic belittling of their role in the independence struggle between 1919 and 1922 are recurrent themes in the *Nutuk*. At least 52 passages are devoted to criticism, innuendo and sarcasm directed against the former opposition leaders.[15] Hüseyin Rauf [Orbay] and Kâzım Karabekir, the most prominent PRP leaders, are singled out for the most vehement attacks. Also, 20 per cent of the text is devoted to the split in the nationalist movement after the proclamation of the republic in 1923 and the emergence of the opposition. This process is described as a dark plot, even an attempt at a coup d'état, inspired primarily by Rauf. In this context it is only logical that the story of the *Nutuk* more or less ends in early 1925, for by June of that year the opposition was effectively crushed.

The events of 1925–6 are summarized by Atatürk in one short paragraph:

> Of course, all these activities ended in a success for the republic. The rebels were crushed. But the enemies of the republic did not accept that the great conspiracy had reached its final pages. They undertook one more vile attempt. This attempt showed itself as the Izmir attack. The courts of the republic once more succeeded in saving the republic from the hands of the attackers.[16]

If we accept that the *Nutuk*'s real character is that of justification and even a kind of apology for a, still hotly debated, political purge, we will not be surprised to find that in some places it gives us a rather lopsided view of historical realities. Let me try to summarize where in my view this is most obviously the case. More important than any number of details are those parts of the account that implicitly or explicitly have given us a warped view of the history of this period because they suggest either ruptures or continuities that really were not there.

The speech begins with Atatürk's landing in Anatolia. His first words are: 'On 19 May 1919 I landed in Samsun.' He then depicts the situation of the Ottoman Empire at that moment: exhausted and in despair, with only some local groups calling for resistance against the dismemberment of the empire. This picture distorts reality in a number of ways. First, the regional resistance committees were formed at the behest of a central organization founded and manned by the CUP, which most probably also enabled Atatürk's own appointment as army inspector for east and central Anatolia. The resistance movement was over six months old by the time he arrived in Anatolia. Atatürk describes the Unionists as usurpers who tried to take over his independent Anatolian organization, while in reality it was *he* who gradually managed to get a grip on the organizations *they* had founded. So in his version the continuity between the period before the end of the World War (the second constitutional period) and the national resistance movement is blurred.[17]

Second, Atatürk throughout his speech suggests that the independence struggle was waged in order to establish a new national Turkish state. He says this plan informed all his actions but that it was a 'national secret' that could only be revealed piecemeal. As he carried out his far-reaching reforms (abolition of the sultanate and caliphate, proclamation of the republic, moving the capital to Ankara etc.), former collaborators with limited views of the future deserted him. The distortion involved here is that we lose sight of the fact that the independence struggle was waged in the name of the continued independent existence of (a part of) the Ottoman Empire in a period when the capital Istanbul was under occupation. The large majority of those who took part (including most of the cadres) undoubtedly saw themselves as fighting for 'king and country'. It is significant that the campaign medals with which soldiers were decorated after the battle on the Sakarya in 1921 were Ottoman ones, and equally significant that the sultan's birthday was officially celebrated in Ankara until 1922. Atatürk may well have cherished the idea of establishing a Turkish national state, but this certainly is not what motivated the movement as such.

A third important distortion is the continuity that is suggested between the national movement of 1919–22 and the RPP in 1927. The independence struggle had been directed by the Great National Assembly, which had opened in April 1920 and was composed of former Ottoman parliamentarians, who had managed to escape Istanbul, leading military officers, former provincial party bosses of the CUP, notables and religious leaders. In the elections for the second Great National Assembly in the summer of 1923 only candidates handpicked by Atatürk were allowed to stand and accordingly this second assembly was dominated by his followers, mostly officers and bureaucrats. The representatives in this assembly first met on 9 August 1923. There, they reconstituted themselves as the parliamentary arm of the People's Party (*Halk Fırkası*) and decided that the new party would take over all material and immaterial assets of the national independence movement. The national liberation struggle was thus fully identified with the People's Party and it was this that allowed Atatürk and his circle to denounce those former leaders of the independence movement as traitors when they left the party in 1924.

Not only the text of the *Nutuk* plays a role in this third form of distortion. The place where the speech was held is important as well. Formally, the speech was a report to the congress of the (by then Republican) People's Party and was accepted as such by the congress. In justifying his actions in the years 1919–23 to the representatives of the party founded only in the latter year, those actions become part of the history of the party. To illustrate this point, the 1927 congress is officially always called the 'second congress of the People's Party'. The first congress of the national resistance movement, in Sivas in September 1919, is retrospectively claimed as the first congress of the party.

With the above I hope to have demonstrated that, while it is true that the *Nutuk* has the outward characteristics of a piece of history writing, its form and content are ultimately determined by Atatürk's contemporary political agenda. It is the product of a politician engaging in historiography to vindicate himself, to strengthen his position and seal his hold on power: aims that Atatürk had achieved gradually between 1923 and 1926.

At the same time, historians who engage with the version laid down in the *Nutuk* or even contest its historical character, as I have done here, also involve themselves in a political debate. This is certainly true for Turkish historians who do so, and it is one reason why even those Turkish historians who relate events in a manner that clearly diverges from the *Nutuk* never make a point of saying so. The official Turkish historiography based on the *Nutuk* is to a large extent an instrument to render the social, ethnic and religious divides in Turkish society innocuous. If there is one thing the nation can gather around, it is the heroic period in modern Turkish history and its protagonist, the founding father of the republic. A critical attitude towards Atatürk's role is almost completely confined to groups with an extremist political agenda and in these circles it often degenerates into a mess of conspiracy theories and unconfirmed rumours. It is therefore incumbent on the historian of modern Turkey, who confronts Atatürk's version in the conviction that the Turks ultimately can only benefit from a realistic assessment of their recent past, to be aware of these sensitivities. In this way the decision of a politician in 1927 to act as a historian forces the historian of today to act politically.

2. Young Turk Memoirs as a Historical Source: Kâzım Karabekir's *İstiklâl Harbimiz**

Historians of the Western world generally take it for granted that good historical research, especially when it is concerned with the modern period, has to be based on primary sources. In the language of the historian this nearly always means archives. For the historian of the Middle East, however, it is often impossible to consult the relevant archives. The older collections are often inadequately systematized or catalogued and the modern archives are often seen by the nation states of the Middle East, which guard them, as too sensitive to be opened to researchers, especially to foreigners. This also obtains for Turkey. Up until the late 1980s there, too, access to the archives, even for Turkish historians, was limited. The *Başbakanlık Arşivi* (Archives of the Office of the Prime Minister), into which the Ottoman state archives are incorporated, were for all intents and purposes closed for the period after 1914. Since then, the situation has drastically improved. While not all collections are open to everyone, the access policy is far more liberal, cataloguing has improved a lot and there are now excellent facilities for copying materials.

In a situation with limited access to archives, the historian who strives to evaluate the current representation of historical events in modern Turkey has to look for alternative sources, which can take the place of the archival materials as primary sources, even if only temporarily. These alternative sources include foreign archival collections, published documentary collections,[1] contemporary Turkish and foreign press[2] and the memoirs and autobiographies of the protagonists of the period.

A large number of works in this last-named category have appeared in Turkey in the last half of the previous century, especially in the 1950s and 1960s.[3] They frequently offer facts and opinions about the history of the national independence movement and the Kemalist 'revolution', which differ considerably from those of the generally accepted Turkish historiography. Important was the account of the national resistance struggle published by Halide Edip [Adıvar], which in places was quite critical of Atatürk. Halide Edip was a well-known author and educator, but hardly a leading person in the resistance movement (in that respect her husband, Abdülhak Adnan Adıvar was far more important). Nevertheless, her book, *The Turkish Ordeal*,[4] published in 1928, was very influential – influential, that is, with a European and American audience, as the book was originally written in English and only translated into Turkish a generation later.

As was mentioned in the previous chapter, one can discern in Turkey an 'official' or 'orthodox' historical tradition which has developed since the mid-1920s on the basis of Mustafa Kemal Atatürk's own version[5] and which has ever since been canonized in an endless stream of schoolbooks, official publications and popular histories and guarded jealously by the *Türk Tarih Kurumu*.[6] The dissident autobiographies and memoirs seem hardly to have affected this tradition, if at all, in spite of their sometimes wide readership. Nevertheless, used in combination with other types of sources and with each other, these works may offer the opportunity for an important recasting of the image created by the Kemalist tradition.

The value of these Turkish memoirs and autobiographies for the historian is very unpredictable. It is determined by a number of factors. In the first place there is the character of the author and the motives behind his writing. There are the circumstances in which he writes, and the time-lag between the events he describes and the time of writing. Because of the gradual liberalization of the political climate in Turkey from the 1950s onwards many memoirs have only been published 25–30 years after the events described in them (which is not to say that all of them were only written at that time, of course). There are also wide-ranging variations in the form in which the memoirs are presented. In some cases we are dealing with verbal accounts or notes which have been turned into a book by the protagonist himself or by one of Turkey's many popular historians or journalists with an interest in historical topics, such as Cemal Kutay, Feridun Kandemir or Samih Nafiz Tansu. Examples of this type of work are the memoirs of Ali Fethi [Okyar],[7] an important young Turk officer and later Prime Minister of Turkey, and of Hüsamettin Ertürk[8] and *Kuşçubaşızade* Eşref,[9] both important members of the *Teşkilât-ı Mahsusa* (Special Organization), the Turkish secret service in World War I, which played such an important role in the independence movement after 1918.[10] These kinds of memoirs are generally unsupported by documents and are meant as a form of entertainment for a large public. They should therefore be used only with the utmost caution. At the other side of the spectrum – as far as information and controllability are concerned – are those works which really only consist of a connecting text between (some-times large numbers of) published documents. Examples of this type are Mustafa Kemal Atatürk's own *Nutuk*[11] of 1927 and Kâzım Karabekir's *İstiklâl Harbimiz* (Our Independence War), which was only released in 1968.[12] In the analysis that follows, this last-named work, Karabekir's *İstiklâl Harbimiz*, serves as a vehicle for exploring the potential importance of this type of material.

Before going into its history and contents, it is perhaps useful to give a short biographical sketch of its author, Kâzım Karabekir Pasha (1882–1948), who is undoubtedly one of the major figures in the early history of modern Turkey.

Kâzım Karabekir was born in Istanbul in 1882 as the son of an Ottoman pasha. He received his education at the military schools of Fatih and Kuleli, and subsequently at the Military Academy (*Harbiye Mektebi*) and the General Staff College (*Erkân-ı Harbiye Mektebi*) in Pangaltı. In 1905 he graduated first in his class. At the military academy he made the acquaintance of Mustafa Kemal, the later Atatürk, who was senior to him by one year. In December 1906, when he was an officer with the staff of the Third Army in Macedonia, he joined the *Osmanlı Hürriyet Cemiyeti* (Ottoman Freedom Society). This was the secret committee founded in September 1906 in Salonica, which in 1907 merged with the *İttihat ve Terakki Cemiyeti* (Committee of Union and Progress, or CUP) of Ahmet Rıza in Paris, and in July 1908 brought about the constitutional revolution under this latter name.[13] Kâzım worked closely with Enver in establishing the all important cell in Monastir (now Bitola), but he never played an important political role in the CUP, concentrating instead on his professional career as a soldier. During World War I he fought on the Caucasian front, in Iraq and at the Dardanelles. When the armistice of Moudhros was concluded in October 1918, he found himself in Azerbaijan at the head of a Turkish expeditionary force. Soon after the armistice he was recalled to Istanbul to head the General Staff. This, however, he refused, and he instead assumed command of the Fourteenth Army Corps with divisions in Tekirdağ and Bandırma.

Kâzım Pasha was one of the earliest supporters of the idea to organ-ize a national resistance movement in Anatolia, plans for which were being hatched within the CUP and especially among its military members from October 1918 onwards. In early 1919 he ferried his troops in European Turkey to the Anatolian side. He was convinced, however, that a real basis for a national movement could only be found in the East, out of reach of the Entente powers. In March 1919 he succeeded in having himself appointed

Commanding Officer of the Fourteenth Army Corps (the former Ninth Army) in eastern Anatolia with headquarters in Erzurum. There he immediately supported the activities of the *Vilâyat-i Şarkiye Müdafaa-i Hukuk-u Milliye Cemiyeti* (Society for the Defence of the National Rights of the Eastern Provinces). This organization, founded in Istanbul in December 1918 by a number of prominent Unionists from the eastern provinces, sought to challenge Armenian claims on eastern Anatolia. At the time of Karabekir's appointment, it was in the midst of preparations for the famous congress of Erzurum (July 1919).[14]

In the earliest phase of the national resistance movement (1918–20) Kâzım Karabekir was the key military figure in Anatolia, because his force was the only regular army of any size the nationalists had at their disposal.[15] Kâzım successfully sabotaged the demobilization of his troops and in the autumn of 1920 he used them to force the Armenian republic to recognize Turkish territorial claims and cede the provinces of Kars and Ardahan to Turkey.

Thereafter attention shifted to the western front and Kâzım's role gradually became less important. From 1920 onwards he was nominally a member of the Great National Assembly, although he did not actually attend the meetings. He came to belong to that group of pioneers of the national resistance movement that was gradually cut off from the centre of power from 1923 onwards and that, under the leadership of Hüseyin Rauf [Orbay] (1881–1964)[16] opposed the radical and authoritarian tendencies of the group around Mustafa Kemal Atatürk. In 1924 this opposition culminated in the founding of the first opposition party of republican Turkey, the *Terakkiperver Cumhuriyet Fırkası* (Progressive Republican Party – PRP). Although the initiative for the founding of the party was not his, Kâzım sympathized. He resigned his army inspectorate in order to be able to take up his seat in the assembly[17] and was elected president of the new party, which presented itself as a moderate, liberal-democratic alternative to the governing party, the *Cumhuriyet Halk Fırkası* (Republican People's Party). From the start the new party was under pressure and it was not long before it was closed down after the introduction of the *Takrir-i Sükûn Kanunu* (Law on the Maintenance of Order) in March 1925. During this period of rather unsuccessful opposition, Kâzım remained a figurehead and did not play an active role either in the organization of the party or in the drawing-up of its programme.[18]

A year later the leaders of the PRP were among the groups, which were purged with the trials following the Izmir conspiracy in the summer of

1926.[19] Although Kâzım Karabekir and the other prestigious military leaders who had been involved with the PRP were acquitted, his career was at an end so long as the radical wing around Mustafa Kemal Atatürk dominated the scene.

In the years that followed, he lived in Istanbul, retired and embittered, and devoted himself to writing a large number of books and composing rather unsophisticated music. This life in relative obscurity lasted until after Mustafa Kemal Atatürk's death in 1938. He then made a comeback on the political scene, which served as a form of rehabilitation, but gave him no real power. In 1939 he was elected to the National Assembly again and from 1946 until his death two years later he even served as president of that body.

Of the many books, the manuscripts of which he wrote in the last 20 years of his life, by far the most important is his monumental (1,230 pages!) *İstiklâl Harbimiz*. This book is a richly documented history of the Turkish independence war on the basis of Kâzım Pasha's own experience and his personal archives, more than 1,000 documents from which are included in the text.

The history of the publication of this work is interesting in itself as an illustration of the development of the freedom of the press in modern Turkey. Kâzım Karabekir seems to have collected the materials and to have prepared the manuscript between 1927 and 1933. In 1933 he commissioned the publication of a short synopsis of his memoirs concerning the national resistance movement under the title *İstiklâl Harbimizin Esasları* (The Foundations of Our War of Independence) from the publisher Sinan Omur.[20] But in April of that year the printing was halted on the orders of *Kılıç* Ali (1888–1971) and *Kel* Ali Cetinkaya (1878–1949), two close associates of Mustafa Kemal Atatürk, who had played a prominent role in the persecutions of 1925 and 1926, as members of the *İstiklâl Mahkemesi* (Independence Tribunal) of Ankara.[21] The proofs of the book were collected and burned. However, the materials on which they were based had been rescued and hidden in time.[22] No publication, either of the synopsis or of the complete work was attempted during the rest of Kâzım Karabekir's lifetime, but after the victory of the Democratic Party in the elections of 1950 his heirs considered the political climate more promising and the publication of the memoirs was taken up again. First the *Esaslar* appeared in 1951. After this 'trial balloon' the publication of the larger work could be considered and in 1959 Karabekir's daughters commissioned the publishing house *Türkiye* in Istanbul to print and publish it. The printing of so large a work took considerable time, but in

July 1960 it was offered for sale. For some months it was sold without incidents in spite of the call for a ban in some newspapers. By now Turkey was ruled by the National Unity Committee (*Milli Birlik Komitesi*), a military junta, which had come to power in the coup d'état of 27 May 1960.

In January 1961 the whole situation concerning the publication of *İstiklâl Harbimiz* changed, when the public prosecutor started an investigation and later (in March) brought a lawsuit against the publisher of the book on the grounds of infringement of articles 1 and 2 of law 5816 of 1951, which made defamation of Atatürk's memory a punishable act.[23]

In the indictment 34 passages from the book were quoted in illustration of the charge. The fact that the decision to prosecute was made, however, probably had more to do with the person of the publisher than with the work itself. The publisher, Tahsin Demiray, was a controversial figure at the time as co-founder and first secretary of the Justice Party (*Adalet Partisi*), and the campaign against the book coincided with the first moves to found this party, which was a barely disguised heir to the ousted and outlawed Democratic Party (*Demokrat Partisi*). The trial of Demiray was suspended in October when he was elected to the National Assembly and thus received immunity. In 1965, however, Demiray decided not to stand for re-election and he himself then asked for the trial to be reopened. The case was won on a technicality, for the prosecutor had not decided to take action within six months of the original publication of the book in 1960, as demanded by law.[24] The book was eventually released for publication in November 1968.

İstiklâl Harbimiz is in many ways an anti-*Nutuk*. Both memoirs resemble each other closely in form and they also largely deal with the same subject matter and period, although Karabekir stops in 1922 with the victory of the nationalists over the Greek forces. Of the later period he says: 'The events of later date have been witnessed and are being witnessed by everyone.'[25] The fact that we know that he wrote at least the first version of his memoirs between 1926 and 1933 also makes it probable that the book is a reaction to the *Nutuk* and the mottos both of *İstiklâl Harbimiz* ('*İstiklâl harbi yaptık. Amilleri yazmazsa tarihi masal olur*' – 'We fought the independence war. If its creators do not write it, its history will become a fairytale') and of *İstiklâl Harbimizin Esasları* ('*Yanlış bilgi felaket kaynağıdır*' – 'Incorrect information is a source of disaster') can easily be interpreted as veiled criticisms of the *Nutuk*.

In a number of places the version of history given by Karabekir differs considerably from the one in the *Nutuk*, on which modern Turkish historiography bases itself for this period. The most important differences can be summarized as follows:

1. According to Karabekir, Mustafa Kemal waited and hesitated for too long, before he decided to join his colleagues who were preparing a national resistance movement in Anatolia.
2. When he came to Anatolia in May 1919, Mustafa Kemal tried to bypass the embryonic nationalist organization in the eastern provinces, which was preparing the congress of Erzurum, and to organize a separate national congress in Sivas. Only with difficulty could he be persuaded to come to Erzurum first and to convene the national congress in Sivas only afterwards.
3. Mustafa Kemal forced the movement to take an independent and radical line when he severed all communications with the government in Istanbul, in effect making the national movement independent, while most other leaders still saw it as a temporary emergency.
4. Much attention is devoted to the relations between the Turkish nationalists and the Bolsheviks. As commander on the eastern front Karabekir witnessed the development of these relations at close quarters, but while he realized the importance of Soviet aid, he found Mustafa Kemal too accommodating to the Bolsheviks and their ideas. Lacking the tactical subtlety of Kemal, he was afraid the latter was allowing them to take over the national movement.
5. Mustafa Kemal is accused of developing an authoritarian and extremist attitude, which, Karabekir claims, resulted in widespread mistrust within the movement, especially in the Eastern provinces, where even the nationalist activists were ideologically much more conservative than in the West. This feeling was strengthened by stories about the 'immoral' lifestyle of Kemal and his circle, and it led to attempts to oust Kemal from the head of the movement.
6. Karabekir criticizes Mustafa Kemal's last-minute decision in summer 1920 to call off the operations to recapture Kars and Ardahan due to pressure from the Bolsheviks.

Throughout, Karabekir emphasizes his own role, for instance when he describes his refusal to arrest Mustafa Kemal after the latter had come to Erzurum in 1919, even though he was ordered to do so by the government, and the fact that he continued to support him as leader even when he was dismissed from the army and his army inspectorate was offered to Kâzım himself. This crucial episode, when Mustafa Kemal only survived as leader thanks to the open support of Kâzım Karabekir, is left out of the *Nutuk* completely, but it is well documented in other memoirs.[26]

What can we say about the reliability of *İstiklâl Harbimiz*? When we review the criteria we listed earlier, we come first to the character and the motives of the author. Karabekir comes alive from the pages of his book as a rather limited, honest man with an unmistakable tendency for vanity and self-importance. He certainly was not a far-sighted politician. The book is clearly an attempt at vindication, written at a time when he was very bitter about his forced retirement and the way his role was depicted in the Kemalist sources, and especially in the *Nutuk*. Against this, the book may have been published in the late 1960s, but it was almost certainly written relatively shortly after the events described. It is extensively well documented and the documents appear to have been rendered quite faithfully.

As to the specific differences between Karabekir's version and that of Atatürk, the former is supported by other sources in several important instances. It is true that Mustafa Kemal was not one of the first high-ranking officers to leave for Anatolia in 1918–19 (he was involved in political intrigues in the capital for the first four to five months after his return from the front) and that others persuaded him of the rightness of the 'Anatolian option' and launched him on his way.[27] That he intended to bypass the Erzurum congress and replace it with a national congress of his own is confirmed by other memoirs, too.[28] Traces of criticism of Mustafa Kemal's authoritarianism and radicalism (and of his personal lifestyle) can be found in many places. Such sentiments seem to have been especially strong in the eastern provinces, leading to the establishment of the *Muhafaza-i Mukaddesat Cemiyeti* (Society for the Preservation of the Holy Traditions) in 1921.[29] In Ankara the founders of the *İkinci Grup* (Second Group) in the National Assembly in 1922 were motivated by the same factors.[30] Mustafa Kemal's reputation in this respect strengthened Enver Pasha's standing when the latter tried to return to Anatolia to replace Mustafa Kemal in the summer of 1921.[31] No doubt the attention devoted to this point in *İstiklâl Harbimiz* reflects Karabekir's own religiously conservative attitude, too.

The relationship between the Nationalists and the Soviet Union presents a complicated and fascinating problem.[32] While it is clear that Mustafa Kemal had to walk a tightrope, maintaining good relations with the Bolsheviks (essential for the survival of the nationalist movement) while avoiding 'sovietization' at the same time, it is most unlikely that he ever seriously contemplated founding a Soviet state in Anatolia. He played a very delicate game, which was perhaps beyond the grasp of Karabekir.

In addition to offering these striking differences with the 'official' version based on *Nutuk, İstiklâl Harbimiz* is a mine of information on all kinds of detailed questions. However, I hope that even the few points enumerated above may serve to give an idea of the potential value of Young Turk memoirs like Kâzım Karabekir's for a revaluation of modern Turkish history. In the next chapter Karabekir's memoirs will be consulted again, but this time with special reference to his years before 1908.

3. The Historiography of the Constitutional Revolution: Broad Consensus, Some Disagreement and a Missed Opportunity*

It is a characteristic of most revolutions that the defining moment, the iconic event by which they are remembered, is usually not the point at which the aims of the revolution were achieved, but a 'heroic' event that is taken to signal the start of the revolution. The declaration of independence on the Fourth of July is remembered as the key date of the American Revolution rather than the actual achieving of legal independence in 1783. The storming of the Bastille in Paris on 14 July 1789 has become a national holiday rather than the abolition of the monarchy in September 1792. Likewise, the storming of the Winter Palace in St. Petersburg on 25 October 1917 rather than the ultimate triumph of the Bolsheviks and the establishment of the Soviet Union was celebrated yearly in the USSR.

The constitutional or Young Turk revolution in the Ottoman Empire in July 1908 in many ways is a curious 'revolution'. It did not result in regime change as Sultan Abdülhamit II, who had been on the throne for 32 years, remained so after the revolution. It did not result in the establishment of a radically new revolutionary order, merely in the promise of the palace to act according to the Ottoman constitution adopted in 1876 and to reconvene parliament, which had been prorogued in 1878. This revolution is also an exception to the rule where its iconic event is concerned. What was celebrated during the final decade of the Ottoman Empire and even beyond it, during the national struggle period, was the date (10 July by the old *Mali* calendar, 23/24 July under the Gregorian one) on which the Sultan accepted the demands of the rebels and announced the reconvening of parliament, not any heroic act or event that started off the revolutionary process.

Perhaps the reason for this can be found in the fact that the early phase of the Young Turk revolution was anything but spectacular. There were no masses storming government buildings or braving the bullets of the forces of order; no barricades in the cities, no marches. Instead, what happened was that over a period of three weeks a handful of junior officers took to the hills of Macedonia with bands of between 20 and 200 irregulars – a series of events that went unnoticed in the big cities of the empire and garnered little attention even by the foreign observers of whom there were so many in the region. There were very few casualties, too. Several of the officers sent out by Abdülhamit to suppress the rebels and to investigate the activities of the underground Young Turk network were killed or wounded, but that was it. In fact, with mass action in an urban setting, bloody skirmishes that left many dead, summary executions and a true regime change at the end of it, the counterrevolution of April 1909 (the *31 Mart vakası*) and its subsequent suppression bear far more of the hallmarks of a classical revolutionary situation than does the constitutional revolution of 1908.

The literature

All of this helps explain why the actual run-up to the proclamation of freedom on 24 July receives relatively little attention in the specialist scholarly literature on the period. This literature basically falls into two categories. On the one hand we have the works dedicated primarily to the history of the Young Turk movement between its inception in 1889 and the revolution of 1908. On the other we have the studies concentrating on the Second Constitutional Period, up to 1913 or even 1918. For the purposes of this chapter I have looked at the works by Ernest Edmondson Ramsaur, Ahmed Bedevi Kuran, Yusuf Hikmet Bayur, Feroz Ahmad, Sina Akşin, Aykut Kansu, M.Şükrü Hanioğlu and George Gawrych.[1]

In the first category Ramsaur's *The Young Turks. Prelude to the Revolution of 1908* was for a very long time the outstanding work. As explained in its preface, work on the book started back in 1939, but was interrupted by World War II. The author only managed to return to his project when he was assigned to Turkey by the American Foreign Service in 1948 and the book was finally published in 1957 by Princeton University Press. In contrast to the scholars who followed, Ramsaur was in a position to actually interview some of the people involved in the Young Turk movement, but such interviews do not seem to have been important to him in his rendering of the events of June–July 1908, probably because none of his informants was directly involved in the events of the revolution. It is a bit of a mystery why, having taken the trouble to gain access to 'old Young Turks', Ramsaur should not have approached important eyewitnesses. Many key figures (Talât, Cemal, Enver, Kâzım Karabekir, Niyazi, Rahmi, Bahaettin

Şakir, Dr Nâzım) were dead by the time he returned to Turkey, of course, but people like Eyüp Sabri (died in 1950) and Mithat Şükrü [Bleda] (died in 1957) were still around.

For his account of the events of July 1908 Ramsaur relies on two published sources: Charles Roden Buxton's *Turkey in Revolution* and E.F. Knight's *The Awakening of Turkey*,[2] published in 1909 and 1910 respectively, as well as on newspaper articles and reports of the British embassy in Constantinople. The fact that Ramsaur's work was so long in the making enabled him to make use of the two important studies in Turkish on the subject that appeared in the 1940s. These were Ahmed Bedevi Kuran's *İnkılap Tarihimiz ve Jön Türkler* (1945) and *İnkılap Tarihimiz ve İttihad ve Terakki* (1948), both of which focus to a large extent on the pre-1908 history of the Young Turks. These books by a veteran of the Young Turk movement, who was a partisan of the anti-Unionist faction of Prince Sabahettin, contain a wealth of documents, primarily correspondence within the movement, of which Ramsaur only seems to have made sparing use. On the actual insurrection of June–July 1908, in which he was not directly involved, Kuran has very little to say – just a one-page overview of the best-known facts.

Ramsaur's summary of the events of June–July is very brief (only three pages), but on the whole accurate. What is clear, however, is that he is not well versed in the inner workings of the Committee for Progress and Union (CUP) or its predecessor in Macedonia, the Ottoman Freedom Society *(Osmanlı Hürriyet Cemiyeti)* founded in September 1906. As I will try to show later, he clearly misunderstands the position of Enver and others within the Macedonian underground, possibly because he relies so much on the accounts of adversaries of the CUP, who were not involved in the planning of the revolt.

Ramsaur's description of the early Young Turk movement stood as the main work on the subject in a Western language until the publication in 1995 and 2001 respectively of M. Şükrü Hanioğlu's definitive studies of the Young Turk movement before the revolution, *The Young Turks in Opposition and Preparation for a Revolution. The Young Turks 1902–1908*. Immeasurably better documented, both with archival materials and published works of the Young Turks themselves, these books set a new standard. The actual revolution itself is dealt with on pages 265–78 of the second book. Hanioğlu's account is the most detailed and best documented that we have at our disposal. He uses documentary evidence from both sides – Ottoman government archival documents that were produced as part of the government's effort to gain information on the Young Turk movement and to suppress it, and documents from the CUP later published in the weekly supplement to the Unionist party newspaper *Şurayı Ümmet*. In addition, Hanioğlu refers to the published memoirs of key activists Enver, Niyazi and Kâzım Karabekir.

Of the books dealing primarily with the post-revolutionary period, pride of place should go to Yusuf Hikmet Bayur's monumental *Türk İnkılabı Tarihi*. This ten-volume work, published between 1940 and 1967, was originally planned as a reference work for university teaching on the 'Turkish revolution' (meaning essentially the national independence struggle and the establishment of the republic), but Bayur rightly saw that the history of that period could not be understood or taught properly without first devoting attention to the final years of the empire. His perspective, it should be noted, was a modern and courageous standpoint at the time and one that ran directly counter to official Kemalist historiography. In the end, and in spite of its huge size, the work never progressed beyond the end of World War I. Bayur gives a detailed account of the events of May–July 1908 on pages 436–79 of the first part of his first volume. He himself was only 17 years old and living in Istanbul at the time of the revolution, so he cannot be regarded as having first-hand experience of the events that unfolded in Salonika, Resne (now Resen or Resjna) and the surrounding areas. Bayur was a politician, diplomat and administrator, and his legitimacy as an expert depends primarily on the fact that he was the grandson of Grand Vizier *Kıbrıslı* Kamil Pasha. Even though its first volumes, in which the revolution of 1908 is treated, were available by the time he resumed his research, Bayur's book does not seem to have been used by Ramsaur.

For his account of the revolution Bayur relies heavily on the memoirs of Adjutant-Major (*kolağası*) Niyazi, which were published in Istanbul in 1910 as *Hatırat-ı Niyazi Yahud Tarihçe-yi İnkılab-ı Kebir-i Osmaniden bir Sahife*.[3] For the basically unrelated, but contemporary Albanian demonstration at Firzovik (now Verisovic or Ferisaj), he takes his data from Süleyman Külçe's Firzovik Toplantısı ve Meşrutiyet.[4] Külçe served as adjutant and secretary to General Şemsi Pasha who commanded the Mitrovica garrison and who would be killed in Monastr when he was about to move against Niyazi's guerrilla band.

Niyazi's memoirs also determine the perspective of Feroz Ahmad's account of the revolutionary days in his *The Young Turks. The Committee of Union and Progress in Turkish Politics 1908–1914* published in 1969, which is based on Ahmad's Ph.D. thesis of 1966. The strength of Ahmad's book is undoubtedly in the analysis of the ebb and flow of the influence of the CUP in the high politics of the empire between 1908 and 1914. The revolution itself gets a relatively brief (10 pages out of 165) treatment. Here as elsewhere the author relies mainly on British diplomatic reports and on Ottoman newspapers, but for this part he also bases himself on Niyazi, both directly and through the very full summary of the latter's memoirs included by E.F. Knight in his book.[5] The works of Kuran, as well as the collection of documents from the days of the revolution published in 1956 by İsmail Hakkı Uzunçarşılı[6] are also referred to. For the Firzovik incident, Ahmad like everybody else depends heavily on Külçe's account.

The status of Ahmad's book as the history par *excellence* of the second constitutional period (at least until 1914) in English was rivalled by that of Sina Akşin's *Jön Türkler ve İttihat ve Terakki*, published in Turkish in 1980. In this work, too, the attention devoted to the actual revolution is slight, even more so than in Ahmad's *Young Turks*: 4 pages out of 308 (but it has to be taken into account that Ahmad stops in 1914, while Akşin continues until 1918). Akşin's summary of the main events seems to be based primarily on Niyazi's memoirs, Külçe's book and the histories of Bayur and Ramsaur.

The most recent monographic treatment of the Young Turk period is that by Aykut Kansu in his *The Revolution of 1908 in Turkey*, published in Leiden in 1997. More than any other of the cited works, Kansu concentrates on the revolutionary period itself, its immediate prelude (starting with the tax revolts of 1906) and its aftermath (up to and including the elections of 1908). Yet, again, in this book of 241 pages (excluding appendices) the revolution itself is treated in 12 pages (89–101). The account is based primarily on British diplomatic correspondence, but also on Niyazi and Knight, Bayur and Uzunçarşılı. For Firzovik, Kansu complements Külçe's story with the memoirs of Galip [Pasinler],[7] the officer sent to placate the Albanians at Firzovik, who, as a member of the CUP, in fact convinced them that they should demand the reinstatement of the constitution rather than go home.

Finally, a recent addition to the literature on the revolution written from a different angle needs to be mentioned. That is *The Crescent and the Eagle. Ottoman Rule and the Albanians, 1874–1923* by George Gawrych. Although published in 2006, the book is in fact a reworked and updated Ph.D. thesis defended in 1980. The framework in which the events of 1908 are described obviously is different from that of the others discussed here, as it focuses primarily on Albanian rather than on Ottoman history, but Gawrych's work distinguishes itself from earlier studies of Albanian nationalism in that he makes extensive use of Ottoman sources and emphatically sees the Albanian road to independence as a part of late Ottoman history. This is particularly relevant for two episodes: Niyazi's rebellion and the Firzovik gathering. Where his sources are concerned, Gawrych relies on the 'usual suspects' (Niyazi, Kuran, Ramsaur, Ahmad, etc.) but he makes significantly more use of Albanian authors, notably İbrahim Temo (one of the original founders of the CUP back in 1889) and İsmail Kemal [Vlora] (a Tosk feudal lord and leader of the Albanian national movement).

Consensus

The outline of the story of June–July 1908 is virtually the same in all of the literature reviewed here, although there are a surprising number of minor factual errors in various authors' accounts. The story goes as described below.

After discussions between the external headquarters of the CUP[8] in Paris and the internal headquarters in Salonica, a declaration was drawn up, in which new demands for reforms in Macedonia on the part of the great powers of Europe were rejected and in which the CUP revealed its existence. This declaration was then left at the foreign consulates in Macedonia. This put the Istanbul government on heightened alert and investigations into the existence of the CUP underground network were initiated. Supervising this work was the commander of the Salonica garrison, Nazim Bey, a brother-in-law of Enver. On 11 June, the eve of his departure to Istanbul, where he was to report on his findings, he was shot and wounded by a CUP *fedaî*. After this, the government redoubled its efforts to uncover the plot and as a result Major Enver Bey, who was implicated, had to go into hiding in the countryside. The CUP headquarters took this opportunity to ask him to set up a guerrilla band in the Tikvesh area north of Salonica,[9] where he had made his name in 1906–7 as a successful fighter against Bulgarian bands.

During this time the situation became very tense due to the discussions held between King Edward VII and Tsar Nicholas II in Reval (now Tallinn) on 9–10 June, where a reform plan for Macedonia was known to be on the agenda. Many in the CUP felt they needed to act now or it would be too late. One of them was Adjutant-Major Niyazi Bey, who commanded a battalion in his native Resne. Beginning on 28 June he started preparations to form a guerrilla band on the pattern of the Greek, Bulgarian and Serb bands that had become such a feature of life in Macedonia in the preceding decade. Having received permission from the Monastır headquarters of the CUP, he sprung into action on 3 July. Having lured the largest part of the garrison and its commanding officers out of town by spreading rumours of an approaching armed Bulgarian band, Niyazi with a group of followers broke into the garrison's arms cache and took 70 rifles, ammunition and 600 Turkish pounds. Thus equipped he took a band of some 160 volunteers with him into the hills. The group consisted in part of civil volunteers who thought they were going after Bulgarian Komitadjis and in part of CUP members who had been involved in the plotting since 28 June. Only nine regular soldiers from Niyazi's own battalion were involved.[10] Once in the hills, Niyazi was joined by another 30 volunteers from nearby Prespe.[11] He now stated his true aim, that is, to force the government to reinstate the constitution, and asked who wanted to join him in his struggle. Of the nine soldiers, four decided to return to their barracks in Resne. All the others followed Niyazi. The band, now called the 'National Battalion of Resne', started to roam from village to village, while Niyazi used the excellent telegraph network of the empire to send proclamations to local and provincial officials as well as to the palace demanding the restoration of the constitution.

In response to the rebellion, the government called up fresh reserve battalions in the province of Aydın,[12] and ordered General Şemsi Pasha, the commander of the garrison in the northern border town of Mitrovica and an experienced and loyal Albanian officer with excellent contacts among the Northern (Geg) Albanians, south to Monastir. Şemsi Pasha arrived in Monastir on 7 July and was about to move on to Resne with two battalions and an Albanian volunteer unit, when he was murdered by a CUP volunteer, Atıf [Kamçıl]. This murder is generally seen as the turning point in the revolution, for it eliminated a very dangerous opponent of the Young Turks, who could have mobilized Albanians against them, demonstrated the power of the CUP in the towns, and demoralized the palace, all at the same time.

In the days that followed Niyazi and Enver continued to roam the countryside and send telegrams, while a third CUP band of some 120 men now left Monastir for the direction of Prilep. From 14 July the reserve units from Aydın started to arrive in Macedonia, but CUP agents had worked on them and they proved unreliable for the government. Meanwhile several officers and police officials working for the palace were shot and on 22 July; Niyazi's 'National Battalion of Resne' along with Albanian bands (çetes) as well as a band from Ohrid, led by Adjutant-Major Eyüp Sabri (who had worked closely with Niyazi since early July), launched an attack on Monastir, which resulted in the kidnapping of *Tatar* Osman Pasha, the successor of Şemsi Pasha. In the meantime CUP activists in different places in Macedonia continued to shower the palace with telegrams demanding the restoration of the constitution, but now these took on the character of an ultimatum. The CUP threatened to have its forces march on the capital, if their demands were not met by 26 July. Instead of waiting for an answer, the Monastir branch of the CUP, which was now in control of the town and the most important garrison in Macedonia, proclaimed the reinstatement of the constitution on 23 July. Seeing that his options had run out, Sultan Abdülhamid followed suit that night and the reopening of parliament was announced in the Istanbul newspapers on the morning of the 24 July. The Young Turk revolution had taken place.

Independent from these developments, the gathering of Albanians at Firzovik that started on 5 July (two days after Niyazi took to the hills) added to the sense of alarm in Istanbul and in that sense contributed to the collapse of resistance from the palace. As described in the sources, the gathering was a spontaneous affair, triggered by rumours (which had been circulating for a few weeks) that the Austrian army was coming to the South. A planned picnic in the village of Firzovik for employees of the company that was exploring the building of a potential track for an Austrian railway through Macedonia somehow gave credence to these rumours. Albanians gathered to prevent the picnic. Starting with 3,000 demonstrators from the area, the crowd soon grew to 20,000 and Ottoman officers, led by Galip Bey [Pasinler] were sent to persuade the demonstrators to disperse. Galip Bey was an active member of the CUP, however, and he managed to convince the gathering to take an oath (*besa*) to the constitution, explaining that only a constitutional regime could avert the danger of foreign intervention. A petition demanding the restoration of the constitution, signed by 194 clerics, notables and tribal leaders present, was sent to the palace on 21 July.

Disagreement

In the literature on the revolution, there are two key issues on which the different authors disagree. One is the relative importance of external events, more precisely the Reval meeting and the plans of the European great powers to impose a new regime in Macedonia, on the one hand and of internal pressures, notably the increasing success of the Sultan's security system in uncovering the CUP underground network, on the other. The second is the question of agency. Was the insurgency in Macedonia in June–July 1908 the work of individuals and small groups of soldiers, who were inspired by the existence of the CUP and its propaganda but who acted independently and whose actions were only given the stamp of approval by the CUP afterwards? Or were the different insurrections in Resne, Ohrid, Monastir and Tikvesh in fact orchestrated carefully by the CUP central committee in Salonica and its most important branch, that in Monastir?

Basing ourselves on the state of the art of research in the field as well as on a reappraisal of the accounts of the two key figures of Enver and Niyazi, we can now reach a tentative conclusion on these two areas of disagreement. On the first issue, Ramsaur and Ahmad seem to accord least importance to the Reval meeting between Tsar Nicholas II and King Edward VII on 9–10 June, during which Russia and Great Britain reached far-reaching agreement about the imposition of an autonomous regime in the empire's Macedonian provinces (Salonica, Kosovo and Monastir) with foreign supervision. Ramsaur attributes the revolutionaries' decision to start an open rebellion in June 1908 primarily to the fact that the palace was getting very close to discovering the extent of the CUP underground network. He accords only secondary importance to the news of the Reval meeting. He relates how first Major Enver at the end of June 'disappeared into the hills' rather than obey orders to report to the general staff in Istanbul and then on 4 July (should actually be 3 July), Niyazi 'took to the hills for similar reasons'.

In Ahmad's eyes, Reval gave a greater sense of urgency to the constitutionalists, and constituted a 'psychological influence', but European observers at the time were mistaken when they thought there was a causal relationship between Reval and the revolution. The real origins must be sought elsewhere, that is, in the growing effectiveness of the Sultan's spy network. Akşin accords equal importance to the news of the Reval meeting and to the exposure of the underground networks of the Young Turks, highlighting the role of the regimental chaplain (alay müftüsü), who managed to penetrate the CUP network in Monastir. Bayur, Ramsaur's Turkish contemporary, is rather ambiguous on this point. In his very brief description he says that the rebellion was prepared 'in the atmosphere created by the Reval meeting' but does not go into details. His contemporary Ahmed Bedevi Kuran sees the increased activities of the Bulgarian, Serb and Greek bands as the factor that made the CUP attractive to officers of the Third Army. He says that it was the Reval meeting that forced them to increase their activities.

The more recent authors, Kansu, Hanioğlu and Gawrych, all seem to agree that the rebellion was originally scheduled for a later date (possibly

October or November 1908) but they agree with Kuran that the Reval meeting 'spurred the CUP to push for an early date' (Gawrych) or even 'forced the hand of the committee' (Kansu, quoting Knight). In Hanioğlu's even stronger words: 'Reval compelled the leaders and members of the CUP to risk all and start the revolution.' In his eyes the discoveries of the Hamidian spy network also played a role, but he definitely sees the Reval meeting as the primary trigger. The conclusion therefore seems to be that the revisionism of Ramsaur and Ahmad has in turn been revised, and that expert opinion seems to be leaning once again towards the original opinion of contemporary observers, that is, that the Reval meeting was the primary trigger of the constitutional revolution.

On the second question, that of agency either on the part of the committee or on the part of the individual soldiers who took to the hills, two traditions seem to exist.

Ramsaur is quite categorical in his view that the uprising developed spontaneously in several places at the same time and that the central committee of the CUP in Salonica had not masterminded it. As mentioned earlier, this could be due to the fact that his main sources were people outside the CUP, which leads him to misunderstand the inner workings of this organization. He describes Enver as 'a young officer... not at the time any more important than the average young officer who had become affiliated with the society'. This, however, misses Enver's crucial importance as the man who provided the committee access to the Third Army and its main base in Monastir. Enver had been admitted to the Ottoman Freedom Society (which later merged with the Paris-based organization of Ahmet Rıza to form the CUP) through the mediation of his uncle Halil [Kut] at a very early stage of the development of the organization. He was in fact its twelfth member. On his return to Monastir in 1906 he started a cell there, in close collaboration with fellow officer Kâzım Karabekir. Enver was the central figure in the Monastir organization and it was he, who enrolled officers like Niyazi and Eyüp Sabri, who were to play key roles in the July revolution.

Ahmad continues this tradition of denying the Committee agency. He states that the memoirs of Niyazi were published with the blessing of the CUP and that their bias is 'to exaggerate the role of the Committee in the insurrection'. He points out that Niyazi, in his first proclamations, 'spoke, not as a representative of the CUP as one might expect, but simply as the leader of "my 200 men"'. This could mean, he argues, that the action was that of Niyazi's own initiative and that the Committee only supported the insurrection in the towns, where it was master of the situation, and not in the countryside where it had little influence. Ahmad does not offer any hard evidence for his assertion that the CUP did not initiate the insurrection, however. Gawrych takes Ahmad's approach one step further, stating that 'Niyazi's first proclamation failed to mention the CUP at all.' For this, he refers to Ahmad's statement quoted above, but as we can see, this is not quite what Ahmad says. One glance at Niyazi's actual proclamation (reproduced in his memoirs) makes it clear however, that he explicitly mentions the 'Union and Progress that is a powerful organisation throughout the country'.

Bayur, who, it should be remembered, like Ramsaur's sources, was connected to the anti-Unionist political currents, also attributes agency primarily to Niyazi Bey himself. He points out that Niyazi himself describes the Resne insurrection as his own initiative and argues that Niyazi could hardly have put forward such a claim if it were false at a time when all his friends, who also had been involved in the revolution, were still alive. Bayur makes a clear distinction between Niyazi's actions and those of Enver. He is very disparaging of Enver, saying that he only left Salonica for Tikvesh to go into hiding and to save himself from arrest. He further charges that Enver's actions there were nowhere near as effective as those of Niyazi in Resne and Eyüp Sabri in Ohrid, and that Enver was only made into a hero of the revolution by Talât after the event for political reasons. This interpretation has to be rejected on the basis of what we know about Enver's crucial role within the CUP, discussed above. It is clearly based on political bias.

While Akşin does not address the issue of agency, Kansu and Hanioğlu clearly offer a very different reading of events. Kansu, basing himself here as elsewhere primarily on Knight and Uzunçarşılı, states that 'throughout his operations [he] was acting as the instrument of the Committee' even before July. While the actual initiative to take to the hills may have been his, Kansu posits that he clearly acted and wanted to act as representative of the Committee. Hanioğlu shows that already in mid-June instructions had been sent to CUP branches to prepare for insurrection and that officers were given permission to form bands (çetes). He emphasizes the degree of control on the part of the CUP, even going so far as to doubt the credibility of Niyazi's claim that he wrote the proclamations that were subsequently sent to the central and local authorities himself the day before he took to the hills. On the basis of documents published in Şurayı Ümmet after the revolution, Hanioğlu states that it was the Monastir branch that provided the documents to Niyazi. It is difficult to reconcile this with the claim in

Niyazi's published memoirs, which at the time were not contradicted by the CUP Perhaps and this is only a tentative suggestion, we should make a distinction between the proclamation sent to the palace, the inspectorate general and the governor of Monastir on the one hand and the telegrams sent to local commanders and administrators on the other, with the former being provided by the CUP branch in Monastir and the latter written by Niyazi himself. Internal evidence gives some substance to this hypothesis as the more political and 'official' discourse of the first proclamation is clearly different from the more fiery, direct and personal discourse of the others. The first text is much more programmatic than the others, which make concrete and personal accusations and threats against specific persons. It seems reasonable to attribute the first text to the CUP and the others to Niyazi.

Alone among our authors, Hanioğlu makes use of Enver's memoirs. These were written shortly after the event, in 1909, but remained within the family in the shape of notebooks until their publication as *Enver Paşa'nın Anıları* in 1991.[13] On the basis of these notes, as well as other sources, Hanioğlu concludes that Enver was clearly sent to Tikvesh on a mission by the Central Committee in Salonica and even given the title of 'inspector-general' for the purpose. A close reading of Enver's memoirs indeed shows that he saw himself as acting on behalf of the CUP and that he was provided with instructions, money and texts for proclamations.

The conclusion, to me, seems to be that, while Niyazi may indeed have approached the Monastir branch with the suggestion that he raise the standard of revolt, he did so fully aware that the CUP had already authorized this kind of action. He explicitly asked the branch for permission (which he got two days later, but before he made his move). He remained in constant touch with the Committee and was guided by it. The idea that individual soldiers like Niyazi, Enver or Eyüp Sabri forced the hand of the CUP and that the latter only mastered the situation on the eve of the proclamation of the constitution, in my view has to be rejected, because it is based either on the evidence of politically biased sources (Ramsaur, Kuran, Bayur) or not based on hard evidence at all (Ahmad, Gawrych).

A missed opportunity?

Finally, a comparison between the published memoirs of Niyazi and the unpublished ones of Enver affords us the opportunity to dig a little bit deeper into the actual mechanics of the insurrection. Looking in detail at what both officers did during their campaign in the mountains we can discern the tactics employed by the CUP to gain the support of the population. In my view, the authors reviewed here have not exploited these accounts in full, and as such, have missed an opportunity to draw powerful conclusions about the nature of the constitutionalist movement.

To start with, what officers like Niyazi and Enver do *not* do, is as interesting as what they do. Neither takes to the mountains as commander of his own regular unit. Niyazi commanded a battalion in Resne, but his band consisted of citizen volunteers, who avail themselves of the arms and money of the garrison. Only nine soldiers join him at a time when his band is supposedly going after Bulgarian bandits. Of those, four return to Resne once the true aim of the operation is revealed. As for Enver, he does not take any troops with him and raises a volunteer force in the villages of the Tikvesh region. He steals away from Salonica like a thief in the night, travels in disguise and tries to avoid contact with troops or gendarmes. In other words: these Young Turk officers clearly did not trust their own troops enough to involve them in the insurrection. This is an indication of the enormous chasm between these college-educated officers and the common soldier, who probably was still extremely loyal to the Sultan.

The second point to be made is that both Enver and Niyazi seek to build their support first and foremost among *Muslim* villagers. When Niyazi first headed for the mountains on 3 July, he carefully chose Albanian Muslim villages as his first destination. As an Albanian from Resne and a member of a landowning family, he had, of course, excellent connections with a number of villages, but the religious aspect is as important as the ethnic one here. When he sent his first soldiers into the first village, Niyazi ordered them to recite prayers while moving in, to put the Muslims at ease. Clearly the insurrection is primarily a Muslim movement, and the religious motif is very strong here. The fact that later in the insurrection the officers try to reassure the Macedo-Bulgarian population that the movement is not aimed against them and call upon Bulgarian bands to join them, does not belie this primary focus on the Muslims.

Third, the way officers try to latch on to the concerns of the peasant population is interesting. According to Niyazi, he found strong support for the CUP in some, or even most, of the Muslim villages. This is surprising, as the CUP comprised about 2,000 members in all of Rumelia at the time, nearly all of them urban (with a quarter of the members in Salonica). Enver's memoirs perhaps offer a clue as to how we should read Niyazi's statement. According to Enver, the CUP had no foothold in the villages, but quite a few of the large landowners, who although they lived in town were very influential in 'their' villages, were CUP members and it was their influence that mobilized the villagers in support of the CUP This likely is the reality behind Niyazi's statement as well.

How do the officers mobilize the support of the villagers? Certainly not with abstract rhetoric about constitutionalism. They appeal to the villagers' deep-rooted discontent about a government that imposes heavy taxation but does not deliver either services (i.e. roads, schools) or protection from the countless armed bands roving the region. Niyazi in particular not only offers protection from these bands with his 'national battalion', but he also implements additional measures, forcing local clans to declare a truce in the internecine blood feuds that were endemic among both the Northern Geg Albanians and the Tosk communities of the South. Niyazi presents his 'national battalion' as a patriotic Ottoman band (*çete*), which makes his operation instantly recognizable for similar groups in the mountains and encourages the bands of deserters, criminals on the run and Tosk Albanian nationalists to join him. The fact that he manages to get the support of the most important Tosk band leader Cercis Topulli is a major success in this respect.

The officers also court the villagers by explicitly capitalizing on the already existing fears about foreigners taking control of Macedonia. They constantly point out that the country is in danger and that foreign (Christian) control will mean the end for the Muslim 'majority' in Macedonia. The corrupt and weak government in Istanbul, they argue, does nothing to avert this danger, so the people have to put their trust in the Committee. The constitution is thus presented as the solution to these very real and concrete concerns of the village population.

In assuring themselves of the support of the villagers the officers make use of traditional means. In the Albanian villages Niyazi induces them to take a *besa*, a communal oath, of which there was a strong tradition in Albanian culture. In the Turkish villages of Tikvesh Enver calls together the council of village elders and working through them initiates whole villages into the CUP.

On the basis of the documentary evidence and in particular the memoirs of participants in the revolution we can now know a lot about the actual nuts and bolts of the insurrection that led to the restoration of the constitution. A close and comparative reading of those details may still give us a better insight into the nature of the Unionist movement. That is perhaps the only missed opportunity of the historiography reviewed here. But on the whole research on the revolution has progressed to the point where we are now able to construct a fairly satisfactory consensus view, which is closest to Hanioğlu's interpretation in that it accords an important place to the 'Eastern Question' and more particularly to the Reval meeting in triggering the revolution, and it sees the insurrection as orchestrated by the CUP headquarters in Salonica and its branches in Monastir and Ohrid rather than as the work of individual patriotic officers.

4. The Rise and Fall of 'Modern' Turkey: Bernard Lewis's *Emergence* Fifty Years On*

In 1961 the famous Arabist, Islam scholar and Turkologist Bernard Lewis published a book with Oxford University Press, which was immediately recognized as a classic in its field and would remain a leading textbook for a generation. It was, of course, called *The Emergence of Modern Turkey*.[1] It was a hefty tome (511 pages), based on research executed in England and Turkey during the years 1954–9.

The fact that nearly half a century has passed since the publication of *Emergence* makes it appropriate to take a second look at the book from the perspective of contemporary Turkology. In revisiting Lewis's classic, we can attempt to gauge if, and where, our field has produced different insights and, who knows, progressed when measured against the yardstick of this seminal work.

For me, a closer look at the book which was considered the bible of modern Turkish history when I studied at Leiden University (and for much longer) and which influenced my decision to make this my own area of specialization is of special significance.

Bernard Lewis and Turkish historiography

The first thing that strikes one on making the renewed acquaintance with the book is how many things, which were self-evident 50 years ago, have now become problematic. It starts on with the title page: *The Emergence of Modern Turkey*. What does 'emergence' really mean? Lewis does not address the matter in his preface, but the word surely suggests that we are faced with a spontaneous and gradual process, through which modern Turkey hatches like a chick from its egg. Feroz Ahmad has more recently pointed out that this is a fallacy.[2] For Turkey as we know it is not the inevitable result of a natural development but the product of wilful acts on the part of ideologically motivated leaders. 'Emergence' is not, of course, a value-free term. It suggests not only gradual development, but also the fulfilment of a destiny: the chick was in the egg waiting to be hatched. It also suggests the reaching of a higher phase in history. That is something Lewis does not try to hide. In the first sentence of the preface we read: 'The theme of this book is the emergence of a new Turkey from the *decay* of the old.' The old Turkey is not only old, but decayed as well. What, now, is 'modern' Turkey and what is the old, decayed Turkey which it has come to replace?

To start with the latter, 'modern Turkey' is not just the opposite of 'older Turkey'. The contrast is that between the republic of Turkey, which was founded in 1923 and celebrates its 85th anniversary this year, and its predecessor, the 600-year-old Ottoman Empire. In this respect, Lewis's terminology reflects a tradition which has been well-established since the mid-1920s. The authors of the stream of books written about the new republic had a strong predilection for this and similar descriptions: Eliot Grinnell Mears, *Modern Turkey* (1924); Berthe Georges-Gaulis, *La Nouvelle Turquie* (1924); Kurt Ziemke, *Die neue Türkei* (1930); Jean Deny, *Petit manuel de la Turquie Nouvelle* (1933); Henry Elisha Allen, *The Turkish Transformation* (1935); Sir Harry Luke, *The Old Turkey and the New* (1936); August, Ritter von Kral, *Das Land Kemal Atatürks. Der Werdegang der modernen Türkei* (1937); anonymous, *The New Turkey* (1938); Geoffrey Lewis, *Modern Turkey* (1955); Eleanor Bisbee, *The New Turks* (1956); Irfan Orga, *Phoenix Ascendant. The Rise of Modern Turkey* (1958) and Pia Angela Göktürk, *Werdegang der neuen Türkei* (1983).

Some authors preferred more colourful wordings to oppose new to old: Karl Klinghardt, *Die Schleier Fallen!* (1933); Lilo Linke, *Allah Dethroned* (1937) and Barbro Karabuda, *Goodbye to the Fez* (1959), but the message remains the same. In all of these books the essential opposition between 'old' and 'new', which coincides with the transition from empire to republic, is the framework within which the story of the Turks is told. But what is 'modern'? We shall return to that particular question later.

When we now look at *Emergence*, we immediately notice that Lewis's attitude towards the problem of continuity and change is ambivalent. On the one hand he sees the developments after 1918 as 'a radical and violent break with the past',[3] but on the other he interprets that break as the culminating point of a much longer process of reforms. He writes:

> The Turkish revolution began in a formal sense with the forcible overthrow of an old political order and the establishment of a new

one in 1908. In another sense, however, it had been going on for nearly two centuries.[4]

In this respect, Lewis's work differs from that of the real Kemalist historians, who, like Afet İnan, see the republic as a radically new departure which owes hardly anything to the Ottoman past and which has been created by Mustafa Kemal Pasha Atatürk as a kind of *deus ex machina*.

Lewis fits much better in a generation of scholars who made their name in Turkey after World War II, people like the sociologist Niyazi Berkes[5] and the jurist and political scientist Tarık Zafer Tunaya,[6] who also see in the Republic of Turkey a new and in a sense final phase in Turkish history, but who have an open eye for those who prepared it: the architects of the Ottoman administrative and cultural modernization in the nineteenth century and, especially, the Young Turk movement in the early twentieth century, which, in Tunaya's words, constituted the 'laboratory of the republic'.

Although this approach is certainly much less forced than that of the orthodox Kemalist historians of an earlier generation, it has one important disadvantage. Through it, late Ottoman history almost automatically acquires a teleological character. It turns into 'prehistory' of the republic. This in turn changes late Ottoman history into Turkish history *avant la lettre*, which misrepresents the multicultural, multi-ethnic character of that history in which Armenians, Greeks, Jews, Kurds, Arabs, Albanians and Bosnians all played important parts within a dynastic and religious political system. That Lewis fits into this Turkish-nationalist tendency is shown, for instance, by a passage in his introduction:

> So completely had the Turks identified themselves with Islam that the very concept of a Turkish nationality was *submerged*.[7]

Turkish national identity submerged in an Islamic ocean. This seems to indicate that Lewis sees the Turkish nation as a primordial entity that waited for its chance to shed all Ottoman and Islamic ballast and rise to the surface. Of course, that is the classic way in which nationalists regard nationality. But to modern historians, who have been sensitized by scholars like Benedict Anderson, Eric Hobsbawm and Ernest Gellner to the ways nationalists construct a nation's past as a weapon in their political struggles, it seems a trifle naive. A remark on page 7 is, if necessary, even more illustrative of Lewis's position. He writes: 'The Turkish language, which, despite long subjection to alien influences, survives triumphantly'. Here, Lewis adopts the basic idea of Kemalist linguistic purism, that there exists a pure or 'real' Turkish, which has to be decolonialized and cleansed of foreign influences. Here, too, he seems to see Turkish identity, expressed in the language, as something submerged in something non-Turkish (Ottoman?) but with a latent existence of its own.

Contents and format of *Emergence*

Emergence consists of two parts. Part one is a chronologically ordered overview in nine chapters, starting in the seventeenth century and ending with the coming to power of Menderes' Democrat Party in 1950. Part two is thematically ordered, with each of its five chapters describing a particular aspect of change. Lewis starts his chronological overview with the 'decline' of the empire, itself a notion which has come under attack rather severely in recent years.[8] Then he treats the attempts to restore the state with traditional means, the growing influence of Europe, the bureaucratic reforms of the early nineteenth century, the Young Ottoman movement, Sultan Abdülhamit's long reign, the Young Turks, the Kemalist republic and the republic after Kemal. In the thematic part he deals with changing collective identities, state and government, religion and culture and class structure.

The book is based on literature in English, German, French and Turkish and on published Ottoman authors, whom Lewis quotes frequently and effectively, both in the text and in the notes. Archival materials do not seem to have been used.

Fifty years on

When we now look at the book from where we are nearly 50 years later and try to compare it with the state of the art in the field of modern Turkish history, what transpires? I think there are three aspects, or rather three groups of aspects which play an important role here: intellectual versus total history, chronology and periodization, and the modernization paradigm.

Intellectual versus total history

The first concerns the kind of history Lewis has written and clearly has wanted to write. *Emergence* is first a history of the élite and its instrument of power, the central state, and second an intellectual history, a history of ideas. Whichever chapter we look at, Lewis concerns himself with the members of the administrative and intellectual élite, the development of their thinking, the terminology they used (and partly invented) and the measures they took. Because he concentrates to such an extent on the history of ideas, Lewis seems to work from the premise that people act from ideological motives. Such an approach overlooks the extent to which people use ideas to defend their political and social interests. A logical result is that policy, in the sense of the formulation of aims and the promulgation of laws and regulations gets much more attention than the power struggles in which the Ottoman (and Turkish) policy makers were involved at the same time. Here, Carter Findley's two-volume history, both institutional and social, of the Ottoman civil bureaucracy has given us a much fuller picture.[9]

In *Emergence*, the writing of intellectual history is at the expense of the depiction of social realities. When one reads the passage about the constitutional revolution of 1876,[10] one could be forgiven for thinking that it was Namık Kemal's play *The Fatherland or Silistria* which brought down the old regime, and not the famine in Anatolia, the insurrection in the Balkans or the financial crisis of the state. When Lewis does write about the financial crisis, he sees its root cause in the extravagances of the court[11] (and in this he is clearly influenced by the Ottoman reformers with whom he identifies) instead of in the immense financial burden created by the introduction of a conscript army, the acquisition of modern armaments and the ballooning of the Ottoman bureaucracy. The question how the reforms worked out in the provinces is not really answered, the question what it all meant for the average Ottoman subject is not even posed. We do not discover what the introduction of conscription or the eradication of the plague meant for the people, even though we can assume that developments such as these were far more influential that the ideological constructs of the intellectual élite in Istanbul. Something similar is true for the famous reforms of the age of Atatürk. There, too, we see the reforms exclusively through the eyes of the élite. When discussing, for instance, the prohibition of the Fez or the introduction of the Swiss civil code in 1926, Lewis does recognize that there was resistance, but he does not ask why. The negative reactions are all those of 'Muslim conservatives'.[12]

In all these respects our field has undergone a sea change in the last 25 years. We no longer concentrate exclusively on the central state, on the élite, its ideas and its measures. In these last 15 years, economic history of the late Ottoman Empire has come of age, with French researchers and American and Turkish colleagues attached to the Braudel Centre in Binghamton playing a leading role in this development. Jacques Thobie's impressive 1977 study of French economic interests in the Ottoman Empire[13] was a pioneering effort, but in the 1980s conference proceedings and monographs were published in rapid succession. Something nearly all of these publications have in common, is that they not only chart the developments within the late-Ottoman economy, but also try to place these in the context of the capitalist world economy centred on Europe. This is no coincidence. Many of the historians who have done this work, people like Donald Quataert, Şevket Pamuk, Çağlar Keyder, Huri İslamoğlu and Reşat Kasaba, have been inspired by the ideas of André Gunder Frank and in particular by Emanuel Wallerstein's 'World System' model. It is interesting, however, to note that the best work emerging from this school shows up the inadequacies of that model. Quataert, for instance, shows how Ottoman manufacture, instead of declining or disappearing under the influence of the incorporation of the Ottoman economy into the periphery of the capitalist world system as one would expect, adapted itself and resisted the onslaught of the Europeans through cost control, use of imported commodities and products and exploitation of niche markets.[14] Kasaba shows that the Armenian and Greek bourgeoisie did not, in fact, have a 'compradore' character and that it competed successfully with the metropolitan European capitalists.[15]

Social history is, of course, not entirely separate from economic history. Two of the path-breaking collections in this field, *Economies et sociétés dans l'Empire Ottoman*, edited by Jean-Louis Bacqué Grammont and Paul Dumont in 1983 and *Social and Economic History of Turkey*, edited by Halil İnalcık and Osman Okyar in 1980, show the connection between the two fields even in their titles. Paul Dumont, together with the Turkish political scientist Mete Tunçay, can be regarded as the pioneer of the history of Ottoman socialism, while Quataert has been the first to give us a picture of the lives of Ottoman workers at the railways, in the docks and in the mines.[16] The lowest step on the Ottoman social ladder, that of the slaves, first gained attention in Ehud Toledano's study of the Ottoman slave trade.[17]

Since 25 years, historians have been able to build on solid historical demographic studies, such as those published by Kemal Karpat[18] and, especially, Justin McCarthy.[19] These make use of the data collected by those, who – in McCarthy's words – were the only ones in a position to actually count: the Ottoman administration. Thanks to their work we can now answer questions about the size and composition of the late Ottoman population with a degree of exactness unthinkable 30 years ago. Alan Duben and Cem Behar have shown what is possible in the field of demographic microstudies in their book about the development of Istanbul households.[20]

Apart from the development of social and economic history proper, the work of French Turkologists such as François Georgeon, Paul Dumont and Stéfane Yérasimos has broadened the scope of cultural history in the direction of a history of mentalities which tries to chart society's attitudes and worldview and which merges imperceptibly into social history.[21]

As early as 1973, Halil İnalcık made an attempt to see how the nine-teenth-century reforms were received in the Balkan provinces in his article 'The application of the Tanzimat and its social effects'.[22] Since then, many local studies based on Ottoman archives in the Balkans and in the Arab world have given us a much fuller picture of what actually happened on the ground (as opposed to what Istanbul bureaucrats thought should happen).

The economic history of the republic has made great strides thanks to the work of people like Zvi Yehuda Hershlag, Korkut Boratav, Osman Okyar, William Hale and Şevket Pamuk. We now have a reasonably accurate idea of economic growth, production and income distribution. The same cannot be said for the social history of the republic. Şehmus Güzel and others have done important work on labour relations and the workers' movement,[23] but there still is an almost total lack of history 'written from below', a historiog-raphy which focuses on the experiences of ordinary people and the way they have undergone the modernization process. The most promising attempt so far has been made by Gavin Brockett,[24] who studied resistance to the Kemalist reforms, but it is clear that this aspect of the field awaits further development.

To sum up the first point, I think we can say that the most important development in this sector of Turkology has been that the history of ideas and institutions, of the central state and the élite, has given way to a much broader approach in which history of mentalities, social history, demog-raphy and economics all play a role, although this development has gone further for the late empire than for the republic.

Chronology

The second aspect of *Emergence* that may be considered outdated, concerns the degree of continuity between the Ottoman Empire and the republic and the periodization which follows from it. We have already noted Lewis's ambivalence vis-à-vis this question. He sees the development of modern Turkey as a long-term process, but at the same time he sees a 'radical and violent break' in that development after 1918, when something substantially new emerges in the shape of the national resistance movement in Anatolia. What he loses sight of in this context, is the degree to which this movement and the republic which grew from it was the work of the same circle of Young Turk politicians and officers who had brought about the constitu-tional revolution of 1908, and the extent to which it was the result of con-scious planning on the part of these Young Turks.

I think this is an area where my own work has contributed to a substantial revision. My main conclusion has been that the traditional periodization, which is followed by Lewis, and which sees the 'national struggle' (*Millî Mücadele*) between 1919 and 1922 as the first phase of the history of the republic, is very distorting for two reasons: first, the initiative for this struggle was taken by those same Young Turk leaders who had held power in Turkey between 1913 and 1918; and second, the proclamation of the republic was really the result of a coup d'état within the movement by a radical wing led by Mustafa Kemal Pasha Atatürk. For the large majority – not only of the rank and file, but also of the leadership – the aim of the struggle between 1918 and 1922 was not the founding of a Turkish state but the preservation of the Ottoman Sultanate and Caliphate. In short: the most important dividing line in post-war history is not that of 1918 but that of 1923.[25] In my view, Lewis is therefore wrong when he says (speaking about the situation in 1919): 'A new Turkish state was emerging in Anatolia.'[26]

Recent work by Turkish historians such as Selim İlkin, İlhan Tekeli, Bülent Tanör and Engin Berber on regional resistance movements, by Bilge Criss on Istanbul during the British occupation and by Ahmet Demirel on the first national assembly in Ankara seem to confirm the importance of Young Turk organizations in the national resistance, and thus the continuity with the empire.[27]

An important reason why Lewis is able to characterize the national independence movement as new, is his neglect of precisely that period which has been both the most traumatic time in modern Turkish history and its most formative phase: World War I. Lewis devotes a great deal of attention to the debates among Young Turk intellectuals and publicists on the eve of the World War, but the war itself is dealt with in two sentences:

> It was while they were still discussing this question that, in October 1914, the Turks stumbled into a major European war, as allies of one group of European powers against another. By 1918 it was clear that their time had run out.[28]

Quite apart from the fact that Lewis does not explain anything about this fatal stumble, he thus neglects even to mention the following developments, which all contributed decisively to the way Turkey took shape after the war.

First: The abolition of the capitulations, those centuries-old economic and juridical privileges held by the Europeans and their protégés in the empire and the introduction of a nationalist economic policy, aimed at the formation of a native Muslim class of traders and industrialists. This policy of 'National Economy' (*Millî İktisat*), which has been described in detail by Toprak in his book of the same title and many subsequent books covering the same ground[29] is a direct precursor of the economic policies of the republic which also aimed at the creation of a national bourgeoisie under the protective umbrella of a military-bureaucratic élite.

Second: The intimidation and discrimination of the Young Turk regime which led to the flight of hundreds of thousands of Greeks and the deportation and death of possibly seven to eight hundred thousand Armenians. In the thematic part of his book, Lewis does mention a holocaust of 1916, when 'a million and a half Armenians perished'.[30] This means, incidentally, that in quantitative terms he accepts the most extreme Armenian claims. But he describes the events as a 'struggle between two nations for the possession of a single homeland' and lays no connection between this episode and later history. All too often in the field of Turkology we forget that the modern state of Turkey was built on ethnic cleansing on a massive scale. The historiography on the issue has been in the grip of very emotional polemics between Turks and Armenians for 80 years. Nevertheless, it has to be said that for a long time research, which really gives us a degree of new insight into what happened in those horrible years 1915–17, has been done almost exclusively by Armenian scholars like Vahakn Dadrian and Ara Sarafian. Since 1992 the Turkish sociologist Taner Akçam, who was deeply influenced by Dadrian, has come to the fore as the leading 'dissident' voice on the Turkish side. His work only received international attention when one of his books was translated into English in 2006.[31] Akçam has called attention to the effect this continued silence on the ethnic policies of the Young Turks has had on Turkish society at large. A very painful point that has been raised specifically by Akçam is the fact that so many people who had been deeply involved in the persecution of the Armenians, and who thus had to fear either Armenian revenge or punitive action by the British, became protagonists in the national struggle and thus founding fathers of the republic. At the start of the twenty-first century, the most promising development seemed to be the joint effort made by the Workshop for Armenian-Turkish Scholarship (WATS) to create a platform for discussion based on empirical evidence. Donald Bloxham made a successful effort to situate the Armenian genocide in the framework of imperialist rivalry.[32]

In the same way, Greek scholars like Paschalis Kitromilidis and Alexis Alexandris are the ones who do research on the million and a half Greek Orthodox who lived in Anatolia before 1922. In Turkey only one scholarly study on the population exchange with Greece was published.[33] This reflects the fact that, whereas the 'Catastrophe' of 1922–4 had always been a defining moment in the Greek historical consciousness, attention to it in Turkey remained scant until well into the 1990s.

Third: The loss of the Arab provinces which had been under Ottoman rule for 400 years, coming so soon after the loss (in the Balkan War, which Lewis does not treat in any detail either) of European core provinces which had been Ottoman for 500 years. The loss of these old imperial domains has been very important in the development of a separate Turkish identity. After all, we should not forget that the founders of the republic had all witnessed these events personally, and often at the military front. Since the 1990s we have seen the appearance of a spate of good books about Arab–Turkish relations in this era, notably by Sabine Prätor and Hasan Kayalı.[34]

Finally: the war itself. Justin McCarthy has shown how ten years of continuous warfare turned Anatolia into a land of widows (with a net population loss of two and a half million Muslims and hundreds of thousands of Christians through war, persecution, hunger and disease),[35] while I have tried to show how serving in the Ottoman army itself almost meant a death sentence.[36] At the moment there seems to be a spectacular increase in the interest of young Turkologists in the World War I period.

In conclusion to this point, I would say that we can now see that Lewis, through his neglect for the World War, misses essential steps in the development of modern Turkey.

The modernization paradigm

The third, and at the same time the most important, aspect of obsolescence concerns the paradigm, the fundamental vision of history which underlies *Emergence*. This paradigm is that of modernization. Lewis sees the history of Turkey in dialectical terms as the struggle between an enlightened élite, which is open to the ideas of the West (the *Tanzimat* bureaucrats, the Young Ottomans, Young Turks and Kemalists), and representatives of traditional, mostly religious, values. Slowly and at great cost, the reforming élite of Turkey in the end succeeds in making Turkey a modern country on the European model.

Although he does not explicitly define 'modern' anywhere, it is clear what the concept means to Lewis: the nation state, a constitutional-parliamentarian regime and industrialization. Fundamental to his concept of modernity is that of secularism – the removal of religious elements from government, law, education and culture. Just as for the Turkish Kemalists, modernization and secularism seem to him to be almost synonymous. This, of course, is a key element in the Kemalist tradition. After all, when Niyazi's great work *The Development of Secularism in Turkey* was translated and published in Turkish, its title was *Türkiye'de Çağdaşlaşma* (Modernization in Turkey).

In Lewis's eyes – and this, too, is typical of writers from the modernization school – the march of modern, Western civilization is irresistible. There is resistance, both among the élite and the masses, but that resistance is the rear-guard action of traditional sectors, which in the end will prove to be backward islands in a modernizing society. They are the ones of whom Lewis can say in the context of the proclamation of the republic: 'Not all the Sultan's former subjects were able to view the march of events with the same historical realism.'[37]

In this respect *Emergence* is a typical product of the 1950s and 60s. Since then, contemporary developments in Turkey and in the world of Islam generally have taught us a degree of scepticism. That the secular nation state in Turkey has only been maintained for the last 50 years with the help of four military interventions and continuous limitations on civil liberties, tends to undermine Lewis's optimistic assessment of Turkey as a country where 'westernizing revolution is accomplished and irreversible'[38] and where 'the social changes that preceded and accompanied the rise of democracy have continued and given greater strength and numbers to the new groups and elements whose interests and aspirations are with freedom.'[39]

Lewis's conclusion that Atatürk's nationalism was 'healthy and reasonable', without 'arrogant trampling on the rights and aspirations of other nations'[40] is strange in itself, given the suppression of widespread Kurdish revolts in the 1920s and 30s. But for us, who have witnessed 15 years of open warfare between the Turkish army and the *Partiya Karkerên Kurdistan* (PKK), it is almost surreal. Generally speaking, one can say that it is striking that the problem of the Kurdish community in Turkey is not dealt with in *Emergence*, not even in the chapter on 'community and nation'. This would certainly be impossible in our day. Not only the ongoing propaganda war, but also the work of serious scholars such as Peter Andrews, Martin van Bruinessen and Hamid Bozarslan has emphasized the ethnic complexity of Turkey, which had been hidden from view by the Kemalist nation-building process.[41]

One does not have to look only at the shortcomings and limitations of the secularist and nationalist modernization policies to call Lewis's dichotomy of modern versus reactionary into question. Perhaps the greatest success of Turkey's modernizing élite is the very fact that it has lost its monopoly on political and cultural debate. Through the spread of higher education and wealth a large and vocal middle class has emerged, important parts of which no longer regard a strong religious identity and a modern way of life as incompatible. Social scientists who work on Islam in Turkey, people like Şerif Mardin, Nilüfer Göle and Sencer Ayata have realized that movements such as that of the Nurcus or of the Welfare Party are not simply 'reactionary' or 'fundamentalist'. Quite to the contrary, they argue that these are ideological movements which function in modern industrializing society and try to formulate answers to the problems it poses.[42]

Sadly, the debate among historians of modern Turkey is less sophisticated. The 1993 textbook by Lewis's pupil Feroz Ahmad (which I have mentioned earlier), *The Making of Modern Turkey* is a prime example of the survival of the modernization paradigm with its black and white contrasts and simplifications. Witness for instance the claim: 'Nationalism was accepted by everyone except reactionaries,' or the statement, 'Secularism was also accepted by nearly everyone.'[43]

In Turkey itself, the growth of a strong Islamist movement has led to a polarization in which many intellectuals feel threatened and turn back to the original Kemalist modernization model.

Conclusion

What, then, should be our conclusion both regarding *Emergence* and regarding the development of this part of Turkology over the last 50 years?

I think we can say with confidence that *Emergence* is outdated in a number of ways. Fortunately so, because it means that Turkology has progressed. In three crucial areas we now have a richer and much more complete picture of Turkish history. In the first place people have finally marched into the historical picture. No longer are we only interested in the question of whether the Young Turks were Ottomanists, Islamists or Westernists, we also want to know whether their policies meant people starved; not only do we analyse what 'populism' meant in Kemalist ideology, we want to know whether workers had the right to organize or strike. In the second place we have become aware of the fact that the developments in the late Ottoman Empire served not only an arsenal, or a laboratory, for the republic, but that the Young Turk power élite had set in motion a number of developments which made Turkey what it became after 1923. We realize, or we should realize, that Turkey carries with it the traumas of a state which lost most of its centuries-old core provinces in the spate of five years and could survive only after massive and vicious ethnic cleansing. In the third place, our history writing no longer needs to be caught in the *clair-obscur* of enlightened élite who have been touched with the magic wand of the West on the one hand and religious reactionaries on the other. We can see that modernization, such as that which Turkey has undergone in the last 200 years, is a multi-faceted phenomenon, which evokes very different reactions. Many of these reactions, even if they are advertised as 'Islamic' or 'traditional', do not necessarily signify rejection of the modernizing process. They may even be the form in which modernization can most successfully penetrate an Islamic society.

Nevertheless, *Emergence* remains an imposing tour de force, an elegantly written survey, with a clear central theme, rich in detail and based on astounding erudition. Nowhere is the struggle of the Ottoman, and later Turkish, élite to catch up with the modern world depicted better. The fact alone that the book can serve as the subject for this chapter after nearly 50 years says enough about its qualities.

II. IMPERIAL TWILIGHT

Introduction

One of the pitfalls that threatens any student of twentieth-century Turkish history is the temptation to see the late Ottoman Empire as the prehistory of the Turkish nation state that succeeded it. Of course, no one can deny the important continuities that exist between the last decades of the empire and the early republic (indeed, my own early work in the 1980s was concerned precisely with showing up these continuities), but nevertheless it is dangerous to succumb to the temptation. As we will see time and again in the course of this part, the story can easily become an analysis of contrasts where Ottoman 'failure' and 'decadence' is juxtaposed with Turkish 'success' and 'strength'. Such a view almost automatically sees the early advocates of the 'national' solution as the realists and the ones best attuned to the march of history and too easily forgets that it is precisely these pioneers of nationalism who made other (imperial, multi-ethnic, federated) solutions impossible. Talk of self-fulfilling prophecies!

The history of the last decade of the Ottoman state, the 'imperial twilight' of this part, is one of trial and error. From the last Hamidian decade, the state inherited steady economic growth and fast-growing international trade, which favoured an emerging urban bourgeoisie dominated by non-Muslims, and an expanding state machinery with all its trimmings in the shape of barracks, schools, clock towers and telegraph lines, that was dominated by Muslims. Interreligious tensions, which were at the same time inter-ethnic tensions because in the Ottoman Empire religious affiliation was the primary ethnic marker, were part of the picture and interplayed in complicated ways with the policies of the European great powers. The tensions and dangers were all too visible to the Young Turks who brought about the constitutional revolution of July 1908. As its name indicates, the Committee of Union and Progress (CUP) saw the basic solution for the problems of the empire in two things: a shared Ottoman citizenship of all different ethnic communities and a rational, 'scientific', social and political order – progress in the positivist sense. But after the short-lived euphoria of the summer of 1908 it soon became clear to them how difficult it would be to achieve these aims. The Christian communities had a very different interpretation of Ottoman citizenship, based on a recognition of differences and historical privileges in a decentralized state, from that of the Unionists, who envisaged a unified state on the French pattern. Less than a year after the constitutional revolution the fragility of the Unionists' hold on power as well as their lack of support among the Muslim masses was shown up by the counterrevolution of April 1909 in the capital. Continued unrest and rebellions among the Albanians threatened the already precarious Ottoman position in the Western Balkans, where Albanians had formed the only community that was not the object of irredentist agitation on the part of one of the Christian neighbour states.

The chapters in this part show the difficulties of the environment within which the Young Turks tried to operate: the vast economic, financial and demographic differences that separated the empire from its main European rivals, the resistance the Young Turks met from conservative Muslim public opinion and from communities with a 'national' agenda. These chapters also attempt to show how they tried to deal with this extremely complex situation (for instance in orchestrating the Sultan's visit to Kosovo) and to explain how the environment in which they grew up and gained their first professional experience influenced their world view and their policies. The final chapter in this part describes the legacy this soul-searching of the last years of empire left to one of the many nation states to grow out of the Ottoman Empire: the republic of Turkey. Thus, in the end, although we are back to the question of continuities between the Ottoman Empire and its successor, hopefully the chapters of this part also show how the Young Turks explored the different options available to them as they were trying to preserve and modernize their state against all odds.

the Unionist envisaged a Unified state on the French pattern.

Atatürk was member of the unionist.

modernize

5. The Ottoman Empire 1850–1922: Unavoidable Failure?*

gong o

It is a safe assumption that a state can be deemed to have failed in its primary functions if it is incapable of defending its territory and keeping together its population. Judged by these standards the Ottoman State of the nineteenth- and early twentieth centuries was a failure. Having already lost control of large sections of its territories in the late eighteenth- and early nineteenth centuries to the expansionist Russian Empire on the one hand and indigenous nationalist movements (Serbian and Greek) on the other, the empire suffered two more great waves of territorial losses. First in 1877–8, Romania and Bulgaria came into existence, Bosnia was lost to the Austrians, and the easternmost parts of Anatolia were seized by Russia. Then, from 1912–20, almost all remaining European possessions were lost to the young national states of the Balkans in the Balkan Wars and the Arab provinces were lost to the British Empire in World War I. The possessions thus lost had been Ottoman for nearly 500 years and they all shared an Ottoman legacy.[1] In the case of the Balkans, the lost territories had also been the richest, most advanced and most densely populated provinces in the empire, and had been home to a disproportionate part of the Ottoman ruling élite.

The continued military and political weakness of the Ottoman Empire was very apparent to the European policy makers of the day. After all, the term 'Eastern Question' was used throughout Europe as diplomatic short-hand for the way in which continued Ottoman weakness would ultimately endanger the stability of Europe by creating a power vacuum for competing European great powers to fill.[2] In spite of strenuous efforts on the part of the Ottoman élite to strengthen the state through the adoption of European technology and practice, very few doubted that the empire was moribund.

Contemporary European observers often blamed the continued weakness of the Ottoman state on a lack of understanding on the part of Ottoman reformers about the underlying reasons for Europe's strength. The reformers

59

— Unionists —

Kemalists are continuation of Young Turks.

were depicted as superficial imitators ('Oriental gentlemen') and their efforts described as half-hearted. This harsh judgement was shared by the more radical wing of the Young Turk movement after 1908 and still later by the Kemalist movement in the Turkish Republic.[3] Disillusioned by the failure of the nineteenth-century reformers to halt either the encroachments of European imperialism or the rise of indigenous nationalisms, the Young Turks and Kemalists abandoned the fundamental ideal of the earlier generation, the 'Unity of the Ethnic Elements' (*İttihad-i anasır*) in favour of, first Muslim, and then (after 1923) Turkish nationalism.[4] In their judgement, which was strongly influenced by social Darwinism of a particular kind (focused on nations rather than on social categories), the reformers of the nineteenth century had been naive and unfit to compete in the struggle for survival between nations.[5]

It is probably true that the Ottoman reformers were late in recognizing the power of nationalism and the danger it brought to the empire, but it is questionable whether their policies can really be held responsible for the 'failure' of the Ottoman Empire. In an attempt to paint a more nuanced picture, let us take a fresh look at the two fundamental problems that faced the empire – first, the maintenance of the external position of the empire or in other terms, the 'defence of the realm', and second, the construction of a collective identity, which could underpin imperial rule.

Defence of the realm

The sudden defeats of 1774 and 1792 at the hands of the Russians, after half a century without major wars, left the Ottomans acutely aware of their military inferiority. The disastrous defeat once again at the hands of Russia in 1829, which was accompanied by a flood of Muslim refugees from the Black Sea littoral, made military modernization even more of a priority. Modernizing the army remained the driving force behind the whole complex of reforms, at least until 1856. The transition to an army dressed, equipped and commanded in the European manner began in 1826 with the founding of the 'Trained Victorious Muhammadan Soldiers' (*Muallem Asakir-i Mansure-i Muhammadiye*). Conscription on the Prussian model, with a standing army, an active reserve and a militia, was introduced in 1844. Conscription was by drawing of lots among age classes, as in Europe.[6] The exact nature of the Ottoman conscription system, its strengths and weaknesses will be dealt with in the first chapter of the part on the Great War.

Though the initial impetuses for reform were military modernization and the establishment of a state monopoly on the use of violence, the achievement

60

of these goals required the reformers to cast the net of modernization ever more widely. The building of a modern army necessitated a population census (for efficient recruitment), the construction of barracks and the improvement of roads and bridges. Enhancing state control was dependent on communications, which translated into the building of an extended network of telegraph cables from the 1850s onwards and of trunk railways from the 1880s. The reforms created their own need for modern educational establishments (and a market for their graduates).[7] Thus, the Ottomans created professional colleges to turn out engineers and architects, (military) doctors and veterinaries, accountants and administrators. The utilitarian drive behind the creation of the new schools is shown by the fact that a university on the European model was founded only at the very end of the century – remarkable, considering the enormous development of the Humboldtian university in the European countries, which the Ottomans took for their model, in this very period.

As products of these new schools and members of modernized Ottoman institutions, the bureaucrats of the fast-growing state machinery were socialized into a system of clear hierarchical relationships, division of labour, endless regulation and regular pay. By the mid-late nineteenth century something resembling Weber's model of a rational bureaucracy came into existence,[8] thus paralleling the growth of a European-style officer corps in the army. Much as one may criticize the reforms for their shallowness, half-heartedness or inefficiency, something resembling a modern centralized state nevertheless emerged. Anyone doubting the Ottomans' achievement in this field need only compare the Turkey of the 1920s, when Mustafa Kemal Atatürk unleashed his radical secularist and nationalist programme, with the Iran of the same period, in which Reza Shah Pahlevi established his power monopoly. Reza Shah's policies necessarily aimed at the construction of a modern state where under the last Qajar Shahs royal authority had barely been noticeable outside Teheran and Tebriz. In this sense his position resembled that of the Ottoman Sultan Mahmut II (r. 1808–39) far more than it did that of Atatürk, who inherited a complete and ruthlessly efficient state apparatus, which he could then employ to effect a cultural revolution of sorts.[9]

The introduction of a Western-style army with up-to-date equipment and armaments, the building of a state bureaucracy and the investment in infrastructure, limited as they were, required a dramatic increase in state expenditure. The introduction of conscription in order to compete with European mass armies meant a significant increase in the required manpower. In other words, the two main requirements for successful military reform were money and men.

Money and men

The Ottoman Empire was, of course, an agricultural state. Its two most important sources of tax revenue until 1856 were the tithe (and similar taxes like
the 'sheep tax' – *ağnam resmi*) and the *cizye*, the tax levied on the 'protected'
minorities (the Christian and Jewish communities) in exchange for their right
to live and worship as distinct confessional groups. Taxes were always imposed
on the heads of households and a system of tax farming was in place throughout the empire. In the past tax farms had been sold to the highest bidder for
a period of three years, but in the eighteenth century the lifetime tax farm
(*malikane*) had become the prevailing practice. Successive governments tried
to replace it with direct tax collection throughout the nineteenth century, but
they never succeeded in fully eradicating the tax farming system.[10] While tax
farming was a rational choice on the part of the central government as it eliminated the risk of crop failure and the need for a system of tax collectors, it did
tend to increase the tax burden of the peasants, thus ultimately damaging the
government's tax base. As for tax revenue from the Christian and Jewish communities, the *cizye* was replaced in 1856 with a military exemption tax called
bedel (about which more below) when the Sultan, under pressure from Britain
and France, granted equality before the law to non-Muslims. Customs duties,
excises, tolls, port fees and market fees were among the other sources of state
income, most of them also farmed out to contractors.

Trade with Europe, which had been on the increase since the second half
of the eighteenth century, increased rapidly from 1840 onwards and continued to do so until 1873. Direct investment by Europeans began to grow
significantly after the Crimean war (1853), when the empire was viewed as
a land of opportunity and attracted serious business as well as many adven-
turers. After a period of stagnation, which reflected trends in the world
economy, trade and investment picked up again after 1896.[11]

However, the central government was in no position to profit financially
from this economic expansion. After the signing of the free trade treaty of
Balta Limanı with Great Britain in 1838 (and similar treaties with other
powers shortly after) it lost its freedom of action in the sphere of custom
duties and tolls. The political climate after the Crimean War created favourable conditions for borrowing in the European capital markets, but in 1875
the state defaulted on its external debt and it could only restore its credit by
handing over a number of important sources of income directly to its foreign
creditors, represented by the *Caisse de la Dette Publique Ottomane*, which
was created in 1881.[12] This Public Debt Administration was given direct
access to a number of important revenue sources of the state, thus further

eroding the empire's fiscal position. The war of 1877–8 also deprived the empire of some of its richest provinces in Europe.

We do not have any reliable figures on total state revenue in the nineteenth century. The figures for this period thus have to be regarded as rough estimates. The first reliable budget, which gives realistic estimations of state income and expenditure, was put together in 1909 by the financial wizard in the Young Turk regime, Cavit Bey. This budget reports a state income of just over 25 million Turkish pounds (27.5 million pounds sterling).[13] To see how that compares to the income of those states with whom the empire had to compete, I have taken the state income for Great Britain, France, Austro-Hungary and Russia in 1900, as reported in Mitchell's *Historical Statistics*[14] (which, incidentally, gives no data on the Ottoman Empire). In order to create a basis for comparison, I have used rates of exchange tables, drawn up by Posthumus in 1943,[15] to convert the national currencies into Dutch guilders as a unit of account (only for purposes of comparison). The result is as follows:

Great Britain	1,680 million
France	1,831 million
Austro-Hungary	1,321 million
Russia	2,113 million
Ottoman Empire	330 million

In other words, the means at the disposal of its greatest rival, Russia, were seven times those of the Ottoman state. In any arms race, this would of course be a factor of enormous importance. It also helps to explain the expanding and ultimately crushing debt the Ottomans loaded themselves with. It was not so much the extravagances of the court, as both European and Ottoman critics assumed, but battleships, guns and salaries, which accounted for massive state spending.

A similar picture emerges when we look at the problem of manpower. Like the figures for state income, estimates of the Ottoman population are similarly uncertain. By the beginning of the nineteenth century the population had probably been in decline for over a century, and numbered about 26 million.[16] The need for more effective taxation and the introduction of military conscription turned counting the population into a priority. The first census was taken in 1831–8, but it was reasonably accurate only in a number of central provinces. The quality of the censuses improved over the next 70 years, but the

Ottomans always undercounted their population and in the more inhospitable areas under marginal state control, such as Kurdistan, Albania or Yemen, the numbers were little more than guesses. On the eve of World War I, the population was stated to be slightly in excess of 21 million, but if all the outlying areas are included, a number some five million higher is probably closer to reality.[17] On the face of it, then, the population numbers for 1800 and 1914 are much the same. But when Ottoman territorial losses of the nineteenth century are taken into account, these roughly equal figures reflect a completely different reality. Though the Ottoman population had experienced strong growth in the 1880s and 1890s, huge tracts of land were lost in the peace settlements of 1878 and 1913. These lost territories were among the most densely populated in the empire. If these provinces had remained within the Ottoman fold, natural growth would have seen to it that the empire's population in 1914 would have been around 42.5 million instead of 26 million. The empire was caught in a vicious circle: loss of land meant loss of income and population, which in turn decreased its ability to defend itself and led to more loss of land.

Comparisons are telling here. The populations of the major competitors of the Ottoman Empire all grew significantly over the century, as this table shows:

	1851	1901
Great Britain	27.3 million	42.5 million
France	35.8 million	38.5 million
Austria/Austro-Hungary	30.7 million	45.2 million
Russia	N/A	126.4 million (1897)
Germany	41 million (1871)	56.4 million
Ottoman Empire	32 million (1844)	26.0 million

(*Source*: Mitchell's *Historical Statistics*)

In other words: populations, which had been comparable in size to that of the Ottoman Empire in the early nineteenth century, were 30–50 per cent larger at the end of the century, while the population of the eternal rival Russia was five times that of the Ottomans.

Looked at in purely military terms, however, the Ottoman situation was far worse, given the huge number of individuals granted exemption from Ottoman military service. Certain categories of Muslims were exempted, like religious scholars and students, pilgrims or residents of Istanbul or the holy places. But the main exempted group was that of the non-Muslims. From the start in 1844, the empire had only conscripted Muslim men into its army. This continued to be the case even after full equality before the law had been introduced in 1856. Until 1909, Christians and Jews continued to pay a special exemption tax (*bedel*) instead of serving in the army. As Christians and Jews made up close to 40 per cent of the population until 1878, this reduced the recruitment base of the army in a major way. They constituted 20 per cent even as late as 1914. Thus, the actual recruitment base of the army consisted of the male, sedentary, Muslim population. No wonder, then, that the actual recruitment rate was among the lowest in Europe: in peacetime only 0.35 per cent of the population was conscripted each year. Fully mobilized, 4 per cent of the population served, as opposed to, for instance, 10 per cent in France in World War I.[18]

Industrial base and transport infrastructure

The army's primary problem did not stem from a lack of modern hardware; much of the money borrowed by the state was in fact used to buy modern European arms. But the lack of an industrial base meant that equipment and most of the munitions for the Ottoman guns had to be imported. As wars grew more industrial starting with the American Civil War, the lack of an industrial base became an ever more severe handicap. When World War I broke out, the empire still did not produce heavy artillery shells. Although the country was a cotton producer, it did not even have the capacity to produce enough bandages.

There are no data on overall Ottoman industrial output, but if we look at one vital precondition for industrialization, coal production, a very clear picture emerges. Coal production in the major Ottoman mining area, the Ereğli coalfields near the Black Sea shore, more than doubled after French interests started developing the local mines in 1896, and by the early 1900s it stood at about 600,000 tons per annum.[19] Compare this to the coal production of some major European countries in 1900:

Great Britain	229.0 million metric tons
France	33.4 million
Austro-Hungary	11.0 million
Russia	16.2 million
Ottoman Empire	0.6 million

(*Source*: Mitchell's *Historical Statistics*)

Oil could have been an alternative to coal, but the Ottomans did not have this luxury. Ottoman troops took the oilfields of Baku in 1918, when they were still among the most important oil producing areas in the world, but the government was forced to withdraw its troops a few months later under the armistice of October 1918. Of course, some of the Ottoman Arab provinces would later become major oil producers, but, although important oil reserves had been discovered in Mesopotamia before the war, exploitation did not start until after the peace settlement, when these areas had already been lost to the empire.

One final element that had significant impact on the empire's ability to defend itself is that of rail transport, an element which had proved decisive in other contexts, such as the Franco-Prussian war of 1870. In 1914, the Ottoman Empire was still largely dependent on coastal shipping for transport of bulk goods (something which made it highly vulnerable in case of war). But the importance of railways had been increasing strongly, and on the eve of World War I, the country had 5759 kilometres of railways of all gauges in operation.[20] Once again, though, Ottoman railway capacity was no match for that of major European countries:

Great Britain	32,623 kilometres of rail
France	40,770 kilometres
Germany	63,378 kilometres
Austro-Hungary	22,981 kilometres
Russia	62,300 kilometres
Ottoman Empire	5,759 kilometres

Even India, with twice the surface area of the Ottoman Empire, had nearly ten times as big a rail network. The nature of the Ottoman railway system was also different from that of its European rivals. The railway networks of France and Great Britain resembled a spider's web with lines radiating from the metropolis (Paris or London). This spider's web structure had a strong integrative effect, enhancing state control and increasing outlying population's dependence on the centre. In the continental empires, military considerations (i.e. the necessity to move troops massively and quickly to the borders) had been taken into account when granting railway concessions. In the Ottoman Empire this was not the case for the railways built by foreign interests between 1860 and 1890. These were essentially lines constructed to connect ports with productive hinterlands. Only when the German-owned

Anatolian railway and Baghdad railway were built from 1888 onwards and the Hejaz pilgrimage railway from 1901 onwards, did the empire begin to acquire a network which actually connected the interior to the capital and which could play a strategic role in enhancing state power.

When discussing the ultimate failure of the Ottoman Empire to defend itself effectively, we should remember these numbers. In a struggle with a country like Russia, which was seven times as rich, five times as populous, produced almost thirty times as much coal and had eleven times as big a rail network, who should be surprised at the outcome?

National cohesion

The loss of territory and the ultimate demise of the Ottoman Empire was not the result of external pressure alone, however, but of the interplay of that pressure with separatist nationalism developed by the non-Muslim communities of the empire. The European idea of political nationalism spread in the wake of the French revolution primarily to those communities, which had the strongest overseas or overland trading networks with Europe: the Greeks and the Serbs. After these two had achieved independence (albeit certainly not to the full extent of their territorial ambitions), Bulgarians, Rumanians, Montenegrins, Macedonians and Armenians followed suit. This spread of nationalist ideologies among the intelligentsia of the Christian communities coincided with the spread of European patronage. The Ottomans had always granted the representatives of foreign powers the right to grant protection to a limited number of local employees, primarily to the embassy interpreters (*dragomans*) who were responsible for contacts with the Ottoman authorities and who were recruited mostly from Levantine (Catholic), but also from Greek orthodox and Armenian families. We now know that the number of these protected Christians remained very limited (hundreds rather than thousands) until the late eighteenth century.[21] This changed in the aftermath of the Napoleonic Wars. Between 1820 and 1880 the number of protected Christians, whose status as protégés of a European power was officially recognized by the Porte (the Ottoman government) through the issuance of a diploma (*berat*) grew explosively. This was the period in which each island in the Aegean was reported to have its own Russian honorary consul with its own circle of protégés. The expansion of the protégé system continued until the 1880s, by which time both the Ottoman Empire and the European states had embraced more modern ideas on citizenship and agreed that the protected Christians should opt either for full citizenship of the European protector state or for Ottoman nationality.

The protected status of the Christians at the precise time (1830s–60s) when trade expanded very rapidly, allowed an entrepreneurial middle class to develop. The increased wealth and self-confidence of the Christian middle class in turn was reflected in the creation of an increasingly dense network of institutions – schools, but also gentlemen's clubs, café's, charitable organizations and (towards the end of the century) sports clubs, which allowed the expression of a distinct sociability of the non-Muslim communities.

By the 1860s, the very visible increase in wealth and status of the Christian communities gave rise to a Muslim backlash. This expressed itself on a popular level in mob violence, of which the best-known example is the pogrom in Damascus in 1860. On an élite level the Muslim reaction took the form of the 'Young Ottoman' movement.[22] This was created by young and middle-ranking Ottoman bureaucrats in 1865. The central idea of the Young Ottomans (whose ideas otherwise show a great deal of variety and inconsistency) was that reforms should not be based on imitation of the West, but on a true and modern understanding of Islam, the premise being that Islam was a rational religion receptive to scientific innovation and that in its original form the Islamic community had been an embryonic democracy. The Young Ottomans advocated the introduction of constitutional, parliamentary rule, arguing that this would give all the different communities a stake in the well being of the empire and thus create a 'Unity of the Elements' (İttihad-ı Anasır). But although a constitutional parliamentary regime was introduced in 1876, the Ottomanist ideology proved to have a very limited appeal. The new social space created by the non-Muslim minorities instead proved to be the ideal breeding ground for ethnic nationalism. When war broke out between the empire and Russia in 1877 over the question of Bulgarian reforms, the relations between Muslims and non-Muslims again were under severe strain. The disastrous defeat in the war of 1877–8 discredited the idea of parliamentary constitutionalism in the eyes of most Muslims, including the Sultan himself.

Faced with the onslaught of nationalism and liberalism, Sultan Abdülhamit II (r. 1876–1909) reacted in much the same manner as did his contemporaries Francis-Joseph of Austria-Hungary and Alexander III of Russia. Over the heads of the middle class intelligentsia, in whose midst the constitutional movement had been born, he reached out to the masses by projecting a paternalistic image and by emphasizing the sacral nature of his rule. The Islamist and Pan-Islamist policies of Abdülhamit have been much studied, but they are interpreted in the context of the political and religious traditions of the Middle East and hence seen as a unique phenomenon. If we look at the East- and Central-European context, however, we notice that Emperor Francis-Joseph very definitely positioned himself both as a father figure and as a Catholic monarch, while Tsar Nicholas II strongly emphasized his role as champion of the Orthodoxy.[23]

In employing these ideological tools, the Sultan was at a great disadvantage when compared to his European counterparts, however. Both the Austrian and the Russian monarchs could effect a certain degree of bonding with the majority and the dominant groups in society. The vast majority of the Austro-Hungarian populations were Roman Catholic and this included the two titular ethnic groups (Germans and Hungarians). While imperial Russia included important minorities of different faiths (Catholic, Georgian and Armenian Christianity, Islam both Sunni and Shi'i), the religious element could be used to cement the bond between the monarch and the vast majority of the population as well as with the sections of society, which dominated economic and political life. The situation in the Ottoman Empire was fundamentally different. The division of labour between the fast-growing state bureaucracy (and army) composed primarily of Muslims on the one hand, and the modern trade and industry sector dominated by non-Muslims on the other,[24] meant that the sultan-caliph could not use religion as a cohesive force in his relation to those non-Muslim groups who dominated the modern sectors of the economy. He did succeed, though, in effecting a degree of bonding with the Ottoman Muslim population. The Christian population of the empire as a percentage of the whole had declined from about 40 per cent early in the nineteenth century to about 20 per cent in the early twentieth century, but that 20 per cent – or rather the bourgeoisie from among that 20 per cent – controlled the vast majority of the industrial sector and a similar percentage of international trade.

The Young Turks who carried out the constitutional revolution in July 1908 and deposed Sultan Abdülhamit nine months later presented themselves as the heirs to the constitutionalists of the 1860s and 70s. Ostensibly, they acted in the name of the 'Unity of the Elements' ideal. In reality, however, both the confidential statements of the revolutionaries before 1908 and their policies thereafter show that they had already become thoroughly disillusioned with this concept and that their real commitment lay elsewhere. It is debatable whether they were already in the grip of Turkish nationalism or inspired by a Muslim-Ottoman proto-nationalism, but it is absolutely clear that the Young Turks of the Committee of Union and Progress (CUP) identified themselves with the interests of the state (which they served as soldiers and bureaucrats) and of the Muslim majority. Their perceived enemy was as much an 'enemy within' as an 'enemy without'.[25]

Almost immediately after the constitutional revolution of July 1908, the CUP started to address the fundamental questions of money and men. On the money front, its possibilities were limited. Its main contribution was the drawing up of a realistic state budget. Cavit Bey, the new finance minister, was able to achieve a significant increase in the tax income, but also a more realistic and much higher level of expenditure, caused in part by the early retirement and paying off of large numbers of servants of the old regime. Attempts by the Committee to negotiate the abolition of the capitulations or the introduction of differential import tariffs (instead of the *ad valorem* ones) were rejected by all European powers, however.

Where manpower was concerned, the Young Turks took the obvious course of eliminating the existing regime of exemptions through new legislation. Discussions about this started soon after the constitutional revolution of 1908, but the legislation was enacted only after the suppression of the counterrevolution of April 1909. In July 1909 military service became obligatory for all male Ottoman subjects. In October, recruitment of conscripts irrespective of religion was ordered for the first time. At this time, the communal leaders of the various Christian communities were by and large still ready to cooperate with the Young Turk regime, even though it was already apparent that their vision of what Ottoman citizenship, the 'Union of the Elements' entailed differed fundamentally from the Young Turks' vision of a unitary state. On the face of it, the Greek, Bulgarian, Syrian and Armenian community leaders agreed to universal conscription, but they added a number of conditions that ran directly counter to the intentions of the Young Turks, that is, to use the army as a melting pot for the different ethnicities. They demanded that units be ethnically and religiously homogeneous, be officered by Christians and – in the case of the Bulgarians – be stationed only in the European provinces of the empire. There was very little enthusiasm for military service among the mass of the Christian population and many of those who could afford it (mostly children of the bourgeoisie) opted to leave the country physically while the recruitment drive was underway or to get a foreign passport, which would render them exempt from military service.[26]

The outbreak of World War I finally gave the Young Turks the opportunity to free themselves from the constraints, which had been preventing the Ottomans from fully exploiting their available resources. On 2 August 1914 the Ottoman government announced that it was suspending payments on the national debt and on 1 October 1914 the age-old capitulations were unilaterally abolished. By this time, however, identity politics, aiming at the creation of, if not a Turkish, certainly an Ottoman-Muslim nation took precedence over economic and military rationality. In other words: of the two problems facing the Ottoman reformers that of national cohesion now completely overshadowed that of financial and human resources.

Economic and fiscal rationality would have dictated the expansion of existing and growing modern industrial and commercial sector, which was almost wholly owned by members of the non-Muslim communities, and the extraction of this surplus through effective taxation. This was no longer an option by 1914, however, after the trauma caused by the Balkan Wars, in which hundreds of thousand of Muslims, including a disproportionate percentage of the political and cultural élite, lost their ancestral homes. The 'National Economy' (*Millî İktisat*) programme launched by the Young Turks in 1914 therefore was primarily the product of ethno-religious nationalism and served a political rather than an economic purpose. It aimed at replacing the non-Muslim entrepreneurs with Muslim ones. As many as 150,000 Greeks were expelled in 1914 even before the outbreak of war, and life was made extremely hard for the remaining Christian entrepreneurs. While it is true that the 'National Economy' programme laid the groundwork for the growth of a native Turkish entrepreneurial class, which came into its own in the republic, for the empire economic nationalism meant a loss in commercial, technical and managerial skills and a fall in productivity.[27]

Military rationality would have pointed to increasing the fighting strength of the army and navy by reducing the number of exemptions, and calling up as many recruits as possible. But here too, the logic of ethnic and religious antagonism prevailed. The Young Turks (not entirely without reason) doubted the loyalties of the Greek and Armenian communities and they were not prepared to run any risks with Greek and Armenian soldiers. This was shown in dramatic fashion when, after the failure – with great loss of life – of the Ottoman winter offensive against the Russians of December 1914–January 1915, the Armenian soldiers were disarmed and reassigned to labour battalions. Most of them were later killed.

The deportation of the Armenian population of Anatolia to the Syrian desert that started in May 1915, and the wholesale killings which accompanied it, contradicted both economic and military rationality. In the countryside of Eastern Anatolia, it destroyed a very important part of the agricultural sector, thus ensuring that the Ottoman army would have to fight without local supplies of food and fodder. Likewise, in the towns a major part of the industrial and commercial infrastructure was destroyed, affecting the productive capacity of the empire as a whole.

The ethnic policies of World War I started a process, which, together with the flight of the Greeks in 1922 and the population exchange executed under the aegis of the League of Nations in 1924, rendered Anatolia far more homogeneous ethnically and religiously. These policies formed the basis for the creation of a successful national state, the Republic of Turkey, but they could not save the empire from collapse.

Conclusion

The reasons for the Ottoman Empire's ultimate failure to sustain its viability thus are manifold. It lacked the manpower, the money and the industrial base necessary to compete successfully with European powers. The prerogatives of the European states under the system of capitulations severely limited its room for manoeuvre in the economic sphere. The division of labour between a vastly increased state apparatus, dominated by Muslims, and a modern industrial and commercial sector, completely dominated by Christians under foreign protection, meant that economic growth could hardly be tapped by the state to increase its resources. At the same time the explosive growth of the number of protected Christians and of their wealth created the social and cultural space in which separatist nationalisms could blossom. By the time the Ottoman élite tried to counter these with emotional appeals to a shared Ottoman citizenship and patriotism in the 1860s, it was already too late. Sultan Abdülhamit's emphasis on the Islamic character of the state during his rule in the 1880s and 1890s served to further alienate the non-Muslims. The Young Turk movement, which emerged in the 1890s and held power between 1908 and 1918, was born out of a Muslim reaction against the perceived failure of the sultan's regime to stop the weakening of the Ottoman state and the encroachments of foreigners and local Christians. When external circumstances gave them the opportunity to act independently, identity politics, or solving the ethnic issue, took priority over increasing the financial and human resources of the state.

6. The Ides of April: A Fundamentalist Uprising in Istanbul in 1909?*

Secularism in the Ottoman Empire

The development of secularism has been a dominant theme in the history of the Ottoman Empire and the Turkish Republic from the early nineteenth century onwards.[1] Prior to the establishment of the Turkish Republic secularization was not a primary aim of the policy makers, but a side effect of the policies formulated, which were aimed at strengthening the Ottoman State through the adoption of European methods. It was not until the mid-1920s that the Republican government under the leadership of Mustafa Kemal Atatürk expressly sought to end the political, social and cultural influence of Islamic institutions and to achieve a total dominance of the secular state over those institutions.

The policies which prevailed during most of the nineteenth- and early twentieth centuries, especially during the period of the *Tanzimat,* or 'reforms' (1839–78),[2] were motivated primarily by two factors: first, the realization by a number of leading statesmen and bureaucrats that the only way for the Ottoman Empire to survive the onslaught of the European nation states was imitation of these states' apparently successful ways and, second, the desire on the part of these statesmen to gain the support of the European powers (especially Britain) against external enemies (mainly the Russian Empire) and internal ones (first of all Muhammad Ali Pasha, the governor of Egypt) through the adoption of measures which would inspire confidence in Europe.

One important element of the nineteenth-century Ottoman reforms, which followed the famous edict of *Gülhane* of 1839, was the creation of a modern conscripted army and navy, equipped with European hardware, and the creation of a bureaucracy along Western, primarily French, lines.[3] Together these reforms enabled the central government to strengthen its hold on the provinces of the empire to a degree which was unprecedented in the history of the Middle East.[4] Even if this in itself did not necessarily constitute a secularizing

73

influence, the establishment of schools and academies for the training of the new civil servants and soldiers did. The founding of these schools undermined the position of the *ulema* in education, culminating in the complete emancipation of the educational system from the control of the *ulema* in 1924.

The second important development of this period was the opening up of the Ottoman economy to the West and its incorporation into the capitalist world system, a process which picked up steam following the Ottoman–British commercial treaty of 1838.[5] This, too, had a secularizing influence, because the legislation and the courts introduced to enable foreigners to trade under conditions acceptable to them, were of a Western type and functioned outside the *sharia,* which, at least theoretically, had been the basis of the Ottoman legal system in the past.

In the third place, the Ottoman reformists felt compelled to comply with Western demands on the very sensitive issue of the relation between Muslims and non-Muslims in the empire, introducing the concept of equal Ottoman citizenship for all. The introduction of this concept, which of course had no place in the *sharia,* was a form of radical secularization, even if it did not strike root in the mentality of the great majority of the Muslim, or indeed Christian population. In the second half of the century, especially after the *Islahat Fermanı* edict of 1856 (which was seen as being issued under foreign pressure), these developments, and the privileged position which the Christian minorities of the empire managed to gain under the aegis of the European powers, led to growing resentment of the *Tanzimat* policies on the part of the Muslim population.[6] This resentment not only found expression in conspiracies, popular uprisings and anti-Christian riots such as those in Syria in 1860, but also in criticism voiced by the emerging Muslim intelligentsia, the second generation reformers who were active in the 1860s and 70s, the so-called 'Young Ottomans'. The Young Ottomans sought to limit the power of the new bureaucrats through the introduction of a constitutional, parliamentary monarchy, which in their eyes was fundamentally consistent with Islam.[7]

The Young Ottoman programme was realized with the introduction of the Ottoman constitution in 1876,[8] but the new Sultan, Abdülhamit II, who had initially appeared receptive to Young Ottoman aims, soon reverted to autocratic rule, suspending constitution and parliament. Abdülhamit, while continuing the modernizations of the *Tanzimat* in many ways, emphasized the Islamic character of his reign and of the empire in an attempt to counterbalance the influence of Western liberal ideas.[9]

During his reign, however, the agitation for a return to constitutional and parliamentarian rule continued, and even gained a far broader basis through the expansion of modern, Western-type education in the empire.[10] The constitutional movement started to expand rapidly in the 1890s, but in 1896 the Hamidian police succeeded in crushing the underground movement and for the next ten years the reformists were active mostly as exiles: in Cairo, Geneva and first and foremost: in Paris. There the movement crystallized into two distinct factions: the nationalist and centralist one around Ahmet Rıza (the Committee of Union and Progress – *İttihad ve Terakki Cemiyeti*) and the liberal and decentralist one around Prince Sabahettin (The League for Private Initiative and Decentralization – *Teşebbüs-ü Şahsi ve Adem-i Merkeziyet Cemiyeti*).[11]

From 1906 onwards, the constitutional movement underwent a new period of growth within the empire, especially within the Ottoman armies in European Turkey. Basically, this was an autonomous growth, but the movement merged with the faction of Ahmet Rıza and adopted the name 'Committee of Progress and Union' in 1907.[12] It later reverted to the better known 'Committee of Union and Progress' (CUP).

The constitutional revolution

In July 1908, the CUP, threatening the Ottoman government with armed intervention, succeeded in forcing the Sultan to restore the constitution and reconvene parliament. But the CUP did not utilize the revolution as a means of taking over power itself. In the Ottoman context of 1908 junior officers and civil servants were simply not acceptable as members of government. Neither did the Unionists see in themselves the ability to govern. Instead they left government in the hands of a senior statesman of the old regime with a relatively liberal reputation, *Kıbrıslı* Kâmil Pasha (1832–1912), and set themselves up as a sort of watchdog committee.[13]

Thanks to their superior organization, the parliamentary elections of the autumn of 1908 resulted in a complete Unionist victory. But here, too, the Unionist influence remained indirect rather than direct, because in many parts of the empire they had to rely on local notables who allowed their names to be put forward as candidates on the Unionist list, rather than on members of the CUP itself.[14]

After the astounding success of the revolution, the CUP was the most powerful force in the country, but increasingly through 1908 and the early months of 1909 it had to contend with two types of opposition. One was that of the followers of Prince Sabahattin, united since September in the *Ahrar Fırkası* (Liberal Party),[15] who had done badly in the elections and felt increasingly frustrated. Kâmil Pasha, who, like the Liberals, resented the pressure of the

CUP, allied himself with this group and relations between him and the CUP became increasingly strained. On 14 February, the CUP succeeded in having the Grand Vizier voted out of office in parliament and having him replaced with Hüseyin Hilmi Pasha (1855–1921), who was close to the Committee.[16] Hereafter a bitter press campaign was started by the opposition, which was answered by the Unionist organs in kind. On 6 April, Hasan Fehmi, the editor of one of the fiercest anti-Unionist papers, *Serbestî* (Freedom), was killed on the Galata-bridge by a Unionist 'volunteer' (*fedaî*). His funeral the next day turned into a mass demonstration against the Committee.[17]

The second type of opposition which faced the CUP was that posed by conservative religious circles, notably the lower *ulema* and sheykhs of the *tarikats*. During the month of Ramadan, which coincided with October 1908, there were a number of incidents and at least two serious and violent demonstrations, during which the closure of bars and theatres, the prohibition of photography and restrictions on the freedom of movement of women were demanded.[18] On 3 April, the religious extremists, who were already active as a group around the newspaper *Volkan* of the Nakhsibandi Sheykh Dervish Vahdeti, organized themselves as the *İttihad-i Muhammedi* (Muhammadan Union), whose president was considered to be the prophet himself.[19] This group organized large-scale propaganda against the policies and mentality of the Young Turks.

The counterrevolution

In spite of all this political infighting and the rising tensions of the past months, it came as a complete surprise to Unionists and foreign observers alike, when, on the night of 12–13 April 1909 an armed insurrection broke out in the capital in the name of the restoration of Islam and *sharia*. Not meeting significant opposition from government, CUP or the Army, the insurgents took over the capital in less than 24 hours. In the capital, the Committee seemed vanquished, but its position in the provinces, most of all in Macedonia, remained intact and within a fortnight troops loyal to the CUP suppressed the counterrevolution and returned the Committee to power. Although the insurrection was suppressed with relative ease, the *31 Mart vakası*, or '31 March incident', as it is known in Turkish history because of its date in the old *Rumi* calendar, made a deep impression on the reformists. The fact that a revolt in the name of Islam had been able to shake the foundations of their regime so easily and quickly came as a rude shock to them. Nearly all the Kemalists, who succeeded the Unionists after World War I and went on to found the secular republic of Turkey, had been members of the CUP. Therefore, the memory, or trauma, of the 1909 revolt was theirs, too. To the supporters of secularism in Turkey the '31 March incident' served as a constant reminder of the danger of Islamic fundamentalism. Even today, whenever the secular system of government of Turkey seems threatened, references to the incident are frequently made.

After a short description of the events of April 1909, and a survey of their possible causes and instigators, I shall address the question whether the qualification 'fundamentalist' is adequate or even helpful in this context. At the same time, I shall try to determine the place of the events of 1909 in the development of the relations between Islam and the State in modern Turkey.

Quite an extensive secondary literature, both scholarly and popular, exists on the subject, much of which is based on memoirs,[20] newspaper reports and foreign archives. The Turkish archives as yet do not seem to have been used for the study of this subject to any extent. A new and far more liberal archival regime was established in Turkey in 1989. Theoretically all the materials pertinent to the events of 1909 should now be open to researchers and this seems indeed to be the case. The cataloguing of the collections has also progressed enormously.

For this occasion I have looked into the Dutch legation reports, kept in the State Archives in The Hague (*ARA*). The coverage given in these records to the insurrection, its prelude and its aftermath is quite extensive (reports being sent daily during the crisis) and, given the limitations of intelligence gathering by a small embassy, the quality is quite remarkable. Even if it offers no startling revelations, it does give a detailed picture of what happened, and a good 'feel' for the period.

The crisis of April 1909 lasted for only 11 days. During the night of 12/13 April, the battalions of Macedonian troops at Taşkışla barracks, which had been brought in only a week before by the CUP to replace the (supposedly less reliable) Arab and Albanian troops,[21] mutinied, after having taken their officers prisoner. Together with a large number of *softas,* students from the religious schools, they marched to the *At Meydanı* where the parliament building stood. During the morning, more and more troops and *ulema* joined them. The government was in disarray and did not dare to send in the loyal troops, but instead dispatched the Chief of Police to listen to the demands of the mob. The spokesmen of the insurgent troops formulated six demands: dismissal of the Grand Vizier and the Ministers of War and of the Navy, replacement of a number of Unionist officers, replacement of the Unionist President of the Chamber of Deputies (Ahmet Riza), banishment of a number of Unionist deputies from Istanbul, restoration of the *sharia*, and an amnesty for the rebellious troops.[22] Confronted with these demands, the Grand Vizier went to the palace in the afternoon and tendered his resignation, which was accepted by the Sultan. The next morning, it was announced that the colourless diplomat Tevfik Pasha [Okday] (1845–1936) had been appointed Grand Vizier. The War Minister in the new cabinet, Field-Marshal Ethem Pasha visited the soldiers at the *At Meydanı,* praised them and promised that all their demands would be met.[23]

The troops and the *softas* celebrated their victory extensively. At the same time, a pogrom against known Unionists developed, resulting in the deaths of at least 20 people, mostly officers, but also two deputies, who were mistaken for Hüseyin Cahit [Yalçin], the editor of the Unionist organ *Tanin,* and Ahmet Rıza. The offices of the *Tanin* were also ransacked.[24]

The Unionists went underground or fled the capital. As a result, the Chamber of Deputies, in which the CUP held the majority, did not have a quorum. Nevertheless, the deputies who did attend at the instigation of the Liberal (and Albanian) deputy İsmail Kemal Bey [Vlora] accepted the demands of the soldiers and at the same time issued a proclamation, saying that *sharia* and constitution would be maintained.[25]

From the first day on, the leaders of the *Ahrar* tried without success to get a grip on events and to prevent the insurrection from moving into a reactionary, anti-constitutionalist and pro-Abdülhamit direction. It should be noted, too, that the higher ranking *ulema* (those who in the ambassador's report are called 'ulema', as opposed to the 'hojas' who supported the revolt), who were united in the *Cemiyet-i İlmiye-i İslamiye* (Society of the Islamic Scholarly Profession) never supported the insurrection and from the 16 April onwards openly denounced it.[26]

The CUP had been driven out of Istanbul, but had kept its position in the provinces, notably in Macedonia, and it started to take countermeasures right away. It organized public demonstrations in the provincial towns, and showered the parliament and palace with telegrams.[27] In Macedonia, especially, it easily won the propaganda battle, convincing the population that the constitution was in danger. From 15 April it started organizing a military campaign against the rebels. The 'Action Army' *(Hareket Ordusu),* as it was termed, consisted of regular units of the Third and Second Armies, reinforced with volunteer units, which consisted mostly of Albanians, led by Niyazi Bey, one of the heroes of the revolution of 1908.[28] By train, these troops were moved first to Çatalca and Hademköy and then to Ayastefanos (nowadays Yeşilköy) on the outskirts of Istanbul.[29]

The Chamber of Deputies sent a delegation to the Action Army's headquarters to try to prevent it from taking the city by force. Unable to obtain a positive response, the members of the delegation decided to stay in Ayastefanos and issued a call to their colleagues to join them. From 22 April onwards both chambers of parliament sat together in Ayastefanos as a 'National Assembly' *(meclis-i umumi-i millî)*.[30]

In the early morning of 24 April, the Action Army began to occupy the city. It did not encounter much resistance – only at the Taksim and Taşkışla barracks did the resistance amount to anything. By four o'clock in the afternoon the last rebels had surrendered.[31] Three days later, the two chambers of parliament, still sitting together, deposed Sultan Abdülhamit, who was succeeded by his younger brother Mehmet Reşat.[32] In the days that followed, two courts martial were instituted, which convicted and executed a large number of the rebels, including Derwish Vahdeti. A number of *Ahrar* leaders were arrested, but set free again under British pressure.

Now, after this brief overview of the events, let us try to summarize the causes of the revolt, the demands of the insurgents and the reaction of the Unionists, in order to establish the character of the insurgency and its place in modern Turkish history.

A fundamentalist uprising?

Several different causes for the events of April 1909 can be discerned. Different groups had become disenchanted with the constitutional regime for different reasons. The overthrow of the old regime in the 1908 revolution had hurt those who had earned a living or enjoyed status as members of the Hamidian apparatus, including the thousands of government spies active in Istanbul, who had supplied the Sultan with their *jurnals* (reports).

The rationalizing policies of the new government, which aimed at ending the overstaffing of government departments, which had been the result of the old regime's policies of favouritism, had already made thousands of civil servants jobless. In a city like Istanbul, where government was the main industry, this had far-reaching consequences.

In the army, the main source of trouble was the friction between the *mektepli* officers, who had been trained in the military schools and academy, and the *alaylı* officers, who had risen through the ranks. The latter had been favoured by the old regime, being paid regularly and stationed in the First Army in and around Istanbul, while the former had been mistrusted (rightly so, because it was these modern educated officers who brought about the constitutional revolution of 1908). Now that the *mektepli* officers had taken over, many of the *alaylı* officers had been dismissed or demoted. Even worse, the whole system of promotion from the ranks was discontinued. The troops themselves, too, had reason for discontent. They were accustomed to the very slack discipline and relaxed atmosphere of the old army, and were now confronted with young officers who wanted to impose Prussian training methods, among other things abolishing the pauses for ablutions and prayers during the exercises.[33]

While no explicitly secularist legislation had been enacted in the eight months since the constitutional revolution, the lower *ulema* clearly felt threatened by the change in atmosphere. One particular measure which aroused feeling among this group was a new measure, stipulating that students at the religious schools who did not pass their exams in time were no longer exempted from military service.[34]

The discord within the Young Turk ranks, with the *Ahrar* opposing what they saw as the irresponsible policies and the monopoly of power of the Unionists, also helped foster an atmosphere conducive to revolt. The debate between the two factions grew more and more fierce in the first months of 1909. These acrimonious verbal exchanges, which could easily spill over into real violence, helped to create a climate in which political opposition came to be regarded as treason. The Dutch legation noted on several occasions that this climate would leave the field open to the conservatives.[35] The exaggerated and immoderate political debate, with its personal attacks, was characteristic both of the Young Turk era and of the Kemalist period. (And even, one might add, of Turkish politics of recent years.)

Finally, the fact that the Unionists were out of touch with important parts of public opinion – and thus were completely taken by surprise by the discontent which existed even among their own Macedonian troops – was also a contributing factor to the crisis. The Young Turks in all guises (Unionists, Liberals and Kemalists) were always very much an enlightened élite, who saw it as their task to educate the masses. Their positivist, liberal and nationalist vision was not supported by what, in a European context, would be considered its natural base, an emerging indigenous bourgeoisie. Instead this vision was forced on a conservative and deeply religious population from above.

Thus, a number of factors can be pointed to as having contributed to a climate, in which the insurrection could take place. But who were the actual instigators? This has been the subject of a lot of speculation, both at the time of the revolt and later.[36]

In all its statements, the CUP characterized the insurrection as an instance of 'reaction' *(irtica)*. It laid the blame squarely on the shoulders of

Sultan Abdülhamit and the religious opposition of the *İttihad-i Muhammedi* of Sheykh Vahdeti. At the time, the hand of the Sultan was also seen in the fact, reported on by the Dutch legation that the insurgents had ample funds and that the soldiers had apparently been paid in gold.[37] Nevertheless, it is clear that throughout the 11-day revolt, the Sultan acted with extreme caution. While he did not openly disavow the soldiers, he never openly supported their demands or tried to lead their movement.

When the Action Army entered the city, he apparently greeted it with relief and ordered the palace troops not to offer resistance. All through the revolt he made the impression of being frightened and demoralized.[38] In his memoirs, he later denied having had anything to do with the revolt.

Conservative opinion in Turkey has sometimes accused the Unionists of staging the whole revolt in order to be able to establish a dictatorship, adducing the fact that the revolt started in the Macedonian battalions as proof.[39] This, however, seems fanciful, in view of the patent unpreparedness of leading Unionists, who had to flee or go underground, some of them just escaping being lynched. No trace of evidence for this thesis has ever been found.

The demands formulated by the insurgents and the evidence presented both before the courts martial and in the memoirs of opposition leaders point to the political opposition, the *Ahrar*, as the prime instigators.[40] The selective way in which the insurgents attacked Unionist individuals and offices also supports this view. At the same time, it is clear that the religious opposition centred around Sheykh Vahdeti and the *İttihad-i Muhammedi* played a very important part in organizing the uprising and in rousing the troops.[41] Most probably the liberal opposition was the original instigator of the revolt. Overestimating its own strength, *Ahrar* thought it could use the religious groups for that purpose, but soon after the start of the revolt, it became clear that it was in no position to exert control. The willingness of one group of basically secularist reformers to form an opportunistic alliance with Islamic groups in its struggle for power with another group of reformers – in the mistaken belief that less sophisticated religious groups can be easily manipulated – is a recurring phenomenon in the politics of modern Turkey.

There were persistent rumours in 1909, reflected in the literature on the revolt, that Great Britain was behind the uprising. The gold distributed among the troops attracted suspicion and attention was drawn to the close links between *Ahrar* leaders and the British embassy. No hard evidence of British involvement has ever come to light, however.

Now, coming to the question of the fundamentalist Islamic character of the revolt, there is no denying that the call for reinstatement of the *sharia* played a large role in the insurrection, which was seen by Unionists and foreign observers such as the Dutch envoy alike as a reactionary Islamic movement. On the other hand, there are good grounds to consider this label inadequate. First, there is strong evidence that the Liberals, who were no more Islamic or fundamentalist than the Unionists, instigated the revolt. Second, there is no relation whatsoever between the call for the *sharia* and the other demands put forward. Third, the insurgents never formulated specific demands for the way the *sharia* should be implemented. Neither did they demand the dissolution of parliament and/or the prorogation of the constitution. It appears that the call for the *sharia* was either a tactical move designed to legitimize the uprising and provide it with a rallying-cry or a kind of 'shorthand' for justice and a return to the good old ways. It should be remembered that the *sharia* had not actually been abolished by the Young Turks.

The CUP, in its counter-propaganda, immediately identified the insurrection as *irtica* (political reaction), which endangered constitution and parliament. This may have been in part a psychological reaction. Both their positivist ideology and their history of struggle against Sultan Abdülhamit's regime had conditioned them to see religious conservatism as the main threat to the realization of their ideals. The 31 March incident seems to have been a genuinely traumatic experience for the Unionists.

It cannot be denied, however, that labelling the insurrection as reactionary and Islamic also had practical political advantages: it enabled the Committee to isolate their opponents by posing as the defenders of the constitution, thereby attracting the support of those Young Turks who shared their secularist outlook but had become disenchanted with the Committee's policies after the revolution. In this way they could eliminate the liberal opposition by identifying them with the insurrection. It also gave them a chance to dethrone Abdülhamit, something which they had not been able to do in 1908 and which was seen by them (and also by neutral observers) as essential to the consolidation of their position.[42]

Both the use of the call for *sharia* as a battle-cry by the opposition and the labelling of the revolt as *irtica* by the Unionists allows for an interesting comparison of the April 1909 counter-revolution with the February 1925 insurrection of Sheykh Sait (a Nakhsibandi sheykh, just like Derwish Vahdeti) in Eastern Turkey.[43] This revolt was at least partly Kurdish nationalist in character and it was motivated by discontent with the social and economic situation in the Kurdish provinces. Nevertheless, the leaders used the call for the *sharia* as a rallying-cry. The rebellion was immediately labelled as *irtica* by the then Turkish government (which consisted of former

Unionists) and subsequently suppressed with the utmost severity. The Prime Minister, Fethi [Okyar], explicitly compared the situation to of the revolt of April 1909 in a speech in the National Assembly.[44] It was on this occasion that, through an amendment to the High Treason Law, the political use of religion was outlawed in Turkey for the first time (it has remained so ever since). The High Treason Law was subsequently used to suppress the liberal opposition within the National Assembly, the Progressive Republican Party, the left-wing opposition outside the Assembly and the opposition press, even though none of these could be linked to the Kurdish rebellion.

Along with the suppression of the socialist, liberal and Kurdish oppositions in 1925, the Kemalist regime intensified its drive to crush institutionalized Islam. Unfortunately, this policy also strengthened the tendency, already evident in 1909, for Islam to become the vehicle for opposition to the policies of an authoritarian state. Likewise, it also rendered supporters of the secular State allergic to expressions of Islamic feeling. This seems to be the vicious circle in which the debate on the relation between Islam and State has been caught in Turkey for much of this century.

7. Sultan Mehmet V's Visit to Kosovo in June 1911*

The context

For the Young Turks of the CUP, whose movement had started in Macedonia in 1906, the situation in that rich but unruly region of the empire[1] in 1910–11 was all but reassuring. Although the constitutional revolution of July 1908 initially had produced rejoicing and reconciliation between the ethnic communities in Macedonia, this had proved short-lived, with agitation and small-scale guerrilla warfare by Serb, Bulgarian and Greek bands recommencing soon after. More worrying from the point of view of the CUP was the attitude of the Albanians. After all, the Committee had originally been an organization of Ottoman Muslims[2] who aimed to strengthen the Ottoman state and the position of the Muslims within it. Most Albanians were Muslims and some Albanians, like the famous Niyazi Bey of Resne (nowadays known as Resen or Resnja)[3] had played leading roles both in the revolution of 1908 and in the suppression of the counterrevolution of April 1909. In the case of the latter, it was military units from Macedonia which, having stayed loyal to the CUP, were instrumental in re-establishing Unionist control.

Nevertheless, attempts by the constitutional regime to strengthen the hold of the state, to make taxation more effective, and to standardize education (in the Ottoman language and script)[4] soon led to disenchantment on the part of the Albanians. The enforcement of military conscription and the disarming of populations also caused great resentment among the Albanians. There were revolts in Northern Albania and Kosovo even in 1909, but in early April 1910, 12 Albanian tribes from the province of Kosovo rose up in arms, led by two tribal chiefs: İsa Boletin, who controlled the Mitrovica area, and İdris Sefer, a chief from Skopska Crna Gora. Led by İdris, 5,000 Albanians cut off the railway between Salonica and Üsküp (now Skoplje) at Kacanik, while İsa led 2,000 rebels against Firzovik (Verisovic/Ferisaj) and Prizren. The insurrection was suppressed with some difficulty by 16,000

Ottoman troops under Şevket Turgut Pasha[5] and by August order had been re-established.[6] The government now took harsh measures to ensure that the area remained under control: all men between the ages of 15 and 60 were registered, with those who were eligible conscripted into the army; Albanian men were disarmed and nearly 150,000 guns confiscated; a new tax on livestock was introduced; and farmers were ordered to widen the windows of their homes (to make them less suitable as loophole).

Nevertheless, rebellion flared up again in February 1911, this time in the area of Dibra. On 24 March, Albanian refugees in Montenegro launched an attack that spilled over into the bordering Skutari (Üsküdar/Skhoder) district. Again Şevket Turgut Pasha was ordered to suppress the rebellion and he arrived with 8,000 troops in Skutari on 17 April.[7] After a difficult campaign the rebels were forced back, but when war with Montenegro threatened, the government ordered the Pasha to declare a ten-day armistice on 17 June. In the meantime, yet another rebellion had flared up, this time among Catholic Albanians more to the South.[8]

The CUP was deeply worried about the situation in Macedonia. One of the reasons they had unleashed the constitutional revolution when they did, in July 1908, was their fear that the European powers would militarily intervene in Macedonia.[9] With the situation in Macedonia all the more precarious, the danger of European intervention certainly had not passed. The Committee therefore decided on a campaign of counter-propaganda built around the most powerful symbol of national unity at their disposal: the figure of the Sultan himself.

Tours of the provinces were not a part of the Ottoman monarchic tradition. Of course, until the seventeenth century, sultans had personally conducted military campaigns which took them through the length and the breadth of their domains. Later sultans had largely restricted themselves to hunting trips. The nineteenth-century sultans who oversaw the process of institutional and legal reforms known as the *Tanzimat*, Abdülmecit (r. 1839–61) and Abdülaziz (r. 1861–76) left their palace with increasing frequency and travelled outside the capital. Sultan Abdülmecit visited İzmir and Bursa in 1845 and Salonica in 1859, a visit during which he was accompanied by his sons, among them the young Prince Reşat – the protagonist of this story.[10] Sultan Abdülaziz had visited Bursa in 1861, Egypt in 1863, and the most famous voyage of all was of course his visit to the Paris World Exhibition in 1867.

During the long reign of Sultan Abdülhamit II (1876–1909), the Sultan had only rarely ventured outside the palace of Yıldız, situated on a hill overlooking the Bosphorus and quite isolated from the capital. He had never made any effort to personally acquaint himself directly with the situation outside the capital or the populations in the provinces. Instead, Abdülhamit relied on his bureaucracy and his extensive network of informers for his intelligence, and on propaganda through the printed media and through the pulpits of the mosques for the projection of his image as just ruler and defender of Islam.[11] The Sultan certainly used modern propaganda techniques to promote his image abroad,[12] but he did not do so by personally boarding ship and going there. Nor did he use the new railway network to tour his country. So, by 1909, when Abdülhamit was deposed, the memory of sultans actually going out to meet their flock was quite a distant one.

Prince Reşat,[13] on the other hand, had already made two very symbolic journeys outside his capital since he had ascended the throne as Mehmet V[14] in April 1909. He had visited the old Ottoman capitals of Bursa and Edirne. But these expeditions had been minor ones compared with the one he was now undertaking.

The expedition to Macedonia was planned meticulously, not only by the government, but also by the palace, especially the palace kitchens, the stables and, of course, the privy purse, the monarch's own allowance from the treasury. For the Sultan and his entourage to move, eat, drink and dress according to their custom, the palace would have to bring everything along for the trip, from kitchen utensils to carriages.[15] The visit was originally planned for April, but the unrest in Albania and the complexity of the preparations had necessitated a postponement.

The imperial visit

The Sultan left Istanbul on 5 June 1911 amid great pomp and circumstance and watched by a large crowd on the banks of the Bosphorus. He travelled aboard the battleship *Barbaros Hayrettin* with part of his entourage, escorted by the cruiser *Turgut Reis*[16] and the steamer *Gülcemal*. After a short stop in Çanakkale, where there was a great demonstration of loyalty on the part of the population, the imperial flotilla arrived before Salonica on the morning of 8 June, a day of continuous rain. There seem to have been worries whether Reşat would be able to withstand the exhaustion of the long trip, particularly the sea voyage to which he was unaccustomed, but according to his private secretary, once at sea he seemed rejuvenated and relaxed and altogether changed from the person he was in Istanbul. He even spoke fluently in public, whereas in Istanbul he had been notoriously shy.[17]

The flotilla was met at sea by a squadron of warships carrying dignitaries, such as the governor of Salonica, the inspectors of the Fourth,
Fifth, Sixth and Seventh Army Corps, and the secretary-general of the
CUP, Haci Adil [Arda]. The steamer *Mithat Pasha* held a special delegation
composed of representatives from all parts of the empire. The fleet greeted
the Sultan with a 21-gun salute, after which he watched naval manoeuvres.
The flotilla then moved into the Salonica harbour escorted by the naval
squadron. After a second 21-gun salute, the *Barbaros Hayrettin* anchored
off the quay and the official reception committee, which consisted of town
representatives and parliamentarians hailing from Macedonia, went on
board.[18]

The Sultan stayed aboard the battleship overnight, but within an hour of
his arrival he despatched his secretary, Halit Ziya Bey [Uşaklıgil][19] and the
inspector of the armies of Rumelia (the European provinces), Hadi Pasha, on
a very delicate mission. They were instructed to go to the villa of the Alatini
family of Salonica industrialists, just outside Salonica, where the former
Sultan Abdülhamit lived under strict house arrest. Reşat apparently felt it
necessary to enquire after the ex-Sultan's health because he was afraid the
latter might see the tour of Macedonia as an affront. For Halit Ziya, meeting
the man who had ruled the empire for 33 years and who had been the hated
enemy of the Young Turks for 20 of them, was an awesome experience, but
the mission proved easier than expected. The ex-Sultan politely wished his
brother success on his trip and used the occasion for some personal requests.
He asked for his son Abid to be allowed to study and to live in Istanbul and
he enquired after a bag full of jewellery which had disappeared when he was
moved from the Yıldız palace to Salonica.

The next morning, the Sultan disembarked, flanked by Grand Vizier
Hakkı Pasha. Two sheep were sacrificed and the *mufti* of Salonica led the
prayers. Then the Sultan, dressed in full military uniform, drove to the main
government building (the *Konak*) in an open carriage. The streets, which
had been newly paved with the houses along the route freshly painted,[20]
were lined with schoolchildren singing Greek and Turkish national songs.
By all accounts, the monarch was greeted warmly, although, according to
the British consul, 'much less so than in the West on such occasions'.[21] The
afternoon was filled with audiences. During these, Evrenos Bey, a local
notable and a scion of the most famous Christian *gazi* dynasty[22] was singled
out for praise by the Sultan, who pointed out how his family had served
his own forefathers back in the fifteenth century – a clear call for loyalty
from the contemporary Ottoman Greek community. Then Reşat received

a delegation from the garrison, whom he greeted saying that 'the army was the soul of the nation'. He also received a delegation from the schools of Salonica.[23] During the day the Sultan received delegations from all over the empire (Skutari, Janina, Erzurum, Trabzon, Crete and Lebanon), who had come to Salonica for the occasion.[24]

Right from the start the CUP made it its business to associate itself as closely as possible with the imperial visit. Rahmi Bey [Arslan] one of the founding members of the CUP in Salonica and also a descendant of the aforementioned Gazi Evrenos, thanked the Sultan for his efforts, to which the latter answered that he was grateful for the opportunity to get in touch with his people. The famous CUP orator Ömer Naci addressed the representatives of the province on behalf of the committee and later the Sultan visited the CUP club, where top Unionists like Talât Bey, Cavit Bey and Mithat Şükrü [Bleda], as well as the historian Abdürrahman Şeref were present to welcome him.

On the morning of 9 June, the Sultan received the *mücahit-i muhterem* (honoured fighter), Niyazi Bey, who in his dual capacity as hero of the constitutional revolution and revered (although politically marginal) member of the CUP on the one hand and ethnic Albanian on the other, was a key figure throughout the whole Macedonian tour. Niyazi Bey was reported as having come to town with 600 well-built men from his native Resne.[25] After the Friday prayers in the Aya Sofya mosque of Salonica, the Sultan distributed 4,500 lira in largesse to benevolent societies, to the poor and to students.[26] In the late afternoon Cavit Bey gave a speech in the public gardens of Beşçınar, which was attended by a large crowd (10,000 people according to the Unionist newspapers) in which he called for unity between the communities and praised the CUP.

On Saturday, 10 June, the Sultan first received a delegation from İzmir. This was followed by a series of audiences with delegations from all over the empire (groups from Crete and Lebanon had already been received). Thereafter leading officials and Unionist politicians were presented with decorations (*Mecidiye* order first class), gold watches and – in the case of the editor of the local paper *Rumeli*, Yunus Nadi [Abalıoğlu] who would later gained fame as the founder of the newspaper *Cumhuriyet* – with a ruby ring.

The programme continued with a visit to the army barracks, where the foundation stone was laid for a monument commemorating the constitutional revolution. The Sultan then received CUP secretary-general Haci Adil [Arda] and praised the CUP for its work. In the afternoon, the Sultan attended a *sema* (religious ceremony) in the *Mevlevihane*, the local head-quarters of the Mevlevi derwish order, of which the Sultan was a devoted member.

In the meantime, an auction in support of the Ottoman Fleet Society (*Donanma Cemiyeti* – modelled after Germany's *Flottenverein*)[27] had been organized in the Beşçınar gardens. Among the items being auctioned were carpets, and the Sultan, at the request of the organizers, agreed to walk over them in order to increase their value.

The Sultan's departure for the interior was on 11 June. The trip to Üsküp was made by train – a seven-hour journey. A pilot train carrying part of the entourage and also Niyazi Bey preceded the imperial train, and it was announced that anyone attempting to come near the tracks between the two trains would be shot on sight. The Sultan boarded the train (on which the director-general of the Oriental Railways, Mr Müller, acted as guard)[28] in the company of CUP grandees Haci Adil and Ömer Naci, and the governors of the Salonica and Kosovo provinces. The military commander and mayor of Üsküp also joined the company. Along the route three stops were made, the first of which was a three-minute stop at Karasulu Kimence to take on water, the second, a ten-minute stop at Gevgili, and the third, a 15-minute stop in Köprülü (Velez). During this last stop an 'old and historic banner (*sancak*)' was presented to the Sultan, who took it in his hand and prayed that 'God make the Ottoman banner ever honoured'. The theme of 'Unity of the Elements' was again brought out in the ceremonies at the station: a Bulgarian girl made a moving speech and a Muslim girl recited a poem. Both were rewarded, the Bulgarian girl being offered an education at the Sultan's expense. Four sheep were sacrificed, after which the governor of Salonica officially handed over responsibility for the Sultan's well-being to the governor of Kosovo.

On his arrival in the capital of Kosovo province, Üsküp, the Sultan was driven in a four-horse carriage (brought from Istanbul) from the station to the government *Konak*, but he was lodged in the arts and crafts school, because that was the most comfortable building around. Upon his arrival, he addressed the local dignitaries, repeating the central themes of his visit. He stated that his aim was the 'mutual understanding of the [ethnic] elements' and that the CUP deserved the gratitude of the fatherland for its services. The Sultan was enthusiastically received by the Albanian population. Albanians performed folk dances after which each of them received a lira. Some 5,000 Albanians had come to the town from villages up to 20 kilometres away, but considerable effort seems to have gone into 'engineering' this Albanian enthusiasm. According to one report, the district governor (*mütesarrif*) of Prizren had given Albanian villagers five days food supplies to enable them to make the trip.[29]

Attempts at reconciliation with the Albanians now took centre-stage, given the Sultan's proximity to areas with an Albanian majority. Two Albanian chiefs who had taken part in the revolts of spring 1910, Süleyman Batuşa and Hasan Aga of Plevlje (Pljevlja), came to swear fealty to the Ottoman throne and were pardoned, but the notorious İsa Boletin, who had been expected, did not show up. Largesse was again employed as a means to win support for the throne, this time not only in the form of donations to charitable institutions (for instance, a promise to build a *medrese* in Priştine/ Prishtina and 300 lira towards the cost of building a school in Firzovik), but also in the form of blood money, distributed to pay off blood feuds. A sum of 30,000 lira is reported to have been spent for this purpose.[30] Another instrument for reconciliation was the granting of amnesties. There had been high hopes among the Christian communities of a large-scale or even general amnesty, but during the visit to Salonica nothing had materialized. Now an amnesty for all except convicted murderers was announced, and 107 Albanians and 134 Bulgarians were released from Üsküp prison.[31]

After the visit to Üsküp, the time had come for what was meant to be the climax of the whole imperial visit: the Sultan's pilgrimage to the *Meşhed-i Hüdavendigar,* the tomb of Sultan Murat I, located on the old battlefield of Kosovopolje near Prishtina. The visit had been publicized widely beforehand. On the day the Sultan left for Salonica, CUP secretary-general Haci Adil issued a statement reminding the population that in the battle of Kosovopolje in 1389, the crusading Christians, 'numerous as locusts', had wanted to throw the Ottomans out of Europe, but that, thanks to the sacrifice of Sultan Murat and his warriors, they had failed. Muslims were called upon to come to Kosovo in great numbers to show their determination to follow Murat's example, and expectations about the number of people attending were very high. In the newspapers, 150,000 or even 200,000 Albanians were reported to be assembling in the plain. The British consul in Üsküp expected 100,000 to turn up.[32]

On 15 June the Sultan left Üsküp for Prishtina by train. During a short stop in Firzovik, two sheep were offered. After three and a half hours, the Sultan arrived in Prishtina, where the mass of people awaiting him had swelled to 300,000, according to Unionist press. Four sheep were sacrificed and an amnesty declared for those who had taken part in the rebellions of 1910 and 1911.

In Prishtina the local Serbian community played an interesting role in the events of the day. A visit by a direct descendent of Sultan Murat I to the battlefield of Kosovopolje, which played (and still plays) such a vital part in the national identity of Serbia, might be expected to meet with strong Serbian resistance. But at this time the Serbs saw the Ottomans as less of a danger than the Albanian and Macedonian/Bulgarian nationalists, and were therefore supportive of Young Turk policies to a certain extent. The Serbian crown prince had originally even been expected to come to Üsküp, but that visit had not materialized, as he had to attend the coronation of King George V in London.[33] In Prishtina, however, the Sultan was serenaded by the choir of the Serbian Orthodox seminary and the Serbian vice-consul Raki had gathered a large Serb crowd.[34]

The next day the royal entourage left for Kosovopolje, arriving there at 10 a.m. Reports on what actually happened there vary widely. The pro-CUP press depicted the meeting as an enormous success and stated that 300,000 Albanians attended. Sir Edwin Pears gives a number of 80,000 in his memoirs,[35] while Halit Ziya, who was present in Kosovopolje, reports that there were about 50,000 people. He says that many more had wanted to come, but that they were stopped for fear of overcrowding.[36] According to British consular reports, however, the Ottomans had real trouble gathering a credible number of people. The Grand Vizier had made a personal request to local notables such as Hasan Bey (a representative for Prishtina) and Beytullah Bey of Gilan, and most of the villagers came from their areas. From places such as İpek (Peç), Djakova and Prizren, where resentment against the repression by the Ottoman army was strongest, only a few official representatives appeared.[37] Indeed, photographs taken during the ceremony and published in the journal *Resimli Kitab* seem to show an attendance of 20,000 people at most.

Facing the mausoleum of Murat I, a historic tent originally belonging to Sultan Selim I (1512–20) had been erected for the Sultan's use. To the right of the tent stood the *mihrab* and the pulpit. After the communal prayer (in which the Sultan took part), the traditional Friday sermon was delivered by a local notable who was at the same time a well-known doctor of Islamic law and a senator, *Manastırlı* İsmail Hakkı Efendi. According to one report the imam Reşit İbrehim Efendi at the same time 'walked through the ranks of the believers, exhorting them to be brothers and reminding them that the late Sultan Murat I, in his testament, had ordered Muslims to love Christians and Jews as their brothers'.[38] Then a declaration by the Grand Vizier was read out. According to Halit Ziya, this was supposed to be translated into

Albanian by *Manastırlı* İsmail Hakkı Efendi, who, however, did not know any Albanian. The ceremonies were ended with a military parade and with the laying of a foundation stone for a new university.

After this high point of the visit the Sultan returned to Salonica via Prishtina and Üsküp, where he changed trains for Monastir (Bitola), the main base of the Third Army. The Sultan's visit of three and a half days to the garrison town was again depicted as a great success by the Unionist press, but according to the British consul he was 'rather coolly received'.[39] Mahmud Şevket Pasha, who, as commander of the First, Second and Third Armies was the military strong man of the empire, and who had joined the Sultan's entourage on 15 June, used the visit to this military centre to give a speech in which he asked the officers not to meddle in politics. The factionalism of the officer corps was by now seriously undermining the discipline of the Ottoman army. In Monastir, too, an amnesty was declared which again fell short of the expectations of the local Christians. Prisoners numbering 108 were pardoned, but 12 others (among them leading Bulgarian nationalists) were banished to Anatolia and the status of 12 others remained unclear. Another interesting event in Monastir was the re-enactment by troops under the command of Niyazi Bey of scenes from the constitutional revolution, notably the entry into town of the constitutional forces on 10/24 July 1908.[40]

After his visit to Monastir, the Sultan returned to Salonica and, after a short stop, he travelled onward to Istanbul, where he was greeted by large and enthusiastic crowds, as the surviving pictures show. The whole town was illuminated to celebrate the return of the monarch and a torch parade was held from Sirkeci to the palace of Dolmabahçe and back. Newspaper editorials commented that many Ottoman sultans had returned to their capital carrying the keys of conquered cities but that this sultan had returned with the keys to the hearts of the people of Rumelia.[41]

Conclusion

What was the Sultan's Macedonian voyage meant to achieve and what did it accomplish? I think we can say that Sultan Reşat's Macedonian journey served four distinct – but interconnected – political purposes: In the first place it was meant to cement ties with the Albanian Muslim population, which was regarded by the CUP as a crucial factor in retaining its hold over the area. After the insurrections of the past year, reconciliation with the Albanians was the most urgent issue on the agenda. The Sultan's visit to Kosovo and the high profile role played by Niyazi Bey throughout served this purpose, as did the amnesties which were declared during the visit and the paying of blood-money. The second, more general political aim was to strengthen the policy of *İttihad-i Anasır* (Unity of the Elements or 'Ottomanism') by the organization of demonstrations of inter-ethnic solidarity in the most ethnically mixed area of the empire; hence the demonstrations of loyalty by Bulgarians and Greeks and references to Gazi Evrenos. Third, the journey served to strengthen the political position of the CUP, which had been losing public support and political power over the past year, through the close and very visible association of the Sultan with leading committee members. Top people of the committee, such as the orator Ömer Naci and CUP secretary-general Haci Adil constantly accompanied the monarch, and the latter expressed his gratitude to the CUP in all four towns he visited. Fourth, the visit, and in particular the ceremonies on the battlefield of Kosovopolje, served the more general purpose of strengthening Ottoman (and more specifically Ottoman-Muslim) national consciousness through reference to historically significant symbols. In this sense, the visit to Kosovopolje was a logical sequence to the Sultan's earlier imperial visits to Bursa and Edirne – the first and second Ottoman capitals.

Apart from its political and ideological content, the Sultan's journey is an interesting phenomenon in its shape. It is an example of something quite novel: attempts of the regime to promote the ruler as a popular figure, highly visible and close to his people. Hence the constant emphasis on the way the Sultan tried to get in touch with his people, showing himself to them and inviting them to join him. Reşat was projected as a 'father of the nation' and he was, of course, very suitable, both physically and mentally, for this role. The years until Reşat's death in 1918 would show many more examples of this use of the monarchy.

It is no exaggeration, however, to say that in the end the tour failed in most of its objectives. In 1912 the Balkan War, the immediate cause of which was the Porte's rejection of Greek, Serb, Montenegrin and Bulgarian demands for far-reaching reforms in Macedonia, put to rest any hopes of achieving a 'Unity of the Elements'. After the collapse of the Ottoman defence, the Albanians opted for complete independence and severed their ties with the Ottoman throne. As for the CUP, it failed to increase its popularity, losing political power in 1912 and only managing to regain it through a coup d'état in January 1913. The efforts to strengthen Ottoman-Muslim consciousness, though, may be termed successful. There can be no doubt that in the ten years between 1912 and 1922 Ottoman-Muslim nationalism became the strongest ideological current in the country. It was discarded, at least on an official level, in favour of Turkish nationalism after the founding of the Turkish Republic in 1923, but in the crucial years when the survival of the Ottoman state was at stake in the Balkan War, World War I and the Independence War, it served as the prime vehicle for mobilization.[42]

8.   Who Were the Young Turks?*

For many years I have cherished the ambition to do some serious prosopographical research, to write a collective biography of the people who played roles in all those crucial and traumatic events of the end of the nineteenth- and the first half of the twentieth century: the constitutional revolution of July 1908, the counterrevolution in Istanbul of April 1909, the guerrilla movement in Tripolitania against the Italian invader in 1911, the Balkan War that broke out in October 1912, the Unionist coup d'état of January 1913, the outbreak of World War I, the persecution of the Armenians in 1915–16, the armistice of October 1918, the almost simultaneous start of the resistance against the break-up of the empire, the independence war of 1920–2, the establishment, first of a republic in October 1923 and then of a dictatorship in March 1925, the purges of 1926 and, finally, the cultural revolution unleashed by the republican leadership in the 1920s and 30s. I have wanted to know who these people were, where they were born and when, where their families came from, what their fathers did for a living, how and where they were educated and what kind of careers they had (apart from their political activities).

In particular, I have desired to study the individuals and the networks that composed the three manifestations of the Young Turk movement: the Committee of Union and Progress (CUP) before 1918, the leadership of the 'national struggle' (*Millî Mücadele*) between 1918 and 1922, and the early republican leadership (up to 1945). How did these three groupings fit together and how were they connected? How, for instance, did Mustafa Kemal fit into the picture?

In spite of the Young Turk's enormous importance in the modern history of Turkey, the literature provides little in the way of answers. The standard works on the period abound in generalizations. Feroz Ahmad calls the Young Turks 'lower middle class' and 'newly emerging professional classes'.

95

Allen says they were 'young officers', which is also Geoffrey Lewis's classification, while Bernard Lewis talks about 'Muslim Turks, mostly soldiers' and 'members of the ruling élite', which is in direct contrast with Stanford Shaw's 'lower class' and 'subject class'. Richard Robinson describes them as 'new technicians, newly awakened intelligentsia, western-oriented army officers', while Sina Akşin[1] summed them up as 'Turks, youngsters, members of the ruling class, western-educated with a bourgeois mentality'. These obviously are very broad, and in some cases contradictory, generalizations.

This chapter is an attempt to be a bit more precise; to draw, if not yet a group portrait of the Young Turks, then at least a preliminary sketch. The underlying premise behind this attempt at a group portrait is that it makes sense to look at the political élite of the period stretching from the 1908 constitutional revolution to the end of one-party rule in the republic as one single group of people. The reason for this is that almost every person of influence in Mustafa Kemal's ruling Republican People's Party had been a member of the CUP and had started his political career in the Second Constitutional period (1908–18).

In order to find out what the Young Turks[2] shared and what distinguished them from one another, I first look at their geographical origins and family background, their age, education and early careers. Here, I divide the Young Turks into subgroups, whose membership in some cases overlap: (1) the founders of the Young Turk movement; (2) the leaders of the 1908 constitutional revolution; (3) the politically active officers in the Ottoman army; (4) the members of the Central Committee (CC) of the CUP; (5) the leadership of the nationalist resistance after World War I and (6) the early republican ruling élite.

The available sources offering insight into these individuals' lives are rich and varied, but at the same time problematical. First, there are biographical reference tools, ranging from printed ones such as İbrahim Alaettin Gövsa's *Türk Meşhurları Ansiklopedisi* (Encyclopaedia of famous Turks) of 1946[3] to the latest web-based ones, such as *Biografi.Net*, as well as a number of Turkish encyclopaedias and more specialized biographical tools, focusing, for instance, on the persons mentioned in Mustafa Kemal's *Nutuk*. These are indispensable tools, but they also pose problems in that the entries are often unpredictable and the data contradictory. As for biographies of the protagonists of the period, they are not very numerous and with few exceptions,[4] do not meet scholarly standards. The number of published memoirs is far greater than that of the biographies. Most of them were first published in serialized form in Turkish newspapers of the 1950s and 60s and later, often much later, as books. The quality of the memoirs varies a great deal, both in their literary qualities and in the information they offer. Newspaper clippings (in particular obituaries) can be very useful. A large and important collection of this type of material, collected by the late İsmail Arar, is held in the International Institute of Social History in Amsterdam. In addition, if the persons under review held administrative positions, their personal data can be found in the collections of *sicilli ahval* of the Ottoman and later Turkish home office. If they were members of the Ottoman parliament or the Great National Assembly of the republic, their personal details are on record. Likewise, if they had a military career, the details of that career, up to the last medal, can be found in the records of the General Staff's personnel section. The military history section of the General Staff has published many biographical details in its journals and in separate publications.

It remains very difficult, however, to trace those people who stayed out of the limelight and did not hold prominent positions in public life, but were very influential nevertheless: some members of the CC of the CUP, the lower ranking officers who, as 'volunteers' (*fedaiin*) did the CUP's dirty work and the party bosses in the capital and in the provinces. Even when the biographical data are easily accessible, as in the case of the military pashas, the details one would like to have, such networks of family and friends or ethnic background often remain out of reach. Given these limitations, this chapter cannot be more than a snapshot of the state of play in this research field.

Let us now turn to the Young Turks and try to discern key commonalities and differences within and between subgroups.

Founding fathers

By the late 1880s the number of students in the modern European-style higher education establishments was growing, due to the expansion of secondary education under Abdülhamit. At the same time disenchantment with the regime was growing among the students in the colleges, given increasing repression after 1882 on the part of the regime and the regime's responsibility for the murder of the 'father' of the Ottoman constitution, Mithat Pasha, in 1885. The British occupation of Cyprus in 1878 and of Egypt in 1882 were also laid at the door of Abdülhamit's regime.

In 1889 a group of four students in the military medical college in Istanbul founded the Ottoman Unity Society (*İttihadi Osmani Cemiyeti*) with the aim of agitating for the restoration of a parliamentary regime, which had been prorogued by the Sultan in February 1878, a mere ten months after the parliament had first convened. They were soon joined by other medical students, who were specializing in the Gülhane and Haydarpaşa hospitals. At the same time, but independently of them, Ahmet Rıza, an agricultural engineer and former director of public education in Bursa, went to Paris to attend the celebrations of the centenary of the French Revolution, an event which served as an inspiration to many Ottoman students and young civil servants at the time. In the years that followed the opposition movement in the empire grew. It spread to provincial centres like Edirne where the lawyer Faik [Kaltakkıran], the Albanian Hoca İbrahim and postal clerk Mehmet Talât formed a cell. Activity outside the empire increased as well, with Ahmet Rıza agreeing in 1895 to act as the president of the Paris branch. In 1896, the underground resistance network, which now went by the name of Ottoman Committee (or: Society) for Union and Progress (CUP) was betrayed on the eve of a coup d'état it was planning to execute. Most of its leading members were sent into internal exile in Tripolitania, and the movement inside the empire would lay dormant for nearly a decade.

But the branch in Paris survived and in the years that followed new 'Young Turks', as they called themselves in the European press, went to Europe, either to study or as political refugees. Some of these already had a reputation, like Murat Bey, who had taught history at the civil service academy (*Mülkiye*) and published the journal *Mizan*. Others were young patriotic students like Mithat Şükrü or Evranoszade Rahmi from Salonica. Muslims from the Russian Empire, who were inspired by İsmail Gasprinskii's *Usul-u Cedid* (New Method) movement of educational reform also joined the society. In contrast, activity in the empire was mostly limited to the illegal distribution of Young Turk journals published abroad.

The opposition in exile, though, was haunted by internal divisions and defections. Tensions came to a head during the 'Congress of Ottoman Liberals' in Paris in 1902, and the movement split into two wings, with Prince Sabahattin founding an offshoot faction, the 'Society of Ottoman Liberals', and Ahmet Rıza continuing to lead the CUP, which was the more nationalist and centrist of the two wings. Ahmet Rıza was more of an intellectual and theoretician than an organizer, and the CUP was only turned into a more disciplined and effective organization in 1905 with the arrival of Dr Bahaettin Şakir, a prominent Unionist and former personal physician to the Ottoman crown prince.

When we look a representative selection of 14 of the most important of these activists of the first generation,[5] we discover that they share a number of important characteristics. With the exception of Ahmet Rıza, Ahmet Saip and *Mizancı* Murat, who were slightly older, all the members of this group were born between 1864 and 1874, the average age being 27 in 1896. All of these 14 important early Young Turks possessed a post-secondary education. In fact: the early Young Turk movement could be described as a conspiracy of medical doctors. No less than eight out of fourteen were trained as military doctors, seven of them in the Military Medical School (*Mektebi Tıbbiyeyi Askeriye*), two went to the War College (*Harbiye*) but one of them was kicked out and went on to study Political Science in Paris, one studied Agriculture in Paris and three obtained higher education in Russia before coming to the Ottoman Empire (one of them also studying in Paris). Interestingly, not one of these Young Turks ever actively served in the army, even though so many of them were trained in military institutions. This strongly suggests they availed themselves of the opportunity to study in the most advanced Ottoman schools (which is what the military schools were) but lacked military ambitions.

When we look at their religious, ethnic and geographic background, we see that they were all Muslims, but only a minority among them were Ottoman Turks. Among the four original founders of the Ottoman Unity Society there was an Albanian, two Kurds and a Circassian, but no Turks at all. Another striking feature is the important contribution made to the movement by immigrants from the Russian Empire. Five out of fourteen had been born in the Caucasus or the Transcaucasian provinces of the Russian Empire, one in Russia proper. Of the others, four hailed from the Balkans, one form Istanbul, one from Bursa (born in a family from Istanbul) and two from Eastern Anatolia. As for the social background of the early Young Turks, they were all urban and literate, but in terms of occupation and social status of their fathers, their origins seem to have been quite varied. We encounter low to middle civil servants, a trader and an industrialist, but also an Ottoman senator, a notable and a tribal chief among the fathers.

Leaders of the 1908 constitutional revolution

With one exception all of the first generation Young Turks lived to see the realization of their goal, the re-establishment of parliamentary, constitutional government, in July 1908. Very few of them were actively involved in this momentous event, however. The roots of the constitutional revolution lay with a group of ten people,[6] who came together in Salonica in the summer of 1906 and founded a secret society, the *Osmanlı Hürriyet Cemiyeti* (Ottoman Freedom Society or OFS), to take up the cause of constitutionalism. The initiative came from first generation Young Turk Mehmet Talât, a native of Edirne, who had been exiled to Salonica in 1896 and was now the chief clerk of the Salonica Telegraph Office. The two people he confided in most were two contemporaries from Salonica, Mithat Şükrü (who had been involved in the Young Turk movement in Geneva) and Evranoszade Rahmi, a scion of a famous family of Rumelian notables, who had also joined the CUP while in France. All three were born in 1873–4, so they were 32 years old at the time the society was founded. While they were all civilians, they realized that success in the struggle depended on the army, so they approached seven army officers. Two of these stood out in that they were both older and higher in rank. They were the director and the French teacher of the local military secondary school: a colonel who was 45 (who like Talât had been involved in the CUP in the early 1890s) and a major who was 40 years old. The other army officers were significantly more junior in both respects; they were captains of between 22 and 29 years old with an average age of 26. In addition to being all male and all Muslim, they all possessed an urban and literate background and all of them except Talât had enjoyed a higher education. Civilian or military, they were all in one way or another in the service of the state.

Another common factor in their background, which would prove to be significant later on, is their geographical origin: Six hailed from the Ottoman Balkans, two from the capital Istanbul, and two from the extreme north-western part of Anatolia (one from Bursa and one from Adapazarı). The complete absence of individuals from the Anatolian inland, Kurdistan, the Arab provinces or the Muslim areas of the Russian Empire makes this group noticeably different from the subgroup of early Young Turks with respect to geographical origin. Like the first-generation founders, though, the status and social standings of their fathers varied from that of landed gentry (Rahmi) to lowly clerk (Talât).

Politically active officers in the Ottoman army

From the start the founders of the OFS actively sought to involve Ottoman army officers stationed in the European provinces of the empire. Although the Inspectorate of the European Armies was headquartered in Salonica, the most important concentrations of officers could be found in the Second and Third Army headquarters in Monastir and Edirne. The officers, mostly captains and lieutenants along with a few majors, who were involved in setting up the first cells of the OFS in Monastir and Salonica, included people like Enver,[7] Fethi [Okyar], Colonel Sadık, Aziz Ali al-Misri (who would end up as Egyptian ambassador to Moscow under Nasser), İsmet [İnönü], Kâzım [Karabekir], Ali [Çetinkaya] and Kâzım [Özalp]. These officers were key players in that they brought the army onto the side of the society and thus gave it its decisive political power.Between late 1906 and the summer of 1908 the number of officers joining the society grew quite fast. At the time of the revolution, the CUP had about 2,000 members, of whom about two-thirds or more seem to have been military men. Of these, maybe three dozen can be considered as politically influential in the inner circles of the committee. Obviously, the exact size of the group is open to debate as there are no strict formal criteria circumscribing the group. Having looked in detail at 21 prominent members of the group of activist officers, I have found some interesting shared characteristics, which overlap to a degree with those of the founders of the OFS.[8]

Geographically, the picture is very clear: Ten of them came from the Balkan provinces, eight from Istanbul, one from the Aegean littoral (Izmir) and one from inland Anatolia. Without exception the young officers came from an urban and literate background. Their fathers had been in the service of the State in one capacity or another, and in the majority of cases the officers were also officers' sons. Social status varied a great deal, making any label like 'lower middle class' or 'establishment' quite meaningless. The fathers of Mustafa Kemal and Enver, for example, were small-time civil servants, while their friends and colleagues Kâzım Karabekir and Ali Fuat [Cebesoy] were children of pashas and quite rich.

In terms of age, these activist officers warranted the label 'Young Turks'. At the time of the constitutional revolution of 1908 they were on average 29 years old, which makes them about seven years younger on average than the group of civilian leaders (or party bosses) around Talât. The age differentials within this group of young officers were very small, with most of them being born in a narrow band between 1878 and 1883.[9] This also means that many of them had known each other as classmates in the military colleges of the empire or during their traineeships in the army.

Although most of the officers were first lieutenants, captains or adjutant-majors at the time of the revolution, their career prospects were very different. Some officers, like Mustafa Kemal (the later Atatürk), Enver, Ali İhsan or Kâzım Karabekir had graduated among the top pupils of the General Staff Academy in Istanbul. They entered the army as Staff Captains and were earmarked for fast-track promotion. They would go on to become generals or at least colonels. Those who graduated from the Staff Academy but did not make the top third of the class, entered the army as 'distinguished captains' with slightly less brilliant career prospects. Those, finally, who graduated from the War College, but whose marks were not good enough

101

for entry into the General Staff Academy, entered the army as lieutenants and would form the middle cadres of the officer corps. Some of these got the chance to go through the Staff Academy later in their careers.

The volunteers

Élite officers like Enver, Kâzım, Fethi and Mustafa Kemal clearly formed a separate subgroup but at the same time bonds of friendship, often based on a shared history as classmates, tied them personally to lower ranking officers. These ties were important and could be mobilized, as indeed they were, most spectacularly by Enver at the start of World War I, when he created the *Teşkilat-i Mahsusa* or 'Special Organization' (a covert group within the War Ministry that facilitated the Armenian massacres) out of the loosely defined group known as the *fedaiin* (volunteers). Already in the run-up to the constitutional revolution some officers volunteered for dangerous missions, like political murders. These officers were organized as a separate unit and continued to do the CUP's dirty work after the revolution. When the Italians invaded Tripolitania in 1911, for example, they flocked there to serve in the anti-Italian guerrilla under staff officers like Enver, Fethi and Mustafa Kemal and one year later, during the Balkan War, they were charged with setting up a guerrilla movement and even an ostensibly independent Muslim republic in Western Thrace. They would later play an important role both in the persecution of the Armenians during World War I and in the resistance movement after the war. A great deal, mostly sensational, stuff has been written about the exploits of this group, but actually we still know very little about the background of most its members, people like *Kuşçubaşızade* Eşref, *Sapancalı* Hakkı, Yakup Cemil, *İzmitli* Mümtaz or *Çerkes* Reşit. We do know, though, that members of the one million strong Circassian minority in the Ottoman Empire, the children and grandchildren of nineteenth-century refugees from the Caucasus, played a key role in this group.[10]

Members of the Central Committee

In September 1907 the Ottoman Freedom Society merged with the Paris-based Committee of Union and Progress to form the Committee of Progress and Union (CPU). In July 1908 it orchestrated a campaign in which several Young Turk officers in different parts of Ottoman Macedonia took the troops under their command out into the field and demanded the restoration of constitution and parliament. When the Sultan responded by deploying troops, the troops' commander, Şemsi Pasha, was murdered in broad daylight by a CUP *fedaî*. Troops brought over from Anatolia were met by

Young Turk agitators on the ships that took them from Izmir to Salonica. On 24 July, the Sultan gave in. The constitutional revolution had taken place.

When elections were organized later in 1908 the CPU, which had by then renamed itself the CUP, won a handsome (albeit somewhat unstable) majority in parliament, and was able to install a government sympathetic to its ideas. The CUP itself, meanwhile, decided to remain a closed, secretive, society ruled by its Salonica-based CC. The party it founded merely consisted of its parliamentary faction and had no independent existence outside parliament.

The members of the opposition who had been sent into internal exile by the Sultan as well as the Young Turk veterans based in Europe came back in triumph, but they soon discovered that they were out of touch with developments in the empire. *Mizancı* Murat, Abdullah Cevdet, İbrahim Temo and even Ahmet Rıza: they all fell out with the CC of the CUP and had to retreat from political life. Murat left for his native Tiflis, while Temo settled in Romania, where he had lived before 1908. At the end of his long life, he would become a member of the senate, but of the Romanian, not the Ottoman one. Ahmet Rıza was first given a seat on the CC because of his undoubted status as the veteran Young Turk leader, but when he voiced criticism of the policies of the CUP he was soon 'kicked upstairs' to the powerless senate. The only two people from among the 'old' Young Turks who really counted politically after 1908 were the two who had reorganized the movement after 1902 and who had been in close touch with the group in Salonica, Bahaettin Şakir and Dr Nâzım. The CC would remain until the end of World War I ten years later the centre of power in the Ottoman Empire. The number of members of the CC numbered from three to twelve and from 1916 a change in the regulations introduced a Central Council (*Meclisi Umumi*), but right to the end the Central Committee (*Merkezi Umumi*) constituted the real centre of power. A total of 26 people served on the CC between 1908 and 1918.[11]

To understand the power structures of the Young Turk era it is not enough to look at the centre alone. For its hold on power the CUP depended not only on its ability to mobilize the army through its officer members, but also on its representatives in the provincial centres. Important members of the CUP, people like *Circassian* Mehmet Reşit (one of the original founders of the Ottoman Unity Society in 1889) in Diyarbakır, Azmi in Trabzon and Evranoszade Rahmi in Izmir held sway in the provincial capitals, and often had a large degree of discretionary power. Rahmi in particular ruled the Aydın province from Izmir as though it was an autonomous region. Apart from infiltrating the structures of the provincial administration, the CUP also set up its own parallel networks. It established Unionist clubs in all the major provincial centres and a network of party bosses, variously called 'responsible secretaries', 'delegates' and 'inspectors.' However, as this chapter is concerned with the core leadership of the Young Turks, the provincial party leaders are not included in the survey. Focus will be on the members of the CUP Central Committee.

When we look at the geographical origins of those Committee members, we see a picture emerging that is by now familiar: out of the 25 people whose origins I have so far been able to find out, eleven hailed from the Balkan provinces, four from Istanbul, four from the Aegean (islands and littoral) and four from Anatolia. One was born in Cairo (as a scion of the Khedivial family), one in the Kurdish areas and one in the Caucasus.

The CC was dominated by the civilian element within the CUP, in particular, Talât. The officers, who had played such a crucial role in the constitutional revolution, the suppression of the counterrevolution of April 1909 and the coup d'état of January 1913, were hardly represented at all except for two of the original 'heroes of the revolution' (officers who had started the rebellion in July 1908): Enver and Eyüp Sabri. The civilian element that dominated the CC was older by about seven years than the military. Civilians and officers alike had at least a college education (with the aforementioned exception of Talât).

Although the members of the CC also had an urban and literate background, their social origins were more varied. Where most of the military officers were sons of officers, we find notables, landowners, postal officials, traders and financial controllers among the fathers of the CC members. However, a paucity of data prevents us from drawing definite conclusions.

The leadership of the national resistance

After the Ottoman defeat in World War I, the paths of the members of the unionist ruling élite diverged. A small group of key leaders, who carried the main responsibility for the entry of the Ottoman Empire into the war and particularly for the persecution of the Armenians (Enver, Talât, Cemâl, Bahaettin Şakir, Dr Nazım and a few others) left the country aboard a German warship. During the de facto occupation of Istanbul by the Entente in 1919–20 some 144 Ottomans were arrested by the Sultan's government or by the British and interned in Malta. Among this group were former members of the CC, former ministers, governors, members of parliament, publicists and prominent military men. The departure of these leaders from the scene, however, did not prevent the emergence of a powerful resistance movement, which had already been in the planning stages prior to the signing of the armistice. Both the central leadership of the CUP and the local party bosses in those areas that seemed in danger of being ceded to the Armenians in the east or the Greeks in the west charged party members with raising public consciousness of the danger and with the preparation of guerrilla warfare.

These people involved with the start of the national struggle do not constitute a new group. They are familiar figures from the preceding era. Three groups in particular seem to have been important: First, politically active military officers (by now mostly colonels and generals, people like Ali Fuat [Cebesoy], Kâzım Karabekir, İsmet [İnönü], Refet [Bele] but also *Deli* Halit, Seyfi [Düzgören], Kâzım [Özalp] or Cafer Tayyar [Eğilmez] – all of them early CUP members; second, CUP party bosses like *Yenibahçeli* Nail, Mazhar Müfit [Kansu], Celâl [Bayar] and *Filibeli* Hilmi; and third, former *fedaiin* from the Special Organization. At the same time as Mustafa Kemal made his much publicized landfall in Samsun on 19 May 1919, the 'second man' of the resistance, former Navy Minister Hüseyin Rauf [Orbay], made a much less obtrusive tour of Western Anatolia, visiting Special Organization veterans, all Circassians like himself, and making Special Organization arms caches available to them. The number of Circassians among the commanders of the resistance is remarkably high: Halit, Ali Fuat, Refet and Rauf were all members of immigrant families from the Caucasus.

The political leadership of the resistance movement, as apart from the military leadership, was formed by the Council of Commissars (*heyeti vükela*), whose members were elected by the National Assembly from April 1920 onwards. This was a rather instable organ, whose membership underwent frequent changes, but if we look at the council of 1920 we see that 17 people served on it.[12] If we exclude İsmail Fazıl Pasha, the general who was elected a commissar out of respect for his support to the national movement in which his son Ali Fuat [Cebesoy] played such a prominent role, they were on average 41 years old in 1920. This makes them very slightly older than the group of military leaders (with which there is some overlap in the shape of Mustafa Kemal, İsmet and Fevzi Pashas). Twelve commissars hailed from Istanbul, the Marmara region, the Aegean or the Balkans, four from the rest of Anatolia and one from the Caucasus. Five can be considered members of *muhacir* families. All except one (Celâl) had a higher education, with the great colleges of Istanbul once more well represented: five came from the *Harbiye*, three from the *Mülkiye* and two from the *Tıbbiye*. Five of the commissars had been educated partly in Europe – in Paris or Berlin. Almost all of them had gained political as well as professional experience under the empire, with no less than seven out of seventeen having served as members of the Ottoman parliament.

The CUP leaders who had fled the country in 1918 never managed to return. The Unionists interned in Malta did return but they were absent at the critical period when the national resistance movement took shape. This allowed a new leadership around Mustafa Kemal Pasha to emerge and assume control over the resistance organization. Having taken over the movement, Mustafa Kemal and his circle successfully beat off attempts by former Unionists to regain control (in 1921) or to make political comebacks (in 1923). Over the period 1925–6 Mustafa Kemal finally established full control by eliminating all those among the former Unionists and former resistance leaders who could provide a credible challenge to his leadership.

The early republican ruling élite

During the first 20 or so years of the republic the trimmings of a democratic parliamentarian political system were in place, although emergency powers gave the government a relatively free hand from 1925–9 and 1939–46. Real power, however, did not lie with parliament but with a small group of politicians, who figured in the top of the Republican People's Party and in the cabinets of the period. The party functioned in practice as a branch of the state, creating a support base for the Kemalist policies and spreading the regime's ideological message.

As for assembling a representative sampling of the early republican ruling élite, the 23 individuals who served in at least a quarter of the cabinets of the first 20 years of the republic are a good place to start. In addition, the long-time president of the assembly, Kâzım [Özalp] should be included in any group of most influential leaders. In view of the overwhelming importance of the army in the founding of the republic, Fevzi [Cakmak], who was Chief of the General Staff through the period should also be on the list.[13]

This is not the whole story, however. During the last ten years of his life (1928–38) Mustafa Kemal Pasha rarely occupied himself with the day-to-day running of the country, concentrating instead on the great reform projects, such as the change of alphabet and the linguistic purification campaign, and embarking on long inspection tours of the country. Nevertheless, he remained the unquestioned leader of the country, and the governing élite who consisted in large part of former military officers continued to adhere to the principle of the 'chain of command'. The fact that the president was so powerful, while at the same time being quite distant from the daily business of government made it possible for his 'kitchen cabinet', a circle of friends, who visited him frequently in his presidential villa, to exert significant influence even if they held no major positions. The members of this group, some ten people who had been close to Mustafa Kemal since his army days and sometimes since his youth in Salonica therefore deserve to be included in any consideration of the élite of the early republic.[14]

The 36 people thus selected show up a number of characteristics that are already familiar to us from our review of earlier subgroups of Young Turk leadership. Geographically, 35 per cent of them hailed from the Ottoman Balkans, 20 per cent from the Aegean, the same number from Istanbul and 11 per cent from the Marmara basin. In other words: fully 86 per cent of them were born in an area that can be considered a cohesive and integrated zone, one which in terms of integration with Europe, literacy, material and cultural development was completely different from that of Central- and Eastern Anatolia. Someone like Evranoszade Rahmi [Arslan], born and bred in Salonica, could easily feel at home in Izmir, where he became the long serving governor, because the cities were very similar in terms of amenities and cultural climate. Central and Eastern Anatolia, the areas adopted as the true Turkish heartland by the Kemalists, brought forth no more than five members of the republican leadership in Ankara. No less than half of the people who led the new republic came from areas that were lost by the empire in the period 1911–13. In a technical sense they were refugees.

With a single exception, the leaders came from an urban environment (the exception being Mahmut Celâl [Bayar], later the third president of the republic). Out of 36, 75 per cent were educated in the great colleges of the empire – 15 of them in the War Academy (*Harbiye*), two in the Military Medical College (*Tıbbiyei Askeriye*) and ten in the Civil Service Academy (*Mülkiye*). The education of two persons I have not yet been able to find out, but six others came from an array of higher education establishments, ranging from the arts faculty of the university to the agricultural college to a school for postal officials. The only member of the élite with a village background, Celâl, was also the only one without higher education. He received on-the-job training in a bank.

In other words: the leaders of the republic, like the Unionists before them, had received a European-styled modern education in secular schools. They all were proficient in at least one foreign language, most often French. People with a traditional religious education are lacking: there was not a single *medrese* student among them.

Conclusion: continuities and discontinuities

The turbulence of the decades spanning the constitutional revolution, World War I, the War of Independence, and the early years of the Republic is reflected in the degree of discontinuity of political leadership at the top level. The constitutional revolution – organized by a group of young civil servants and even younger officers in the Balkan provinces of the empire and followed within a year by a counterrevolution in the capital that had to be suppressed by the army – very quickly led to the sidelining of the leaders of the first generation Young Turks, the men who had been active in the opposition movement abroad since 1889. These pioneers, with a strong intellectual streak, yielded to the men of action. Then, the defeat of the Young Turk-led empire in World War I led to the flight of the top political leaders and the internment of dozens of leading members of the CUP. This gave Mustafa Kemal the chance gradually to establish his supremacy. Having beaten off different challenges of the older leaders and having purged the remnants of the old leadership in 1926, he created a power monopoly for himself and his followers.

However, under the top level of leadership we see a lot of continuity among the political élite of the whole period 1908–45. The three elements that together made up the core of the national resistance movement were military officers with a Unionist background, activists with a background in the Special Organization, and CUP party bosses and organizers in the provincial centres. The leadership of the early republic reflected these three ingredients, with a dominant position for (former) military men. Having been Unionists themselves, they shared the basic characteristics possessed by the top-level of the pre-1918 Unionist leadership. They were Muslim males of varied ethnic descent, Turks being the largest group. On average they were born in 1883, which makes them almost precisely the same age as the officers who had founded the Ottoman Freedom Society in Salonica in 1906, as well as the politically active officers of the CUP and their representatives on the CC. This similarity in age also reflects the fact that the slightly older (by about seven years on average) civilian group around Talât that had dominated the CC before 1918 had been eliminated, partly in 1918 and partly in 1926.

Surprisingly, perhaps, the new Republic, consisting almost entirely of Anatolia, continued to be dominated by people born in the Balkans, Istanbul or the Aegean. Three quarters of the founders of the OFS and the members of the CC of the CUP had hailed from these three areas. We find exactly the same percentage among the republican leaders. Only the politically active officers of 1908 display an even higher percentage (95 per cent!).

Although the position and wealth of their families varied a great deal, the republican leaders just like earlier Young Turk groupings came from an urban background (with a single exception) and from literate families. All subgroups reviewed here share a background in secular, European-modelled higher education, be it military or civil. There were only two exceptions of people who had no higher education but were trained on the job: Talât among the Unionists and Celâl [Bayar] among the Kemalists. One was to become grand vizier, the other president. The only person with a religious *medrese* education was the Unionist *Şeyhülislam* Hayri Efendi. With very few exceptions (Celâl again being one) they made their careers as officers, bureaucrats or teachers in the service of the State they had attempted to save.

9. The Young Turk Mindset*

The constitutional revolution of 1908 and the proclamation of the republic in 1923 were very much the work of a single group, a closely-knit generation of young officers and administrators, who, as we have seen in the previous chapter, shared a number of characteristics in their personal background. There is a common profile to this group of important Young Turks (including both the leading members of the Committee of Union and Progress and the ruling élite of the republic). It consisted of Muslim males, born almost exclusively between 1875 and 1885, with an urban literate background (albeit hailing from different social strata). The majority of them had their roots in the Southern Balkans, the Aegean or the capital, a region vastly different from inland Anatolia and the Arab provinces. Ethnically the composition of the Young Turks was diverse, with a majority of Turks but important components of Albanians and Caucasian immigrants, some Kurds and Arabs. The two factors that, apart from their age, clearly were common to nearly all of them were a higher education in one of the European-type colleges of the empire and a career in the service of the state. The influence of the military in the Young Turk movement was important from 1906 onwards and grew as time wore on: the early republic was completely dominated by the military element, albeit they had by then resigned or retired from the armed forces.

Having thus established a somewhat clearer picture of the Young Turks, their origins, background and age, we can now chart the crucial shared experiences of this group from their adolescent years until the demise of the Ottoman Empire and examine to what extent these experiences may have shaped their mentality and their worldview: their youth in Balkan towns, education, professional experience and political activism.

The Christian bourgeoisie: threat and model
Three quarters of the Young Turks grew up in the 1880s and 1890s in the Balkans, the Aegean or Istanbul. Consequently, they witnessed at close range

the rise of the Christian bourgeoisie in the towns and cities of the empire. The area they hailed from had been integrating into the European economy since the late eighteenth century and trade with Europe had increased at a high rate since the 1830s.[1] It was primarily the Christian middle class that profited, sometimes working with European economic interests, sometimes in competition with them.[2] From the mid-1890s the pace of integration picked up, and by the end of the century the overwhelming majority of the industrial establishments of the empire were in the hands of foreigners or local Christians. The two categories overlapped to a certain extent because many among the Christians who had earlier acquired protection of a European power later opted for full foreign citizenship.[3] In cities like Istanbul, Salonica or Izmir the gap between the Muslims and non-Muslims in terms of wealth, education and lifestyle grew visibly larger. New neighbourhoods with French-style apartment blocks and villas and with tramways and electric light grew outside the old towns. The emergence of the new largely Christian bourgeoisie led to the creation of new sociabilities: gentlemen's clubs, cafés and restaurants, charitable societies and Masonic lodges, parks and promenades, sports clubs and hippodromes.[4] Young Muslims with an urban literate background and an education in modern secular schools lived on the margins of this new world, participating in parts of it but aware of the inferior status they occupied within it. Talât and his friends joined a lodge (partly to shield them from the omnipresent Hamidian secret police) and expounded on the future of the country in the cafés of Salonica. Mustafa Kemal frequented the same cafes of his native town from 1907 onwards. Later, he would stay at the Pera Palas hotel and frequent the Cercle d'Orient club in Istanbul. At the same time the Young Turks were very conscious of the increasing wealth and influence of the non-Muslims, which contrasted with their own situation as young officers and bureaucrats whose pay was often in arrears by months. Their collective identity was certainly formed in opposition to non-Muslims, as is proven by the fact that the Ottoman Freedom Society founded in Salonica in 1906 explicitly excluded non-Muslims.[5] The first 70 members were all Muslims and even when the society expanded its membership in 1907–8 only a handful of non-Muslims were allowed in, almost all of them either *dönme* (Sabbataic Jews) or Vlahs (members of the Romanian-speaking minority in Macedonia). When they took to the mountains in June–July 1908, Young Turk officers first of all mobilized Muslim villages against the threat of a European Christian takeover.[6]

At the same time the Christian bourgeoisie of the Ottoman towns provided these Young Turks with model of modernity. The modernity to which the Young Turks – Unionists and Kemalists alike – aspired is clearly visible in the architecture they promoted and in the rearrangement of the public space. The Unionists had little room for manoeuvre in this field as seven years of their ten-year rule were war years, but when the dust had settled, the Kemalists had the opportunity to rebuild Turkey according to their ideal of modernity. The result was that in every Anatolian provincial town, where the Kemalists in the 1930s laid out new areas, we see parks, cafés, tearooms and theatres. Ankara, the showcase of the new state, had straight (rational) avenues lined with villas that could have been taken from the Balkans, a gentlemen's club, an opera house and a racecourse. The model of modernity they aspired to is also visible in their lifestyle. In their personal attire and behaviour the Young Turks mimicked the example of the Christian bourgeoisie. They dressed in European clothes (something made compulsory for the population as a whole with the Kemalist dress code of 1925) or uniforms. Pictures of wives and daughters of Unionist leaders show them in European dresses, sometimes with 'voiles' replacing the veil, and in the 1920s and 30s the female relatives of the republican leadership are often shown in high heels and sleeveless dresses or fur coats. Enver promoted the boy scout movement and the (originally German) vogue of dressing children in naval uniform reached the Ottoman Empire too. The Young Turks used calling cards, held dogs as pets and went out of their way to learn ballroom dancing. It is hard, therefore, to escape the notion that the Young Turk interpretation of modernity was in fact the European bourgeois way of life, as presented to them in the towns and cities of the Southern Balkans and the Aegean.

Education and revelation

Although many Young Turks had some experience in traditional neighbourhood schools where the Koran was learned by heart, the characteristic feature of their education was that they were schooled in secular Western-type schools both at the secondary and higher education level. This imbued them with a science-oriented and materialist worldview, which is particularly evident among the many doctors in the Young Turk movement. As Hanioğlu has shown, the writings of the Young Turks are full of references to the need for a rational, scientific approach to replace traditionalism.[7] This is actually a more important theme in their writings than politics. From them there runs a straight line to the Mustafa Kemal Atatürk, who pronounced that 'the truest spiritual guide in life is science' (*Hayatta en hakiki mürşit ilimdir*) and that 'the torch that the Turkish nation held in its hand on its road to progress and civilisation, is exact science'.[8]

Learning French in these Western-styled schools opened up entirely new worlds to them, even if the level of proficiency was often mediocre, and we know that they used this knowledge to read, not only textbooks, but also French journals (in particular the popular illustrated ones) and books. Besides information on the wider world the periodicals also serialized novels in the shape of *feuilletons*.[9] What they took from this literature is a penchant for romantic activism, for great and heroic acts and a high regard for youth. The Young Turks were quite young in a literal sense when they came onto the scene in 1908, but they were also the first generation of Ottomans to see youth as an asset. Being young and well-educated, they felt they understood the world much better than older people and believed that their youth was a factor that legitimized their actions.[10] This was in stark contrast to the worldview of earlier generations of Ottomans, who saw a positive relationship between old age and authority. That the emphasis on the key role of the young persisted in the republic is shown best by the final paragraph of Mustafa Kemal's great six-day speech of 1927. In the famous section of the speech, *Gençliğe Hitabe* (Address to Youth), which can still be found inscribed all over Turkey, the president emphatically entrusts the Turkish youth with his legacy.[11]

Seeing as the Young Turks by and large owed their career to their higher education, it therefore makes sense that they believed in the power of education to produce progress and enlightenment. This belief in education was particularly important as a constituent element in the self-view of the Kemalists, who often portrayed themselves as educators of a backward population. When the new alphabet was introduced in 1928, Mustafa Kemal Pasha gave public lessons explaining it. Pictures of him with blackboard and chalk are still among the most popular items in the Atatürk iconography.

It was also during their time in college that most of the Young Turks discovered the existence of a constitutional opposition movement. By word of mouth they were made aware of the banned works of the constitutional movement of the 1860s, the Young Ottomans and especially of the fiery calls for reform and patriotism of Namık Kemal. Handwritten copies were passed from student to student in the dormitories. After 1896, the journals of the Young Turk movement abroad (papers like *Meşveret*, *Şurayı Ümmet* or *Osmanlı*) were read and distributed illegally in the colleges. They propagated a message of political opposition in the name of constitution and parliament, and called for renewal on the basis of science and rationalism. Most of all they attacked the sultan's government for failing to defend the empire against foreign encroachments.[12]

For some of the Young Turks, particularly those who stayed in Europe, the sudden discovery of one particular European thinker became all-important. One has to remember that these people were not academic theoreticians or researchers (even if some of them came to hold chairs in universities), but were instead activists on the look out for a solution that would save their state and bring about a reinvigoration of Ottoman society. There was an urgency to their quest for a philosopher's stone that made them impatiently embrace a single idea or thinker uncritically, once they thought they had found it. This happened to Ahmet Rıza with Auguste Comte and his disciple Pierre Lafitte, to Prince Sabahattin with Camille Demolins and Frederic le Play, to Abdullah Cevdet with Gustave Le Bon and Ludwig Büchner, and to Ziya Gökalp with Emile Durkheim.

Guerrilla warfare and the Third Army

The officers that graduated from the War College and the General Staff school had to do their practical field training with one of the Ottoman armies. Nearly all of them served at one time or another with the Third Army, which was garrisoned in Albania, Kosovo and Macedonia. Here they were confronted with the ongoing guerrilla warfare of Greek, Serbian, Albanian, Macedonian and Bulgarian bands that was endemic in these areas. These Greek, Bulgarian and Serbian bands often acted in the name of nationalist demands, even if their actions were indistinguishable from other robber bands. The continuous small-scale, but sometimes atrocious, confrontations between Ottoman army units and these bands constitute the dominant professional experience for most Young Turk officers up to 1911. Some of them, like Enver, gained fame through their exploits in this struggle. Though the guerrilla bands were not able to defeat regular army units, what made them so dangerous in Ottoman eyes was that the unrest they created could attract foreign interference. Macedonia was already under foreign tutelage of the combined European powers since the Mürzsteg agreement of 1903,[13] and officers from different European countries acted as inspectors of the Ottoman gendarmerie, something that hurt the national pride of the young officers a great deal.[14] As in any typical guerrilla situation it was very difficult for the army to distinguish between the bands themselves and the population that sheltered them, thus increasing the officers' mistrust of the Christian communities as a whole. For people whose identity formation had already taken place in the context of the growing divide between Muslims and non-Muslims in the towns, their experiences in the Third Army, fighting Christian bands, of course reinforced that aspect of their development.[15]

At the same time, the Young Turk officers had a grudging admiration for the fierce nationalism of the bands and for the effectiveness of their methods of warfare. Simply put, the Young Turks learned their lesson. Already in May–June 1908, the CUP had decided to start 'Ottoman national bands' on the pattern of the Greek, Bulgar and Serb bands.[16] When Italy invaded Tripolitania in 1911and regular Ottoman forces could not reach the province (the Italians had mastery of the sea and the British would not allow troops to cross Egypt), a few dozen Unionist officers, staff officers like Enver, Fethi and Mustafa Kemal as well as many Unionist *fedaiin*, went there to organize guerrilla units composed from Arab tribes from the interior. Likewise, when the Balkan War broke out in October 1912, the *fedaiin* were charged with starting a guerrilla in Western Thrace, an area populated by Muslims and contested between the Ottoman Empire, Bulgaria and Greece. This group of Young Turk officers and *fedaiin* behind these guerrilla movements formed the nucleus of the Special Organization officially founded in 1914.[17] When an allied breakthrough at the Dardanelles seemed imminent in 1915 and again, when defeat in the World War I had become inevitable in 1918, the CUP leadership prepared the ground for a guerrilla war in Anatolia. When that guerrilla war started in 1919 under the aegis of the Society for the Defence of the National Rights of Anatolia and Rumelia (the national resistance led by Mustafa Kemal Pasha), the volunteers of the Special Organization played a leading role, applying the lessons they had learned in the Balkans.[18] The importance of the Balkan experience before 1908 can also be seen in the Turks' adoption of the Serbian and Bulgarian terms for this type of guerrilla band: *Çete* and *Komitacı* respectively, terms still in use (with very negative connotations) in Turkey today.

Initiation into the CUP

Between September 1906 and July 1908 a few hundred young officers serving in the Second and Third Armies were sworn in as members of the underground resistance known, first, as the Ottoman Freedom Society and then as the Society for Progress and Union (the more familiar name of Society (or Committee) for Union and Progress was reintroduced after the revolution). Initiation into this society was strictly regulated and ritualized. The new member was introduced by a guide (*rehber*) and brought to a house at night, to be interrogated by three members in masks and gowns. He then had to swear loyalty and silence on pain of death over a Koran and a revolver.[19] The ritual, which shares many characteristics with the initiation rites of European secret societies like the Italian *Carbonari*, the Greek *Philiki Hetairia* or the

Serb *Black Hand Society*, clearly had religious overtones and we know from the personal recollections of the Young Turks that it was an experience they never forgot. They were imbued with a feeling of belonging to a dedicated vanguard with a mission; it is not unusual to find references in their memoirs to the *cemiyeti mukaddes* (holy society).[20] For some it created bonds of loyalty that would outlast the CUP itself, which was formally disbanded in 1918.

Revolution and counterrevolution

For the lower-ranking officers in their late twenties, toppling in three weeks the regime of an autocratic monarch who had been on the throne since before they were born and becoming the masters of an empire that still stretched from Albania to the Yemen must have been a heady, indeed an intoxicating, experience, giving a sense of unlimited possibilities for those who were bold enough to try. Belief in the force of the human will to change things is a characteristic of Young Turk leaders like Enver and Mustafa Kemal and in their eyes it contrasted sharply with what they saw as the fatalism of the conservative masses.

But if the revolution of 1908 was a euphoric experience, the counterrevolution of April 1909 (or '31 March incident') was one of the most traumatic ones in any Young Turk's life. The fact that the Unionists, who saw themselves as the saviours of the country and who had been hailed as the 'Heroes of Freedom' (*hürriyet kahramanları*) eight months before, proved helpless in their own capital in the face of a rebellion by dissatisfied soldiers from the battalions they had themselves picked for garrison duty and a bunch of religious students, came as a tremendous shock. Even though they succeeded in re-establishing order with the help of loyal army units from Macedonia within a fortnight, it left them with an acute sense of vulnerability. From this time onwards, *irtica* (religious reaction, or something we would now perhaps call 'fundamentalism') would become their worst nightmare. They were left with the feeling that it would always be possible for reactionary figures to mobilize the ignorant masses against the forces of progress with an appeal to Islam. Later, when rebellions or manifestations against the Kemalist regime occurred that had religious overtones, as in the Sheikh Sait rebellion of 1925 or the 'Menemen incident' of 1930, the former Unionists who made up the republican élite immediately referred to the experience of April 1909 in their efforts to understand what was happening. Even today, when the secularist establishment of Turkey feels under threat, references to the '31 Mart incident' surface in speeches and newspaper headlines.[21]

In the service of the state

Almost without exception the Young Turks made their careers in the service of the Ottoman state. This factor undoubtedly left a deep imprint on their worldview. As had been pointed time and again, the most urgent question they faced was: 'How can this state be saved?' As we have seen in the chapter on the *Historiography of the Constitutional Revolution* (Part I), the event that triggered this revolution in 1908 was Great Britain's offer (at the meeting in Reval (Tallinn) between Edward VII and Tsar Nicholas II) to support full autonomy under a Christian governor for the Macedonian provinces, a solution that would have fatally weakened the empire in Europe. Likewise, saving the State (as well as their own position) was behind the Unionist coup d'état of January 1913, behind the decision to join Germany in the World War and behind the national resistance movement in 1919. For the Unionists saving the state was conditional on strengthening the position of the only really dependable part of its population, the Ottoman Muslims and, increasingly, the Turks, and the claim to be acting to save the state ultimately legitimized every kind of measure.

The state-centred view of the Young Turks also meant that they almost automatically saw the state as the engine for change in society. The only Young Turk faction that looked beyond the state was Prince Sabahettin's 'League for Private Initiative and Decentralization'. In Sabahettin's eyes the key to progress lay in the development, through education, of an enterprising and individualistic élite. His ideas were attractive to the Christian communities because of his advocacy of far-reaching decentralization, but he only had the support of a small minority of the Young Turks and played only a marginal role after the revolution. After the counterrevolution of 1909 he had to leave the country. The Kemalists were very firmly in the statist tradition of the Young Turks, seeing the interest of the (republican) State as something of transcendent value. That is also a legacy that is still very much with us today.

The military mind

At least two-thirds of the early Unionists were soldiers by trade and it is not surprising that their approach to problem resolution should reflect their military background. Handan Nezir has shown how German military thinking (primarily that of Colmar von der Golz, who trained generations of Ottoman officers) as well as the Russia's military defeat in 1905 at the hands of a non-Western power, the Japanese, deeply influenced this generation of officers.[22] They gleaned from these sources the idea that the modern state should be built on a 'nation in arms' and that the strength of the state could only be ensured by creating a nation of soldiers. The idea that the Turks *should become* a nation of soldiers became very popular in the Unionist media after the outbreak of the Balkan War in 1912. Even in respectable ladies' journals, the readers were exhorted to bring up their sons as soldiers for the fatherland. The idea that the Turks actually are a nation of soldiers, or even a soldier race later became an integral part of Turkish republican nationalism and it still lives on even today in nationalist circles. One of the best-known marches and one that every recruit has to learn by heart during the first weeks of military training is 'Every Turk is Born a Soldier' (*Her Türk Asker Doğar*).[23]

Coupled to the idea of the nation in arms was a particularly grim Darwinist worldview, clearly derived from thinkers like Gustave Le Bon (who was very popular among military men worldwide), which held that a struggle for survival was underway in the world, in which nations had to earn the right to exist. When we look at what Young Turk writers say about the defeat in the Balkan War or the Armenian genocide, this aspect stands out. These writers, for instance, posit that the Ottomans lose out in the Balkans because they have failed to train their children to be soldiers and to hate the enemy. In the same vein, the Armenians forfeit the right to exist because in a struggle to the death they prove to be the weaker ones. Mustafa Kemal later uses this same rhetoric, albeit in a different context, when he urges the Turkish nation to modernize and develop: the Turks have to earn the right to exist in a world of competing nations. If they fail, stronger nations will devour them.

Losing the ancestral land and the adoption of Anatolia

With half of the Young Turk leaders hailing from areas lost to the empire in 1911–13, the loss of the Balkan provinces and the Aegean islands constituted a trauma of the first order. To much of the Ottoman élite, the Balkans (*Rumeli*) was their home, their ancestral land. It is perhaps useful here to remind ourselves just how long some of the main towns and cities of the Balkans had been in Ottoman hands: places like Prishtina, Üsküp (Skopje), Monastir (Bitola) and Salonica (Thessaloniki) had all been conquered between 1385 and 1390 and so had an Ottoman past stretching back more than 500 years. There was a strong consciousness of this fact and a feeling that the legacy of the glorious forefathers had now been lost. This is visible, for instance, in the lines of one of the best-known poems of the famous poet Yahya Kemal Beyatlı, himself born in Skopje in 1884:

> When I passed my youth in Balkan towns
> I felt a yearning with every breath

I took. Byron's sad melancholy rules my heart then.
In youth's daydreams I roamed the mountains
Breathed the free air of Rakofça´s fields.
I felt the passion of my raiding ancestors
Every summer, for centuries, a run to the North
That has left a thundering echo in my breast.
While the army was in defeat, the whole country in mourning
A conqueror's thought entered my dreams every night
Feelings of melancholy, a sad remnant of the flight.[24]

It would not have been surprising had a strong irredentist movement, aiming to reconquer the lost territories, developed among the Ottoman élite after 1913. This, however, was not the case. The attack by the Balkan states caused enormous bitterness and both the periodicals and the literature of the years 1912–14 are full of calls for revenge.[25] But these emotions did not result in any strong revanchist political movement for reconquest (as in post-1871 France). Though reversing the losses of 1913 was part of the war aims formulated by the Ottoman government when it joined German by in World War I, this had no practical effect, as drawing Bulgaria into the orbit of the Central Powers (and thereby opening up the vital supply route between Germany and the Ottoman Empire) took precedence over rearranging the borders in the Southern Balkans. After World War I and the Turkish victory in the independence struggle (1919–22), the Turkish delegation to the Lausanne peace conference sought a plebiscite in Western Thrace (the area west of the Maritza river populated by a Muslim majority) and the return of the Aegean islands adjacent to the Anatolian coast, but did not make demands concerning Macedonia. When Greece, Britain and France refused to grant the plebiscite in Western Thrace or the return of the Aegean islands, the delegations acquiesced. The National Assembly in Ankara then ratified this decision.

After 1923, during the Kemalist republic, relations between Turkey and its Balkan neighbours actually became quite good. While a distinct Rumeli identity can be discerned in literary products such as Yahya Kemal's poem, in the naming of shops and restaurants, in the performance of Macedonian music at President Atatürk's dinner table, and, after the introduction of family names in 1934, in the naming of families, by and large the 'generation of 1880' did not react to the loss of their homeland by focusing on the lost provinces. Instead the Young Turks after 1912 invested their emotional capital in the discovery and adoption of Anatolia as the new fatherland and fostered a deep mistrust for the non-Muslim communities whose loyalty to the empire now seemed very doubtful indeed.

A new interest in Anatolia can already be discerned immediately after the constitutional revolution. It is visible in historian Ahmet Şerif's reports from Anatolia published in the Unionist daily *Tanin* (Echo) in 1909, which opened the eyes of many city dwellers to the harsh realities of life in Anatolia. After the loss of the Balkans in 1912, Mehmet Ziya Gökalp, the leading ideologue of the Young Turk era, propagated the idea that the peasants of Anatolia represent 'true' Turkish culture and values as opposed to the 'Byzantine' and 'Arab' high culture of the Ottomans. In 1916, the 'Toward the People' (*Halka doğru*) movement, inspired by the same sort of idea, started in Izmir. In the republic this was to develop into the idealization of the Anatolian peasant (*köylücülük*), symbolized by Atatürk's dictum 'the true master of this country is the peasant.'

The feeling that Anatolia was the 'Turk's last stand', the homeland that had to be secured at all cost, underpinned Unionists and, later, Kemalist attempts to homogenize the population of Anatolia and turn it into a land for Turks only. This process started in 1914, with the expulsion of over 150,000 Greek orthodox from the Aegean seaboard in retaliation for the expulsion of hundreds of thousands of Muslims from the Balkans, and culminated in the Armenian genocide of 1915–16. It is no coincidence that refugees both from the Balkans and from the Caucasus played a critical role in the persecution of the Armenians. The Young Turks' nervousness about the future of Anatolia is demonstrated also by the fact that in late 1916, very shortly after the end of the major Armenian persecutions, the Turkish nationalist 'Turkish Hearths' (*Türk Ocakları*) organization, which was closely linked to the CUP, sent an emissary to Anatolia to investigate whether the heterodox Muslims living there, such as Alevites and Tahtacis, were in fact converted Christians and thus of doubtful loyalty.[26] This illustrates the fact that Anatolia was relatively unknown to the Macedonians who made up the core of the CUP. As Talât Pasha himself admitted:

> We are at the head of a nation. But Anatolia is a closed book to us. I think we first have to learn what is in it and then to provide services that suit this nation.[27]

Those Armenians who remained or returned after the end of World War I, were largely killed or forced to flee by a campaign of intimidations during the war of independence. The Turkish victory over the invading Greek army in September 1922 led to a mass panic among the Greek Orthodox of Western Anatolia, with three quarters of a million people crossing the Aegean aboard almost anything that could float. The agreement concluded between Turkey and Greece in Lausanne in 1923 not only saw to it that the remaining Greek Orthodox of Anatolia were forcibly exchanged with the Muslims of Greece (with the exception of the community in Eastern Thrace), it also legitimized and made permanent all population movements that had taken place since October 1912 (the start of the Balkan war).

The independence struggle after World War I was waged in order to 'safeguard the national rights of Anatolia and Rumelia' and the leaders of the resistance, including Mustafa Kemal Pasha, made a conscious effort to identify Anatolia as the historic home of the Turks, whose earth had been coloured red by the blood of the 'martyrs' since the first Turkish conquest in 1071. Emotional appeals were made to the populations to defend the fatherland. After the proclamation of the republic, the cult of Anatolia persisted and, particularly in the 1930s, the old Anatolian civilizations, such as that of the Hittites, were claimed as Turkish, thus staking out a historical claim to the territory older than that of the Greeks, Armenians, Arabs or Kurds.

The adoption of Anatolia as the true homeland of the Turks went deep, and it was a feeling shared even by many who were not Kemalists. Turkey's most famous modern poet, Nazım Hikmet [Ran], a communist and an internationalist who many times fell afoul of the Kemalist authorities, spent years in Turkish prisons and died in Moscow, in one of his best-known and loved poems, *Vasiyet* (Testament), expresses his wish to be buried in an Anatolian village:

> Comrades, if I am not granted to see that day
> If I should die before freedom comes
> Lift me up and carry me
> Bury me in an Anatolian village cemetery.[28]

The poet who wrote these lines in 1953 was born in Salonica in 1902 and first set foot in Anatolia when he was 18 years old (and left again for Russia after nine months)!

Victory from the clutches of defeat

One of the most amazing episodes in the history of the Young Turks is the resilience they showed after the crushing Ottoman defeat in World War I. A significant number of officers and party bosses were determined to resist the attempts of the victorious Entente to dismember the country. The Unionists who had fled abroad, in particular Enver, immediately started to organize support for the resistance and to plan a worldwide struggle against British and French interests through a network of former agents resoundingly called the 'General Union of Islamic Revolutionary Societies'. It is easy to dismiss these plans hatched in Berlin coffee houses as fanciful and adventurist, but then again: only a couple of years earlier Lenin had been hatching plans for worldwide revolution in Zürich coffee houses and been dismissed as a dreamer. Mustafa Kemal's defiance of the British and French in Anatolia was also dismissed as reckless adventurism by many at the time. The point is that from the moment the armistice was concluded, the Young Turks found the energy and the determination to continue the struggle. This is something unheard of in any of the other defeated countries of World War I. Where did they find this strength, this belief in their cause? I think the answer can be found at least partly in the history of the previous five years.

In January 1913, with the Bulgarian army at the Çatalca lines 30 miles from Istanbul, the Unionists had taken over power when the government seemed ready to cede Edirne and most of Eastern Thrace to the Bulgarians. Their first attempts to turn the tide and break through the Bulgarian lines failed, but later in 1913, when the Bulgarians were at war with the Greeks and the Serbians, they went on the offensive and Enver could make a triumphant entry into Edirne. Then, in February and March 1915 a large Franco-British battle fleet attacked the Dardanelles in order to break through to Istanbul, join forces with the Russians and put the Ottoman Empire out of action. Everyone, including the Unionists themselves, expected them to break through and emergency measures were taken to relocate the government to Konya, but then, on 18 March, the Entente suffered such severe losses that they gave up. The attack was broken off. All through 1915 and 1916 the Russian army, that had inflicted a devastating defeat on the Otomans at Sarıkamış in December 1914, continued its march through Eastern Anatolia, taking Erzurum, Trabzon and Van. The road to Istanbul seemed open to it, when the Russian revolution broke out. The Russian army melted away and the Ottomans regained all their losses and more at the treaty of Brest-Litovsk.

In other words: the Young Turk leaders had witnessed a number of occasions where disaster seemed unavoidable, but where through totally unexpected developments, the tables had been turned in a miraculous fashion and they had emerged victorious. I am convinced that these examples were in the minds of those people like Enver or Mustafa Kemal (and many others), who in 1918–19 decided that the battle had been lost, but that the war could still be won.

Conclusion

The Young Turks we have discussed in the preceding pages formed a remarkable generation, a generation who took fate into their own hands – and in doing so determined the fate of others. We have tried to answer the question of who they were by looking at their background, their shared experiences, and the mental attitudes and worldview they displayed. Having established these, an effort was made to detect linkages between their background, their experiences and their ideas. It is not my intention to 'prove' that some ideas derived directly from elements in the biography of the Young Turks. This would be quite impossible. After all, one can establish who the Young Turks were and what they did, but not why they did it; at best why they said they did it. One can trace the reasons for their actions in their memoirs, but then again, memoirs most often are means at vindication, so who is to tell whether the reasons given were actually the decisive factor at the time? So, no definitive proof is claimed or aimed for. Instead, this chapter is an attempt to suggest, hopefully convincingly, that there is something that can usefully be called the 'Young Turk mindset' and that it can be explained and understood better by taking into account the life stories of those involved. Understanding the mindset of the Young Turks is relevant to our reading of modern Ottoman and Turkish history, because it concerns the ideas, not of academics, but of people who actually held power for half a century and who to some extent were able to shape their society according to their vision. This is true as much for the policies executed during World War I as for the nation building process and 'cultural revolution' of the Kemalist republic.

10. Atatürk as a Unionist*

In the historiography of modern Turkey the relationship of Mustafa Kemal [Atatürk] with the Committee of Union and Progress (CUP) is depicted as very contentious. While it is recognized that Mustafa Kemal was a member of the CUP and remained so until the dissolution of that organization in 1918, his disagreements with the leadership of the CUP, both before and during World War I are emphasized. The 'storyline' is usually that of rivalry between two military leaders, Enver Pasha on the one hand and Mustafa Kemal on the other, with Enver cast as an irresponsible and vainglorious gambler and Mustafa Kemal as the prescient voice of reason, who was disregarded for reasons of political and personal jealousy. This version of events ultimately seems to go back to Kemal's published memoirs of 1922 and 1926, which stem from an era when he was establishing his hold on the political system of the new republic and purging potential rivals, who were all former Unionists. Kemal's position and prestige made sure that this version of history took hold, but perhaps seeing recent history in terms of a comparison between the two supreme military leaders of the age, one of whom had presided over the collapse of the Ottoman Empire and the other over the emergence of the Turkish republic, was a tempting paradigm in itself. The very fact, however, that this version of history originated in, and was so closely linked to, the political struggles of the period, makes it imperative that we should look at the evidence afresh and form ourselves an independent opinion of what exactly was Kemal's place in the CUP, dealing also with the issue of the supposed rivalry with Enver.

This is precisely what I aimed to do in the second chapter of my 1984 book *The Unionist Factor*. However since then almost 25 years have passed and important new biographies of Atatürk[1] as well as monographs on topics like the Ottoman officer corps, the Balkan War and the Ottoman Empire in World War I[2] have appeared. So it is, I think, a worthwhile exercise both to summarize the findings of the 1984 chapter and the evidence presented in the more recent literature to get at a clearer picture of Mustafa Kemal, or Atatürk as we have come to know him, in his Young Turk days.

Kemal joined the CUP in February 1908 with membership number 322.[3] This in fact means that he was the 232nd person to join, as the CUP, to make itself look stronger and more attractive to prospective members had decided to number new members joining after the initial ten from 111 upwards.

By the time he joined, the CUP was already well established and had a clear leadership, consisting of the founders of the Ottoman Freedom Society in Salonica (people like Talât, Rahmi and Mithat Şükrü), some of the members of the Paris-based Committee of Progress and Union with which the OFS had merged in September 1907 (people like Bahaettin Şakir and Dr Nâzım) and the founders of the CUP branch in the most important military centre, Monastir (Enver, Kâzım Karabekir, Ali Fethi [Okyar]). Kemal was not among the leading strata of the society and this is something that probably rankled with him, as he may well have seen himself as one the initiators of revolutionary activity in Macedonia. Here is why.

Like many of his colleagues, he had been involved in embryonic secret societies, both in Damascus in 1905 and in Salonica, 1906. Between February and May 1906, Kemal used extended sick leave to visit his hometown of Salonica, where he met with some former classmates (Ömer Naci, Hüsrev Sami and Hakkı Baha) and founded the Fatherland and Freedom Society (*Vatan ve Hürriyet Cemiyeti*), which was intended as a branch of another small secret society that he had founded in Damascus the year before. After Kemal's return to Syria, this society proved to be stillborn, but some of its members soon after became important in the OFS/CPU/CUP. Ömer Naci was among the founders of the OFS in September 1906 and he and Hüsrev Sami were sent to Paris to negotiate the merger with the CPU a year later.

In September 1907, Mustafa Kemal managed to secure a posting in Salonica and a transfer from Southern Palestine, where he was stationed at the time. From September 1907 until June 1908 he served on the staff of the Third Army in Salonica. In early July 1908 he was appointed inspector of the railway line between Salonica and Skopje, a position that gave him mobility and allowed him to fulfil a role in the internal communications of the CUP. This proved important when shortly after Enver took to the hills and started the constitutional revolution in the Tikvesh area and Kemal was used as the messenger, who brought him both arms and a document from the Central Committee, appointing him 'General Inspector of the Internal Organisation and Executive Forces in Rumeli'.[4]

During the revolutionary days of July 1908 Mustafa Kemal did not come to the fore as one of the leading representatives of the committee. He was not one of the 'Heroes of Freedom' whose image was reproduced in journals and on picture postcards. On the other hand, he clearly was closer to the centre of power than most ordinary members of the CUP (and there were about 2,000 of them in July 1908). This was due not so much to his own position or activities, but to his friendship with fellow officers Ahmet Cemal (the later Cemal Pasha), Ömer Naci and Ali Fethi [Okyar], who *were* at the centre of things.

Several sources suggest that Mustafa Kemal was one of the members of the CUP, who, after the revolution, pleaded for a complete disengagement of the army from politics and he seems to have made enemies by his insistence on this point at the first post-revolutionary congress of the CUP.[5] Soon after, in September 1908, he was sent by the Committee to Tripolitania on a mission to explain the revolution to its inhabitants and build support for the CUP. Mustafa Kemal claimed that the Unionist leaders intended this mission to be a kind of exile, but this seems unlikely. In the first place it was a short mission so if the intention as to remove Mustafa Kemal from either Salonica or the capital, it was not very effective and in the second place the mission was not unimportant. Tripolitania was the empire's last African possession and it was well known that Italy had designs on the province. Had the deeply religious Arab population of the province rejected the Young Turks or openly rebelled against the new regime, that would have created a serious embarrassment and might have led to the loss of the province. At the same time, it must be said that, while Mustafa Kemal was thus given an important political assignment, the plum jobs went to others: Ali Fuat [Cebesoy] was appointed military attaché in Rome, Ali Fethi in Paris, Hafız Hakkı in Vienna and Enver in Berlin.

After his return from Tripolitania, Mustafa Kemal was appointed chief of staff of the 11th Reserve Division in Salonica. When the counterrevolution broke out in Istanbul in April 1909, the CUP gained the support of General Mahmut Şevket Pasha, the commander of the Third Army and inspector of the European Armies, who had his headquarters in Salonica. He ordered the 11th Reserve Division to advance by rail to the Çatalca lines 30 miles west of Istanbul as part of what was called (possibly on the suggestion of Mustafa Kemal)[6] the 'Action Army' (*Hareket Ordusu*). So, in the first phase of the operations against the insurgency Mustafa Kemal played quite an important role, but his position was not that of commander or chief of staff of the whole Action Army, nor did he command the 11th Reserve Division. When the army had achieved its first objectives, Mahmut Şevket Pasha himself came over to take up the command for the march into the city. He brought with him his own staff including Ali Fethi, Enver and Hafız Hakkı, who had been recalled from their diplomatic postings for the purpose. Mustafa Kemal, the same age but junior in rank and with less political clout, was expected to serve under them in the divisional staff. Again we see the same pattern: Mustafa Kemal was a prominent Unionist officer, who was trusted with a key position during the life and death struggle of the CUP with its opponents, but he was definitely second rank when compared to figures like Enver, Cemal, Hafız Hakkı or Fethi.

After the suppression of the counterrevolution Mustafa Kemal served in an officer training unit in Salonica and then on the staff of the Third Army. In 1910, as an adjutant-major he temporarily commanded the 38th Regiment in Salonica because of illness of the commanding officer and in 1911 he served on the staff of Mahmut Şevket Pasha during the suppression of the Albanian rebellion of that year. In September 1911 he was appointed to the general staff in Istanbul, but he never took up his post as he left for Tripolitania once more on 11 October.

The Italians had invaded Tripolitania on the flimsiest of pretexts and occupied the coastal areas. Their naval superiority made it impossible for the Ottoman government to send an expeditionary force, but a number of Unionist officers decided to go to the province to organize resistance from the desert. Some, like Fethi, went by way of France and Tunisia, but most went through Egypt, disguised as civilians. Mustafa Kemal travelled with his old friend Ömer Naci and two Unionist *fedaî*s, Yakup Cemil and *Sapancalı* Hakkı. In Egypt he fell ill, but having recovered he joined another old friend (and distant family member) Nuri [Conker] and crossed the border into Tripolitania. Between December 1911 and October 1912 he fought with distinction in the guerrilla war against the Italians. His headquarters were opposite Derne in Cyrneaica and he served under Enver, who had overall command of the operations in North Africa and whose headquarters were nearby. Although they seem to have worked well together professionally, relations between the two men seem to have soured during their months in the desert. By the time they got back to Istanbul the problems between them seem to have been well known within army circles.[7]

Many of the volunteers who fought in North Africa belonged to the *fedaî* ('self sacrificing volunteer') wing of the CUP. They were mostly lower ranking officers, who were used in the most dangerous missions. In 1914 the volunteers would be reorganized by Enver into the 'Special Organisation'

(*Teşkilat-i Mahsusa*), but Mustafa Kemal seems to have been quite close to a number of them as well. We already noted that he travelled to Egypt in the company of two notorious *fedaî*s and in Tripolitania he fought side by side with Ali [Çetinkaya], the man who would later become a close collaborator and notorious as president of the independence tribunal of 1926. Some of Mustafa Kemal's close friends, like Nuri [Conker] and Hüsrev Sami [Kızıldoğan] and his long serving adjutant Cevat Abbas [Gürer] were all 'volunteers'.

The Ottoman officers were still in North Africa, organizing the anti-Italian resistance, when the Balkan War broke out in October 1912. When the news of the war reached Tripolitania, it was first decided that Enver would return to Istanbul and that Mustafa Kemal would take over, but when the extent of the disaster that had befallen the Ottoman arms became clear, most of the officers decided to return and they left Enver's younger brother Nuri [Kıllıgil] in charge of the guerrilla war. By the time they arrived back in the capital, the Bulgarians had occupied Thrace and the Ottoman armies held the Çatalca line to the west of Istanbul, the encircled fortress city of Edirne and the Gallipoli peninsula. Enver was appointed chief of staff of the Tenth Army Corps, the strategic reserve with divisions in Istanbul, Izmit and Bandırma. Fethi was made chief of staff of the Bolayır Army Corps that defended the Gallipoli peninsula, while his friend Mustafa Kemal served under him as the head of operations on the army corps staff.

Militarily the situation was deadlocked and in December an armistice was concluded. When the negotiations broke down, the great powers, on the initiative of Great Britain communicated an ultimatum to the Porte on 17 January, in which the Ottoman Empire was asked to acquiesce in a new border along a line running from Enez on the Aegean to Midye on the Black Sea coast. This implied the loss of the old capital city of Edirne, a town that was still in Ottoman hands. When signs began to emerge that Kamil Pasha's government might accede to the demands, the CUP leaders, who had been exposed to persecution by Kamil and his cabinet for months, decided to act. On 23 January they executed a coup d'état and took over power. The decision for the coup was taken in a small inner circle of Unionists. Some leading Unionist officers in the field, like Enver and Fethi had been consulted beforehand and as Fethi opposed the plan, he was left out of the final preparations. Enver, on the other hand, personally led the coup.

The weakness of the army left the new government just as powerless to regain the lost territories as the old one had been. In order to satisfy the demands for offensive action, the chief of the general staff İzzet Pasha now decided to execute a plan prepared by the staff for an amphibious operation against the Bulgarian troops opposite the Gallipoli peninsula. The plan envisaged a combined operation of the Bolayır Corps and the reserve, the Tenth Corps. The Bolayır Corps (commanded by Fahri Pasha with Fethi and Mustafa Kemal on his staff) would engage the Bulgarians in front of Bolayır, while units from the Tenth Corps, commanded by Hurşit Pasha with Enver as chief of staff, would simultaneously land in the rear of the Bulgarian army facing the Gallipoli peninsula at Şarköy and İnce Burun. The operation was planned in detail and extensively rehearsed in January. After a week's delay due to storm it was executed in the second week of February, but it ended in disaster. The Bolayır Corps attacked the Bulgarians at the agreed time without checking whether the Tenth Corps had actually arrived and the Tenth Corps was half a day late in landing due to the late arrival of the Ottoman battleships that were to provide covering fire. In the end, the landings went relatively well and the Ottomans established a beach head west of Şarköy, but by that time the Bolayır Corps had been mauled by the Bulgarians, losing half its strength in casualties. This put an end to any idea of catching the Bulgarians in a pincer movement and after three days the expeditionary force was recalled. Amazingly, and thanks to Enver's staff work, it escaped almost unscathed. After re-embarking, the Tenth Corps was ordered to Gallipoli to strengthen the now depleted forces on the peninsula.[8]

Now an acrimonious debate started between Gallipoli and Bolayır. Both army corps commanders and their staff officers entered the blame game with gusto. When Hurşit Pasha was appointed commander of the whole Dardanelles force, Fahri Pasha, Fethi and Mustafa Kemal all handed in their resignations to the vice-commander in chief (İzzet Pasha), who in turn notified the Grand Vizier on 20 February. Mahmut Şevket Pasha decided that the situation was so serious that he needed to go to Gallipoli in person to settle the affair. On 21 February he heard all parties and then relieved Fahri Pasha, who seemed to be the most quarrelsome and who was responsible for the fiasco at Bolayır, of his command. He intended to take Enver with him to serve as head of operations on the general staff in Istanbul, but the chief of that staff, İzzet Pasha now intervened and asked the Grand Vizier to discuss the matter with him before taking such a step. The reason was that İzzet had by now received letters of resignation, written on the 19th (before Mahmut Şevket's visit to Gallipoli), from Fethi and Mustafa Kemal and a memorandum in which they demanded a resumption of the offensive against the Bulgarians in order to save Edirne. İzzet submitted both to Mahmut Şevket.[9]

The existence of this memorandum has been known to modern historians since 1968 when Mithat Sertoğlu found it among the papers of Mahmut Şevket Pasha and published it,[10] but neither he nor later Turkish authors seem to see its true significance. Sertoğlu does not link it to the controversy following the failed Şarköy operation, but simply interprets it as an exhortation to liberate Edirne. Later Münir Aktepe in the 1970s and Naim Tufan in the 1990s have interpreted the memorandum as a plan of action for the amphibious operation of 8–10 February, in other words: as a text written before that date.[11] This interpretation has to be rejected, however. The document is dated 4–5 February (*Şubat*) 1328 according to the old (Rumi) calendar, which means it was written on 18/19 February 1913 according to the Gregorian calendar, that is, after the Şarköy action. The amphibious operation anyway had been planned and prepared from early January onwards. Tufan's assertion that the Fethi and Mustafa Kemal wrote '4–5 Şubat 1328' by mistake and really meant '4–5 Şubat 1913' is not substantiated and extremely unlikely for Ottoman officers of the time. In addition the memorandum recommends the immediate transfer of the troops 'that are in Gallipoli harbour' to the Çatalca front and those troops (the Tenth Army Corps) only arrived there *after* the Şarköy expedition. In the end this recommendation was followed and the whole Tenth Corps with Fahri Pasha and Enver was shipped to the Çatalca front. Fethi and Mustafa Kemal were persuaded – either by the Grand Vizier or by Talât, who also got himself involved, to remain in their posts in Bolayır.

The events of February, described in such detail here (and in much more detail by Aktepe and Tufan), deserve our attention for two reasons. In the first place, it illustrates the extent to which discipline within the officer corps of the Ottoman army had broken down under the impact of politicization (a point also emphasized by Tufan). A row between three young officers, two of them lieutenant-colonels and one a major, was solved not by disciplinary measures but through the direct involvement of the chief of the general staff and the Grand Vizier. Instead of coming in for a punitive posting to Basra or the Yemen, Fethi and Mustafa Kemal, who had been partly responsible for a disastrous defeat, handed in their resignation *and* wrote a memorandum in which they made demands in a peremptory tone for a different strategy, were *persuaded* to remain in their posts.

The second point, and the one directly relevant to the subject of this chapter, is that it allows us to place Mustafa Kemal within the CUP. During the whole episode he emphatically sided with his friend Fethi against Enver, with whom he seems to have been on bad terms since their time in

North Africa. The documentation makes it very clear, however, that the row was considered by all concerned to be one between Fethi and Enver, with Mustafa Kemal very much in a supporting role. That figures: Fethi was higher in rank than Mustafa Kemal and equal in rank to Enver. They were both army corps chiefs of staff and lieutenant-colonels. Mustafa Kemal was a major in charge of a section of the staff. Fethi and Enver were both important military members of the CUP inner circle, so much so that Fethi had been consulted during the planning stage of the coup d'état in January. Mustafa Kemal was close to – but not in – the inner circle. While they resigned together and wrote their memorandum together, it was Fethi, who, a year later, was to publish a booklet (that seems to have escaped the attention of historians so far), called *Bolayır Muharebesinde Adem-Muvaffakiyetin Esbabı. 'Askeri Mağlubiyetlerimizin Esbabı' Muharririne Cevap* (The Reasons for the Lack of Success in the Battle of Bolayır. An Answer to the Author of 'The Reasons for Our Military Defeats'). In the booklet he defends himself against the accusation that it was the staff of the Bolayır Corps that had ruined the operation by going on the attack without waiting for the Tenth Corps in order to claim the honour of defeating the Bulgarians.[12]

Clearly, the events of February 1913 mark the breakdown of relations between Fethi and Mustafa Kemal and Enver, which was unfortunate for the former as in the next months Enver was to emerge as the undoubted leader of the military within the CUP. In June the Bulgarians attacked their former allies Greece and Serbia and the Ottomans decided to make use of the opportunity to liberate Edirne. By joining the advance cavalry that was nearing the city unopposed, Enver managed to position himself as the liberator of Edirne. Mustafa Kemal was engaged in a sideshow, commanding the troops that broke out of Bolayır to conquer the port of Dedeağaç. On 4 January 1914, Enver was appointed minister of war. Fethi drew his conclusions. Rather than serve under Enver he left the army. He was offered the post of secretary-general of the CUP, but instead opted for the post of ambassador to Sofia. Mustafa Kemal was clearly under a cloud as well because of his support for Fethi and he was persuaded by the latter and by Ahmet Cemal to join him in Sofia as military attaché.

Mustafa Kemal stayed in Sofia until after the entry of the Ottoman Empire in the World War in November 1914. He then asked for a military command, a wish that was granted with his appointment as commander of the Nineteenth Division that was being formed in Tekirdağ for service on the Gallipoli peninsula.

The military career of Mustafa Kemal in World War I is covered in detail in the major biographies. He played an important role, first as commander of the Arıburnu section and then of the whole Anafartalar front during the Dardanelles campaign in 1915. His success as a front line commander under Esat Pasha and General Otto Liman von Sanders was known within the army. The journal *Harb Mecmuası* (War Journal) honoured him with a full-length photograph, but he was not known to the wider public. The Dardanelles campaign in 1915 gave him a reputation in the army as a very able commander, but also as a hypersensitive and quarrelsome colleague. He had constant problems with the German officers, with Enver and ultimately also with Liman. Again he had to be dissuaded from resigning. The pattern remained the same throughout the war. Mustafa Kemal served with distinction as commander of the Sixteenth Army Corps in Eastern Anatolia in 1916 and then as commander of the Seventh Army in Palestine in 1917 under Von Falkenhayn and again in 1918 under Liman von Sanders. After the Ottoman retreat from Syria and the armistice of Moudros, he succeeded Liman as commander of the remnants of the Syrian armies. All this time he was involved in activities that at the very least undermined military discipline and which can often also be called political.

The trouble started when he left the Anafartalar front on 'sick leave' and returned to Istanbul in November 1915. He approached a cabinet minister, Ahmet Nesimi, to voice his criticism of the military situation and in particular of the German role. The minister apparently simply told him to address his complaints to the general staff. He also reported the conversation in a meeting of the cabinet.[13] In 1916, while serving on the eastern front Mustafa Kemal circulated a cipher telegram to the other commanders in the East, again criticizing the conduct of the war and asking them to take concerted action. Vehip Pasha, the commander of the Second Army and a man who was close to Enver, intercepted the cable and notified Enver Pasha in Istanbul. Enver reacted by offering Mustafa Kemal a choice: either to refrain from further political activity or to resign from the army and to enter politics officially. In case he chose the latter alternative, Enver was prepared to offer him a seat in parliament. It was a clever way of turning the tables on Kemal, who had so forcefully advocated a separation between army and politics back in 1908.

The same year Kemal's name came up in connection with the attempted coup d'état of Unionist *fedaî* Yakup Cemil.[14] After his arrest, the latter told his interrogators that he had wanted to replace Enver with Mustafa Kemal. There is no further indication of any involvement on Mustafa Kemal's part, but one of the other conspirators, a Dr Hilmi, who was also arrested and interrogated, sought refuge with Mustafa Kemal at his headquarters in Silvan, north of Diyarbakır. Mustafa Kemal gave him a position on his staff and thus granted him protection.[15]

Mustafa Kemal had had strained relations with the German officers in Gallipoli. As a proud Turkish nationalist he deeply resented the overbearing attitude of many of the Prussian officers. In 1917, this showed itself again when he was appointed commander of the Seventh Army and had to serve under Erich von Falkenhayn. This former chief of the imperial general staff had been replaced by Von Hindenburg after his failure at Verdun and transferred to the Syrian command in 1917. He relied solely on his German staff and understood little of the circumstances in the Ottoman Empire and did not consult his Ottoman commanders. Mustafa Kemal not only found this treatment unacceptable, he also opposed the, in his eyes totally unrealistic, offensive strategy agreed by Enver and Von Falkenhayn. On 20 September 1917 he sent a long report to the war minister, detailing his criticism. Not content with sending this report to Enver, he also went over the war minister's head and sent a copy to the cabinet.[16] When he received only a formal reply from Enver, he resigned his command. When also refused the offer of the command of the Second Army in Eastern Anatolia, he was recalled and put at the disposal of the general staff in Istanbul. Back in the capital he seems to have teamed up with his old friend Fethi again, both of them trying to find a hearing with Talât and to turn him against Enver.[17]

Mustafa Kemal stayed away from the front lines for almost a year, only returning to Syria, again to command the Seventh Army, in August 1918. By that time Von Falkenhayn had been replaced with Liman von Sanders, who handed over his command to Mustafa Kemal at the time of the armistice.

The object of this short chapter is not to tell the story of Mustafa Kemal's life in the last decade of the empire. That has been done far better elsewhere. The aim is to establish what was his place within the CUP. In order to do that, we have first to understand the structure of the CUP. This was not a monolithic organization with a single powerful leader. Nor was it led by a 'triumvirate' as contemporary European observers often thought. Enver dominated the Unionist officers in the army after 1913 and Talât dominated the civilian wing of the CUP throughout, but the organization they headed was a complicated whole of interlocking and overlapping networks. As we have seen, Mustafa Kemal joined the CUP relatively late and was not part of the first echelon of the military wing of the CUP. He did not come to the fore in any of the big events of the first five years of CUP rule: the constitutional revolution, the suppression of the 31 March rebellion, the *Babı Ali* coup or the retaking of Edirne. Of the members of CUP with access to power, he seems to have been particularly close to Ali Fethi and to a lesser extent to Cemal Pasha, with whom he worked closely in 1908 and again in 1917. His relations with Enver seem to have soured during their tour of duty in Tripolitania in 1911–12 and especially as a result of the botched Şarköy-Bolayır operation of February 1913, in which Fethi and he jointly opposed Enver.

This meant that Mustafa Kemal was positioned very badly – politically – from 1913 onwards. After the liberation of Edirne, Enver's star rose quickly and Fethi had to go into exile as ambassador to Sofia. From late 1914, Cemal Pasha took over the Syrian front, which meant that he was almost all-powerful in Syria and Palestine but also that he lost most of his influence in the capital. Mustafa Kemal was left without effective protection. His spirited defence of the Anafartalar front gained him a reputation in the army (although he was never the highest commander on the Dardanelles front, or even the second or third highest), but it brought him little in the way of influence within the CUP. In 1916–18 he served with distinction, although without spectacular results on the Eastern Anatolian and Palestine fronts, but he also gained a reputation as a trouble maker through his constant breaches of army discipline and his political meddling. Still, as I said back in 1984, 'the really amazing thing is that he was kept in important positions in the army at all. In what other army could an officer, who had laid down or refused a command four times, openly criticized the high command, not only to his military superiors, but also to [a minister], the cabinet and the head of state and whose name had been mentioned in an attempted coup d'état have finished up commanding an army group?'[18]

The answer, I think, lies in two factors. The first is that the CUP was so powerful that prominent members were almost untouchable under law or army discipline. This showed itself very clearly in 1913, when chief of staff and full general Ahmet İzzet Pasha had to conclude that it was impossible to discipline two quarrelling lieutenant-colonels and a major because they were prominent Unionists. The second factor has to be that the internal structure of the CUP with its intricate web of interlocking networks made it very difficult to take action against a prominent member of one of the factions, without setting off a chain reaction. Talât, the ultimate 'people manager' kept his hold on the CUP precisely through his ability to manipulate and cajole the different factions and to play them against each other without alienating any of them.

Was there a rivalry between Enver and Mustafa Kemal, as the latter suggested in his memoirs and has been assumed by many later historians and biographers? Not really. Mustafa Kemal never came close to challenging Enver for the leadership of the military wing of the CUP. Cemal, Fethi and Hafız Hakkı all were much more serious rivals to Enver before his meteoric rise in 1913. Mustafa Kemal's memoirs seem to show that he developed an 'Enver complex' but there is no evidence that this was reciprocal. Nor is there any evidence that his career suffered or that it was sabotaged by Enver or other circles within the CUP. His career shows a normal pattern of promotions. He was made a brigadier and a pasha in 1916, after his successes at the Dardanelles, at the age of 35. Perhaps a promotion to lieutenant general would have been on the cards in 1918, but then again: he spent almost a year without active duty in 1917–18. The postings he received were substantial, including the command of an army corps, an army and, finally, an army group. Where he was thwarted, was in his ambition to influence government policy and the conduct of the war in general. For that, he lacked the political clout.

Mustafa Kemal's lack of political access during World War I would become his greatest asset after the war. When the Unionists looked for a commander with an excellent military reputation, who was a Unionist and a nationalist, but without too close an association with the wartime policies of the CUP, he was their man. It was his own political acumen and tactical brilliance, as well as the fact that the top echelon of the CUP had either fled abroad or been arrested by the British, that allowed him to emerge as the unquestioned leader of the Turkish independence movement.

11. The Ottoman Legacy of the Kemalist Republic*

The Kemalist experiment of the 1920s and 30s was both a classic example of nation building and a daring modernization project. The state that emerged in the shape of the Republic of Turkey in 1923 had to be built on the basis of a population that was 90 per cent Muslim, but ethnically mixed, impoverished and numerically decimated. To turn this mass of people into a nation, to make citizens out of subjects and to install a sense of patriotism in the population was one of the two main aims of the Kemalists. The other was to make society 'modern' (*muasir*) and 'civilized' (*medeni*). Both of these terms, which at times were used as synonyms, referred to contemporary European civilization, which the Kemalists, like the radical 'Westernizers' among the Young Turks before them, considered the only viable civilization in the world. These goals could only be reached by enlightening the masses, which required forcing organized religion to relinquish its hold on people's minds. That is, unless religion could be used as a state-controlled channel to spread the message of enlightenment.

The policies that resulted from this ideological programme, such as the abolition of the mystical fraternities (*tarikat*) and the introduction of the Swiss civil code to replace the religious law (sharia or *şeriat*), constituted such a far-reaching form of interference in the daily and personal lives of the citizens, that they aroused both resentment and resistance. If we want to understand the Kemalists and their policies, we must take a step back and look at their shared past, in other words at the final years of the Ottoman Empire. That period shaped the future leaders of the republic as well as the country they tried to reshape. Both the material circumstances and the ideological toolkit available to the Kemalists were products of the constitutional period after 1908 and the decade of war between 1912 and 1922.

The new borders

One look at the map suffices to make clear that in geographical terms the new republic was very different from the empire of even 1912. The Arab provinces which had formed part of the empire for 400 years had been lost, as had the southern Balkan ('Rumelian') provinces which had been Ottoman since the fifteenth (and in some cases, the fourteenth) century, and had produced the bulk of the Ottoman bureaucratic and military élite. Losing such important areas clearly was a traumatic affair. At the same time, it is important to understand the nature of the new borders. They were not 'natural' borders in any sense, but determined by the political and military realities of 1918. The national borders were laid down in the 'National Pact' (*Misak-i Millî*) adopted by the last Ottoman parliament in February 1920. In essence these were none other than the armistice lines of October 1918 (although confusingly two versions of the text seem to have been in existence from the very start, one calling for independence of the Ottoman-Muslim majority within the armistice lines and the other within and without the armistice lines).[1] In other words: the territory of the republic was that which was still under Ottoman control in 1918, a fact which was recognized in so many words by Mustafa Kemal Pasha, the leader of the national resistance movement.[2] It is important to note that in 1918–19 not even nationalist officers like Mustafa Kemal objected to the terms of the Armistice of Moudhros as such – they objected to the violation of these terms by the allies, primarily the British.[3] These infringements in part consisted of the occupation of territory, which had still been in Ottoman hands at noon on 31 October, when the armistice formally came into effect. The most important of these were the occupation of areas around Mosul in the East and around Iskenderun on the Mediterranean. Who held what in the inland areas of the Syrian desert was completely unclear. This would later create problems during the peace negotiations in Lausanne in 1922–3. At Lausanne, the Turkish delegation argued for a new southern border, which would run from a point south of Iskenderun on the Mediterranean coast, along the Euphrates and then on to the Iranian border, thus including the province of Mosul in the new Turkey. As we know, it was unsuccessful in its demands. Arbitration by the League of Nations awarded the province of Mosul to Iraq in 1926, but Turkey managed to regain the district of Iskenderun (or *Hatay*) in 1939. The border with the French protectorate of Syria was determined in Lausanne as it had been in the Franco-Turkish agreement of 1920, and ran just south of the track of the Baghdad railway. As for the Arab provinces under British occupation on the day of the armistice, the 'National Pact' demanded a plebiscite, but not automatic inclusion in the post-war Ottoman state. While disillusionment with the attitude of the Arabs during the World War I probably played a role, the leadership in Ankara was also realistic enough to see that reconquest of the Arab lands was beyond their means. There were attempts to cooperate with Arab nationalists in 1919–21, but inclusion of the former Arab provinces (Damascus, Baghdad, Basra, Hejaz) was never seriously contemplated.

On the Caucasian border, the National Pact demanded a plebiscite for the three provinces of Kars, Ardahan and Batumi. These had been lost to Russia in 1878, regained after the collapse of the Russian army in 1918, and lost again to the British and their Armenian and Georgian allies in 1919. The Turkish nationalist general Kâzım Karabekir reconquered Kars and Ardahan in a short war against the Republic of Armenia in 1920–1, thus making the plebiscite superfluous in these two provinces. This left only the fate of Batumi to be decided. The threat of a clash with the Red Army and the need for Soviet military and financial support led to a compromise with Russia, which left Batumi and its hinterland in the hands of Soviet-controlled Georgia.

In the West, the National Pact foresaw a plebiscite in Western Thrace (*Garbi Trakya*) with its Muslim majority. At Lausanne, the Turkish delegation also forwarded the claim that a number of Aegean islands adjoining the Anatolian mainland should be ceded by Greece. Like the demands for inclusion of Iskenderun and Mosul, these claims, too, were rejected. In the end, the Turks acquiesced, although the fact that the Lausanne treaty left sizeable Turkish and Muslim communities outside the new national borders caused acrimonious debates in the Turkish National Assembly.[4]

Thus, in essence the borders of 1918, which were recognized in the peace treaty of Lausanne in 1923, were no different in principle from those established in 1878 or in 1913: They corresponded to that which the Ottomans had managed to hold on to and were not the result of any principled choice for a 'Turkish' homeland. In this sense the borders of Turkey were very different from the lines drawn in Eastern Europe after 1918, which at least pretended to do justice to the right to self-determination of nations. The Republic of Turkey, created within the former Ottoman borders, was still a multi-ethnic, multi-lingual society, with a large majority of Turks and significant minorities of Kurds, Arabs and many smaller groups. It was far less multi-ethnic that it had been, however.

Demographic change

The population composition of the new state was very different even from that of the same geographical area in late Ottoman times. This was the result of large-scale migration and warfare in the decade prior to the proclamation of the republic in 1923. The demographic effects of the ten years of warfare between 1912 and 1922 cannot be overstated. Mortality among the Anatolian population had been incredibly high. The Ottoman army had recruited most of its soldiers from among the peasant population of Anatolia. As such, the Anatolian peasantry composed a very large proportion of the 800,000 fatal casualties of the campaigns in the Caucasus, Gallipoli, Palestine, Mesopotamia, Galicia and Romania. Roughly half of these casualties, as we shall see in more detail in the next section of this volume, were due to disease, rather than warfare. Furthermore, from the spring of 1915 onwards, eastern Anatolia had become a war theatre itself. This had led to great suffering among the Muslim population, in part because the retreating Ottoman armies stimulated the spread of epidemics, notably typhus in winter and cholera in summer.[5] The decade of war also brought an end to the old Christian communities in Anatolia, primarily those of the Greek Orthodox and the Armenians. The Armenian community was ravaged by the large-scale persecutions organized by the Young Turks in 1915–16. Massacres, death marches and neglect combined to kill some 800,000 Armenians, which probably constituted at least 40 per cent of the community as a whole.

World War I had been followed by an independence war during which campaigns had been fought in the east and the west, in addition to guerrilla action in the south and the west, and civil war between supporters of the Istanbul government and the nationalists in the interior. On the western front the retreating Greek forces had committed large-scale atrocities against the Muslim population and some of the advancing Turkish troops had acted with comparable brutality against the Greek Orthodox.

As a result of war, epidemics and starvation, some 2.5 million Anatolian Muslims, as well as up to 800,000 Armenians and some 300,000 Greeks, had lost their lives. All in all, the population of Anatolia declined by 20 per cent through mortality – a percentage 20 times higher than that of France, which was the hardest hit western European country in World War I. The effects of war and disease were spread unevenly, however: in some eastern provinces fully half of the population had perished and another quarter were refugees. There were 12 provinces, most of them in the west, where more than 30 per cent of adult women were widows.[6] Turkey after the war was an empty country. Travellers who visited the country in the 1920s and 30s, like the young Turkologists whose exploits are described in Part IV, remark without exception on the desertedness of its countryside.[7]

Apart from mortality, the Anatolian population of the new Republic also showed the effects of large-scale migration. All through the nineteenth and early twentieth centuries Muslims had fled, or been forced to flee, from territories, which were lost by the empire to Christian states: Russia, Romania, Bulgaria, Serbia and Greece. Eventually, these people had been resettled in Anatolia (often on former Armenian properties). These refugees and their children now comprised about a third of the post-war population. The loss of the predominantly Christian areas and the immigration of Muslims had meant that in 1913, for the first time in its entire history, the Ottoman Empire had a Turkish majority.

During and after the World War almost all of the surviving Armenians left the country for Russia, France or the United States. In the aftermath of the Balkan War up to 200,000 Greeks (out of 450,000 living on the Aegean coast) had been forced to leave Western Anatolia. Three quarters of them returned in the wake of the Greek occupation in 1919.[8] When the Greek army in Anatolia collapsed in 1922, almost the whole of the Greek community in the west, fled to Greece. This situation was made official with the agreement on the exchange of populations (the *mübadele*), which was annexed to the peace treaty of Lausanne. Under this agreement the last remaining Greek Orthodox communities of Anatolia, mainly those of the Black Sea coast (the 'Pontic' Greeks) and the Karamanlis (Turkish-speaking Greek Orthodox from Central Anatolia), were exchanged for the Muslim community in Greece. In total about a million Greeks left Anatolia in 1922–4, and about 400,000 Muslims from Greece came in. The migratory movements of during and following the war resulted in a net population loss of 10 per cent, which should be added to the 20 per cent loss due to mortality.

The changes in population also meant that from a cultural standpoint, Anatolia in 1923 was a completely different place from what it had been in 1913. The larger Christian communities were practically gone, and the population of about 13 million was now 98 per cent Muslim, compared with 80 per cent before the war. Linguistically, only two large groups were left: Turks and Kurds, though half a dozen smaller but still important language groups endured. The country was also more rural than it had been with only 18 per cent of the population living in towns of 10,000 or more inhabitants, as opposed to 25 per cent before the war.[9] This reflected the fact that the Christian communities had been more heavily urbanized. They had also completely dominated the modern sector of the economy. The cotton mills of Çukurova, the silk of Bursa, the exports of figs and raisins in the West, shipping, banking, the railways, hotels and restaurants – all had been almost exclusively in the hands of Christians before the war. In 1923 Turkey was not only a country almost without managers and engineers – it was a country almost without trained waiters, welders or electricians. It would take at least a generation to rebuild the skills that had disappeared.

A new state?

The republic created out of the ruins of Ottoman Anatolia in October 1923 was, of course, legally and formally a new state. It was only one of the many new states which were created out of the Ottoman Empire and carried part of the Ottoman heritage with them. Comparisons with the experiences of other successor states in the Balkans and the Arab World (such as that pioneered by Carl Brown in his *Imperial Legacy. The Ottoman Imprint on the Balkans and the Middle East*) are helpful in understanding the way the Ottoman heritage continued to play a role in the 'new' states. At the same time, it is evident that in some ways Turkey is a very different heir to the empire from, say, Syria or Albania. It was created by the dominant ethnic and cultural elements of the empire and it inherited not one of the limbs, but the head and heart of the empire, its cultural and administrative centre. It inherited a disproportionate part of the military and civil bureaucracy, and of the people with political experience.

One could argue that this position made defining the identity of the new state more, not less, difficult than in any of the other successor states, which could distance themselves from the Ottoman past by redefining it as a foreign occupation and seek inspiration from a mythical 'national' golden age that preceded the Ottoman conquest. In this respect, the Turkish experience can perhaps be usefully compared to that of Austria. Where pre-war inhabitants of the German speaking parts of the Habsburg Empire had thought of themselves both as German and as subjects of a Catholic and dynastic empire, the élite of the new republic of Austria almost had to invent a 'small Austrian' identity from scratch. So the Turks, too, who had thought of themselves as Muslim subjects of an Islamic empire, now had to start thinking of themselves as Turks.

The following section turns to the legal, political and institutional aspects of this transition.

The legal framework

On the face of it, the question of when the change from empire to republic took place seems easy enough to answer. After all, the Republic of

Turkey (*Türkiye Cumhuriyeti*) was proclaimed on 29 October 1923. But the Ottoman sultanate had been abolished almost a year earlier, on 1 November 1922. The delegation dispatched to the Lausanne conference that month represented 'the government of the Great National Assembly'. Very well, but what state was that the government of? One could argue that it was, in fact, the Ottoman Empire, because the imperial constitution of 1876, as modified in 1908–9, remained in force until the promulgation of the new republican constitution of April 1924. Nor had the dynasty altogether disappeared. After the deposition of the last sultan in November 1922, his cousin Abdülmecit Efendi had been proclaimed caliph. The concept of a purely religious caliphate was alien to both Islamic and Ottoman tradition, however, and there can be little doubt that in the eyes of the population Abdülmecit was as much a monarch as Vahdettin, the last Ottoman Sultan, had been. Many in the leadership, too, felt an emotional bond of loyalty to the dynasty which they and their forefathers had served.[10] This was, in fact, the main reason why the republican leadership decided to abolish the caliphate in March 1924.

On the other hand, as early as January 1921, the national assembly in Ankara had proclaimed the 'Law on Fundamental Organisation' (*Teşkilât-i Esasiye Kanunu*). This law has generally been regarded by Turkish historians as the first republican constitution. In Turkish politics, it has been seen as the ultimate source of political legitimacy; both the future leaders of the Democratic Party in their famous *dörtlü takrir* ('Memorandum of the Four') of 1945, which helped usher in the era of multi-party politics the following year, and the generals who staged a coup against the Democrats in May 1960 in their first official statement referred to this law in an effort to justify their actions. Strictly speaking, this view of the law as Turkey's first republican constitution is incorrect. The Ottoman constitution was not abrogated in 1921 and the Law on Fundamental Organization was primarily an instrument to enable the nationalist de-facto government in Anatolia to function, while Istanbul was occupied. It was in force alongside the Ottoman constitution.[11] At the same time, it cannot be denied that the law, with its emphasis on unrestricted popular sovereignty vested in the nation and exercised solely by the national assembly on the nation's behalf, is an expression of republicanism in the radical tradition of the French revolution, and sits awkwardly with a system of constitutional monarchy.[12]

In the one-year period between the abolition of the sultanate and the proclamation of the republic, Mustafa Kemal Pasha in his public statements said that the nationalists had founded 'a new state', although at this time he still maintained that it resembled neither a monarchy nor a republic and was, in fact, *sui generis*. The term 'Türkiye', which had been used occasionally as a synonym for 'Ottoman Empire' by him and others, now became the sole term describing the country.[13]

The conclusion, therefore, has to be that in the legal sense the transition from empire to republic was a gradual one, which took place between February 1921 and April 1924.

The leadership

As we have seen in the previous chapters of this part, political leadership, both of the resistance movement (1918–22) and of the republic (1923 onwards), consisted of a well-defined group of people, who shared a number of characteristics. Their most distinctive characteristic, though, was that they were all products of the modern educational establishments of the empire, created by the *Tanzimat* reformers of the nineteenth century.

Apart from their social characteristics, we have seen that they also shared a number of experiences. Almost without exception they were former members of the Committee of Union and Progress (CUP) and played a role in the politics of the second constitutional period (1908–18). They were bound together by a common past which included a number of the greatest upheavals in modern Ottoman history. Most had participated in the constitutional revolution of 1908; the suppression of the counterrevolution of April 1909 by the 'Action Army' (*Hareket Ordusu*); the organizing of Bedouin resistance in Tripolitania against the Italian invaders in 1911; the Balkan War disaster of 1913; the World War and the resistance movement after the war. For the typical leading Kemalist politician of the 1920s these were all part of his personal curriculum vitae.

The great military victory of August–September 1922 made Mustafa Kemal, who had been granted the title of *Gazi* by the Grand National Assembly one year before, the undisputed political leader. In the years after the proclamation of the republic, more particularly between the promulgation of the 'Law on the Maintenance of Order' (*Takrir-i Sükûn Kanunu*) in March 1925 and the political trials of June–August 1926, the remaining members of the top echelon of the former CUP as well as those commanders of the national resistance movement who had played a leading role in the start of that movement (in some cases even before Mustafa Kemal Pasha arrived in Anatolia) were eliminated physically or politically.[14] From then on, Mustafa Kemal Pasha ruled unchallenged. Gradually, younger men were brought into the political centre, but throughout the years of the Kemalist single party state and to a certain extent even into the 1950s, the key positions remained in the hands of individuals who had made their political and military careers during the Young Turk era.

The state apparatus

In the execution of its policies, the political leadership could count on the support of the large bureaucratic and military apparatus which had been built up under the empire from the 1840s onwards. This is not to say that the Kemalists took over the servants of the empire without some purging of the ranks, a practice that had been utilized by the Young Turks in the years before. Civil servants who had compromised themselves by corruption or spying on behalf of the Hamidian regime were thrown out after the constitutional revolution of 1908. Likewise, many of the officers who had risen from within the ranks under the old regime had been purged by Enver Pasha in 1913–14 and replaced with officers who had graduated from the modern military colleges. In the same fashion, the Kemalists, too, resorted to purges. On 25 September 1923, Law 347 was passed, which enabled the dismissal of army officers who had not joined the national resistance movement. Three years later, on 26 May 1926, a similar law was passed (Law 854) for civil servants. But with respect to the application of these laws, the scope of the purges seems to have been fairly limited and as early as 24 May 1928, Law 1289 created a review panel for officers and civil servants who felt they had been wrongfully dismissed.[15]

In essence, therefore, the army of the republic was the army of the late empire. And it was this army, and certainly also the gendarmerie, which allowed the republican regime to extend its control over the population and land to a degree the empire had never achieved.[16] In fact, one could argue that it was this establishment of effective control, more than any of the famous Kemalist reforms (clothing, alphabet or calendar), which heralded the arrival of the modern state in Anatolia. As for the bureaucracy, it was by and large the imperial bureaucracy. In the early years of the national struggle, the nationalists weeded out members of the provincial bureaucracy who were considered unreliable because of their links to the Istanbul government. The persons concerned were mostly provincial and district governors (*valis* and *kaymakams*), who had been political appointees. But on the lower levels the provincial administration remained intact, and this enabled the nationalists to conscript soldiers and raise taxes in the areas under their control. Another branch of the bureaucracy, the Ottoman telegraph service, proved itself loyal to the nationalists, rendering sterling service to the nationalists, and as such its ranks also remained largely the same. Though the Kemalists secured the right at the peace conference of Lausanne in 1923 to ban 150 undesirable Ottoman Muslims from the country, these 150 names (a number that by the way was totally arbitrary) were only filled in with some difficulty more than a year after the conclusion of peace.[17] There was a number of army officers and bureaucrats among those banned, but obviously it concerned only a very small number of people.

In the field of finance, the republic inherited two separate bureaucratic structures from the empire. One was the Ministry of Finance, which had been thoroughly modernized under the Young Turk finance minister Cavit Bey, and the other the administration of the Ottoman Public Debt, which since 1881 had taken control of the collection of taxes, duties and excises in areas such as the sale of tobacco, tobacco products, salt and fisheries on behalf of the European creditors of the empire. Although the new Turkey shouldered part of the Ottoman debt at the peace of Lausanne in 1923, the autonomous operation of the Public Debt Administration was terminated and the existing monopolies were taken over by the Turkish state. In 1932 they were united under the Directorate of Monopolies. The monopolies provided vital income for the new state in the 1920s and 30s.

Of all the branches of the state bureaucracy, the one to undergo the greatest change under the republic was undoubtedly the religious institution. The passing of the law on the unification of education in 1924 and the introduction of a European-style family law in 1926 meant that the secular state now took direct control of these important fields and that the role of the religious establishment contracted accordingly. The abolition of the caliphate and the simultaneous replacement of the office of the *Şeyhülislam*, the highest religious authority, by a directorate under the prime minister, certainly meant that the upper echelon of the religious establishment lost much of its room for manoeuvre. But it should be noted that the reforms of 1916, when the *Şeyhülislam* had been removed from the cabinet and had lost his jurisdiction over the sharia courts, the foundations (*evkaf*) and the religious colleges (*medreses*), had already severely circumscribed its function. The fact that Mustafa Kemal Pasha could push through his reforms almost without opposition from the senior clergy is testimony to the degree to which the Ottoman religious establishment had already been bureaucratized and brought under state control in the late Ottoman Empire.

Not only were these key branches of the state inherited by the republic, but the means of filling the ranks of these branches also remained virtually unchanged. The great schools of the empire, modelled on the French *grandes écoles*, which had bred the officers and civil servants of the *Tanzimat*, Hamidian and Young Turk eras, continued to do so under the republic. The military academy, which was provisionally relocated to Ankara during the national struggle, moved back to Istanbul in 1923 and then moved one final time to Ankara in 1936, all the while retaining its function and way of working. The same is true for the civil service academy (*Mülkiye*), which was reconstituted as the Political Science Faculty in Ankara in 1935. It continued to provide the state with its governors, diplomats and administrators. In time both institutions also became centres of Kemalist indoctrination, where nationalism, republicanism and secularism were articles of faith for staff and students alike – a situation, which continues to this day.

The Unionists had tried to reform the *medreses*, by including science in their curriculum, but the Kemalists thought they were beyond redemption and closed them down in 1924. From now on, the education of religious specialists was in the hand of the Faculty of Theology of the university in Istanbul and of two dozen *imam-hatip okulları* (schools for prayer leaders and preachers), but the former was closed down in 1935 and the latter over the years 1930–31. The decline in the level of religious learning only became apparent when the older Ottoman-educated generation started to fade, however, something which can be roughly dated from the mid-1940s.

The party

A new instrument at the disposal of the Republican regime was the People's Party (*Halk Fırkası, Halk Partisi*), which from 1925 onwards was the only legal political party in Turkey, save a three-month, dual-party period in 1930. Of course, political parties themselves were not entirely new; the country had been ruled by a one-party regime in 1908 and 1913–18. But these prior experiences with political parties differed in a few major respects: in the second constitutional period power ultimately rested with the secret, extra-parliamentary committee, which dominated both the parliament and the cabinet. In the republic, the People's Party, created by Mustafa Kemal in the national assembly, functioned to a large extent as an annexe to the state. Between 1925 and 1929, the emergency legislation in force meant that the parliamentary party abdicated all of its powers to the cabinet, so, ironically, the parliamentary party exercised no power at all during the time when most of the radical reforms were adopted. In these years reform laws were usually adopted unanimously or with very large majorities, but the number of votes cast was often less than half of the total.[18] From 1930 onwards, the People's Party, especially through its educational arm, the People's Houses

(*Halk Evleri*) became an instrument for indoctrination and mobilization, but it always remained under tight state control. This culminated in the formal unification of state and party in 1936. The CUP had also reached out to the public through its 'clubs' and through the branches of the 'Turkish Hearth' (*Türk Ocağı*) movement, but these had never been under the kind of central state control that the People's Houses were under during the republic.[19]

Ideology

If it is true that there was a high degree of continuity in political leadership and the state apparatus, the picture is more complicated where the aims and underlying ideology of the regime are concerned.[20]

Before the outbreak of the Balkan War in 1912, the heated ideological debates among the Young Turks, all of whom were preoccupied with finding a way to save the Ottoman state, had centred around two main questions. The first concerned the degree of Westernization needed to strengthen state and society, and in particular the way in which the use of Western science and technology could be reconciled with continued adherence to Turkish culture and Islamic civilization. As Mardin and Hanioğlu have shown, the vast majority of Ottoman intellectuals (who were at the same time in the service of the state) came to believe from the mid-nineteenth century onwards that Westernization was the only way to achieve material progress and political strength.[21] Equally widespread was a belief in modern science and biological materialism. Relatively few Young Turks were committed positivists in the strict sense (Ahmet Rıza being the best-known example), but nearly all were influenced by positivism in a broad sense. Its combination of belief in progress through science and intellectual elitism appealed to the Young Turks, many of whom were influenced by LeBon's deeply distrustful ideas on mass psychology.[22] Without exception, however, Young Turk thinkers defended the idea that 'real' Islam (which they contrasted with the obscurantism of the clerics of their day) was receptive to, and quite compatible with, science. Even if they were not religious men themselves, they regarded religion as an important 'national cement'.[23] As such, the question over whether the republic could reconcile borrowing from Europe with the maintenance of an Islamic value system constituted a key part of this debate.

The second question occupying the minds of Young Turk authors was that of the communal basis of any future Ottoman state, with debates centring on whether this future state should be based on a single nationality, on a voluntary union of nationalities or perhaps on religion. By the early twentieth century, sincere belief in a 'Union of the (ethnic) Elements'

(*İttihad-ı Anasır*) was probably limited to some Greek, Arab and Albanian intellectuals and the 'Liberal' group led by Prince Sabahattin. The vast majority, certainly of the Unionists, already before the 1908 revolution subscribed to a kind of Ottoman Muslim nationalism in which the dominant position of the Turks was taken for granted. While there was a growing awareness of Turkishness among the Young Turks, they seem to have regarded it as one facet of a complex identity in which being an Ottoman and a Muslim played equally important parts. From the start the organizers of the 1908 revolution opened up their ranks to non-Turkish Muslims, but not (or at least not automatically) to non-Muslims.[24] Contrary to what is often supposed, Pan-Turkism was popular only among a very small circle of intellectuals in which Russian émigrés played a dominant role. Islamist or Pan-Islamist sentiments were used politically by the Unionists, but played almost no part in their ideological make-up.

The Young Turk thinkers, their intellectual debates and the journals which formed the mouthpieces of the different currents have been described in detail.[25] However, with the outbreak of the Balkan War, these theoretical questions paled in significance. There was a national emergency and the most important issue now was the mobilization of all national resources. What was deemed 'national' was no longer in doubt by the end of 1912: the empire had been attacked by a coalition of Christian Balkan states, the loyalties of the Ottoman Christian communities were questionable at best and the big powers of Europe did not lift a finger to help the empire in distress. When the Young Turks organized the war effort through countless political, social, economic and cultural organizations, all of which carried the title *millî* ('national'), it was clear what this term meant: by and for the Ottoman Muslims. Defining the national as Ottoman Muslim continued throughout the years of World War I (which was also officially declared a *Jihad* and which was partly fought out as a brutal ethnic/religious conflict in Anatolia) and beyond. The proclamations of the national resistance movement in Anatolia after 1918, for example, make it abundantly clear that the movement fought for the continued independence and unity of Ottoman Muslims. The religious character of the movement was often remarked upon at the time, with religious ceremonies accompanying every major event. It was the only period in recent Turkish history when the country knew prohibition of alcohol.[26]

After the war had been won in 1922, this ideological orientation changed quite suddenly. With the passing of the national emergency the need for mass mobilization had also passed. The debates conducted before 1912 now resumed their importance and here the republican regime made some very deliberate choices. In the debate over the degree of Westernization needed, Mustafa Kemal and his circle identified themselves with the position of the most extreme 'Westernists' (*garbcılar*) of the Young Turk era, who held that European civilization was indivisible and should be adopted in toto.[27] There was no attempt to harmonize European civilization (*medeniyet*) with Turkish culture (*hars*), although these terms, which had been coined by Ziya Gökalp to differentiate between the acquired *Gesellschaft* and the organic *Gemeinschaft*[28] remained in use. In fact, the Kemalists envisaged a cultural revolution in which not only the 'high' Islamic civilization would be exchanged for that of Europe, but also the 'low' or popular culture would be transformed. Like the Young Turk ideological writers, Mustafa Kemal insisted that Islam was a 'rational' religion and adaptable to the contemporary world, but there was no attempt to turn a 'purged' Islam into a major constituent of the republican ideology. The *Jadidist* ideas of Akçura and Ağaoğlu were rejected along with Gökalp's proposals for a Turkified Islam and Said Nursi's ideas on Islamic moral rearmament. Instead, secularism (*laiklik*, derived from the French laique) became one of the main planks of Kemalist ideology. Scientism and biological materialism (as well as social Darwinism) occupied a more prominent place in Kemalist thinking than they had in that of the Unionists. Witness Mustafa Kemal's famous dictum, 'the only real spiritual guide in life is positive science' (*müspet ilim*), or the passage in his 1933 anniversary speech, where he proclaims that 'the torch, which the Turkish nation holds in its hand while marching on the road towards progress and civilization, is positive science.'

On the issue of national identity, a radical choice was also made. Ottomanism obviously no longer was an option. But the Muslim nationalism which had been championed from 1912–22 was now also abandoned, as it sat awkwardly with the ideal of wholesale adoption of European civilization. Instead an immense effort at nation-building within the borders of the new republic was made, based on the idea of a 'Turkish' nation. Although Turkish nationalism was territorial and based on a shared Turkish language and culture (with nationality being open to anyone willing to adopt these), a romantic idealization of the Turkish national character, with racist elements, became more and more important in the 1930s (in line with developments in Europe). In practice, the adoption of Turkish nationalism led to the forced assimilation of the 30 per cent or so of the population which did not have Turkish as its mother tongue.

One aspect of ideology where there was marked continuity between the Unionists and the Kemalists was in their firm rejection of the role of classes and class struggle. Both Unionist and Kemalist policies aimed at the creation of a national bourgeoisie and rejected any kind of change in property relationships. The CUP had reacted to the wave of strikes after the constitutional revolution of 1908 with repressive legislation, and its 'National Economy' programme after 1913 had been geared towards the creation of a class of Muslim traders and industrialists under state protection.[29] Corporatism gained a measure of popularity among the political élite both between 1913 and 1918 and in the early years of the republic. The creation of societies of traders and artisans by the CUP after it had disbanded the old guilds was an expression of the importance attached to professional organizations. This interest continued into the republic, but proposals, such as those put forward by the nationalist ideologist Gökalp, to base the political system on corporatist structures, were rejected.[30] Instead, the republic adopted a vaguely defined notion of 'populism' (*halkçılık*) or national solidarity, which was partly derived from the Russian *Narodniki* and partly from the romantic nationalist *Halka doğru* (Towards the People) movement, founded in Izmir in 1916.[31] In practice, the republican regime supported the capitalists and left both peasants and workers at the mercy of the ruling coalition of officers, bureaucrats and large landowners and the 'national' bourgeoisie which gradually grew up under its protection. Socialism, trade unions and strike action: all were banned under the Kemalist republic and land redistribution did not become a government policy until 1945.

III. THE GREAT WAR

Introduction

It has long been a consensus opinion in European historiography that World War I marks the end of the long nineteenth century, the end of the Edwardian age of self-confident belief in progress and ultimately of European global dominance. It marked the end of an old world order and led to the disappearance of four empires. Eastern Europe was broken up into newly created nation states and the Near East into British and French mandates that would become very problematic nation states a generation later. World War I has left an indelible imprint on European memory as the first industrial war, a war in which killing itself became an industrialized process.

For the Ottoman Empire and Turkey the war and its sequel (the 'national struggle' or 'liberation war', which lasted until 1922) also are the formative experiences of the era in that without them, modern Turkey could not have come into existence. Nevertheless, and with the single exception of the issue of the Armenian genocide, it remains the most understudied period in twentieth-century Turkish history. In Turkey, outside a very limited circle of purely military historians, World War I was eclipsed by the story of the national struggle, which generally has been set in the context of the emergence of the Turkish republic rather than in that of the war of which it was in essence a prolongation.

The chapters in this part seek to add to our knowledge of the Ottoman war experience, putting the focus on those who bore the brunt of the fighting: the conscripted soldiers who, under conditions of almost inconceivable hardship, managed to beat the British army four times, in Mesopotamia, Palestine and Gallipoli. The last three chapters in this part focus on the end of the war, in particular the armistice, and the national resistance that followed it, demonstrating that that struggle was not waged in the name of any new Turkish nation state but instead was very much a struggle for empire and Islam. The last chapter reflects the truth that nations are built not only on collective memory, but also sometimes on collective silence about the past.

12. The Ottoman Conscription System in Theory and Practice, 1844–1918*

The introduction of conscription in the Ottoman Empire was closely linked to the introduction of a European-style army, but it did not coincide with it. The first attempt to create an army, which was trained, equipped and dressed in the contemporary European fashion, was made by Sultan Selim III in 1792. His *Nizam-i Cedid* (New Order) army by all accounts was quite an impressive achievement. Starting from a strength of about 2,500, the corps quickly expanded to 22,685 men and 1,590 officers by 1806, with half of them stationed in the capital and the rest in provincial centres in Anatolia. When pressure against him and his new army on the part of the old army establishment, primarily the Janissaries, mounted, however, the Sultan succumbed without any attempt to use the considerable strength of his new army and disbanded the corps in 1808.[1]

The *Nizam* troops constituted a professional army. They were not recruited on the basis of universal conscription, but rather in a fashion reminiscent of the system introduced by Peter the Great in Russia or the *Bunicheh* system in Persia.[2] Governors and notables in Anatolia (not in the Balkans or the Arab provinces) were required to send contingents of peasant boys to Istanbul for training. Those enrolled in the corps remained under arms for an unspecified period.

The reforming Sultan was toppled in 1808, but the arguments for a wide-ranging reform of the army remained as compelling after Selim's demise as they had been before. The great defeats of the Ottoman army against Russia in 1774 and 1792 had exposed its weakness; the Napoleonic wars and especially the actions of the French and British troops in Egypt and Syria in 1798–1800 had made a deep impression on those who had witnessed them; and, from the 1820s onwards, the successes of the Pasha of Egypt, Mehmet Ali, with his French-trained army served as a source both of inspiration and envy.[3]

When Sultan Mahmut II finally felt secure enough to take up the military reforms of Selim III in 1826, he first tried to avoid the clash with the army establishment, which had been fatal to Selim, by forming his modernized army from the active parts of the Janissaries (most of whom by this time were not soldiers at all, but shopkeepers who held a Janissary pay ticket and thus enjoyed the privileges of the military ruling class). When this, too, met with stiff opposition and even open rebellion, Mahmut had the Janissaries shot to pieces in their barracks. The next day the venerable corps was formally disbanded (although in some provinces Janissary troops continued to exist into the 1840s) and the forming of a new army, the *Muallem Asakir-i Mansure-i Muhammadiye* (Trained Victorious Mohammedan Soldiers), was announced.

The new army, which was modelled entirely on the earlier *Nizam-i Cedid* corps, quickly grew from 1,500 to 27,000 men. The army was organized along European lines, with the basic units being the regiment (*tertip*, later *alay*), consisting of three battalions (*tabur*). Once again, this was a professional army manned by volunteers and peasants recruited by the Sultan's officials in the provinces. There was no real system of recruitment, but the ranks of the army would be filled according to need. Each year the requirements of the army would be determined in a decision (*kararname*) of the imperial council and then communicated to the provincial authorities, who were left a free hand in the way they filled their quota.

Recruitment age was between 15 and 30 years and, once recruited, the minimum term of service was 12 years. After 12 years the soldiers could opt for a civilian life, but in order to qualify for a pension, soldiers were obliged to serve until overtaken by old age or infirmity.

Parallel to the *Mansure* army, a second modernized unit was formed out of the old corps of Imperial Gardeners (*Bostanciyan*) who for centuries had guarded the imperial palaces and the seafront along the Bosphorus. They were now reconstituted as an Imperial Guard, called the *Hassa* (Special) army, whose strength reached about 11,000 by the end of the 1830s.[4]

In July 1834, a further momentous step in the modernization of the army was the establishment of a reserve army or militia, based on the Prussian 'Landwehr', called the *Asakir-i redife-i mansure* (Victorious reserve soldiers), or *Redif* for short. In each province between ten and twelve battalions were established, manned with able-bodied men of between 23 and 32 years of age. They trained twice a year and added their strength to the regular army (now again generally known as *Nizamiye* (Regular), which name was reintroduced officially in 1841) in times of war. Initially composed of 57,000 men in 1834, the *Redif* after a reorganization in 1836 grew to 100,000 men. During the nineteenth century the main task of the *Redif* was that of keeping law and order in the countryside. In conformity with the Prussian regulations of 1814, the *Redif* had its own separate officer corps, whose members at first were drawn from the younger members of the local notable families (who were supposed to take the role of the *Landjunker* in Prussia). These officers served for two days a week and received a salary one quarter of that of equivalent regular army officers.[5]

Universal conscription on the modern European model began to be discussed towards the end of Mahmut II's reign and there can be no doubt that this time the role model was very much Mehmet Ali, whose well-trained army of conscripted Egyptian peasants had shown its superiority over the *Mansure* army in Syria in 1831–3.

The 'Military Council' (*Dâr-i Şûrâ-yi Askerî*), which was established in 1837, a year later proposed that a five-year term of military service should be introduced and this suggestion was incorporated in the famous 'Imperial Edict of Gülhane', the reform charter promulgated in 1839. The edict noted that up to now the burden of defence had fallen unequally on different provinces and that lifetime service had damaged the population as well as the quality of the army.[6] The passage in question reads:

> As regards military matters, for the above-mentioned reasons these are among the most important. Although it is the duty of the subjects to provide soldiers for the defense of the fatherland, it is also true that up to now the size of the population of a province has not been taken into account and because some [provinces] had to provide more [soldiers] than they could, others less, this has become the cause of all kinds of disorder and chaos in useful occupations such as agriculture and trade. As life-long service for those who enter the army causes loss of zeal and decline in the population, it is necessary with regard to those soldiers who will be recruited in each province according to need, to establish some good rules and to establish a system of alteration with a term of service of four to five years.

This led to the new army regulations, which were promulgated in September 1843 under Rıza Pasha. Primarily inspired by Prussian regulations, with some French influences, this established a regular *Nizamiye* army manned by conscripts (*muvazzaf*), who served for five years (later reduced to four, three and – finally – two years), and a reserve army (*Redif*), manned by those who had completed their service with the regular army and those who had drawn a low number in the *kur'a* (drawing of lots). The term of service in the *Redif* was seven years, during which time the reservists were called up for training for one month a year. When this proved too disruptive, this was later changed to once every two years. Each of the five armies into which the Ottoman Army was divided – the Guard, Istanbul, the European provinces, Anatolia and the Arab provinces – had its own separate reserve attached to it.[7] The *Redif* army would continue in this fashion until 1912, when a decision was taken to merge it with the regular army. Due to the upheavals of the Balkan War, this merger only took place in the course of 1914.[8]

The system of conscription was first established in detail under the *Kur'a Nizamnamesi* (regulation on the drawing of lots) of 1848. It put the strength of the army at 150,000 (two classes), which meant that, with five-year service, the army needed to recruit 30,000 men a year. This quota consisted of volunteers and conscripts. Conscription took place through the drawing of lots among those eligible on the basis of sex, health and age. Those, whose names were drawn, were drafted into the *Nizamiye* army, while the others were relegated to the *Redif*, without first having to serve with the regular army.

The system remained more or less unchanged until the new army regulations were proclaimed in August 1869 under Hüseyin Avni Pasha. Under these regulations the army was now divided into three categories: the *Nizamiye* (regulars), the *Redif* (reserve – *Landwehr*) and the *Mustahfız* (guards reserve – *Landsturm*). The regular army was divided into two classes: conscripts (*Muvazzaf*), composed of men who were performing their four-year, full-time service, and active reserve (*İhtiyat*), composed of those who, having had completed these four years, remained under arms for one to two years in their region of origin and acted as a kind of permanent 'backbone' to the local *Redif* battalion. The total active land army of the Empire after the changes of 1869 is put at 210,000; 150,000 under arms and 60,000 in the active reserve.

Those who had completed their service with the regular army, those who had been allowed to return to their homes because they were sole breadwinners and those who were over 32 years of age served with the *Redif* for a further six years, as did those whose name had not come up to begin with. In 1869, the strength of the reserve was foreseen as being slightly over 190,000.[9]

The *Mustahfız* (guards) reserve was the least active, least well-armed part of the army. It was not expected to take the field in times of war, but rather to take over garrison duties and maintain law and order when the regular army and the reserve were at the front. It consisted of (relatively) able-bodied men who had done their service in the *Nizamiye* and/or *Redif*. They served for eight years, between the ages of 32 and 40. Total strength was 300,000.

In March 1870 the whole system of recruitment was reviewed and codified in a new *Kur'a Kanunnamesi* (Conscription Law), promulgated in 1871. This remained the basic set of regulations until after the constitutional revolution of 1908, but some of its provisions were modified during the army reforms of 1879 (after the disastrous defeat in the war against Russia) and 1885–7 (when the German military advisors led by Colmar Freiherr von der Goltz worked in Istanbul).

The law consists of 77 articles, grouped in seven chapters: General ground rules for the conscription; Reasons for exemption from military service; Treatment of those who dodge the draft or intend to use tricks to escape from military service; Execution of the draft; Measures to be executed after the draft; Conditions for the acceptance of volunteers in the army; and Conditions pertaining to the people who send replacements or pay the exemption tax.

The way the draft should be executed is described in great detail: First, conscription councils are formed in each recruiting district (which coincided with the *Redif* districts). Three months before the drawing of lots is to take place, the population records are checked and lists of possible recruits drawn up. All those who figure in the records are then ordered to appear in person in the district capital. After those who can show that they have a right to exemption on the basis of health or other reasons have been separated, all those who are going to be included in the draft are arranged around a square or open place. Two bags are put in the centre, one filled with envelopes, each containing a small piece of paper with the name of one of the men on it; the other, with an equal number of pieces of paper in envelopes. Depending on the number of recruits needed, that number of slips of paper in the second bag is inscribed with '*asker oldum*' (I have become a soldier), the rest being blanks. The envelopes are then taken from the first bag, and the names read, one after each other and they are matched with a paper from the second bag. This goes on until all the slips with *asker oldum* on them, have been read.[10] Later legislation, such as the military service law of 1916 is even more detailed and specific. Under article 14 of this law all males who have reached age 18 before the first of March in any given year have to report in person and in the company of their village headman to the authorities in the district capital before the end of October. Recruitment starts on the first of May and includes all those who have turned 20 before the first of March.[11]

It seems, however, that these procedures were not always followed in areas such as Albania or Kurdistan, where feudal relationships were strong. According to one British military report, the conscription in Albania was purely a façade and recruits were really selected and sent by their tribal chiefs.[12]

In the reforms of 1879 (which also introduced the division as the basic unit of the army) the term of service with the infantry of the regular army was brought to six years, of which three were spent under arms and three in the active reserve. The period of service in the *Redif* was brought down from eight to six years, of which three were classed as *Mukaddem* (vanguard) and three as *Tali* (rear). Service with the *Mustahfız* likewise was reduced from eight to six years. In 1887 the *Redif* districts were reorganized.

At the end of empire, the Young Turks changed the term of service with the regular army again: in 1909 it was brought down from three to two years for those soldiers serving in particularly severe climes – with the Sixth Army in Iraq and the Seventh in Yemen.[13] With the passing of the last Ottoman conscription law in May 1914, the term was brought down from three to two years for the whole infantry, but as mobilization started almost immediately afterwards, this measure was not implemented.

The problem of exemptions

In introducing conscription as the basis for its recruitment system, the empire faced the same problems as European states. Conscription presupposed the existence of a fairly reliable census to determine where the potential manpower could be found. Producing a reliable census required a sizeable growth in the state, and especially the provincial, bureaucracy. A census in the strict sense of the word, that is, a population count of the whole empire at one and the same time, remained outside the possibilities of the Ottomans until the very end of the empire. Only the republic was able to introduce it in 1927. The Ottomans had a tradition of population registration, however, and the first one of modern times (counting only male heads of households) was held in the years 1831–8. A second registration, specifically for the purpose of enabling conscription to work, was conducted in 1844. As actual counting was impossible in many areas due to lack of manpower or to popular resistance, particularly on the part of tribes, the results were no more than a rough estimate, and certainly a serious undercount of the population. European writers working from the 1844 results put the total population of the empire (excluding Africa) at about 32 million. The much more reliable data from the later nineteenth century, particularly the registration carried out between 1882 and 1890 and published in 1893, give a total of about 17.5 million, which is not entirely incredible given the large losses in land and population of 1877–8, but certainly represents an undercount.[14] For 1914, at the beginning of the last large-scale war ever fought by the Ottomans, the number is put at 18.5 million for the core provinces[15] or between 23 and 26 million, if all of the outlying provinces are included.[16]

The lack of an accurate census made it especially difficult for the Ottoman authorities to compel those who were liable to serve to take part in the draft. Although some wars, such as the 1897 war with Greece and the 1912 Balkan War did arouse enthusiasm in some places, resulting in quite large numbers of volunteers,[17] under normal circumstances military service was very unpopular. This was due primarily to the length of service. The lack of manpower, especially in combination with the attrition caused, not so much by the great wars, but by the never-ending guerrilla warfare in Albania, Macedonia, the Hawran and above all Yemen, meant that conscripts were very often kept under arms for far longer than their legal term. Some reports describe conscripts serving for ten years and more.[18] Even when there was initially an enthusiastic response, this tended to evaporate very fast when recruits were faced with conditions in the army.[19] The lack of an industrial base meant that the state had the greatest difficulty in feeding, clothing and equipping its soldiers. Pay was regularly in arrears. The conditions under which the army had to fight in wartime were atrocious. In the 1877–8 Russian war, in the Balkan War of 1912–13 and in World War I large parts of the army were starving and many more soldiers died of cholera, typhus and dysentery than did of wounds.

In the countryside it was relatively easy to go into hiding, even for those who were registered. 'Leaving for the mountains' to stay out of the hands of the representatives of the state was a well-established tradition in the Ottoman Balkans and Anatolia. Like other countries, therefore, the empire had a system of heavy penalties for draft dodgers and people who hid or helped them. The regulations adopted in 1909 also included a system of material and personal sureties, whereby those who had no property were required to have a male family member (father, brother or uncle) vouch for them.[20]

What made the manpower problem even more serious is the exceptionally large proportion of those exempted from military service. Broadly speaking, one can say that there existed two types of exemption: individual and collective. Groups which were exempt were: women; non-Muslims (formally until 1856, in practice until 1909); inhabitants of the holy places,

Mecca and Medina; religious functionaries and students in religious schools; and a whole range of professional groups. Exemption from the draft was a prime attraction of membership of each of these groups. It is even reported that young men went on pilgrimage to Mecca when recruitment threatened. The regulations of 1871, 1886, 1909 and 1916 all contain provisions about exemptions. The 1916 regulations are particularly specific, with long lists of exempted professions. Some of these (i.e. top civil servants, judges, *muftis*) are exempted under all circumstances, while others (i.e. lower ranking civil servants, policemen, railway clerks) are exempt except in case of mobilization.[21]

Nomads, even if not legally exempt, by and large were so in practice. Istanbul with its outlying districts (and a population of over a million) also did not deliver a single soldier to the army.[22] The Ottoman army, therefore, was an army of sedentary Muslim men and, as over 80 per cent of the population was rural even at the dawn of the twentieth century, primarily one of sedentary Muslim peasants.

Individuals who belonged to those sections of the populations which were obliged to serve could claim exemption if they could show that they were *muinsiz* (without support, or the sole breadwinner in their household). The actual regulations are quite complicated and interesting as they clearly reflect the realities of life and family relationships of the time, as in these examples:

> The father-in-law is not to be considered as the supporter of a husband, but he may be so considered in a case where the wife inhabits the home of the father-in-law of her husband (i.e. of her own father).
>
> A young married man whose wife is dead or divorced leaving children is exempted. The care of the latter is the duty of the young father, even though natural supporters of the young woman exist, as for example, her father, father-in-law and brother. This is in order that the orphans may not be allowed to fall into the hands of the stepmother.[23]

The essential point was that those men who could not be replaced as breadwinners of their household were considered *muinsiz*, and therefore exempt.

Those who were not without support could only escape conscription by a lucky draw or through payment. Anyone drawing a blank for six years in a row and so escaping service in the regular army was enrolled in the reserve, but any Muslim man liable to serve, could also buy exemption. The first conscription law of 1848 allowed conscripts to send a personal replacement (*bedel-i şahsî*). In other words, they could send someone else if they could force, persuade or pay anyone to go in their place. The 1870 regulations, while still mentioning personal replacement as a possibility, also detail the way in which service could be bought off. Exemption could be bought for 5,000 kuruş or 50 gold lira (a very considerable sum at the time). Those seeking exemption were not allowed to sell land, house or tools in order to pay.[24]

This payment, called *bedel-i nakdî* (cash payment-in-lieu) in the sources, should not be confused with the – much lower – sums paid by non-Muslims until 1909. Those who had bought their exemption, like those who drew a lucky lot, were declared reservists, until a change in the law in 1914, which stipulated that they should serve for six months with the active army and only then be classified as reservists. The same law of May 1914 also made the *bedel* applicable in peacetime only, but it seems doubtful that the Ottoman government, always hungry for money, actually suspended the practice during World War I. The regulations for payment of the *bedel* also found their way into the first military service law of the republic (of 1927), but by then the amount was determined as 600 lira.[25]

With the famous exception of the Janissary corps, which had been recruited from among the Christian peasantry (but whose members converted to Islam), primarily in the European provinces, the empire had only rarely employed non-Muslims for its land forces. Traditionally the bearing of arms had been the prerogative of the ruling élite, the *Askerî* (military) servants of the sultan. When lack of manpower forced the government to start arming members of the subject class (*reaya*) in the form of irregulars (*Levent*) drawn from the peasantry and the town roughs, this use was again confined to Muslims.

The reform edict of Gülhane in 1839, the first conscription law of 1844 and the regulations of 1871 all specified that all Muslims (*bilcümle ahaliyi müslime*) were liable to serve in the army. At that time, the idea that non-Muslims should be allowed, or forced, to serve seems to have been as alien as the idea of female soldiers. But the reform edict, which Ali Pasha drew up in 1856 in close cooperation with the French and British ambassadors and which formed the empire's entry ticket into the 'Concert of Europe', emphasized equality between Muslims and non-Muslims. Application of this principle meant that the discriminatory practice of conscription would have to cease and non-Muslims would have to take part in the drawing of lots as well.[26] In reality, there was very little enthusiasm for the idea on either side. The army feared that an intake of Christian peasants would burden it and that non-Muslims would damage morale. This was a serious point, because, as all observers of the Ottoman army between 1850 and 1918 agree, the fighting spirit of the Ottoman troops was to a very high degree religious. Attacks were always carried out under simultaneous shouting of '*Allah, Allah*' and '*Allahüekber*' (God is great). It would be hard to envisage a religiously mixed army do the same. Most Muslims, especially in the countryside, disliked the idea of Christians bearing arms (one observer compares their feelings to those in the southern United States on the equality of blacks).[27]

Most Ottoman Christians were equally unenthusiastic. By and large they felt themselves to be subjects of the Ottoman state, not members of an Ottoman nation. The idea of Ottoman nation building (known at the time as the before mentioned idea of the 'Unity of the Elements') was embraced only by a small, mostly Muslim, élite.

The Ottoman government, finally, had the strongest incentive of all to not conscript non-Muslims. The reform edict's emphasis on equality before the law meant that the *cizye* tax, which Ottoman Christians and Jews traditionally paid as a tribute to the Islamic state, had to go. Although the number of Ottoman Christians dropped considerably during the last century of the empire due to the loss of European provinces, they still represented nearly 30 per cent of the population in Abdülhamit's reign and close to 20 per cent on the eve of World War I. Not surprisingly, the *cizye* was the second most important source of tax revenue (after the tithe) for the state. No wonder, then, that the state actually preferred that the Christians pay an exemption tax (first called *iane-i askerî* – military assistance, and then *bedel-i askerî* – military payment-in-lieu), rather than serve. Thus, the non-Muslim exemption tax remained universal practice until 1909. The *bedel* was much lower than that required of Muslims and just like the *cizye* before it, it was paid collectively by Christian and Jewish communities to tax-farmers and, later, salaried treasury officials.

That the recruitment of Christian subjects into the army was rejected as an option before 1909 is shown very clearly by the text of the 1870 regulations, even though, as Tobias Heinzelmann's recent research has shown, it was an option that was discussed in the highest echelons of the state in the first half of the nineteenth century.[28] The first article of the 1870 regulation reads:

> All of the Muslim population of the Well-protected domains of His Majesty are personally obliged to fulfill the military service which is incumbent on them.

There is no mention of non-Muslims anywhere, which clearly suggests that in the Ottomans' eyes they did not come within the compass of the military service law.

Military service for non-Christians thus remained a theoretical option until 1909. This is not to say that there were no Christians in the army – there were, but they were in the officer corps, primarily in the medical corps, which consisted in large part of Armenian and Greek army doctors who held the ranks of lieutenant and captain.

The Young Turks, who came to power in July 1908 and for whom unity and equality between the different ethnic 'elements' of the empire was a top priority, started work on the change of the recruitment law soon after they had suppressed the counterrevolution of April 1909 in Istanbul. In July 1909 military service was made compulsory for all Ottoman subjects. At the same time a number of Muslim groups – for instance, not only students in religious colleges who had failed their exams, but also the inhabitants of Istanbul – lost their exempt status. In October 1909, the recruitment of conscripts irrespective of religion was ordered for the first time.[29]

The reactions of the Christian communities to the new law were mixed, but there was no real enthusiasm anywhere. The spokesmen of the Greek, Syrian, Armenian and Bulgarian communities agreed in principle, but with the all-important proviso that the members of their communities serve in separate, ethnically uniform units officered by Christians. The Bulgarians also insisted on serving in the European provinces only.[30] This was totally unacceptable to the Young Turks, who saw it as just another way to boost the centrifugal forces of nationalism in the empire – the opposite of what they were aiming for. In response to the compulsory service requirement, many young Christian men, especially Greeks, who could afford it and who had the overseas connections, opted to leave the country or at least to get a foreign passport.[31]

Those who could not leave, change their nationality, or pay the much higher *bedel-i nakdî* (along with well-to-do Muslims), were indeed recruited when World War I broke out, but the Ottoman government continued to mistrust its Christian subjects to such an extent that almost without exception they were left unarmed. Instead they served in labour battalions, doing repair work on the roads and railways and, especially, carrying supplies to the front.

The result of the extensive system of exemptions employed was that the empire, already far less populous than its rivals, drew less conscripts from its relatively small population as well. Its yearly required intake of recruits in

1913–14 (when the term of service was still three years) was 70,000 or about 0.35 per cent of the population. In reality the intake was probably lower. In Bulgaria the ratio at the same time was 0.75 per cent. Fully mobilized, as in early 1915, only 4 per cent of the population was under arms and on active duty, compared with, for instance, 10 per cent in France.[32] The actual strength of the army on the eve of World War I is not altogether clear, but it is certain that it was relatively small by contemporary continental European standards. The reports of the British military attaché for 1910 give the peace strength as 300,000 and service in the regular army as three years. This means that 100,000 recruits per year were needed, but the actual annual contingent was put at 90,000, of which 50,000 were really enrolled after exemptions. This meant that the actual peacetime establishment was only about 150,000 and the inclusion of large numbers of *redifs* was necessary to bring the army up to strength. A British report written in 1914 puts the peace strength of the army at 230,000 before the Balkan Wars and 200,000 thereafter. Larcher, on the other hand, states that in 1914 the active army was composed of two classes of about 90,000 each, which would mean an army of between 180,000 and 200,000 men.[33] The peacetime establishment of the Russian army (which also recruited a low percentage of the population, but could afford it because of the sheer size of that population) was five times its size in the early twentieth century. The Austrian army was at least twice the size of the Ottoman one.[34]

When fully mobilized, the Ottoman army was of course much bigger – this, after all, was the main advantage of the conscription system, but mobilization was painfully slow, taking four to five months to complete (if transport to the front is included). The mass mobilizations of 1912 and 1914 showed up all the inherent weaknesses in the Ottoman system. The slow mobilization of 1912 (mainly due to lack of good roads, but also to confusion and the inability of the armies to absorb, equip and feed the reservists) meant that the Balkan War had been lost before the troops from the Asiatic provinces could even reach the European fronts. With only one single-track railway available for supplies and troop movements, the troops at the front (only 30 miles from the capital Istanbul for most of the war!) were starving, and when the Syrian reserves finally arrived the cholera they brought killed off a significant number of them. At the outset of the war there seems to have been very little enthusiasm, but nevertheless a genuine and quite widespread readiness to serve, but this evaporated quickly under the circumstances. Even during the first days of marching after leaving their depots, the supplies ran out. Troops had to live off the land and large-scale desertions started.[35]

The outbreak of World War I in 1914 again saw a very slow process of mobilization (even slower than that of the Russians). This time it had to take place in winter, which made the whole process more burdensome, especially in Eastern Anatolia. On the other hand, warfare was practically impossible in winter on the Caucasian front and if Enver Pasha had not squandered 72,000 soldiers' lives (out of 90,000) by ordering an attack over the mountain passes at Sarıkamış, the Ottoman Army could have been at full wartime strength in the spring. Once again, the call to arms was answered relatively well, in Anatolia if not in the Arab provinces. But as in the Balkan War, the conditions in the army (payment with worthless paper money, undernourishment, lack of medical care, epidemics of typhus, cholera and dysentery, bad or non-existent clothing and shoes) were so bad, that desertions soon started to become a problem of enormous proportions. By the end of the war the number of deserters was four times that of soldiers on the front. Desertion rates and the World War I experience of the Ottoman soldier are the focus of the next chapter of this volume.

The conclusion would seem to be that the Ottomans, over a period of 60 years and as part of a more general programme of modernizations, managed to put in place a sophisticated system of recruitment through conscription modelled on that of Prussia/Germany, but the lack of infrastructure and an industrial base meant that they could not really cope with the mass army they had so diligently created. Conscription failed as an instrument of Ottoman nation-building, too. The system of exemptions through the *bedel-i nakdî* and the *bedel-i askerî* meant that the burden never fell equally on all Ottoman subjects. Even after these reforms, the Ottoman army remained an army of Anatolian Muslim peasants, in a sense foreshadowing the establishment of a Turkish nation state in Anatolia after World War I.

13. The Ottoman Soldier in World War I*

The limits of the sources

For some 35 years now, in the prolific field of World War I studies a certain
approach to the history of the war has been popular; an approach which is
epitomized by Martin Middlebrook's famous *The First Day on the Somme*
(1971) and by the various works of John Terraine. This is the attempt to
write the war's social history, to examine the war experience from below,
through the eyes of the men who served in the trenches, the people who
drove the ambulances, the women who filled the shells in the factories.

In the case of Europe, there is ample material available for this way of
writing history: letters and diaries, stories, poems and paintings, autobiographies and oral history. Where the Ottoman Empire is concerned, though,
the situation could not be more different. The reason is a simple one: the vast
majority of the common soldiers of the Ottoman army were illiterate.[1] Even
as late as 1927, four years after the establishment of the Turkish republic and
a decade after the war, only 10.6 per cent of the whole population was able
to read and write. This overall average hid vast differences, however. While
of the men in the towns of over 10,000 inhabitants 41.5 per cent was able to
read and write, at the other end of the scale only 1.4 per cent of the women
in the villages could do so. As 80–85 per cent of the population lived in the
countryside and as the vast majority of the recruits were villagers, the most
relevant statistic is that of the 11.4 per cent of male villagers who were literate.[2] Sometimes non-commissioned officers (sergeants) functioned as the
official scribe for a company, writing letters which were dictated to them,
but it was more usual for new arrivals from a village to the front to bring the
news orally – and for discharged or convalescent soldiers from a particular
area to take messages back the same way.[3] This means that the Ottoman
soldier has not left much in the way of written monuments: no letters home,
no diaries. Naturalist painting of course was not a Middle Eastern tradition,

167

being frowned upon by Sunni Islam, so we have no sketches. Oral history has come into fashion in Turkey, but only in the last 25 years – more than three decades too late to be of much use for the study of World War I.

We do have a number of sources, which tell us something about the conditions in which the Ottoman soldier tried to survive, but with one exception they are typical 'top-down' documents, which view the war from the standpoint of high-ranking officers. There are scores of memoirs and autobiographies of Ottoman officers (Ali İhsan Pasha Sâbis, Cemal Pasha, Ahmet İzzet Pasha [Furgaç], Selâhettin Adil Pasha, Halil Pasha [Kut], Mustafa Kemal Pasha [Atatürk], Kâzim Pasha Karabekir and others), German officers (Liman von Sanders, Kress von Kressenstein, Kannengiesser, Von Gleich, Guhr, Guse, Von Seeckt and others), and even Austrian ones (Joseph Pomiankowski). An important source for the recollections of the members of the German military mission serving in the Ottoman Empire, some 18,000–20,000 men in all, is the journal *Mitteilungen der Bundes des Asienkämpfer* (Bulletin of the Society of Veterans of Asia), later rechristened *Orientrundschau*, and the yearbooks of the same society, entitled *Zwischen Kaukasus und Sinai* (Between Caucasus and Sinai).[4]

The complexities of the German–Ottoman alliance have been studied exhaustively, but these studies are essentially diplomatic, not so much military in nature.[5] As far as histories of the Ottoman war effort go, there is the large-scale official history, published by the War History and Strategic Studies Directorate of the General Staff in Ankara,[6] but relatively little in the way of regimental histories or histories of specific battles or fronts, as far as World War I is concerned. Most efforts in this field in Turkey seem to be concentrated on the independence war, which followed between 1919 and 1922. World War I does receive some attention in the historical sections (*tarih kısmı*) of the journal *Askerî Mecmua* (Military Journal) published by the Military Press in Istanbul between the wars, as well as in some 131 publications on the war published in Turkish up until 1955. This amounts to 0.2 per cent of the number of titles on the war published in English, French and German during the same period, and since then, interest in the war does not seem to have revived to any large extent in Turkey.[7]

In European languages the only detailed history of the Ottoman war for 70 years was Maurice Larcher's *La guerre turque dans la guerre mondiale* (Paris, 1926). It has now been joined by Ed Erickson's *Ordered to Die. A Study of the Ottoman Army in the First World War* (Westport, 2001). For the economic and social history of the war, Ahmet Emin [Yalman]'s *Turkey in the World War* (Yale, 1930) is indispensable.

The Turkish General Staff archives are almost completely closed to foreigners (and to most Turkish scholars as well). Among the foreign archives, the German military archives (*Bundesarchiv-Militärarchiv* or BA-MA) in Freiburg are obviously the pre-eminent sources. However, these too have their limitations. The German Empire as such had hardly any national (imperial) ground forces. Only its navy, air force and colonial troops were imperial forces. The rest of the army consisted of the contingents of Prussia, Bavaria, Württemberg and Saxonia, which operated as separate units and were put at the disposal of the imperial general staff in case of war. It follows that the German Empire had no central military archives. Of the contingents, the Prussian one was of course by far the most important. Unfortunately, 98 per cent of the documents pertaining to the Prussian army were destroyed in an allied air strike on Potsdam in April 1945. As the large majority of the German officers serving in the Near East was Prussian, this is a great handicap. For the much smaller number of Bavarian officers (among them Kress von Kressenstein), it is worth consulting the Central Archives of the Bavarian Free State in Munich, in which the documents of the Royal Bavarian Army have been preserved. I have also consulted the political reports from the Constantinople embassy in the Dutch state archives. The Netherlands being neutral, these reports continue throughout World War I and at times yield interesting insights.

But what all these sources have in common is that they share a 'top-down' vision, which keeps us distanced from the realities of the war experience. This vision views casualties as a manpower problem rather than as something involving pain and death. The only officers who do devote considerable attention to the living conditions of the soldiery are the German medical doctors who served in the empire.[8]

The one source which may be said to give us the soldier's voice – albeit indirectly – is formed by the daily and weekly 'intelligence summaries' of British military intelligence on the Egyptian and Mesopotamian fronts and of the British expedition forces in Salonica, the Dardanelles and Persia. These intelligence summaries are based on agents' reports and debriefings of neutral travellers, but also on interrogations of Ottoman prisoners of war (POWs) and deserters, and on letters to Ottoman POWs. (If this seems in contradiction with the earlier statement about the vast majority of the Ottoman soldiers being illiterate, it should be remembered that relatively many of the POWs and deserters were Armenians and that literacy among the Armenians and Greeks, even in the countryside, was very much higher than among the Muslims.[9])

The Ottoman army: size and composition

The most amazing thing about the Ottoman army in World War I is that an army which had been beaten comprehensively by four small Balkan states a year earlier, managed to fight for as long as it did and as well as it did. During the war, the general opinion among the British and French was that this was wholly due to the efforts of the German officers and troops serving in the empire; but in reality it was also the result of the reforms pushed through in the year following the Balkan War by the Young Turk leader and Ottoman War Minister Enver Pasha, and his German advisors. These reforms entailed the retirement of a large number of older officers, many of whom had risen from the ranks, and their replacement with modern educated younger officers. According to German observers, this new generation of officers knew the theoretical bases of modern warfare extremely well and thanks to them, the level of staff work in particular was greatly improved. However, often their whole experience had been in the general staff, and as such lacked command experience. They now took over units in the field for the first time.[10] That the army generally performed far better when it defended than when it attacked, was due mainly to the lack of experienced non-commissioned officers (NCOs) who could lead and inspire the units. Too many of these had died in the Balkan War of 1912–13.[11]

The army these officers had to lead into battle was burdened with two almost insurmountable problems right from the start: lack of manpower and lack of communications. We shall return to the lack of communications later, in the context of a discussion of the army's supply situation. Lack of manpower had been a problem for the Ottomans all through the nineteenth century, that is to say: once they came up against large conscripted European armies. The Ottoman population, even though it had been growing quite fast over the last 30 years, was still comparatively small: about 19 million people in the core provinces and, if the outlying areas (where no reliable census existed) are included and the undercount of the Ottoman census system is taken into account, perhaps between 23 and 26 million in total.[12] Not all Ottoman adult males were equally available for military service, however. The non-Muslims (Christians and Jews, about 20 per cent of the population in 1914) traditionally had paid an exemption tax (the *bedel*). Many Muslims also made use of this possibility, but for them the exemption tax was considerably higher, so those who managed to raise enough money mostly came from among the more affluent town dwellers.

From 1909, the Young Turk government had started to enforce the conscription for non-Muslims as well, but in practice the majority of eligible

Christians still managed to avoid military service, paying the higher rate Muslims paid. Those who did serve, though, could not rise above the rank of lieutenant, with the exception of army doctors who held the rank of captain.[13] During the war the poorer Christians who could not pay the exemption fee generally were employed in unarmed labour battalions.[14] Just like the other armies of the day, the Ottoman army had labour battalions (*amele taburları*) included in both its peacetime and its mobilized strength. These battalions were attached to the inspectorates of lines of communication (*menzil müfettişlikleri*) of the seven armies into which the Ottoman army was organized. The number of labour battalions varied throughout the war, but between 70 and 120 units seem to have been active at any given time.[15] Total strength may have varied between 25,000 and 50,000 men.[16] The primary functions of the labour battalions were transport and road repairs (carrying and digging). Apart from these primary functions within the field army, labour battalions also fulfilled a number of functions for the Office of the Quartermaster General (*Levazim Dairesi*) of the armed forces. These were partly industrial, with a number of munitions, arms, shoes and clothing factories in and around Istanbul run as military establishments (as they had been even in peacetime).[17] They were partly artisanal (repair shops, bakeries) and partly agricultural, with labour battalions formed to replace peasants sent to the front, especially in the vital grain-growing areas of Central Anatolia. These last named units, which seem to have been formed from non-Muslims, but also from women, played an important role in increasing the area under cultivation, which had dropped by two-thirds in the first year of the war due to lack of manpower.[18] This was especially important, because the supplies of Russian and Romanian wheat, which had been the main sources for the provisioning of Istanbul, had dried up in the first years of the war as well.

By and large the labour battalions were composed of Armenians – one source puts them at 75 per cent,[19] but also Syrian Christians and Greeks. These Christian minorities, whose loyalty was suspect in the eyes of the Ottoman army, were obvious candidates for recruitment into these unarmed and guarded battalions.[20] With respect to the Armenian recruits, at first only younger (age 15–20) and older (age 45–60) males were put to work, with those aged 20–45 drafted into the regular army. But the decision of 25 February 1915, in the wake of the failure of the Ottoman army's eastern offensive and the defeat of Sarıkamış, to disarm all Armenians in the army for fear that they would collaborate with the Russians obviously meant that many of those Armenians who had been recruited into the regular army units were now transferred to the labour battalions as well. This certainly

171

was the practice on the Caucasian front, though it may not have been universal, as we find mention of Armenian soldiers serving in the front line on the Sinai front as late as the spring of 1916.

Eyewitnesses describe atrocious conditions in the Armenian labour battalions. Like Muslim soldiers, Armenian recruits were underfed, exhausted, suffering from disease,[21] though support units like the labour battalions, as well as fortress garrisons, were even worse off than the front soldiers.[22] The mistreatment of Armenian recruits in the labour battalions in the winter of 1914–15 was but an extreme case of what was going on throughout the army.

These labour battalions, though not created for the specific purpose of killing off Armenians, certainly facilitated the process once the massacres started in April 1915. The massacres were aimed primarily at the Armenian male population, and at this point there were tens of thousands of Armenian men, who were already assembled and under guard of armed soldiers. They did not stand a chance once the decision to attack them was taken. The timing and method of the killings seems to have differed from place to place, however. On the Caucasian front, with the Russian army on the attack, the priority was to make the Armenians harmless and to prevent them from deserting to the enemy.[23] After the disarming most were sent to join labour battalions, but many were simply kept under guard in prison-like circumstances and eventually marched off to their deaths. The actual killing is reported as having been the work both of soldiers and gendarmes, and of Kurdish tribes. The former are described as taking groups of 50 to 100 Armenians to secluded spots and finishing them off with bullets and bayonets.[24] The latter lay in waiting to attack the convoys on the road.[25] On other fronts, such as the Dardanelles and the Sinai, as well as on the construction sites of the Baghdad Railway, the Armenians seem to have continued their work in the labour battalions until the end of 1915 and even the summer of 1916. It is probably correct to say that the killing off of the Armenian soldiers was concentrated at either end of the great terror campaign of 1915–16. Those in the East were among the first to fall victim, even before the deportations started in earnest in May 1915, while others were part of the last sweep, aimed at those who, until then, had been considered indispensable. Of course, for the army being deprived of workers and carriers wrought havoc on its logistics. No wonder that a prominent general like Vehip Pasha, the commander of the Caucasus front, instigated court martial proceedings against those responsible for killing all of 'his' Armenian labourers, who were engaged in road repairs.[26] But once the fury was unleashed, rational arguments, even if they were based on the interests of the army, ultimately fell on deaf ears. This was for instance the case with the Baghdad Railway Company, which depended on the skilled Armenian workers and clerks for its smooth operation. It fought hard and with some success to protect its own employees from deportation, in the face of growing pressure from the Ottoman government. This resorted to the deportation of wives and children as a means to put pressure on the workers. The railway company ultimately failed to protect the construction workers in the tunnels through the Amanos range from deportation and death, in spite of the vital strategic importance of these tunnels.[27]

Some Armenian soldiers seem to have escaped deportation by converting to Islam. Sarafian estimates that between 5 and 10 per cent of the Ottoman Armenians escaped the death marches by converting, either voluntarily (if one can call it that, in view of the circumstances) or under government pressure, but the practice of (forced) conversion is usually associated with Armenian women and children who were taken into Muslim households or orphanages.[28] The practice of forced mass conversion seems to have existed in the army as well, however, as an eyewitness account from the Sinai front in the spring of 1916 relates. Apparently, quite significant numbers of Armenian soldiers agreed to become Muslims, change their names and be circumcised in field hospitals and dressing stations, and this was an occasion for official celebrations.[29]

Not only the Christians were kept separate. As far as I have been able to make out, the units of the Ottoman Army were ethnically uniform up to the level of regiments or even divisions. German officers routinely speak of 'Arab divisions' and 'Turkish divisions'. The British reports do the same. We frequently find statements such as 'the 51st division is composed of good Anatolian Turks and Kurds' and 'the 141st and 142nd divisions are Arab and Syrian'.[30] This is only to be expected as regiments had their own regular recruiting areas. There were exceptions – we do find evidence of mixed units – but this most probably was due to the fact that in the last phase of the war many units were so far below strength that they had to be broken up and merged with other ones.

Arab troops, of which there were many, were primarily used for garrison and lines of communication duties, but sheer lack of manpower meant that, increasingly during the war, the Ottoman government had to use Arabs from Syria and Iraq in front line fighting units. By the end of the war four out of ten divisions on the Palestine front were Arab. But Arab troops were considered inferior to the Turkish troops, as evidenced by the exchange of prisoners of war. The Ottomans used to insist that they be given 'real

Turkish troops, not Arabs' in exchange for British troops and offered only Indian troops in exchange for Arabs.[31] In Liman von Sanders's opinion the Arab troops were not necessarily bad, but needed 'just but strict command'.[32] Kress considered them 'more lively and intelligent, but less reliable' than the Anatolian troops.[33] Some of the nomad tribes of the empire, notably Kurds, did contribute to the war effort, but largely as irregular cavalry units which were only loosely attached to the regular army and their usefulness seems to have been extremely limited.[34] So the burden of military service in the regular units posted to the front line fell overwhelmingly on the Turkish peasant population of Anatolia, which constituted about 40 per cent of the total population, or nine to ten million.

After deduction of those who could pay the exemption tax, about 100,000 men were called up for military service each year and of these only about three quarters actually joined the army, most of the others being rejected for reasons of health.[35] This meant that the peacetime strength of the army was about 150,000 (two classes). There is a lot of uncertainty about the mobilized strength of the army, but probably the maximum number of men actually under arms at anyone time was slightly under 800,000.[36] Mobilization, however, was extremely slow and took at least six months to be fully effective. (As we have seen in the previous chapter, this meant that even after full mobilization, only about 4 per cent of the population was under arms and on active duty.[37]) In the course of the mobilization males between the ages of 19 and 45 were called up. By 1916, however, the age limits had been extended to 15 and 55 respectively and, according to British reports by mid-1917, 12 per cent of the total were between the ages of 16 and 19.[38] In April 1915, a new military service law tried to reduce the number of exempted males, but it remained possible to pay instead of serving, albeit that the amount was now an astronomical 50 Turkish pounds. Shortly afterwards even Muslim foreigners residing in the empire were made eligible for military service (under the pretext that they too should take part in the holy war, *cihat*, proclaimed by the Sultan in 1914), but they could buy it off for 45 pounds.[39] These measures, though undoubtedly lucrative, did little to strengthen the army.

Offensive strategy

Neither the Ottoman nor the German military leadership took the manpower problem into account when deciding on the strategy to be followed. Even though lack of manpower in the face of the Russian army was a major headache, the German high command imposed an offensive strategy on the Ottoman government. The German chief of the general staff, von Moltke, told Enver Pasha on 10 August 1914 that it was the task of the Ottomans to draw away the largest possible number of British and Russian troops from the European battlefields.[40] The German military attaché in Istanbul, Von Lossow, energetically supported this line, but the head of the German military mission in the Ottoman Empire, Liman von Sanders, favoured a defensive strategy.[41] Enver, whose personal relations with Liman were never good, sided with Moltke and Lossow and the offensive strategy, which he opted for from the outset wasted human life on a grand scale. The greatest disaster was Enver's ill-conceived winter offensive towards the Russian fortress of Kars in December 1914. The troops were forced to cross mountain ridges deep in snow and as a result of the combined effects of cold, starvation and typhus, a mere 12,000 of the 90,000 troops of the Third Army who took part in the attack survived into spring. The attacks on the Suez canal in February 1915 and August 1916, and the attempt to round the Russian flank in Eastern Anatolia through an adventurous offensive in Persia, although much less costly, were also irresponsible adventures which brought no tangible results. The decision to hold on to Yemen and the Hejaz (with the holy cities of Mecca and Medina) was a purely political one, which left the army stretched out along a thousand mile single-track railway and tied up a large garrison in Medina. Finally, the decision to send Ottoman divisions to fight in support of the Austrians in Galicia and the Germans in Rumania perhaps enhanced Ottoman prestige with its allies, but it was a luxury the country could ill-afford.

The high point of the Ottoman war effort of course was the Gallipoli campaign of 1915. After the repulse of the Franco-British attempt to force the straits by naval force alone had ended in a totally unexpected Ottoman victory, the Ottoman army just managed to block the allied attempt at a breakthrough overland on the Gallipoli peninsula. There can hardly be any doubt that this was a great strategic victory, which gave the empire a new lease on life (or prolonged its misery, whichever way you choose to look at it). The victory over first the British fleet and then the allied expedition force was a tremendous morale booster for the Ottomans, but in the long run it broke the back of the army. The Dardanelles campaign cost the Ottomans nearly 90,000 dead and 165,000 wounded and sick (by their own official figures which are certainly an underestimate),[42] almost all of them from the best-equipped and most experienced divisions in the army. In spite of the carnage at the Dardanelles, the Ottoman army reached its peak numeric strength at the beginning of 1916, the year the British General Sir Charles Townshend had to surrender to the Ottomans at Kut al-Imara. But in terms of quality the damage caused by Gallipoli could not be repaired. After 1916, quality went down and numbers started to dwindle: In winter 1916, when the unfortunate Third Army in Eastern Anatolia sustained attacks by much superior Russian forces in terrain where neither its supply trains nor its medical service could follow, it was thrown back and lost both Trabzon and Erzurum. Following the defeat a large part of the Third Army simply melted away. According to one source, the Third Army alone had 50,000 deserters at this time.[43]

The Second Army lost about two-thirds of its strength (over 60,000 men) on the southern section of that same front (the Muş-Bitlis area) in the winter of 1916–17.[44] As a result the total number of combatants fell to 400,000 in March 1917 and 200,000 in March 1918. When the armistice was signed in October 1918, less than 100,000 troops remained in the field.[45]

Disease

This dwindling of the numeric strength of the army was due mainly to two causes: disease and desertion. Malaria, typhus, typhoid, syphilis, cholera and dysentery were rampant.[46] Especially in winter the ubiquitous lice carried in clothing and upholstery caused typhus to spread all along the routes to the front, killing soldiers, Armenian deportees and Muslim refugees alike. Among the Ottoman troops casualties were very high. Without treatment, the disease killed about 50 per cent of those affected. Even among the Germans, who were very well cared for by their own medical service, mortality was 10 per cent. The delousing ovens built by the Germans were excellent, but they remained inoperative a lot of the time due to lack of firewood, which also hampered the heating of washing water.[47] Summer saw the spread of malaria, which was especially bad along the Black Sea coast and the Bosphorus, in some places in Anatolia (such as Ankara and Konya) and, most of all, around Adana and İskenderun – an area through which all of the troops destined for the Mesopotamian and Syrian fronts had to pass. In late summer and autumn, cholera, caused mainly by contaminated drinking water, was the great killer.[48] In the dry months the soldiers drank from the remaining stagnant pools and besides, they preferred defecating close to open water because it was customary to wash afterwards. Syphilis and gonorrhea were also widespread, with Istanbul, Izmir and Beirut being mentioned specifically as sources from which the infections spread. These venereal diseases were treated in the battalions and sufferers were not hospitalized.[49] The German army surgeons, through efficient inoculation programmes, but even more through the introduction of basic hygiene, managed to bring down the number of sick soldiers quite drastically where they were active, but the Ottoman medical service often lacked even the most basic materials. Especially in the first two years of the war, practically all medicines and equipment had to be imported. The biggest problem of all, however, was the lack of sufficient and healthy food. This made the troops vulnerable to disease and it made recovery in hospital very difficult. We shall return to the food problem shortly, but the combined effect of the factors mentioned here was that nearly seven times as many men died of ill-ness as who died of wounds during the war.[50] One report on the Third Army (Eastern Anatolia) states that in March 1917 its hospitals held 16,956 sick compared with 1,340 wounded.[51]

Desertion

In terms of loss of available manpower, however, desertion was an even bigger problem for the army than was disease. Though all armies engaged in the fighting of the 'Great War' encountered the problem of desertions, in the Ottoman case it reached unmanageable proportions. By December 1917 over 300,000 men had deserted.[52] By the end of the war the number stood at nearly half a million. This is a number over three times that of the deserters from the far larger German army. Where European armies lost between 0.7 and 1.0 per cent of their total mobilized strength to desertion, the percentage for the Ottoman Empire is at least twenty times as high. According to Liman, every single division that was transported or marched to the front lost thousands from its original strength. Bavarian officer Kress von Kressenstein in October 1917 reported that the 24th Division that had left Istanbul with 10,057 men had arrived at the Palestinian front with only 4,635. Nearly a quarter of the soldiers in the division had deserted before it reached the front. The others were either hospitalized or poached by other units along the way.

Most of these deserters as a rule did not go over to the enemy, although especially in the second half of the war the number of Armenians and Arabs who deserted to the British increased sharply. Most recruits fled while en route to the front or while escaping from enemy armies on the march, especially when they passed close to their hometown or village. They roamed the countryside, living off the land and turning into robber bands. Further troops had to be detached in ever greater numbers to deal with the insecurity these bands created behind the frontlines.[53] The population often sympathized with the deserters and hid them in their homes.[54] When deserters were caught, they generally were punished only lightly and returned to their units as soon as possible in order not to deplete the strength of the army any further. As early as May 1916 we find a Dutch embassy report stating that the army had replaced prison sentences with corporal punishment in the field.[55] Only rarely do we find reports of deserters being executed, but the army did try to make it difficult to desert. Troops, especially those consisting of Arab recruits, were mistrusted so much that they were sometimes brought to the front unarmed, and under armed escort of Turkish guards.[56] In Syria extreme coercion had to be used, with Arab soldiers sometimes being marched to the front in chains. Also, in Syria as well as in Palestine, Bedouins were offered a reward of five Ottoman pounds for every deserter they captured and returned.[57]

Pay, arms, equipment, food and fodder

Why did so many Turkish soldiers desert, even though they were considered good soldiers and (as was pointed out to them many times) there was a specific Quranic injunction (8:15–16) against leaving the battlefield? In 1917, Liman primarily blames the policies of the army. Since the beginning of the war training had been neglected. Depleted units had been brought up to strength with raw recruits. Units were constantly being broken up and reassembled and therefore lacked cohesion and team spirit. Soldiers also did not know or trust their officers and had very little idea of what was going on. 'They only knew that they were being sent somewhere where things were going wrong,' states Liman.

At heart, though, both the troops' tendency to desert as well as their vulnerability to disease was in large part a result of the lack of basic care for their welfare: the troops were ill-paid or not paid at all, worn out marching, undernourished and badly clothed. Time and again lack of pay and lack of food are mentioned as reasons to desert in the British reports.[58] Theoretically, the soldiers were paid 5 kuruş a month during the first year and 10 a month during subsequent years,[59] but in reality they were paid very irregularly. Sometimes pay was in arrears for three months.[60]

While the troops seem to have been well armed, the same cannot be said for the rest of their equipment. Footwear seems to have been an especially serious problem, which is mentioned time and again in the reports. It was not unusual for Turkish troops to fight – and march – barefoot or with their feet covered in rags.[61] The fact that the Russians who were captured on the eastern front all turned out to be wearing boots was a tremendous source of envy for the Ottoman soldiers.[62] As a matter of fact, the war is still known as 'the barefoot war' in Syria.[63] Reports describe how on the

Palestinian front no new shoes had been available for almost a year. As a last resort, the troops in the front line were given yellow Bedouin slippers, which were bound to the feet with throngs. Those on garrison duty had to make do with shoes made of straw, with wooden soles.[64] Nor was the situation much better where uniforms were concerned. Most soldiers were dressed in rags.[65] In March 1918 one deserter said that the troops on the Palestinian front had not received new clothing for 15 months.[66] The Turkish journalist Falih Rıfkı Atay, who served under Cemal Pasha on the Fourth Army staff in Syria from 1915 to 1918, vividly describes the contrast between the lack of everything on the Ottoman side and the plentiful supplies over which the British disposed. Soldiers halted in the middle of the battlefield, under intense enemy fire, to rob dead British soldiers of their boots and, in at least one incident, an Ottoman regiment after a successful attack on a British trench, returned unrecognizable, having exchanged their own rags with British uniforms taken from the dead (most of them did not take to the short trousers worn by the British, though).[67]

Theoretically, the army should have been adequately fed. In spite of the fact that the production of foodstuffs dropped by 40 per cent during the war, mainly due to lack of manpower, Anatolia had a wheat surplus, and Syria had adequate supplies overall except after the disastrous locust plague of 1915.[68] Throughout the war, the Ottoman Empire exported wheat to the Central powers as payment for deliveries of armaments. The German army reckoned that the Arab provinces produced enough grain to support the local population and the armies on the Palestinian and Mesopotamian fronts. Official figures at first sight support this idea. The official daily rations of an Ottoman soldier consisted of: 900 grams of bread, 600 grams of biscuit, 250 grams of meat, 150 grams of bulgur (broken wheat), 20 grams of butter, and 20 grams of salt.[69]

The reality, though, was very different. Although it varied a great deal it was never anywhere near as good as these figures suggest. Each year the government would announce the percentage of the harvest of basic foodstuffs (mainly wheat and barley), which it would need. On the average this was between 40 and 50 per cent, 10 per cent of which was collected as tithe, the rest being bought, but at official prices, not market value. Because the actual purchase of wheat and barley was decentralized and done by the commissariat of each army, and because transport was such a tremendous problem, the food situation of the different armies varied enormously, depending on whether they were close to, or far away from, grain-producing areas.[70] This was the case, for instance, on the Palestinian front, where the troops on the east bank of the Jordan in as-Salt were supplied from the rich grain growing area of the Hawran, while the troops to the west of the Jordan in Nablus and Jaffa went hungry. The amount of bread the troops were given daily, for instance, is given as follows in different reports:

Comparison of Daily Bread Rations	
Dardanelles, 1916	900 grams
Palestinian front, 1918	350–600 grams
Damascus, 1918	500–600 grams
Haifa, 1918	900 grams
Mesopotamia, 1918	300 grams

When and where wheat was scarce, bread was made of wheat mixed with barley or ground beans. In addition to the bread, the troops generally received two warm meals a day, one in the morning and one in the evening. These meals consisted of flour soup or bulgur. Sometimes there was meat or stew, but a ration of meat once a week seems to have been the rule and in outlying stations it could be once a month. When there was meat, it had to be shared out among a lot of people: according to one report the daily supply was one ox or four sheep for 450 men. Most often, though, the meat was camel meat, as dead camels were not in short supply. Unlike the officers, who had their field kitchens and cooks, the men were catered for by sergeants, who, with the help of a couple of men from each company, doubled as butchers and cooks. Of course, food had to be cooked and bread had to be baked – with wood. Officially each soldier was entitled to 700 grams of wood a day, but we find one report of a mess officer on the Palestinian front which gives a picture of the difficult reality. This mess officer, a man by the name of Abdüllatif, threatens to resign as he has never received more than 300 grams of wood per soldier and the supply is now down to 100 grams. He does not know how the food is to be cooked.[71]

Whenever possible, the soldiers complemented their diet with dates, figs, raisins or olives, but on the whole the diet contained very little in the way of vegetables or fruit. Scurvy therefore was a serious problem, with soldiers' teeth falling out and large sores forming in their mouths or even through their cheeks.[72] According to one report, 20 per cent of the army was affected by scurvy.[73]

On the eastern front the food shortage was exacerbated by the deportation and massacre of the Armenian population, which created an agricultural wasteland in the very area where the Ottoman army had to operate.[74] In Western Anatolia the food situation was badly affected by the deportation of Greeks from the coastal plains in 1915.[75]

Animals of course suffered as much as people, as feeding the tens of thousands of camels, oxen, mules and horses in areas where grazing was impossible, proved an almost insurmountable problem.

Everywhere, the troops on the front line were better fed than those on garrison or lines of communication duty. It has to be remembered, though, that even they were better off than the civilian population, especially in the towns. The overall food situation seems to have been worst in the winter of 1917–18, though from the spring of 1918 onwards, the effects of the armistice with Russia and the opening of the Black Sea began to be felt and the harvest of May–June 1918 was exceptionally good almost everywhere.[76]

As for the impact of the food shortage on desertion, Liman assesses that the supply situation was not a driving factor. But the reports we have on the mobilization for the Balkan War in October 1912 seem to suggest otherwise. British consuls state that conscripts had reported for duty at the depots in large numbers, but that after a few days march, when supplies ran out, the hungry troops started to desert in droves. Consistently supplying the troops in Palestine, Mesopotamia and Eastern Anatolia with food, medicines, clothing and even cooking fuel proved beyond the means of the Ottoman state, and hunger and disease were widespread. It stands to reason that if the lack of provisioning was a reason to desert in 1912, it must certainly have been so five years later.

If sheer misery and hunger was a driving force behind the mass desertions, the Ottoman soldier also had opportunities to escape that his European counterparts lacked. In countries like Britain, France or Germany soldiers were under constant surveillance from the moment they reported to the depot to the moment they reached the front. Once at the front they had little opportunity to escape, as the densely populated hinterland was patrolled constantly by a vigilant military police on the lookout for 'stragglers'. In the Ottoman Empire, by contrast, the troops were slowly moved thousands of kilometres through sparsely populated terrain, marches of a month or more not being exceptional. Many soldiers used the opportunities this afforded them. In Liman's words 'they jump out of the train just like they flee from the marching columns in complicated terrain or from the camp.' This is perhaps the most important difference with the situation in the European countries during World War I. The Ottoman Empire may have been involved in a modern, industrialized war that forced it to mobilize all of its resources, but its war effort was not accompanied by a modern mobilization of the population through effective propaganda and indoctrination. In the Ottoman Empire an effort was made, with German assistance, to set up a propaganda machine, but it barely reached into the (almost completely illiterate) countryside and by and large failed as an effort at mobilization. As such, villagers felt more akin to the peasant lads on the run than to the state or the army.

Transport – the biggest problem of all

The one single factor which, more than anything else, was responsible for the disastrous supply situation was the lack of transport facilities. Before the war the empire had been dependent on the sea for internal transport of bulk goods and the British blockade now made shipping impossible anywhere but in the Black Sea and the Sea of Marmara. Even in the Black Sea shipping, for instance of coal from the Ereğli coalfield, was often interrupted by the actions of the Russian fleet.

The railways were totally overburdened. There were only 5,700 kilometres of railway (one kilometre per 304 square kilometres of territory – the figure for France was one in ten and for India one in sixty).[77] They were single track everywhere and the key connections between Anatolia and the Arab provinces through the Taurus and Amanos mountain ranges had not been completed yet (the crucial tunnels through the Taurus were only finished by September 1918). The railway was normal gauge down to Rayak (east of Beirut) and low-capacity narrow gauge from there southwards. This meant that supplies imported from Germany or Austria (for instance, almost all artillery shells) had to be unloaded and reloaded seven times before they reached the front: first they had to be shipped across the Bosphorus and put on the train at Haydarpaşa on the Asiatic shore; then they were taken by train to Pozantı; carried by trucks or camels across the Taurus ridge; reloaded on board a train in Gülek and taken to Mamure (a stretch of railway that was within reach of British naval guns) and then loaded onto camels to cross the Amanos range, or – after the completion of the tunnels through the Amanos in early 1917 – put on open narrow gauge carriages to be carried through them. The completion of the tunnels through the mountains was delayed by six months when the deportation of the Armenians, who made up almost all of the skilled workforce, was ordered in 1915.[78] They were replaced in part by British POWs who had been captured in Mesopotamia. East of the Amanos range, the camels or narrow gauge carriages had to be unloaded and the supplies reloaded aboard a normal train in İslahiye; this train then went as far as Rayak, where everything had to be unloaded and reloaded again because of the change from normal to narrow gauge rolling stock. The British computed that the line from Rayak to the front at Beersheba could handle a maximum of nine light trains a day.[79] No wonder, therefore, that it often took between four and six weeks to get from Istanbul to the Palestinian front by rail and seven to get to the front in Mesopotamia.[80] The fact that all of the fronts were fed through the bottleneck of Istanbul also made the supply situation extremely vulnerable, as was shown when the ammunition depot in Haydarpaşa blew up on 6 September 1917. Twelve ammunition dumps, and oil and petrol tanks exploded and all of the stocks of rubber and medical supplies as well as 300 freight cars went up in smoke. This delayed the start of the *Yıldırım* operations for months.[81]

In Anatolia the railway to the East extended some 60 kilometres beyond Ankara and ended at Çerekli. From there to Erzurum, the main Ottoman fortress in the East, was 35 days marching.[82] Efforts to extend the railway towards Sivas were underway but remained unfinished by the end of the war. The Eastern front (always optimistically called the 'Caucasian front') was supplied mainly from the railheads at Ulukışla and Rasülayn, both about a month's march away from the front line at Erzurum.

There was an acute shortage of locomotives (Turkey had only 280 of them) and of coal to stoke them with. Instead the locomotives had to be fired with dwindling supplies of wood and large sections of the olive groves in Syria were cut down for this purpose.[83] Wood being bulkier than coal, the locomotives had to stop frequently to refill their bunker and they had to reduce speed in order to save fuel. Thus, the 200 kilometre stretch from Aleppo to Homs took 26–28 hours and from there to Rayak another 10–20.[84] Damascus–Aleppo took 3–4 days as opposed to 17 hours before the war.[85] Carrying capacity was insufficient (troops were transported 60 men to a freight car)[86] and freight cars often were allocated on the basis of corruption and political influence.

The roads were so primitive that the lorries, which the Germans and Austrians sent in considerable numbers, constantly broke down. According to Yalman, even ten years after the war, their wrecks could still be encountered everywhere along the roads.[87] Where the roads were adequate, the lorries ran at a maximum speed of 30 kilometres per hour.[88]

There also was a lack of transport animals. The Ottoman Empire bred excellent riding horses and useful, albeit small, pack horses, but draught horses had to be imported.[89] For draught animals, the army mainly relied on oxen (one heavy gun needing eight) or mules. For carrying it relied on camels. It had between 5,000 and 10,000 (the estimates vary) of these animals in service behind the Palestinian front alone. But they were reared by the Arab Bedouin, and had to be paid for in gold. Paper money was unpopular everywhere and in the settled areas those who refused it faced heavy penalties, but the Bedouin could not be coerced in this way.[90] Anyway, from 1916 onwards many of the Arab tribes were in open revolt, and even before the standard of revolt was raised by the Sharif of Mecca in June 1916, the most important tribal federation in Syria, the Anazi, were already refusing to sell camels to the army. The Shammar, more to the east, did deliver camels in large quantities, but they could not cross Anazi territory. Hence, 'shaggy' or Anatolian-type camels had to be brought in from the north, taking up more precious space on the railway.[91] The condition of the army camels seems to have been quite bad, the animals being overworked and underfed.[92]

Corruption

As a result of the lack of transport facilities, not only the availability but also the price of foodstuffs differed widely (in 1916 wheat was over six times as expensive in Istanbul as it was in the central Anatolian grain-growing area of Konya). As such, fortunes could be made by those who managed to get hold of freight cars – and a government permit to use them.[93]

Corruption was widespread and encouraged by the fact that army commanders received the money for their army as a lump sum, with complete discretionary powers as to how to spend it – as one German observer put it: 'on food for his troops, or on building a cinema'.[94] Officers, who had the right to buy a certain amount of flour from government stocks, often managed to get extra supplies, which they sold on the market.

The graft on the part of government employees was only to be expected. The war years were a time of high inflation (the cost of living index in Istanbul more than quadrupled) and salaries were low. In addition, several different extraordinary levies were imposed, which were subtracted consecutively from the salaries: 25 per cent 'war fund'; 5 per cent 'red crescent fund'; 5 per cent 'aviation fund' and 5 per cent 'defense of the faith fund'.[95]

As a result of the combined effect of disease and desertion, the actual strength of most of the units by 1917 was at or below 50 per cent of their nominal strength, with battalions numbering 300–400 troops, regiments 800–1,500 and divisions between 2,500–4,000.[96] Reports indicate that a loss of about 50 per cent between departure of a division from Istanbul and arrival at the front was not unusual.[97]

The voice of the soldier

The numbers do indeed tell a tale, a tale of extreme hardship, which again makes one wonder at the ability of this army to keep on fighting so well for so long, but still the voice of the Turkish soldier remains largely unheard. While the figures concerning disease, desertion, the availability of food and the like tell us something about what the soldiers had to go through and how they coped, they do not tell us much about the psychology involved, or in other words about morale. It is a striking fact that in spite of the horrendous conditions there were no significant mutinies at all among the regular troops. Indeed, sometimes British reports, while stating that morale was very low among the civil population, say that it was high among the troops. But what exactly did this mean?

One authentic expression of feeling on the part of the soldiers we do have is contained in the songs, which were popular in the trenches. Many of these were older than the war itself, with melodies taken from already known songs and new lyrics reflecting the experiences of 1914–18 added. This is the case with, for instance, the *Çanakkale Türküsü* (Dardanelles Song), one of the best known of them all. Even when the songs were new, though, they reflected the experience of the past hundred years rather than that of just World War I.

The great wars against the Russians of the nineteenth century (1828–9, the Crimean War, the disaster of 1876–8) and the attrition caused by continuous small-scale warfare against rebel-bands and tribes in places as far apart as Albania and Arabia, meant that those who were unfortunate enough to be conscripted into the Ottoman Army and who did not have the means to buy off conscription, had very little chance of returning alive. Thus, the prevailing sentiment in the lyrics of the songs is that those who went on campaign had no chance of returning and that they would die in some far off desert. The symbol that came to represent this feeling, as well as the idea that young lives were being wasted to defend some unknown faraway place, was the Yemen.

Yemen and the 'Yemen songs'

After the Ottoman reoccupation of the Yemen and its capital, Sana'a, in 1872 the country remained unruly, with major insurrections in 1882, 1898 and 1904. Constant harassment by Arab bands cost the Ottoman army anywhere from a few hundred to a few thousand casualties a year all through this period. It was the major rebellions, though, that really caused large-scale slaughter: the 1904–5 rebellion left 30,000 out of 55,000 Ottoman

185

troops dead. The period 1910–11 saw another rebellion, with the mortality rate rising once again to between 30 and 50 a day. It is clear, therefore, that the Yemen had earned its bloody reputation.[98]

Especially popular among the troops serving in Syria, Palestine and Mesopotamia were the 'Yemen Songs'. There are at least a dozen with names like 'Does grass grow in Yemen?', 'The Band is Playing', 'The Mobilization Song', 'The Exercise Song', 'No Water Flows in Yemen', 'No Cloud in the Sky', 'On the Road to Yemen', 'In the Desert of Yemen' and, of course, 'The Yemen Song'.[99] The feelings expressed in these songs are not startlingly original, but they are telling: There is no heroism here, and no patriotism. Nor do the songs express the kind of dogged determination of contemporary Western front hits such as 'Pack up your troubles' or 'Keep right on to the end of the road'. More than anything they express a feeling of homesickness, hopelessness and doom, of being sacrificed. In the eyes of the people who sang these songs, being called to the colours was a death sentence. At the same time the songs convey a sense of resignation.[100] So perhaps that is what the relatively high morale of the Ottoman troops was about: a feeling that they had nothing to lose as they felt they were as good as dead anyway. Perhaps it was this that gave them their ability to fight so well, especially when on the defensive, in the face of overwhelming odds.

The death toll

In many cases, of course, they were right about their chances of survival. There is much that is not clear about the casualties of the Ottoman army. Probably about 325,000 Ottoman soldiers were directly killed in action.[101] The number of wounded varies in the sources, with both slightly over 700,000 and about 400,000 cited. The latter number may refer to those permanently injured when the war ended, while the former probably refers to the number of people registered in field hospitals. Of the latter, nearly 60,000 died from their wounds. The number of soldiers who died of various diseases was nearly seven times as high at over 400,000. How many people were still ill when the war ended is unclear. So the 'net loss' (to use the term of the British reports) may have been 785,000. To this number over 250,000 people missing or captive and roughly half a million who had deserted, must be added.

These numbers mean that for an Ottoman soldier the risk of dying, both from wounds and from disease, was very much higher than in any of the European armies. Of the 1,037,000 battlefield casualties, 385,000 or 37 per cent died (325,000 killed in action plus 60,000 who died on wounds

in hospital). To put this percentage into perspective, we can compare this number to the well-documented British and Franco-British losses in some of the most notoriously murderous campaigns of the war where mortality was much higher than average. Of the casualties sustained on the famous first day of the Somme offensive in 1916, 33 per cent were fatal; for the Flanders campaign of 1917 the number is 25 per cent and for the atrocious Gallipoli campaign it is 'only' 16 per cent. And this, unlike the Ottoman total, includes persons missing in action.

Of the number of admissions to field hospitals for various illnesses (if that is the way the number of sick given in the Ottoman statistics should be read), 400,000 ended in death. This means that, quite apart from battlefield casualties, about one-seventh of the total mobilized strength of the army succumbed to disease – a percentage unheard of on the western front. Malaria was by far the most widespread of the diseases, but dysentery and typhus were the greatest killers.

These numbers make dismal reading. On the other hand, it has to be said that the Ottoman soldier had an infinitely better chance than any soldier on the western front to escape the mass slaughter of the front altogether by deserting. One has to agree with Larcher that the desertion of over half a million men must have constituted a major factor in the success of the Turkish struggle for independence between 1918 and 1922. Not that all of the deserters of 1914–18 willingly or enthusiastically served Mustafa Kemal Pasha,[102] but instead of sacrificing themselves in an ultimately doomed cause, through their desertion they had lived to fight another day – when it really mattered for the survival of an independent Muslim Turkish state in Anatolia.

14. The Ottoman Empire and the Armistice of Moudhros*

Each year Turkey has a day of national mourning on 10 November. This, however, has nothing to do with the celebrations and commemorations that take place all over Europe one day later. This day, 10 November, is the anniversary of the death of Mustafa Kemal Pasha Atatürk (1881–1938), Turkey's first president. The next day, 11 November – the day that the armistice treaty was signed between the Allies and Germany thus ending Word War I – carries no special meaning in Turkish collective memory.

For the Ottoman Empire the end of World War I came on 31 October 1918. It was triggered by the almost simultaneous collapse of the Macedonian and the Palestinian fronts. The Allied attack on the Macedonian front, which started on 15 September, resulted in a breakthrough when whole regiments of the Bulgarian army simply left the trenches and revolted. Two weeks later, on 29 September, Bulgaria was forced to sign an unconditional armistice, that is to say: with the terms to be established unilaterally by the Allies. The collapse of the Bulgarian front left European Turkey, including the Dardanelles and the capital Istanbul, open to attack, for the Ottomans had no means of defence left as this section of the front was held by less than five weak divisions.[1] On the Palestinian front, British Commander Edmund Allenby's forces had broken through on 19 September. The Ottoman forces had to beat a hasty retreat to the north of Aleppo, losing two-thirds of their strength.[2]

The real cause of the collapse was total exhaustion. The Ottoman Empire was essentially an agricultural state, which had thrown itself head over heels into an industrialized war. The result was that, while the empire proved able to field a large and fairly modern conscripted army, it was not capable of supporting it adequately. The previous chapters of this section have shown that means of transport were completely insufficient, food, clothing (especially shoes) and medical care were totally inadequate, and diseases were omnipresent. The conditions in the army affected morale to the extent that, by the end of the war, over 400,000 men had deserted and the army numbered about 100,000 men or only 15 per cent of its peak strength reached in early 1916.

Conditions in the army were very bad, but as the needs of the army overrode everything else, the living conditions of the civilian population were if anything worse. Official consumer price inflation during the war was 400 per cent, but many articles were available on the black market only, where prices were, of course, much higher.[3] Shortages of food and fuel made life particularly hard in the cities. The persecution of the Armenian and Greek communities also had a detrimental effect on the economy, as the commercial and professional middle classes of the empire hailed to a very high degree from these communities.

To sum up the situation: by mid-1918 the empire was exhausted militarily, economically, financially and morally. Public discontent, especially with the very visible corruption and profiteering on the part of the protégés of the ruling Committee of Union and Progress (CUP), was rising fast. In an effort to defuse this discontent, the CUP relaxed its hold over parliament and lifted political censorship to allow criticism of profiteers and corrupt officials to be vented.[4]

The breakthrough in Macedonia convinced the Young Turk leadership and especially Grand Vizier Talât Pasha (who had witnessed the chaos in Bulgaria on his return from Berlin) that the war was lost. The cabinet decided to ask for an armistice and, pinning its hopes on President Wilson's 'Fourteen Points', it approached the Americans through Spain's mediation on 5 October. When no reply was received and the British and French troops in Thrace kept moving steadily forward, approaching the Maritza river, the Young Turk cabinet resigned on 8 October. It was succeeded by a cabinet headed by one of the Ottoman Empire's top military officers, Field-Marshal Ahmet İzzet Pasha [Furgaç], who was trusted by the Young Turks as a nationalist, though he had never been a member of the CUP himself. His cabinet, which took office on the 14 October, was politically neutral, and included a small number of important CUP politicians, but none of the people who were closely identified with the wartime policies of the committee.

The new cabinet immediately made another attempt to open negotiations with the Allies, this time by sending General Townshend, who had been held as a prisoner of war on the island of Prinkipo near Istanbul since the fall of Kut in 1916, to meet with Admiral Calthorpe, the commander of the Mediterranean Station of the Royal Navy, whose squadron lay at anchor in Moudhros harbour on the island of Lemnos. On 23 October, five days after the start of Townshend's mission, Calthorpe informed the Ottoman government that he was empowered to negotiate on behalf of the Allies. That Admiral Calthorpe was empowered to negotiate on behalf of the Allies in spite of the fact that the supreme naval command in the Mediterranean had been in French hands throughout the war, amounted to recognition of Britain's dominant role in the Ottoman war theatre.

The next day the Ottoman delegation, consisting of Lieutenant Colonel Sadullah (Chief of Staff of the Eighth Army), Reşat Hikmet Bey (Secretary General at the Foreign Office) and Hüseyin Rauf Bey (Navy Minister and head of the delegation) left for Moudhros, where they arrived on the 26 October. The Ottoman delegation was armed with cabinet instructions, which, considering the hopeless situation of the Ottoman army seemed to display a certain lack of realism. They agreed to the opening of the straits, but demanded that foreign warships not remain in the Marmara Sea for more than a day, claimed full responsibility for the maintenance of law and order and rejected any foreign interference and the landing of troops, demanded the preservation of sultanate and caliphate, accepted only administrative (but not political) Allied control in the occupied (i.e. Arab) provinces, and even demanded financial assistance for the empire.[5]

The actual negotiations took place aboard Calthorpe's flagship *Agamemnon* in Moudhros harbour. Although the admiral made it known right at the start that no substantial alterations to the Allies' already agreed upon set of conditions would be entertained, the talks lasted for four days because the Ottoman side did what it could to mitigate some of the toughest conditions. In doing so it tried to remain in touch with the cabinet in Istanbul, but this proved very difficult. Attempts of a British cable ship to lay a connection to Çeşme on the Anatolian mainland failed because of bad weather, so the delegation had to communicate by wireless transmissions to the Ottoman wireless station in Okmeydanı (Istanbul). They only managed to get instructions regarding the Allied conditions on 29 October and again on 30 October. The Ottoman worries, as reflected in these instructions, centred on three points: First, while they were prepared to accept that the fortifications on the Dardanelles and the Bosphorus would be occupied, they tried to get assurances that this occupation would be executed with British and French troops, without participation of the Italians and particularly the Greeks. Second, the Ottomans wanted guarantees that the capital Istanbul itself would not be occupied. Third, they were extremely worried about possible abuse of articles 7 and 24 of the armistice agreement. Article 7 stated that, when faced with a situation in which their security may be endangered, the Allies would have the right to occupy any strategic point, while article 24 said that, in case of disturbances in the six 'Armenian' provinces, the Allies reserved the right to occupy any part of these provinces. In Ottoman eyes, these articles opened the door wide for attempts by Greek or Armenian nationalists to provoke Allied interference. They therefore requested that article 24 in particular be kept secret. This, however, was rejected by Admiral Calthorpe, who pointed out that the principles laid down by President Wilson made secret diplomacy of this kind a thing of the past.[6]

In the end the Ottoman delegation decided to accept the 25-point armistice text without major alterations, even though it did not have full authorization to do so. It did, however, persuade Admiral Calthorpe to write a personal letter, intended only for the eyes of Rauf Bey, the Grand Vizier and the Sultan, in which he promised on behalf of the British government that only British and French troops would be used in the occupation of the Straits fortifications. In addition, Calthorpe said that he had strongly recommended to his government that a small number of Ottoman troops would be allowed to stay on in the occupied areas as a symbol of sovereignty. Finally he said that he had conveyed to his government the urgent requests of the Ottoman delegation that no Greek troops be allowed to land either in Istanbul or Izmir and that Istanbul should not be occupied as long as the Ottoman government could protect Allied lives and possessions there.[7]

The delegation left the *Agamemnon* on the evening of 30 October and reached Izmir by noon the next day. After telegraphic communication with Istanbul they now received the cabinet's approval for the signature of the armistice.

When we now try to gauge the immediate popular reaction to the conclusion of the armistice, we have to make a clear distinction between the Muslims of the empire and the Christian communities. It should come as no surprise that the latter were elated. The loyalty of the Greek and Armenian communities to the Ottoman state was in grave doubt even before the war and the ethnic policies of the wartime government, which resulted in the deaths of up to 800,000 Armenians and the flight and expulsion of hundreds of thousand of Greeks, had caused both communities to look upon the Allies as liberators. This had been clear even in 1915, when foreign observers in Istanbul noted the Christians' great hopes of an Allied breakthrough in Gallipoli and their disappointment when that failed to materialize.[8] It was also apparent in the way the Allied commanders were greeted when they entered Istanbul after the war. General Franchet d'Esperey, the French commander of the *Armée de l'Orient* (the army of Salonica) entered the city astride a white stallion donated by the Greek community and the whole Christian part of the city (Pera, or modern Beyoğlu) was decorated with Greek, Italian, French and British flags.

The Ottoman government was well aware of these sentiments. When the delegation returned to Istanbul on 1 November, Rauf Bey was met by a group of newspaper editors. He agreed to speak to them, but only off the record. He emphasized the delicacy of the situation and implored the editors to avoid publishing anything that could raise tensions between the communities or give the Ottoman Christians (*malûm unsurlar* or 'certain elements') an excuse to start disturbances and call for the help of the Allies under article 7. The newspapers complied and anyway, from the next day there was another issue which diverted public attention from the armistice: the flight, during the night and aboard a German submarine, of the wartime leaders Enver, Talât and Cemal. When word of their flight got out on 2 November, the cabinet (which still contained a small number of former members of the Young Turk Committee of Union and Progress) was accused of conniving at their escape. It was the sign for a general assault by the press on the Committee and its wartime policies, in which all the anger and disappointment of the public was vented.[9]

Among the Muslim population, reactions to the armistice were more varied than among the Ottoman Christians. Those who bore responsibility for the conduct of the war, such as the leading echelons of the Committee and the members of parliament, were of course disenchanted with the formal recognition that the war was effectively lost, but the public seems to have been relieved, rather than anything else, by the armistice.[10] One can point at several reasons for this relief.

The main reason obviously was the fact that the war had finally ended. The war had never been popular. While a defensive war against the Russians could count on a great deal of popular support, war against the British and the French, who had enormous prestige and cultural influence among the urban Ottoman élite, even when the empire was linked politically to Germany, was seen by many as unnatural and even suicidal. The hardships endured during the final years of the war had dissipated what enthusiasm there had been.

Another reason for relief lay in the comparison between the armistice of Moudhros and the armistice imposed on Bulgaria just before, which amounted to an unconditional surrender of that country. Seen in that light, the conditions of the Ottoman armistice were favourable in that they left the defeated empire with a qualified independence and some dignity.

The fact that the empire survived *as an empire* with the revered institutions of the sultanate and caliphate intact was a consolation. Looking back from where we are, the Ottoman Empire is only one of the great continental empires to disappear in the wake of World War I, but we should not forget that in 1918 the Ottoman dynasty, unlike that of the Romanovs, the Habsburgs or the Hohenzollerns, did manage to hang on to its throne.

Finally, there was a widespread belief in British fair play on the one hand, and in the promises of a new world order based on the principles enunciated by President Wilson on the other. Quite a few members of the Istanbul bourgeoisie enthusiastically joined the 'Society of the Friends of England' or the 'Wilsonian League' after the war and there was much talk of the benefits of an American mandate.[11]

Perhaps the most striking point, when one reads the contemporary declarations and speeches where the armistice is discussed, is this: the armistice was not in itself seen as unjust or unacceptable, even by those nationalist Young Turk officers who would go on to lead the national resistance movement in Anatolia and eventually found the Turkish Republic. There were clear worries about the elasticity of articles 7 and 24 and as early as November 1918 the population in those areas that could be disputed by the Greeks (in the west) and the Armenians (in the east and south) was being mobilized to resist those claims. But the armistice as such was not a bone of contention among the Ottoman élite. There was no feeling, as there was to be in Germany, of betrayal or injustice.

Turkish historiography has conditioned us to juxtapose the defeat of 1918 and the armistice that ensued with the triumph of 1922, which resulted in the armistice of Mudanya and then, in 1923, the peace of Lausanne. Armistice, occupation and the treaty of Sèvres with its complete dismemberment of the Ottoman state and huge concessions to Greeks, Armenians, Kurds, Italians and French now all seem part of one dark page in Turkish history. That Hüseyin Rauf Bey, the chief of the Ottoman delegation in Moudhros, emerged as the leader of the political opposition against Atatürk in the young Turkish Republic after 1923 and that he was purged in a political trial in 1926, gave added impetus to the tendency to see the armistice as a piece of treason, to which no true Turk could or should have put his signature.[12]

In reality, though, the immediate reaction to the armistice on the part of the Ottoman Muslims was generally one of relief and hope. It would be the Allies' policies, in particular the decision to allow Greek troops to land in Izmir in May 1919 and the occupation of Istanbul in March 1920, rather than the armistice as such, which turned public opinion against the Allies and eventually persuaded the majority to throw in their lot with the nationalist resistance. When we read the speeches and declarations of Mustafa Kemal and other resistance leaders from this period, we see that these are full of complaints and indignation about the way the Allies, especially the British, abused and exceeded the terms of the armistice.[13] That the Greek occupation of Izmir galvanized public opinion is well known. It gave rise to mass protest rallies in Constantinople and to armed resistance in Anatolia. The occupation of Constantinople, however, was an equally traumatic experience. Both memoirs and novels show the anger and dismay experienced by Ottoman Muslims at the almost colonial way they were treated in their own capital by the officers of the Entente and their Greek and Armenian protégés.[14]

15. Renewal and Silence: Post-war Unionist and Kemalist Rhetoric on the Armenian Genocide*

It was 25 years ago that I published my first book, *The Unionist Factor.*[1] The theme of the book was the continuity between the Young Turk period in Ottoman history and the history of the early republic. It charted the way in which leading members of the Committee of Union and Progress (CUP) built the national resistance movement after World War I and the way in which Mustafa Kemal Pasha gradually managed to take over this movement and concentrate power in his own hands by eliminating his former Unionist colleagues.

Generally, the book was received quite favourably, both in Turkey (after its Turkish translation appeared as *Milli Mücadelede İttihatçılık*) and abroad. One day, an Armenian friend and colleague of mine brought to my attention a review in an Armenian journal (which he had kindly translated) that, although on the whole quite favourable, was critical on one important point. In the eyes of the author of the review, the analysis of the power struggles within the Unionist/nationalist camp lacked a historical context. In the words of the author, I had 'depicted figures in an empty landscape'. He referred to the fact that I had described the political developments of the period without taking into account the persecutions of Armenians and their aftermath in Anatolia – events which in his mind had created the backdrop against which the Unionists acted.

At the time, I thought the criticism misplaced. Although I had no intention of denying the Armenian 'holocaust' (to quote Bernard Lewis),[2] my book simply had not been about that. It was about something else. Later, however, I came to realize that the reviewer had been right. Study of the ideological changes that occurred between 1908 and 1928 made me aware of the degree to which identity formation in this period had been defined by the opposition between Muslims and non-Muslims, a process in which religious identity had become an ethnic marker and which ultimately resulted in the emergence of a fierce Ottoman-Muslim nationalism.[3] As Deringil and Yavuz have shown,[4] the foundations for this had been laid during the reign, and through the policies, of Sultan Abdülhamit II, but it was the ten-year period of war between 1912 and 1922 that gave rise to mass mobilization of the population on this basis.

This mass mobilization was effected by a Young Turk leadership, both civilian and military, that overwhelmingly hailed from the Balkan provinces and the Aegean littoral. Although they are never denoted as *muhacir* (refugee), a term reserved for lower class migrants, many of them were in effect refugees after the loss of the Dodecanese to Italy in 1911–12 and the Balkan War of 1912–13. The same is true for the first generation of leaders of the Republic of Turkey.[5] In the years that followed they had to grapple with this trauma of territorial loss and military defeat, and find a new basis for their identity. From 1913 onwards, the reaction of the Young Turk leadership to the loss of their ancestral lands seems to have manifested itself in four different ways, which were not mutually exclusive and in fact often overlapped:

Irredentism: perhaps surprisingly, political irredentism was relatively subdued, although the hope of recovering at least some of the lost territory did play a role in the decision to go to war in 1914.

Pan-Turkist escapism: the loss of a real empire in the West certainly encouraged dreams of a virtual empire in the East, especially after war with Russia had broken out, but to my mind the importance of Pan-Turkism in the events that followed has been drastically overstated by Armenian scholars.

Resentment: there is no doubt that the resentment against the Christian minorities that had been growing since the 1860s and had become very tangible after the constitutional revolution, was given a strong impetus by the sometimes blatantly disloyal behaviour of the Christian communities in the Ottoman Empire during the Balkan War. We can certainly detect a discourse of revenge, violence and hatred in the Turkish writings of this period.[6]

The discovery of Anatolia as the true Turkish fatherland: there had been a rise in interest in Anatolia since the constitutional revolution, but after 1912 it was embraced as the true home of the Turks even, or perhaps primarily, by those (like Mustafa Kemal) who had been born and bred in south-eastern Europe and discovered their new homeland when in their thirties. The same can be said for the smaller but also influential group of immigrants from the Caucasus and the Black Sea littoral.

The combination of resentment against the Ottoman Christian communities and the adoption of Anatolia as the new homeland made it crucial for the Unionists to make sure that Anatolia was and would remain an Ottoman-Muslim land. These sentiments served as the impetus for the policies of ethnic cleansing that started in the summer of 1914 with the expulsion of the Greeks from the coastal areas in the west. It is certainly no coincidence that the man in charge of these expulsions, Mahmut Celâl, was a son of refugees from Bulgaria, as was the main architect of the Armenian massacres, Dr Bahaettin Şakir.

In the post-war environment, when the carve-up of Anatolia by the Entente and their Greek and Armenian clients seemed imminent, the leaders of the resistance movement that emerged from November 1918 onwards once again had recourse to mobilization on the basis of an ethnicized religious identity. The dominant discourse of the movement between 1919 and 1922 is one of 'us' and 'them', in which the other is defined as the non-Muslim. In fact, as I have argued elsewhere, it is precisely in the post-war era, under Mustafa Kemal's leadership, that Muslim nationalism reaches its climax, something illustrated and symbolized by the text of Mehmet Akif's strongly Islamic 'Independence March' of 1921, which paradoxically went on to become the national anthem of the secular republic.[7]

In other words, and to turn back to where I started, I must now concede that my Armenian reviewer was right: one can only fully understand the post-war policies of the former Unionists who made up the national resistance movement by taking into account the experiences that shaped them in the preceding period. Of these, the persecution of the Armenians is no doubt one of the most important. Leaving this out indeed risks turning the nationalist leaders into figures in an empty landscape.

Time, then, to look again at the impact of the Armenian massacres on the post-war attitudes of the Unionists. I want to do this by looking at their public statements in order to establish to what extent an effort was made either to distance themselves from, or conversely to justify, the ethnic policies of the war years. After all: if this was the defining moment in their immediate past, they would have to deal with it one way or another, when trying to find a new political role in the post-war environment.

Post-war statements on the persecution of Armenians

The public statements of Unionists in the post-war environment were issued in two contexts: (1) the activities of Unionist parliamentarians in new parties and parliamentary groupings that can be regarded as successors to the *Party of Union and Progress* (the CUP's parliamentary party that was ostensibly merged with the committee in 1916); and (2) the embryonic national resistance movement that was to a large extent based on the local branches and Unionist clubs in the provincial centres. Of course, individual former Unionists quite often played a role in both of these settings. The activities of the secret underground networks,[8] such as *Karakol* (the Guard), founded in October 1918 at the behest of Enver and Talât Pashas, no doubt would be a fascinating context for the study of Unionists' post-war sentiments and attitudes, but as these networks did not produce public statements, they fall outside the purview of this chapter.

The heirs to the Party of Union and Progress

Two political parties were clearly identified at the time as being heirs to the old Party of Union and Progress, which had dissolved itself at its final congress on 5 November 1918: the Renewal Party (*Teceddüt Fırkası*) and the Ottoman Liberal People's Party (*Osmanlı Hürriyetperver Avam Fırkası*).

The Renewal Party was founded by the Unionists present at the final CUP party congress on 9 November 1918. Although the party officially denied that it was a continuation of the CUP, its takeover of CUP assets, such as organizational networks, real estate (the clubs) and cash detracted from the credibility of this claim.

The party published a detailed party programme (prepared by a commission during the CUP's last party congress), containing 175 articles on all aspects of internal and external policy.[9] This is in some ways a very interesting document. In part it reads like a constitution, not as a party programme at all, suggestive perhaps of the degree to which the Unionists had come to identify themselves with the state. The first section, consisting of 33 articles, describes the principles underpinning the Ottoman state order and its main institutional elements. It deals with issues like sovereignty, the role of the dynasty, state religion and language and the fundamental rights of the citizen. The party itself is not mentioned even once in this whole section.

The document is also interesting in the way it presages some of the later reforms of the Kemalist republic. Article 22 announces the abolition of all civilian honorary titles (*Pasha, Bey, Efendi* etc.). Article 54 calls for the introduction of a national anthem, an official name and arms for the state (all of which the Ottoman Empire never had). The next article, 55, states that the constitution will be modified to comply with the principles of national sovereignty (*hakimiyeti milliye*) and parliamentarism. This of course reminds one of the Law of Fundamental Organisation, adopted by the assembly in Ankara in early 1921, with its famous first article 'Sovereignty belongs unconditionally to the nation' (*Hakimiyet bilakaydüşart milletindir*). Article 70 calls for a reform of the calendar, article 96 for the introduction of family names and article 118 for a reform of the Turkish language, all of them ultimately realized under Atatürk in the 1920s and 30s. Improvement of conditions in the countryside is sought through the reclamation of marshland (article 130) and the abolition of the tithe (article 159) precisely in the way the republic was to do.

In other words: the party programme of the Renewal Party is quite an elaborate and also a forward-looking document, which announces a number of bold policy initiatives. It also seems to be totally divorced from the reality of late 1918. There is no mention of the war, of the dire economic circumstances of the country or, indeed, of the persecution of Armenians. Security of life, honour and property is emphasized as a common right of all Ottoman citizens and the rights of minorities are guaranteed (articles 3–6) but no mention is made of any past transgressions, let alone of the need to deal with the past and punish the culprits. This is remarkable, as everyone knew that the Entente powers had announced they would take action on this issue once the war was over.

The Liberal People's Party had come into being as the result of a split within the CUP. It was founded in mid-October 1918 by Mustafa Kemal's old friend Ali Fethi [Okyar] and Hüseyin Kadri, the member of parliament for Karesi, who, together with a small group of Unionist parliamentarians, announced their departure from the CUP. Although all its members had a Unionist background and were even invited to the last party congress of the CUP after they had split off, the Liberal People's Party was not a successor of the CUP in the sense that it took over CUP assets as the Renewal Party did.

The Liberal People's Party, too, published a very detailed (94 articles) party programme immediately after its foundation.[10] Like that of the Renewal Party, its first sections are strongly reminiscent of a constitution and describe the state order rather than formulating any party policies. In the rest of the document we encounter many of the elements present in the programme of the Renewal Party, although it lacks the more radical reform proposals of the latter – surprising, perhaps, if one bears in mind that Mustafa Kemal was close to the party and even became co-owner of the party newspaper *Minber* after his return from the Syrian front.[11]

Like the programme of the Renewal Party, that of the Liberal People's Party seems to have been drawn up with great care, but in complete isolation from the realities of the day. Those realities – rocketing inflation, severe shortages, displaced persons, mass desertions – are not mentioned, and there is no call for any kind of reckoning, redress or persecution of the culprits of the Armenian massacres. This is perhaps more surprising in the case of the Liberal People's Party than in that of the Renewal Party, as Ali Fethi's group had officially and openly resigned from the CUP and thus could be expected to feel more freedom in this respect.

Both parties were closed down on the orders of the government in May 1919 because they were considered direct successors to the CUP, but they were quite active and vocal in parliament and outside it in the early months of 1919.

The Anatolian resistance movement

By the time the parties were closed, the efforts to organize a resistance movement in Anatolia, based partly on the network of Unionist clubs and branches and partly on the infrastructure of the army, were well underway. The Congress of Sivas (4–11 September 1919) was the first attempt to unite all the regional resistance initiatives in a common national front, and it was there that the 'Society for the Defence of the National Rights [a reference to President Wilson's *Fourteen Points*] of Anatolia and Rumelia' was founded. The congress was completely dominated by people with a Unionist background, but like the parties discussed earlier, those present made a point of denying any continuity between the CUP and themselves, even going so far as to swear a solemn oath that they would not revive the CUP.

The formal declaration of the congress formed the basis of the 'National Pact', the nationalist programme that was officially adopted by the final Ottoman parliament four months later. Unlike the documents produced by the parties in Istanbul, this declaration was very much focused on the actual events and circumstances of the day. What did this text have to say about the Armenian issue? The text refers to the Armenians and Greeks explicitly in article 3 and implicitly in article 4. Article 3 states that struggle against the attempts to found independent Greek and Armenian entities (*Rumluk ve Ermenilik*) on Ottoman soil is legitimate, and article 4 promises equality before the law to non-Muslims, but rejects the reintroduction of the capitulations.[12]

It could be argued that the document deals with the current situation and with political goals and that it is therefore natural that it should not refer to the events of the immediate past. One could, however, expect the issue of the persecution of the Armenians to come up in the discussions on the oath not to revive the CUP. This oath was debated quite seriously, opinions being divided between those who merely wanted to swear not to work for personal gain or party political interests and those who expressly wanted to mention the CUP.[13] Some of those who supported the latter option, like Bekir Sami [Kunduh] or Rauf [Orbay]) referred to the 'Unionist nightmare' and to the 'disasters to which the CUP had led the country', while others like Mehmet Şükrü said that the CUP had had an exalted idealist programme, which still commanded respect in the greater Turkic and Islamic world and that it would be unjust to reject its legacy just because of the misdeeds of a few individuals. Ultimately, the argument that there was a great deal of suspicion in the country that the congress would revive the CUP and that it was therefore necessary publicly to vow not to do so, carried the day, on the understanding that the oath would be valid only for *the duration of the congress*. The interesting point is that at no time during these discussions was the treatment of the Armenians mentioned, not even by those who were most critical of the CUP. The same is true for Mustafa Kemal's opening speech at the congress, which set out the necessity of organizing national resistance. He mentioned the Armenians but only to say: 'In the East the Armenians have begun their preparations to expand their state up to the banks of the Kızılırmak and even now their genocidal policy has started to reach our borders.'[14]

This set the tone. In the first public speech Mustafa Kemal gave after establishing his headquarters in Ankara in December 1919, he again warned about the dangers facing the country both from the victorious Entente and from the non-Muslim minorities, and especially from the combination of the two. He firmly rejected the idea that the Turkish nation was an oppressor (*zalim*), praised the tolerance shown by the Ottoman Muslims in the past and had this, and only this, to say about the Armenian massacres during the war:

Whatever has befallen the non-Muslim elements living in our country, is the result of the policies of separatism they pursued in a savage manner, when they allowed themselves to be made tools

201

of foreign intrigues and abused their privileges. There are probably many reasons and excuses for the undesired events that have taken place in Turkey. And I want definitely to say that these events are on a level far removed from the many forms of oppression which are committed in the states of Europe without any excuse.[15]

All the classic elements in the defence of violent aggression are here: they asked for it, it was not really so bad and anyway, others have done the same and worse.

Conclusion: the dog in the night-time

In a sense the outcome of these findings resembles Sherlock Holmes' famous 'curious incident of the dog in the night-time'. In other words: when we scan the policy documents of those post-war organizations that had a clearly Unionist character for references to the persecution of the Ottoman Armenians barely two years earlier or for attempts to either express regret or justify the events or unequivocally distance the said organizations from them, we draw a complete blank. As is well known, there were those in the post-war Ottoman environment who did call for the culprits of the genocide to be brought to justice. These were not limited to the Liberal opposition (people like Ali Kemal), and also included the Young Turk *eminence grise* Ahmet Rıza. But the two parties that directly sprang from the bosom of the CUP did no such thing. Both the Renewal Party and the Liberal People's Party came up with detailed, one might even say, remarkably mature policy documents, but one looks in vain for a single reference to the treatment of the Armenians in the immediate past. This is the more surprising for Fethi Okyar's Liberal People's Party, as that group was a dissident grouping that had broken away from the CUP before its last party congress. The same is true for the leadership of the national resistance movement in Anatolia. The language employed with regards to the Armenians and Greeks where their political or territorial claims are concerned, in Erzurum, Sivas and Ankara is quite uncompromising and references to the events of 1915–16 are completely lacking save for the one very severe statement of Mustafa Kemal in Ankara, quoted in *extenso* above.

In this respect, the argument, sometimes voiced even by concerned historians, that Turks do not have to fear a reopening of the debate on the Armenian issue, because the republic is clearly distinct from the late empire and that Mustafa Kemal 'has never spoken in support of the genocide', sounds rather weak. When it mattered, in 1918–20, Mustafa Kemal never spoke out against the genocide either and he surrounded himself with people, his own bodyguard Topal Osman among them, who were quite notorious for having blood on their hands. His keynote address in Ankara in December 1919 put the blame squarely on the victims.

Taner Akçam, a Turkish sociologist who has written extensively on the Armenian genocide, provides a somewhat dubious explanation for this dog that didn't bark. In a recent article,[16] Akçam argues that the attitude of the Turkish nationalists after the war can be explained by the fact that the British at the same time conducted an aggressive imperialist policy aimed at the destruction of the empire AND took the initiative in opening the case against the people responsible for the genocide. So closely identified were the two that supporting the legal persecution of the Unionists became an unpatriotic act by association. His argument is that a different policy on the part of the British, which would take seriously the national aspirations of the Turks, might have allowed Mustafa Kemal's nationalists to distance themselves from the Unionists who were responsible for the genocide. I have to say that I very much doubt if this is realistic. After all the party programmes of the Renewal Party and of the Liberal People's Party (with which Mustafa Kemal was associated) date from before the arrival of the British. Still, both parties denied themselves the opportunity to distance themselves from the crimes committed during the war. The Unionist underground organization *Karakol* was founded as early as October 1918 to smuggle arms and people to Anatolia with the twin aims of strengthening any future resistance and to keep those who were at risk of arrest out of the hands of the British. It thus linked the two elements of national resistance and sabotaging the persecution of Unionist officials right from the start.

I fear that it was simply impossible for Unionists in 1918–19 to distance themselves too visibly from the crimes of 1915–16 and those who had committed them. Those crimes occurred at the height of the period in which the population had been mobilized by the Unionists themselves on the basis of a Muslim-Ottoman identity, an identity that had been formed in continuous and conscious opposition to the Ottoman Christians. The Unionists depended on this sentiment for their grass-root support and could not afford a break with the past. This was as true for Mustafa Kemal and his men in Anatolia as it was for the politicians in the capital. Therefore, the silence of the post-war documents on the issue does not, I think, indicate a conspiracy of silence, an effort to cover up the past. Nor

203

does it indicate that the Armenian massacres had become a taboo. Quite simply, I think the most logical explanation is that for an effort to generate political support among the Ottoman Muslims, whom they clearly regarded as their constituency (witness Rauf Bey's statement in Sivas: 'the aim of the Defence of Rights Association is to unite the Muslim population'), discussing the massacres was counterproductive and thus politically irrelevant.

The Kemalist republic

In the first few years of the republic, the Armenian issue does not seem to have been discussed at a political level. When Mustafa Kemal finally decided to deal with the remaining Unionist leaders and eliminate them once and for all in the show trials conducted in the summer of 1926, they were fiercely castigated by the Independence Tribunal before which they had to appear for the way they had dragged the Ottoman Empire into World War I, for acts of corruption during the war and for their behaviour in the after-war years, but not for their ethnic policies. In other words: even when an effort was made to publicly disgrace the former Unionist leaders, the treatment of the Armenians apparently was not considered something to disgrace them with in the eyes of the Turkish public.[17] One could argue that Mustafa Kemal did condemn them for the treatment of the Armenians in his well-known interview with the 'Swiss reporter' Emile Hilderbrand that was published in the *Los Angeles Examiner* on 1 August 1926, in which he is supposed to have said that 'they should have been made to account for the lives of millions of our Christian subjects who were ruthlessly driven en masse, from their homes and massacred...'. There can be serious doubt, however, about the authenticity and reliability of this text, and even if it should be authentic, it was meant for foreign consumption. The fact remains that the massacres did not figure in the actual trials or in Mustafa Kemal's statements to the Turkish public.[18] On the contrary, in the very year when these Unionist leaders were purged, the Turkish national assembly adopted a law granting pensions to the widows and orphans of the Unionist leaders who had been murdered by Armenian revenge killers in 'Operation Nemesis' and of those hanged by the military tribunal of Nemrut Mustafa Pasha in Istanbul in 1919.[19]

That no need was felt to distance oneself from the perpetrators of the genocide in the early republic is also shown by another interesting example. In 1936, ten years after the purges, veteran journalist and editor Hüseyin

Cahit Yalçın published a series of biographical portraits of people he had known in the paper *Yedigün*. Among the people whose portrait Yalçın draws, is the man now generally considered the architect of the genocide, Dr Bahaettin Şakir. Yalçın first describes Bahaettin's character:

> Bahaettin Şakir had become a single hard unit through his exploits, like a piece of steel that had been toughened in hardship, deprivation and pain. He solved his whole life and all political problems with a sharp and decisive reasoning: What wasn't black was white; a man who wasn't good, was bad – forever. Subtle differences, vague colours did not exist in his eyes. One could say he lived far removed from reality and from the world. In him there was an ideal of freedom that formed life's driving force and goal. For him this had become a creed. He had buried himself in that ideal, that creed, had withdrawn from the human world and had made himself a world in the abstract and the absolute.
>
> In the assemblies and central committee meetings of the Committee of Union and Progress Bahaettin Şakir was always the most ardent supporter of the most radical measures. He could not envisage sacrificing ideas or opinions to reach a compromise. In his view, there was no world, there were no opponents, no problems, just an ideal and a creed, and the process of moving towards it with decisive steps without thinking of anything.

And then he goes on the openly address the question of Bahaettin's role in the Armenian question:

> What is Bahaettin Şakir's role in the deportations? Even in our most intimate meetings this issue was not made clear to us. I have no clear, definitive opinion, but based on a word here that escaped from his lips when we discussed other matters, a thought there that came out, involuntary gests, subtle and slight, even imperceptible, indications, which aroused suspicion in a person, one idea imposed itself on me with great strength: that he was the prime shaper and executor of the deportation business. I am strongly convinced that he prepared the ground when he travelled the East by himself, took the basic decisions and that, while he worked to put his own personal ideas into practice, his position meant that his orders were

taken to be orders of the Central Committee and of the government and that in the end he carried some of his influential friends in the government with him. *That is why, if one day it would be necessary to revive Bahaettin Şakir's memory, the provinces in the east will be more than ready to put up his statue.* [my italics][20]

First of all, this statement is interesting for its contents. It is clear that this old Unionist has no hesitation in describing Bahaettin's role quite openly (even if it is the deportations rather than the killings that are being discussed here). That the Armenian policy was not discussed openly in his presence is entirely credible. After all, Hüseyin Cahit was certainly trusted by Talât's circle up to a point, but he was not one of the people who had been actively involved in the planning of the constitutional revolution and definitely not a member of the innermost circle of power. He also probably gives too much credence to the idea that Bahaettin worked on his own. The important thing, however, is that he concludes that Bahaettin must have been the one who was primarily responsible and then goes on, not to blame him or to distance himself from him, but instead to suggest that his memory should be honoured.

The most interesting aspect of the publication is of course that it was published at all. In 1936 Kemalist Turkey had one of the most draconian press laws in existence, which even prohibited 'any publication at odds with the general policies of the state'. Censorship was strictly enforced, so we may assume that a statement like the above was published with the implicit agreement of the government.

In short: in the early republic the political and intellectual élite felt just as little need to distance itself from the genocide and its perpetrators as had been the case in the immediate post-war environment. In the years 1918–22 the continued need to mobilize the Muslim population of Anatolia had made any serious reckoning with this aspect of the immediate past an impossibility. After the proclamation of the republic it was the composition of the ruling élite that precluded it. Turkey was ruled by an élite that consisted of bureaucrats and military officers with a Unionist background, who overwhelmingly hailed from the Balkans and had adopted Anatolia as their new fatherland because they had nowhere else to turn. Quite a few of the people in central positions of power (Şükrü Kaya, Kazım Özalp, Abdülhalik Renda, *Kılıç* Ali) had been personally involved in the massacres, but the ruling élite as a whole depended for its position (and in fact had done so since the start of the national resistance movement) on a coalition with provincial notables, landlords and tribal chiefs, who had profited immensely from the departure of the Armenians and the Greeks. It was what Fatma Müge Göçek has called an unspoken 'devil's bargain'.[21] A serious attempt to distance the republic from the genocide could have destabilized the ruling coalition on which the republic depended for its stability.

IV.   TOWARDS THE NATION STATE

A)

1) The Republic of Turkey was grounded/established by a gang of soldiers under the leadership of M. Kemal Atatürk.

2) These were the soldiers & members of administrative elite of the Ottoman Empire, the other of the West.

3) In definition of the western identity the Ottoman Empire was the main marker as the leader of the Muslim (mainly Sunni) World.

4) The Sultans were also Caliphs of the Ummah.

~~has power to mobilise~~
spiritual leader & also political leader, have power to mobilise (billions of Muslim) at least in theory ---

B) Ottoman Empire
• a Multilingual & cultural/ethnic empire.
• stretching from Caspian Sea to the Sad shes, covering MENA (geopolitically strategic geographies).
~~that~~ until 17. century - Crimea then decline ...
then gradually started loosing some of these lands

↳ Young Turks
↪ How can the empire be saved?
   - Modernisation ⇒ Westernisation
   ¿ Binding elements ⇒ 3 TOL - (Sijes?) ↓

Introduction

Out of the decade of war that was the subject of the previous part came a new state, the Republic of Turkey proclaimed on 29 October 1923.

The story of this new state is a paradox. On the one hand there is an undeniable continuity between the empire and the republic at the level of political leadership and that of the state apparatus (both bureaucratic and military). On the other hand, the political and cultural élite of the young republic opted for a radically different definition of its own identity: they decided to be Turks and to take Turkishness as the basis their new national state. This identity was then imposed gradually on the population through a process of nation building in which, as in similar processes the world over, historiography and linguistics played a key role, as did suppression of alternative or even sub-identities.

The process through which first Ottomanism and then Islamism lost their appeal and were replaced with Turkish nationalism is often described as a logical process of elimination in which Ottomanism, still the rallying cry of the 1908 revolution, lost its credibility because of the disaffection of the Ottoman Christian communities during the Balkan War and Islamism had to be jettisoned after the Arab revolt, leaving only Turkism as a viable option. The chapter on 'Ottoman Muslims, Young Turks and Turkish Nationalists' suggests a different rationality, based on the predominant concern of the Young Turks, that is, to save and strengthen the state they served rather than on an ideological preference per se. In the war years (1912–22) this imposed the need to turn to Ottoman Muslim nationalism (in which 'Ottoman Muslim' served as an ethnic marker rather than as a religious category) in order to mobilize the population of Anatolia. After the wars, the same underlying logic, that of saving and strengthening the state, in the eyes of the Kemalists imposed the need for radical modernization and secularization. Turkey had to become 'civilized' in order to survive. As the population no longer had to be mobilized for war, the appeal to Islamic sentiments lost its relevance.

Within a few years after the victory in the independence war, the movement split into a moderate and a more radical faction, but as the chapter on the Progressive Republican Party (PRP) shows, the argument was about the political system rather than about conflicting ideologies, as both the ruling People's Party and the opposition PRP fundamentally shared the same modernist and secularist agenda, which had its roots in French positivism and ultimately the enlightenment. Where the PRP was closed down in 1925, the (Republican) People's Party went on to become the most important tool for the Kemalist state in spreading the nationalist, modernist and secularist message of that state. The party never gained ascendancy over the state but it was important for the institution-building of the republican regime and provided a training ground for politicians and administrators.

While the republic had a secularist agenda, which went way beyond that of the *Tanzimat* era or even of the Young Turks, at the same time it reinforced the control over Sunni Islam that the empire had already exercised. The chapter on 'Islam in the Service of the Caliphate and the Secular State' investigates this uniquely Turkish ambivalence in the relationship between state and religion.

All of these chapters deal with ideologies and policies formulated at the centre, be it the central committee of the CUP, the leadership of the national resistance movement or the government of the early republic. This is fairly typical, not only of my own work, but of the field in general. The historiography of the Kemalist republic is completely dominated by the centre, its ideas, its plans and ambitions and its infighting. It is healthy, therefore, to also include at least one chapter that looks at the actual impact of the reforms on the country at large after 15 years of Kemalist rule. The chapter based on the travelogues of Anhegger, Tietze and Linke is an attempt to look away from the centre and it yields some surprising results, clearly demonstrating how important it is to distinguish between the policies of the centre and the realities on the ground. Six years after its original publication there is still a great need for studies on the impact of the Kemalist regime on the population outside the major towns. There have been some attempts to look at the history of modern Turkey through the lens of local communities, as in Michael Meeker's very important anthropological study *A Nation of Empire* (which combines anthropological with historical methodologies)[1] and some younger scholars are trying their hand at subaltern history of the period, but the difficulty of this approach is that there is a great scarcity of authentic source materials so that one is forced to get at the people's voice through the records of the authorities of a very authoritarian state.[2] There can be little doubt that the subaltern history approach that has been so fruitful in the case of Indian history in spite of all its difficulties,[3] still holds a lot of promise for the field of Turkish studies.

212

16. Young Turks, Ottoman Muslims and Turkish Nationalists: Identity Politics 1908–38*

When did the Turks start identifying themselves primarily as 'Turks'? More specifically, when did they begin to see the state to which they belonged primarily as the political home of the Turks, instead of as the Ottomans' state or the Islamic Caliphate? For the majority of the population, those questions are impossible to answer. At the time the Republic of Turkey was established only slightly over 10 per cent of the population was able to read and write, and sociological and anthropological field work really took off only in the post-World War II era. Yet even if we confine ourselves to the ideological make up of the élite, or just to that of the political leadership, the questions remain very complicated.

The Young Turks

All through the nineteenth century, nationalism proved a debilitating virus for the multinational Islamic state that was the Ottoman Empire. As it infected first the Serbs and the Greeks, then the Bulgarians and the Armenians, nationalist agitators tried, in many cases successfully, to provoke intervention by the major powers of the day (Russia, Britain and France) to further their aims. Meanwhile, successive Ottoman governments seemed powerless to halt the disintegration of the empire in the face of the combined efforts of those Ottoman Christian nationalists and foreign diplomats.[1] From the late 1880s onward, young (junior) Ottoman bureaucrats, who had been educated in the modern, European-style colleges of the empire and often had studied in Europe as well, became increasingly restless under the apparent impotence of the government they served, in the face of this double nationalist and imperialist challenge. People with such a background founded the Young Turk movement in 1889, the centenary of the French revolution.

The Young Turks started a campaign of agitation and subversion to overthrow the autocratic Sultan Abdülhamit II and establish a constitutional, parliamentary regime (with which the Ottoman Empire had a few months experience before the Sultan suspended it in 1878). Establishing such a regime, they hoped, would cut the ground from under the feet of both the nationalist separatists and the European imperialists, taking away their arguments for intervention in the internal affairs of the empire. As Hanioğlu has shown, however, their espousal of constitutionalism clashed with their elitism.[2] Their background as members of the administrative élite and their adherence to positivism, with its fundamentally undemocratic attitudes and deep-rooted mistrust of the masses, led them to see themselves as an enlightened élite on a mission to educate their people. In their eyes, the constitution was an instrument and an emblem of modernity, but not a goal per se. The history of both the second constitutional period and the Republic would show that when the Young Turk and Kemalist leadership faced a choice between modernization and genuine democracy, they always opted for the former.[3]

During its first 15 years, the Young Turk movement largely confined itself to holding meetings, writing pamphlets and distributing illegal newspapers. Then in 1906 a new activist organization based in Salonica, the 'Ottoman Freedom Society' (*Osmanlı Hürriyet Cemiyeti*) started to spread throughout the officer corps of the Third and Second Ottoman Armies in Macedonia and Thrace. The following year it merged with the most influential Young Turk organization abroad, the Committee of Union and Progress (*İttihat ve Terakki Cemiyeti*), and at the request of the leadership of the unified society, the officers in Macedonia and Thrace raised the standard of revolt in July 1908, forcing the Sultan to reinstate the parliament and constitution.[4]

Ideological debates

Under Abdülhamit, extremely strict censorship had banned any political discussion from the Ottoman media. Although some public debate had been kept going by the Young Turk emigrants in Europe, until 1906 they remained preoccupied with scientific and cultural questions and despised 'pure politics'.[5] Their primary concern was to instil a positivist mentality and worldview in the Ottoman public so they had given scarcely any thought to what their political programme would be once the constitutional-parliamentary system was reinstated.

214

Binding element! [handwritten]

After the revolution of July 1908 the situation in the empire changed dramatically. The number of newspapers and magazines increased thirty fold, fostering a very lively debate about all kinds of questions. The one question, however, that occupied the Young Turks more than any other was 'How can this [the Ottoman] state be saved?'[6] In this context they addressed two sets of problems: how the empire could be modernized sufficiently (and sufficiently quickly) to take its place among the leading powers of the world and what would be the binding element, on which the state would be built (what Bernard Lewis has called 'the questions of corporate political identity').[7] In the historiography of Turkey, the debate on the second question traditionally is depicted as a contest among three currents of thinking: Ottomanism, (Pan-)Islamism and (Pan-) Turkism. This representation is as old as the debate itself, going back to the famous essay 'Three types of policy' (*Üç Tarz-ı Siyaset*) published by the Tatar Yusuf Akçura in the Turkist 'émigré' paper *Türk* in Cairo in 1904,[8] although modern scholars generally have failed to appreciate that Akçura's position at the time was highly exceptional.   *3 currents of Thinking* [handwritten]

Ottomanism was the idea that all of the different ethnic and religious communities of the Empire would coalesce into one Ottoman citizenry and remain loyal to the Ottoman dynasty if only Muslims and non-Muslims were granted full equality before the law and parliamentary representation. Its adherents themselves called it the *İttihad-ı Anasır,* or 'Unity of the Elements'. This ideal, which originated in the 1860s, had been the official ideology of the Ottoman Constitution of 1876[9] as well as of the constitutional revolution which restored it in 1908, but it is debatable how many of the revolutionaries actually believed in Ottomanism.

The second of the three currents, Islamism, took the community of Muslims, the *ümmet,* as its basis and saw return to Islamic values and Islamic law as preconditions for a regeneration of the Ottoman state. It, too, had its origins in the intellectual movement of the 1860s. Pan-Islamism, the expansionist version of this ideology, had gained popularity and government backing under Sultan Abdülhamit II (1876–1909) and aimed at strengthening the bonds within the Muslim world community under the aegis of the Ottoman Sultan/Caliph. The Young Turks in exile constantly wrote about the cultural, social and economic development of the Islamic community, interpreting Qur'an and tradition in a positivist and materialistic way,[10] but they did not develop an Islamist political programme. Soon after the revolution and 'liberation' of July 1908, the Committee of Union and Progress (CUP) became deeply suspicious of Islamist political activity when activists of the

'Muhammadan Union' (*İttihad-ı Muhammedi*) led a failed attempt at coun-terrevolution against the constitutional regime in April 1909. This counter-revolution and the ease with which it swept the Young Turks from power in the capital before they managed to reinstate the constitutional order by force of arms came as an enormous shock.[11] The Young Turks were quite prepared to use Islam, however, especially to strengthen the international position of the empire, having the Sultan proclaim Holy War (*cihat*) in 1914.[12]

Turkish nationalism was the youngest of the currents and really not one, but two different movements. The older was Pan-Turkism, which originated among the Tatars of Kazan on the Volga, of the Crimea and of Azerbaijan and was brought to the Ottoman Empire by Russian émigrés after 1908. Emphasizing the common historical roots of the Turkic peoples (including the Ottomans), its programme consisted of the cultural and political uni-fication of these peoples.[13] From 1911 onwards, Pan-Turkist nationalists had their own organization in the 'Turkish Hearths' (*Türk Ocakları*) which were closely linked to the CUP. The younger Turkish nationalist movement romantically idealized the Anatolian peasants as the 'real Turks', whose vir-tues should be rediscovered and adopted by the Ottomans. It gained impetus after 1913 and particularly with the founding of the *Halka Doğru* (Towards the People) movement by the CUP in 1917.[14]

Some authors, taking their cue from Niyazi Berkes' highly influential work, *The Development of Secularism in Turkey*, have described the debate as being among 'Islamists, Turkists and Westernists'.[15] These were indeed the labels used during the second constitutional period (mainly by opponents of the movements in question), but they confuse the issue. In fact, the debate about the degree of Westernization permitted, or needed, for the empire's survival and regeneration was quite different from, and ran right through, the debate on corporate political identity. Among the Islamists in particu-lar there was wide variation between those prepared to accept considerable Westernization in order to strengthen the Islamic community and those who rejected any kind of innovation.[16] Conversely, the positivist Westernists dif-fered in the extent to which they tried to clothe their ideas in Islamic ter-minology or reconcile them with Islamic doctrine. Berkes' discussion in the part of his book entitled 'In Search of a Fulcrum' actually concerns finding a fulcrum for the regeneration of society rather than its political identity.

The traditional representation of ideological development

Most traditional accounts of the debates on national identity depict the Young Turks as gradually discarding both Ottomanism (because the

216

Greeks, Macedonians, Bulgars and Armenians did not renounce their nationalist claims in exchange for equality after the constitutional revolution) and Islamism (because first the Albanians and later the Arabs developed separatist movements of their own). Turkism then remained the only option. During World War I, especially after the Russian Revolution seemed to open the way to Central Asia, the Pan-Turkist variety gained strength with Enver Pasha, the Young Turk *generalissimo* and war minister, as its strongest advocate. After the defeat in the World War Turkish nationalism still remained the only option, but the Turkish resistance movement led by Mustafa Kemal Pasha, the later Atatürk, opted for Anatolian Turkish nationalism and rejected irredentist claims. This, roughly, is how the ideological development of the Young Turks has been described from the 1920s onward by influential writers such as Toynbee and Luke and in many textbooks of today, such as those by Stanford Shaw and Geoffrey Lewis.[17]

Hanioğlu, however, takes a different view. He maintains that the CUP centre in Paris was gradually converted to Turkish nationalism before the constitutional revolution, in the period 1902–6, so that by 1906 'CUP propaganda realized a nationalist focus'.[18] Hanioğlu also states that this change was accomplished under pressure from groups formed to counter the Greek and Armenian committees, which themselves were working in the empire at a time when Balkan Turkish journals claimed that 'Islam and nationalism had merged into a single construct.' In view of what I hope to demonstrate later, the fact that the changeover to nationalism was made in these circumstances is highly significant, for it leads me to doubt that the nationalism of the Young Turks was truly 'Turkish'.

Young Turk ideology and CUP policies

The ideological debates of the second constitutional period have been the subject of extensive study, both inside Turkey and outside Turkey and rightly so. They form an important experimental phase in the modern history of Turkey. By contrast, there never has been any attempt to relate the ideological debates of the years between 1908 and 1918 to the actual policies of the Young Turks in those years. When the policies are mentioned, it is only to point out that they were inconsistent, seeming to be Ottomanist at one point and Islamist or Turkist at others. In others words, there seems to be a tacit assumption that the ideological constructs of journalists, educators and academics formed the frame of reference for the political leadership of the Young Turks and thus determined their actions and the role they played in the creation of modern Turkey. But in my view this is very questionable. It is quite conceivable, indeed probable, that the politicians formed their policies under the impetus of fast-changing political realities of the day and used the ideological toolkit available to them in an essentially pragmatic manner.

Although the people who actually brought about the revolution in 1908 formally belonged to the same CUP to which most of the émigrés in Europe belonged, since 1906 the character of the organization had changed dramatically. In 1906 the arrival in Paris of Dr Bahaettin Şakir and Dr Nâzim gave the CUP organizational strength and an activist programme, and in the same year the 'Ottoman Freedom Society' (*Osmanlı Hürriyet Cemiyeti*) was founded by Mehmet Talât and his circle in Salonica. As the new group built up a network among the officers of the Ottoman army in Europe, it kept in close contact with Bahaettin Şakir and Nâzim and in 1907 decided to adopt the hallowed name of the older organization. This 'new' CUP was now dominated by activists, not publicists, that is, by Bahaettin Şakir, Tâlat and Enver, not Ahmet Rıza, Abdullah Cevdet and *Mizancı* Murat. After the revolution the latter were honoured (in some cases), but not trusted with any real power.[19]

Although the activists had not written about ideological issues to any great extent and probably were not that interested in them, for a decade and a half (1908–23) their actions largely determined the course of Ottoman history. If we are to understand the history of the period (and its legacy), therefore, it is essential that we understand what made these Young Turk politicians tick, but we have to take their actions as our point of departure, rather than try to place them in the Ottomanism-Islamism-Turkism paradigm. The activists of the CUP, who had been the strongest political force in the country from 1908 to 1913, held a monopoly of power between their coup d'état in January 1913 and the Ottoman defeat in World War I in October 1918. Subsequently, until 1922 former CUP leaders initiated and shaped the national independence movement, which fought off attempts to hand parts of Anatolia to the Greeks and Armenians, and in October 1923 gave rise to the Turkish Republic.[20] Consequently we can learn from that movement how the Young Turks used political power and whether the Ottomanism-Islamism-Turkism debate really did influence or even determine the course adopted by the Young Turk political leaders.

The argument of this chapter is threefold. First, I contend that, if we look at the actual policies of the decennium 1913–23, those policies do not,

[handwritten: Turmoil of the years 1912-22 & psyche of people]

in fact, seem to relate very closely to any of the ideological currents described above. Second, given that discrepancy, the policies – rather than the ideological debates – are what shaped both the Turkey that emerged from the turmoil of the years 1912–22 and the psyche of its people. I shall try to demonstrate this point by discussing four of the most important developments of those years: the attempts to nationalize the economy, the persecution of Ottoman Christians during World War I, the struggle for independence after the war, and finally the population exchange of 1923–4. Third, I shall briefly analyse the nationality concept of the early Republic, to determine where it constituted a break with the immediate past.

[handwritten: a break or continuity ?]

National economy

The programme of the 'National Economy' (*Millî İktisat*) launched in 1914,[21] constituted a break with the economic policies pursued between 1908 and 1913, which had been liberal in the classical sense. Between 1903 and 1913, the Young Turks by and large had expected economic development to result from free market policies, but growing disillusionment with the liberal countries of Europe, as well as increased German influence, engendered a shift to economic nationalism. At the start of the World War, with the European powers occupied elsewhere, the Unionists unilaterally abolished the capitulations on 1 October 1914.

The Young Turk government now proceeded to build a strong 'national' bourgeoisie by forming entrepreneurial cadres from among the Muslim traders, guild members and even bureaucrats.[22] They then encouraged the members of this embryonic bourgeoisie to accumulate capital by exploiting the wartime market conditions that made extensive profiteering possible. The 'National Economy' programme gained impetus from 1915 onwards. As 80 new joint-stock companies were founded between 1916 and 1918 with the active support of the CUP, traders and small businesses were organized into large societies and encouraged to invest their profits in the new companies.

The war created an extraordinary demand for all kinds of goods, especially foodstuffs, because the empire was cut off from its traditional suppliers Rumania and Ukraine. The rising demand, in turn, created new wealth in the countryside, but not through the operation of market forces alone. The CUP government and army held a monopoly or railway transport, so only provincial merchants with good political connections managed to get the necessary freight cars to transport wheat to Istanbul or to the army.

219

While this policy led to the intended capital accumulation by the Muslim traders, large landowners and Unionist functionaries, the price for it was, of course, paid by consumers and by Greek and Armenian businessmen, who did not have political backing like their Muslim competitors. The non-Turks were forced to use Turkish in their administration and to take Muslims onto their boards as all kinds of pressures were brought to bear on them by the government and by the Unionist 'secret army', the *Teşkilât-i Mahsusa* (Special Organization).[23] Approximately 130,000 Greeks from the western coastal zone alone left for Greece, and many Armenians decided to emigrate as well, leaving their companies to be bought by the new Muslim businessmen (or would-be businessmen) at far below their market value. Celâl Bayar,[24] who was in charge of the 'nationalization' (*millileştirme*) campaign in Izmir/Smyrna, quotes in his memoirs a report by a Special Organization agent describing the removal of the 'internal tumors' whose 'treacherous and shameless greed' endangered the country – in other words, how the Greeks were driven out of business.[25]

The persecution of the Armenians

As is well known, the Young Turks' confrontation with the Christian communities during the war was not limited to the business sector, for beginning in early 1915 they carried out a large-scale persecution of the Armenian community. There is a voluminous, but also very polemical, literature on the subject, both by Armenians and by Turks and supporters of the Turkish position. Nevertheless, I think the testimony of the survivors, the reports of German and Austrian officials (allies of the Young Turk government of the day), and the proceedings of the post-war court martial in Istanbul, which tried a number of people accused of involvement in genocide, all offer convincing evidence that an inner circle within the CUP used the deportations (which were horrendous enough in themselves) to execute a planned 'ethnic cleansing' or genocide of the Armenian population. While many Ottoman provincial and military officials opposed the killings, the provincial party chiefs and special emissaries pushed them through, utilizing the forces of the Special Organization.[26]

The persecution of the Armenians can be understood only in the context of the traumas suffered previously by the Muslims of the empire, fully one quarter of whom were either fugitives from Russia and the Balkans or the children of fugitives. Those same Young Turks who ordered and executed the wholesale killing of Armenians had seen the European provinces where many of them were born and raised lost in the Balkan War. They joined the CUP while serving in the fight against separatist Greek, Macedonian and Bulgarian bands in Macedonia and Thrace, and now they were convinced that what had happened in the Caucasus and the Balkans was about to repeat itself in Anatolia. In this sense the genocide was a product of the reactive Muslim nationalism that motivated the Young Turks.

At the same time, the persecution of the Armenians shaped and polarized identities in Anatolia. After the massacres, no Armenian could regard himself wholeheartedly as an Ottoman citizen. The thousands of Muslims who had been directly involved in the persecution and the hundreds of thousands who had witnessed them, could no longer envisage living in anything but a Muslim state. This was, of course, especially true for the CUP functionaries from top-level politicians, military leaders and provincial governors down to the Special Organization thugs who did the actual killing. These people then were the first to support the struggle for continued Ottoman Muslim independence in Anatolia, known in Turkish historiography as the *Millî Mücadele* (National Struggle) or *Kurtuluş Savaşı* (Liberation War). It is no exaggeration to say that the period of the national independence movement (between 1918 and 1920) and the subsequent war for independence (between 1920 and 1922) was the zenith of Ottoman Muslim nationalism.

The national independence movement

The Ottoman Empire, having been defeated by the British in Palestine and Mesopotamia, was forced to conclude an armistice on 30 October 1918. In the following months and years successive governments in Istanbul considered close cooperation with the victorious Allies as their only option. Leading members of the Young Turk Committee of Union and Progress, who had been in power before and during the war and had foreseen the dismemberment of what remained of the Ottoman possessions, however, had prepared the ground both for armed resistance and for the mobilization of public opinion even before the war ended. 'Societies for the Defence of the National Rights' were founded in many different places, nearly always by members of the local branches of the CUP, sometimes in conjunction with the representatives of their province in the capital. These local Unionist leaders co-opted notables, such as *müftüs* (Islamic legal advisors) and *eşraf* (officially recognized descendants of the Prophet Muhammad, members of the local élite) onto the boards of the societies which emphatically declared their non-partisan status. The first thing the societies did was to organize a regional congress whose participants were invited, rather than elected, from among the notables and Unionist party bosses. All in all, 28 of these congresses were held between 5 November 1918 and 9 October 1920, 3 of them in 1918, 17 in 1919 and 8 in 1920.[27] Not surprisingly the resistance societies organized earliest and were most active in areas under the greatest threat of cession to Greece, Armenia or one of the victorious Allies: the six easternmost provinces (which were claimed by the Armenians), Cilicia (claimed by France *and* the Armenians) and the mixed areas in the west around Izmir (Smyrna) and in Thrace that Greek Prime Minister Venizelos claimed for his country.

The Republic of Turkey proclaimed in October 1923, which developed into a Western-oriented, secularist and Turkish nationalist state, had its roots in the Anatolian resistance movement of 1918–22, so modern Turkish historiography, shaped as it has been by the nation-building policies of the early republic, sees the resistance as Turkish nationalist from its start. Indeed the period of the resistance movement (1919–22) is relegated to the status of prehistory of the Republic. This is clear not only in the periodization used by Turkish textbooks, but also in the fact that the first nationwide congress of the resistance movement at Sivas in September 1919 is retrospectively claimed as the first congress of the Republican People's Party, which was founded by Mustafa Kemal Pasha (Atatürk) only in 1923. Although Western historiography on the whole has taken its cue from this Turkish interpretation, the important role of religion in the 'nationalist' mobilization of the Anatolian peasantry was recognized as early as 1936 by the unrivalled authority on the Turkish independence movement, Gotthard Jäschke,[28] and 20 years later by Dankwart Rustow.[29] Rustow emphasizes that the national independence struggle had a strong Islamic flavour and was waged until the end in the name of caliphate and sultanate. Kemal Karpat has also pointed to the identification of nationalism with religion among the Turkish population,[30] and recently this aspect has been emphasized by Binnaz Toprak.[31] The two last named authors, however, see the role of Islam as that of a tactical instrument. They speak about the political use of religion by an implicitly non-Islamic, or not primarily Islamic, leadership, and they see the leaders' Islamic rhetoric as the translation of abstract notions, such as the 'nation', into the discourse of the peasant population.[32] Feroz Ahmad makes a slightly different point when he says, 'The nationalists were forced to use Islamic propaganda *by an appeal to religious sentiments.*

in order to counter Istanbul's propaganda against them.'[33] All of these authors thus seem to agree that the rural population of Anatolia could only be won over to the cause of the resistance by an appeal to religious sentiments. But is it really true that what we have here is a 'translation' of a nationalist message?

If we try to look at the movement afresh, without taking into account its eventual outcome, a different picture emerges from the avowed aims of its founders. In the week after the armistice was concluded, on 5 November 1918 the *Millî İslam Şurası* (National Muslim Council) was founded in Kars, the chief town in the three eastern provinces, which had been Russian between 1878 and 1917, were reconquered by the Ottoman army in 1918, and now were expected to be ceded to the Armenians at the peace conference in Paris. The new organization's name is significant. Although the word 'şura' undoubtedly is a translation of the Russian term 'soviet', 'Islam' appears to be a synonym of 'Muslim' in the usage of the leaders of the council (thus denoting the person or persons rather than the belief system, a usage that still is current in Turkey).[34] The stated aim of the council was to prevent 'the splitting up the Muslim population living in the Caucasus' (*ahâli-i islâmiyye'nin tefrik-i ictimaları*).[35] Like all of the later congresses of local 'Defence of Rights' societies, they produced material 'proving' that the majority of the population in their area had been Muslim even before the war. This was essential because all such societies and, indeed, the later nationwide resistance movement based their claims on President Woodrow Wilson's 'Fourteen Points' and the principle of self-determination for 'the Turkish parts of the Ottoman Empire' embedded in them.[36] The organization in Kars, which had changed its name to 'Temporary Government of the South Western Caucasus', was suppressed by the British on 17 April 1919. Subsequently the torch of resistance passed to organizations in Trabzon and Erzurum further to the west. Held in July 1919, the congress of Erzurum, representing the seven easternmost provinces,[37] generally is considered the real starting point of the resistance movement. It is, therefore, important that we look closely at the statutes of the 'Organization for the Defence of the National Rights of the Eastern Provinces', which convened the conference, as well as at the proclamation and decisions of the congress itself.

According to article 1 of the statutes that the organization submitted to the governor of Erzurum to comply with the empire's Law on Associations, its goal was 'to defend the historic and national rights (*hukuk-u tarihiye ve milliye*) of the Muslim population' (*ahâli-i islâmiye*).[38] The report issued by the local congress held in Erzurum on 17 June in preparation for the regional one held one month later refers to 'the Muslims who form one nation (*millet*), consisting of Turks and Kurds'[39] and to 'the Muslim majority consisting of Turks and Kurds who for centuries have mixed their blood in an intimate relationship and who form the community (*ümmet*) of one prophet'.[40] The statutes of the society organizing the Erzurum congress, however, speak about 'all Islamic elements (*bilcümle anasır-ı islâmiye*) of the population'[41] and say that 'all Muslim compatriots (*bilumûm islâm vatandaşlar*) are natural members of this society.'[42] A few passages in the Erzurum documents mention Turkish as an ethnic identity, but even in most of these, the concepts of 'Turkish and Islamic' are closely linked. Just as it described the Turks and Kurds as forming one community (*ümmet*), the proclamation of the local Erzurum branch countered Armenian claims that the Turks 'have only ever destroyed civilizations' by saying that '(Erzurum) was a pasture of Turkish tribes and that Islam had sent its light as far as this area when it first appeared'. The Seljuk dynasty had spread 'Turkish culture and Islamic civilization' (*Türk harsını ve islam medeniyeti* – a formula taken directly from the writings of the Young Turk ideologue Ziya Gökalp).[43] The proclamation goes on to say that the Armenian population of the eastern provinces has never been above 15 per cent and that 'the voice of truth, which had risen from the other side of the ocean (meaning President Wilson) will never recognize the right to rule over these lands of any nation but the Turks.' Here, the use of 'Turks' may simply be borrowed from the American original of President Wilson's Fourteen Points. Although in the congress report of the Erzurum branch the Turks are described as 'an oppressed race' (*mazlûm bir ırk*), that use of a racially based concept of ethnicity seems to have been extremely rare.[44]

What the society aims to achieve in political terms is made abundantly clear: it portrays itself as the 'guard of the Islamic Caliphate and the Ottoman Sultanate' and the 'real protector of the Muslim rights'.[45] The latter term, *hukuk-u islamiye*, appears to be a synonym for the better known and more widely used *hukuk-u milliye* (national rights). The Muslims it represents want to remain part and parcel of the Ottoman Empire. Apart from the terms one would expect in this context ('Ottoman state' or *devlet-i Osmaniye* and 'Ottoman rule' or *hakimiyet-i Osmaniye* as well as the above-mentioned 'Ottoman Sultanate') the society states it desire not to be separated from the 'Ottoman and Islamic community' (*camia-i Osmaniye ve islamiye*).

In the Western Anatolian regions that were in danger of cession to Greece, the Muslim population was dominated more clearly by a Turkish majority. There Kurds are not explicitly mentioned in the documents put out by 'Defence of Rights' organizations, but at the congresses of Balıkesir and Alaşehir, which were held almost simultaneously with that in Erzurum (in July and August 1919 respectively), the resolutions address 'our beloved Turkish and Muslim compatriots' and talk about 'our Turkish and Islamic fatherland (*Türk ve müslüman olan memleketimiz*) and our holy ground colored red by the blood sacrificed for our religion'. In different places within the same proclamation first 'our innocent Muslim brothers and sisters' and then 'all of our Turkish brothers and sisters' are mentioned. Similarly the 'compatriots of Anatolia' (*Anadolu vatandaşlar*) work with 'religious and patriotic feelings' (*hiss-i dinî ve vatanperverî*).[46]

In September 1919, after an abortive attempt in June, a congress purporting to speak on behalf of all the regional resistance initiatives in Anatolia and in European Turkey was finally convened by Mustafa Kemal Pasha in Sivas.[47] It adopted the resolutions of the congress in Erzurum and likewise made Muslim solidarity the basis of all activities to preserve existence of 'our state which belongs to the Muslims'.[48] As in Erzurum, the documents emanating from the congress in Sivas make very clear who the enemy is: 'movements which strive for the establishment of Greek or Armenian entities (*Rumluk ve Ermenilik*) on Ottoman soil'. Yet the terminology also makes clear that the members of the congress were not against Greece (*Yunanistan*) or Armenia (*Ermenistan*) as such, but only against Greek or Armenian entities within the armistice lines. Indeed, Mustafa Kemal Pasha, the president of the congress and of the representative committee, himself stated in an interview on 25 October 1919 that the nationalists 'were in favor of an Armenia outside the Ottoman borders'.[49] What the congress demands is that those parts of the empire inhabited by a Muslim majority be recognized as inseparable from each other and from 'the Ottoman community', for the 'Islamic elements' (*anasır-ı islâmiye*) living there are 'true brothers' (*öz kardeşler*) who respect each other's racial (*ırkiye*) and social rights.[50] Article 6 of the same document adduces another argument and another definition of the area that should remain united and independent, speaking about '(these lands) where cultural and civil superiority belongs to the Muslims (*harsî ve medenî faikiyet*)'. As had the Erzurum congress it thus uses a formula that echoes the thinking of Ziya Gökalp.[51]

In his own speeches and declarations during the early phase of the struggle, Mustafa Kemal Pasha was extremely cautious when describing the national basis of the movement; his central terms were *millet* ('nation') and *millî* ('national'). In his 15-minute opening speech at Sivas the terms occur 41 times, but, as Rustow has remarked, they undoubtedly still had religious connotations for most Ottoman Muslims.[52] This point recently has been repeated by Feroz Ahmad, who notes that 'millî came to mean national… through evolution.'[53] Indeed one could argue that even today the *millî* in *millî görüş* carries a very different meaning from that in *millî piyango* – in other words: that the religious and national meanings of the term have continued to exist side by side and that, if we are to use Darwinian concepts, the older species has not died out.

In his opening speech at Sivas Kemal explained that the Allies were breaching the conditions laid down in the armistice and encroaching upon the rights of the Ottomans every day. Next he described the inactivity and treason of the central government in the face of the injustices perpetrated by the Allies and argued that, therefore, the nation could find salvation only in its own spirit (*ruh*). Although, according to Kemal, the congresses at Erzurum and Sivas represented this 'national spirit' (*ruh-u millî*), the religious flavour was there, too: The Greek oppressors have entered 'the innermost shrine of Islam (*İslam'ın harîm-i ismet*) in the Western Anatolia'. In addition, he spoke about the preservation of the 'sacred things' (*mukaddesat*) of the nation and the country.[54] This latter term later became identified with the conservative religious wing within Kemal's national movement, which founded the '*Muhafaza-i Mukaddesat Cemiyeti*' or 'Society for the Preservation of Sacred Things' in Erzurum in March 1921.

In December 1919, the leadership of the resistance movement, the 'Representative Committee' headed by Mustafa Kemal, moved from Sivas to Ankara, which had a more central location and a direct rail link with the outside world. In a speech to notables in Ankara,[55] immediately after his arrival, Kemal again related how the Allies had trampled underfoot both the principles laid down by President Wilson and the original conditions of the armistice. He then described the work of the congresses at Erzurum and Sivas and set out the goals of the movement: 'saving the fatherland from dismemberment and the nation from captivity' (*vatanın inkısamdan ve milletin esaretten tahlisi*).[56] Again Kemal constantly used the term 'nation' (*millet*). First, he mentioned the 'Ottoman state and nation' (*Osmanlı devlet ve milleti*) which seems to indicate a political definition of the concept, but he went on to give a definite religious meaning to *millet*, albeit without actually describing the nation as 'Muslim' or 'Islamic'. He apparently took its Muslim character for granted. For instance, he rejected claims that 'our nation' was oppressive by pointing out that 'our nation' had granted the non-Muslims every freedom ever since the conquest of Constantinople.[57] He very much spoke in terms of 'us' and 'them' as in *biz, bizimle beraber yaşayan anasır-i gayrimuslime* ('we and the non-Muslim elements living among us').[58] By implication, the 'we' must have meant 'we Ottoman Muslims'.

Kemal did not use the ethnic concept of nationality at the time he moved to Ankara. The word 'Turk' does not occur in the text of his speeches, so in this respect he appears to have trod even more carefully than the congresses did in their official statements. He did use the term 'Turkey' (*Türkiye*) several times to describe the country for whose liberty the fight was being waged, something we do not see in the earlier documents from Kars, Erzurum or Sivas. It could be misleading, however, to read into this an indication that Kemal was already thinking of a new Turkish state to replace the Ottoman Empire. True, he later claimed to cherish this ambition as a 'national secret' (*millî sır*) that he could not divulge until the time and public opinion would he ripe for it,[59] and although there is no contemporary evidence to support his claim, it is quite conceivable in light of his later policies. But in his speech in December 1919 he also referred to the persecution of the Armenians in 1915–17 as *Türkiye'de zuhûra gelmiş şayan-i arzu olmayan bazı ahval* ('Some undesirable events which have occurred in Turkey')[60] apparently using 'Turkey' simply as a synonym for 'Ottoman Empire'.

Kemal employed two arguments to defend the 'national borders' (*millî hudud*) laid down in Sivas. First, this was the area controlled and defended by the Ottoman army on the day of the armistice. Furthermore, 'this border delineates the part of our fatherland inhabited by Kurds and Turks. To the south of it live our Arabic- speaking co-religionists.'[61] He proceeded to express his solidarity with the Arabs and wished 'our co-religionists (*dinda ş-larımız*), our brothers and sisters', success in their efforts to liberate every corner of the 'world of Islam' (*alem-i İslâm*) without making their liberation part of his own programme.[62] Parting with the Arab provinces does not seem to have been a problem for the leadership of the resistance movement, who simply did not see them as part of the fatherland. Even before the end of the World War many of the Young Turk officers and administrators serving in the Arab provinces had come to realize how tenuous were the cultural, social and political links between those areas and the Ottoman centre.[63] In many memoirs Turkish officers depict the Arab troops as very much unreliable. The Arab troops felt they were being sacrificed in a cause they did not understand, and the Arab population often appeared to be hostile. In short, because nearly all of the leading cadres of the national movement had served in the Arab provinces during the war, they were far too disillusioned to harbour any dreams of re-establishing Ottoman rule there.

The official demands of the national resistance movement were laid down in January 1920 in the so-called National Pact (*Misâk-i millî*).[64] Adopted by the last Ottoman parliament on 28 January 1920 and published three weeks later, it remained the official statement of aims of the resistance movement until the conclusion of the Peace of Lausanne in 1923. This document closely follows the provisions of Erzurum and Sivas. It demands the right of self-determination through a plebiscite for the population of the Arab provinces, Western Thrace (i.e. west of the Maritza River) and the three easternmost provinces of Kars, Ardahan and Batumi. Its central statement, however, is that:

The totality of the parts within the lines of the armistice[65] which are inhabited by an Ottoman Muslim majority, which is united in religion, race and origin,[66] and imbued with feelings of the fullest mutual respect and sacrifice and with full consideration for each other's racial and social rights and circumstances, forms a whole whose partition cannot be accepted in reality or in law for any reason whatsoever.

(*Bu mütareke hattı içinde dînen, ırkan ve aslen müttehit yekdiğerine karşı hürmet-i mütekabile ve fedâkarlık hissiyatiyle meşhun ve hukuk-u ırkiye ve ictimaiyeleriyle şerait-i muhitiyelerine tamamiyle riayetkâr Osmanlı İslam ekseriyetiyle meskûn bulunan aksamın heyet-i mecmuası hakikaten veya hükmen hiç bir sebeple tefrik kabul etmez bir küldür*).[67]

The population exchange

The victory of the Defence of Rights movement was recognized, after difficult and long drawn out negotiations, in the Peace Treaty of Lausanne (1923). The ambitions of the National Pact were not realized completely in Lausanne, but its main demand, unity and independence for the Muslims within the armistice lines, was largely met. Lausanne also meant a major step in the direction of the creation of a homogenous Muslim state.

In appendix 6 of the Lausanne treaty, signed on 30 January 1923, Turkey and Greece agreed upon an exchange of populations. Mass migration had, of course, been a feature of the history of the region for a century. Over 2 million Muslims had migrated from the Caucasus to the Ottoman Empire rather than remain under Russian rule; 800,000 Muslims had fled from Bulgaria and Rumania in 1877–8 and 400,000 had emigrated to the empire during and after the Balkan War of 1912–13. The same Balkan War had led to increased pressure on the Greeks of the Ottoman Empire, over 130,000 of whom had decided, or been forced, to leave for Greece in 1913–14. Many of the surviving Armenians, too, had fled the country. The agreement of January 1923 thus constituted the final act in a long drama in these ethnically, linguistically and religiously mixed lands.

The significance of the population exchange, therefore, is not that it was a novelty. Even the mechanism of a formal exchange of populations between states was not new as Greece and Bulgaria had concluded a very similar agreement in 1919 (with the significant difference that under that agreement the exchange formally was on a voluntary basis). From the viewpoint of this chapter, what was significant in 1923 was that the criterion for deportation was religious affiliation and nothing else. According to the first article of the agreement:

> From the First of May, 1923 a start will be made with the forced exchange of the Turkish citizens of Greek Orthodox faith who live on Turkish soil with the Greek citizens of Muslim faith who live on Greek soil ... [68]

All told, over 1.2 million Greek Orthodox were exchanged with 400,000 Muslims and the exchange included those Greek Orthodox citizens, the *Karamanlı*, who spoke only Turkish.[69] As a matter of fact, however, the population exchange agreement put an official seal on something that already had taken place, for most Greek inhabitants of Western Anatolia had already left the country, and the communities exchanged, apart from the *Karamanlı*, mostly hailed from the Black Sea Coast. That Greeks and Turks alike were of the opinion that it was Orthodox Christians and Muslims who could no longer live together, again indicates the total dominance of the religious component in the identities shaped in the preceding decade.

Conclusion

My conclusion, therefore, would be that the political and military leaders of the crucial decade under review were guided not by Ottomanism, not by Turkism and not by Islamism. The Young Turks were not guided by Ottomanism because they did not desire to win over the non-Muslim communities by granting them equal rights; quite the opposite was true. They consistently aimed at reducing the Greeks and Armenians' position in society in order to become masters in their own Ottoman Muslim house. Turkism they espoused only in the sense that the majority of Ottoman Muslims, certainly in the west of the country, were Turks and the terms 'Turkish' and 'Muslim' often were interchangeable or used in juxtaposition (*Türk-Müslüman Unsuru*) there unlike in the mixed areas of the empire, where the term *Müslüman* covered Turks, Kurds, Arabs and other groups. Indeed the role of expansionist Pan-Turkism to my mind is vastly overrated, especially by Armenian historians, as it was never widespread. The dominant ideology of the Young Turk politicians of the decade under review was not Islamism either. At first sight this statement may seem surprising after so much evidence of the Muslim character of the policies of the decade. Islamism, however, was not only about taking the Islamic community, the *ümmet*, as the basis for corporate political identity, but also about basing state and society on Islamic values and Islamic law. No trace of these aims is found in the policies of the CUP. On the contrary, once the Unionists were in power, they reduced the influence both of the doctors of Islamic law and of the Islamic law (*şeriat*) itself. The head of the religious hierarchy, the *Şeyhülislam*, was even removed from the cabinet during the World War. Instead Pan-Islamic rhetoric was used, both in the World War and in the War of Independence, only as a political expedient to help strengthen the position of the Ottomans.

Instead, the Unionists were motivated by a peculiar brand of Ottoman-Muslim nationalism, which was to a very high degree reactive. It was defined in a particular and antagonistic relationship between Muslims who had been on the losing side in terms of wealth and power for the best part of a century and Ottoman Christians who had been the winners. The Unionists' ideology was nationalist in the sense that they demanded the establishment of a state of their own: before 1918 they took every step to make the existing Ottoman state the Muslims' own and after 1918 they fought to preserve what remained of that Ottoman Muslim state and to prevent it from being carved up. But the nation for which they demanded this political home was that of the *Ottoman Muslims* – not that of all of the Ottomans, not only that of the Turks and certainly not that of the Muslims of the world. In other words, what we see here is an ethnicizing of religion; the movement was political and not religious, but the nationalist programme is based on an ethnicity whose membership is determined largely by religious affiliation. That is why the Muslim nationalism of the Young Turks could go hand-in-hand with secularist modernizing policies.

The policies of the Unionists were not inconsistent. Ottomanism, Islamism and Turkism were tools to be used to strengthen the position of the Ottoman Muslims (as was Westernization), not ends in themselves. The Unionist politicians, therefore, felt free to use any and all of these ideologies as they saw fit to accomplish their ultimate goal of establishing a strong, modern and unified state.

The legacy inherited by the Turkish republic

The predominance of Muslim nationalism in the formative phase of modern Turkey (the years of the Balkan War, World War I and the war for national independence) is highly relevant to understanding the way the Turkish Republic developed after 1923. According to the traditional teleological account of the Young Turks' ideological development, they discarded Ottomanism and Islamism after 1908 out of disillusionment with the attitude of, respectively, the Christian minorities and the Muslim Albanians and Arabs, leaving Turkish nationalism their only option – and therefore their dominant ideology – after 1913. Creation of a Turkish national state ten years later then was the logical outcome of this development. This account, however, does not explain why the Kemalist regime, which established the secular national state, met with so much stubborn opposition from large parts of the population and even from parts of the national movement itself and why it was voted out of office as soon as that population gained the right to express itself in free elections after World War II. On the other hand, the problems of the Kemalists become understandable if we accept that the formative phase in the development of modern Turkey was a decade totally dominated on the level of politics and of public opinion by an anti-Christian, and especially an anti-Greek and anti-Armenian, Muslim nationalism. In 1923 the Anatolian Muslim population had managed, against all odds, to secure the continued existence of a state of their own in Anatolia, but from 1923–4 on the Kemalist leadership of the Republic broke the bonds of solidarity forged during the preceding ten years and opted instead for far-reaching secularization and for Turkish (as opposed to Ottoman-Muslim) nationalism and nation building.

More research is needed on the reasons underlying the change, but there can be no doubt that the decision was deliberate to seek a new Turkish

Why?

national and secular corporate political identity in order to replace the Ottoman-Muslim one. There was certainly nothing inevitable about it, and the switch was far too sudden to be explicable on the basis of any underlying socio-economic process. One can only assume that the crucial question the Young Turks had faced about corporate political identity lost some of its urgency once independent survival had been secured and the society had become relatively homogeneous in religious terms, so then the question of 'catching up with Europe' again moved to centre-stage. In the debate about Westernization, Kemal and his circle belonged to the radical wing of the Young Turks who believed implicitly in a popularized version of nineteenth-century European positivism. In their eyes only scientific rationalism could form the basis for the modernization leap Turkey would have to make, and only a nation state could give Turkey the coherence needed to compete with the national states of Europe. Because they thus emphasized secularism in their thinking on modernization, they did not find a nationality in which religion was the dominant factor a suitable basis for a nation state. Now that the danger to independence had passed and they could create what they considered the ideal circumstances for successful modernization, they opted for secular Turkish nationalism. This of course precluded any idea of Kurdish autonomy.

Kemalist nation-building

As early as 1923 laws, government proclamations, and the statutes and programs of the People's Party – the direct successor of and heir to the Defence of Rights movement – had ceased to speak of 'Muslims' or 'Kurds and Turks.' The third article of its 1923 statutes states: 'Every Turk and every outsider who accepts Turkish nationality *and culture* [Italics: EJZ] can join the People's Party.'[70] Two years later, on 8 December 1925, the Ministry of Education announced in a proclamation on 'Currents trying to undermine Turkish unity' that use of the terms *Kürt, Laz, Çerkez, Kürdistan* and *Lazistan* would be banned.[71] Subsequently article 5 of the party programme of 1927 declared spreading the Turkish language and culture to be a guiding principle because 'among compatriots unity of language, of feelings and thoughts forms the strongest tie'.[72]

In 1931, at the second (officially, 'third') party congress, 'nationalism' was included among the Six Arrows (*Altı Ok*) that formed the basic principles of the People's Party and were included in the party programme. In the secondary school history text *Tarih* (History), the fourth and final volume of which appeared in the same year, 'Turk' is defined in the context of the second 'arrow': 'Any individual within the Republic of Turkey, whatever his faith, who speaks Turkish, grows up with Turkish culture and adopts the Turkish ideal, is a Turk.'[73] The Kemalist concept of nationality was thus firmly based on language, culture and common purpose ('ideal'). As a result, authors who place the nationalism of the Turkish Republic fully within the traditions of the French Revolution, with its emphasis on national self-determination and its legalist-voluntarist definition of 'nation', claim that Turkish nationalism is in no way based on racial or religious characteristics and that therefore anyone is free to join this nationality.[74] It is not quite so simple, however, because of the way the central concept of 'culture' is defined.

There are surprisingly few texts from the Kemalist period that describe the national basis of the new state. Mustafa Kemal Pasha so constantly appealed to Turkish national pride, exhorting his people to show the world what Turks could accomplish, that the inscription on the monument in Ankara's Güven Park, '*Türk, Çalış, Güven, Öğün!*' (Turk, Work, Trust, Be proud!) well summarizes many of his speeches. Nevertheless, he did not try to define the identity of the nation in either his six-day speech of 1927 or in the speech he gave in 1933 on the tenth anniversary of the Republic, from which is taken the famous dictum '*Ne mutlu Türk'üm diyene!*' (How fortunate is the one who can say 'I am a Turk'). Rather, in most of the speeches *muasir* (modern) and *medenî* (civilized) are the central terms, indicating the Kemalists considered the issue of national identity settled and that, after a decade in which Young Turk leaders had been preoccupied with national survival, they had returned modernizing society to the central position it had held before 1912.

Other texts from the early Republic, where one would expect a high ideological content, also yield very little reflection on the problems of nationality and nationalism. *Ülkü* (Ideal), the journal of the *Halk Evleri* (People's Homes) that were the educational arm of the People's Party from 1932 to 1951, concentrates almost entirely on spreading general knowledge. The booklet *İnkılâp Dersleri* (Revolutionary Lessons) by Recep Peker, the general secretary and 'ideologue' of the People's Party, is equally barren in this respect although Peker obviously is an ardent nationalist defending the 'national state' and a statist, one-party regime with a strong leader. He refutes internationalism, Marxism and liberalism, and he praises the 'national unity' of the Turks, but he does not devote a single paragraph to the nature of modern Turkey's 'corporate political identity'. Still, Peker emphatically rejects expressions of minority identities, such as 'Kurdism' and 'Circassianism', arguing they are 'false conceptions' resulting from historical oppression and that the minority groups are too small numerically to form a nation.[75]

One of the very few people to address the philosophical implication of the kind of nationalism adopted by the Kemalists after 1923 was the Kemalist ideologue Tekin Alp (Moise Cohen) who discusses the Kemalist concept of the nation in his book *Le Kémalisme* published in 1937.[76] He points out that the programme of the People's Party sees unity of language, culture and ideal as constituting the nation and says that these have replaced the older concepts of nationality based on race or religion. Because Tekin Alp considers unity of ideal the self-evident prerequisite for nation-building and language as part of culture, he discusses only the cultural element in detail. Drawing on Ziya Gökalp's distinction between culture (*hars*) and civilization (*medeniyet*),[77] Tekin Alp states that culture consists of the sentiments and attitudes adopted from earliest childhood onwards from one's parents and immediate surroundings, but civilization is the high culture consciously learned at a later age, which is international and can be changed at will. In this Tekin Alp is the archetypal Kemalist.

Tekin Alp seems to be unaware of the inconsistencies in his description of culture and its role in the nation. On principle, the change over from an Islamic to a European civilization was possible in his (and Gökalp's) thinking as 'civilization', like 'ideal', was something one could consciously adhere to. Changing one's culture (*hars*), however, is intrinsically impossible because in Tekin Alp's own words, it is 'natural and so to speak biological'.[78] He quotes with approval Meyer's description of culture as 'a product of history, which one cannot create at will'. In other words, culture in this understanding is an exclusive category as much as race: you either belong or you do not. Asking Kurds, Arabs or Circassians to adopt Turkish culture is, therefore, an impossible demand even in the eyes of the ideologues of Kemalism. Because adoption of Turkish culture was a prerequisite for being a member of the Turkish nation, both in Tekin Alp's eyes and according to the statutes of the People's Party, it posed a problem the Kemalists could not solve. The Muslim nationalism of the period before 1923 was a genuine popular movement, which made possible the mobilization of the masses, but it was unsuitable as the glue to hold together a society modernizing itself on the basis of secularism and positivism. Although the imposition of Turkish nationalism fitted in with this

234

modernization project, it was based in part on an organic view of 'Turkish culture' and not fully on a voluntarist/legalist concept of nationality. This Turkish nationalism could only exclude significant parts of the population within the new borders from full and equal membership in the nation and lead to a politics of assimilation.

17. Were the Progressives Conservative?*

Conservatism as a political philosophy

As a doctrine, conservatism is notoriously hard to define, partly because its adherents explicitly reject doctrines as the basis for politics. Nevertheless, it is probably justified to say that those who have sought to establish philosophical foundations for political conservatism from Edmund Burke,[1] through (Lord) Hugh Cecil and (Lord) Hailsham[2] to Roger Scruton[3] in the 1980s, have shown a remarkable consistency in what they see as its central characteristics. Burke, the father of conservatism as an ideology, developed in his *Reflections on the Revolution in France* six themes, which have remained characteristic of conservative thought ever since its publication in 1790: the importance of religion; the danger of inflicting injustice on individuals in the name of reform; the reality and desirability of distinctions of rank and station; the inviolability of private property; the view of society as an organism, rather than a mechanism; and finally, the value of continuity with the past.[4]

Central to the concept of conservatism is the notion that legitimate rule is based on established patterns of governance (what Scruton calls 'established usage'[5]) rather than on a mandate or any other form of 'contractual' relationship between the rulers and the ruled. This notion of transcendent authority made an institution like the House of Lords, with its core body of members selected on the basis of hereditary peers, acceptable, yes even desirable to British conservatives.[6] It was also the aspect of conservative thinking, which lay at the heart of Metternich's restoration in Europe between 1813 and 1848.

Karl Mannheim, the pre-eminent student of continental conservatism, sees the transition from semi-conscious traditionalism to conscious political conservatism as a result of the emergence of the class-based capitalist society. The expressions of this dynamic movement vary over time and from place to place, but conservatism's underlying worldview is based on a very stable set of attitudes. These include a strong attachment to the individual, the concrete, the qualitative, the historical and the organic, and a rejection of the collective, the abstract, the quantitative, the programmatic, the mechanistic and the universal.[7]

In its nineteenth- and early twentieth-century form this ideology, or rather: set of attitudes, opposed the political and philosophical movements, which took their inspiration from the enlightenment (in particular Rousseau) and the French Revolution, that is to say: liberalism and socialism in their many guises. Under the leadership of modern political leaders, such as Disraeli in Britain or Bismarck and Windthorst in Germany, conservatives managed to reach out to the lower middle class and sections of the proletariat and build mass parties, often in close collaboration with the churches. In the Netherlands, for instance, the first modern mass party to be founded (in 1876) was composed of a breakaway section of the reformed protestant church. Its conservative credentials showed in its name: Anti-Revolutionary Party – the revolution in question being the French Revolution of 80 years earlier!

That conservative, and conservative Christian parties not only managed to survive in the twentieth century but actually thrive, has to be attributed to their ideological flexibility, which allowed them to adopt, first social democratic ideas on the welfare state and social security and then extreme free-market liberalism, which had been the complete antithesis of conservative thinking a century before.

Political and philosophical conservatism in the form described above was never a powerful influence in the Ottoman Empire or in the early Republic, and only gained force in Turkey in the second half of the twentieth century. One strand of direct influence, though, can be seen in the League for Private Initiative and Decentralization of Prince Sabahattin, which, in spite of the fact that it advertised itself as 'Liberal' in Europe, owed more to the ideas of the anti-revolutionary, aristocratic and catholic conservatives around Frederic Le Play in France than to any genuine liberals. After all: like them, Prince Sabahattin saw a central role for a reinvigorated 'aristocracy', which he equated with the provincial notables (*ayan*) in the regeneration of the Ottoman Empire, a role modelled on that of the British aristocracy in the management of the British Empire.

The main body of Young Turk writers and politicians, united (if that is the word) in the Committee of Union and Progress (CUP), consisted of people, who stood firmly in the traditions of the enlightenment and the French Revolution. They greatly admired the French revolutionaries (it is no coincidence that the Committee was founded in 1889, the centenary of the revolution) and some of their attitudes can certainly be described as Jacobin. But the main ideological influence on their worldview derived from a popular form of late nineteenth-century positivism, mixed with Büchnerian materialism.[8] Their greatest source of inspiration was Gustave LeBon, the founder of 'mass psychology', whose popularity among the French right (military officers in particular) was due to a deep-rooted fear of 'the masses' (*la foule*), engendered by the events following the 1870 Paris commune.[9] The ambiguity of the Young Turks' view of the French Revolution echoes that of the Positivists themselves. These rejected violent and revolutionary change (as well as democracy), but advocated a secularism and rationalism that was clearly rooted in the enlightenment and the ideals of the revolution. Their rationalism was intimately linked to their scientism. After all, the essence of positivism lies in its assumption that universal laws akin to the laws of science underlie the evolution of societies. The Unionists and later the Kemalists clearly share this secularist, rationalist and scientist, but at the same time authoritarian and elitist outlook. They were inspired by late nineteenth-century thinkers, who regarded popular democracy as outmoded, but at the same time their project was ultimately a social and political 'grand design', which was based on rationalism, guided by universal truths, and involved radical change – all things abhorred by true conservatives like Burke.

It is clear, therefore, that measured by the aforementioned criteria for conservatism, the Unionists and Kemalists did not qualify. They did not advocate an organic view of society, legitimized by tradition and religion. They did not reject abstract reasoning or a mechanistic view of social change. The policies of the period 1913–18 (i.e. ethnic cleansing and the 'National Economy' programme) and even more those of the 1920s and 30s were inspired by utopian views on an ideal society of the future. Nor did the Young Turks reject the social contract. Far from it. No better proof of the indebtedness of the Kemalists to the French Revolution can be adduced than the fundamental political principle enshrined in the Law on Fundamental Organization of 1921: 'sovereignty belongs unconditionally to the nation' (*hakimiyet bila kayd-ü şart milletindir*). This idea was, after all, copied directly from the French revolutionary Declaration of the Rights of Man (*Déclaration des droits de l'homme et du citoyen*) of 1789.

The accusations levelled at the Progressive Republican Party

In the political debates and power struggles of the mid-1920s, out of which the short-lived Progressive Republican Party (PRP) was born in November 1924, 'conservatism' as a philosophical concept played no role of importance.

This should come as no surprise, as the debates were part of a struggle within the Kemalist movement, which had been started by Unionists after World War I and only gradually acquired an identity of its own.[10] As we have seen above, the Unionist-Kemalist current in Turkish politics, from which the PRP emerged, was squarely in the tradition of the French Revolution as well as in that of positivism. Those who can reasonably be regarded as true conservatives in the Turkish context, the followers of Sabahattin and the monarchists, had been all but excluded from the political debate years before, with the nationalist victory in the war of independence in August 1922, the abolition of the sultanate in November 1922 and the changes to the High Treason Law of April 1923. This is not to say that the anti-modernist or anti-rationalist currents in European philosophy, the ideas of people like Friederich Nietzsche or Henri Bergson, were entirely without influence in Turkey, but their following consisted of small groups of intellectuals without serious political influence.[11]

When the PRP emerged in November 1924, it was criticized, or rather attacked, quite fiercely by Mustafa Kemal Pasha and his followers. Three different accusations were levelled at the party.

The first argument was that it was not a real party with a real programme, but in fact a creation of opportunistic generals and politicians (Mustafa Kemal's old comrades in arms in the independence war), who were jealous of Kemal's success and could not stomach the idea that they had been sidelined while new (and often younger) followers of Kemal took over the most influential positions after the conclusion of the war of independence. Proponents of this argument charged that the PRP leaders, by claiming that they had a right to be heard in post-war political decisions on the basis of their earlier merits in the war of independence, were in breach of the democratic order and were advocating junta-style government 'just like in China'.[12] The Kemalists levelled this accusation against them in particular at the time of the proclamation of the republic by the national assembly in October 1923, a year before the establishment of the party. By coincidence, most of the leading figures in the independence war, such as Hüseyin Rauf, Refet, Dr Adnan, Kâzım Karabekir and Ali Fuat, were in Istanbul at the time of the proclamation, but were not consulted on the decision, only learning of it like the public at large, when they heard cannons being fired in celebration. When they criticized the proclamation decision, with the charge that it was not the name of the political system, which was important, but instead its democratic content, their opponents labelled them as disloyal and inspired by personal resentment.

Mustafa Kemal echoed these sentiments in his *Nutuk* of October 1927. There, he describes the establishment of the PRP as the outcome of a plot hatched by ambitious generals in the summer of 1924. Generals like Kâzım Karabekir, Ali Fuat, Refet and Cafer Tayyar had been awarded positions as deputies in the National Assembly in the elections of 1923, but they did not actually exercise their mandates, because they also held active command positions in the army at the same time. According to Mustafa Kemal he realized that he was faced with a plot when the generals first tried to win over the army and then the representatives in the National Assembly and, through friendly media, public opinion. He describes how he called the generals' bluff by forcing them to choose between their military position and their political role as representatives in the assembly. Faced with the choice, they opted to leave the army and this was the first step on the road to the establishment of an opposition party.[13]

The second argument used at the time was that the Progressives were not honest conservatives but crypto-monarchists. Mustafa Kemal himself used this line in his interview of 21 November 1924 with Maxwell Macartney of *The Times*. There he said that he would have respected the opposition if it had come out with an openly conservative programme, but that as it was, its political programme was more or less identical with that of his own Republican People's Party (RPP), thus proving that the opposition was not sincere. If this were really their programme, he charged, they could just as well have stayed within the RPP. Instead, on the basis of what he knew about especially Rauf Bey's loyalty to the former caliph and his critical stance towards the republic, he suspected them of being closet monarchists, whose real aim was to restore the Ottoman family to the throne.[14]

The loyalty of the PRP leaders, particularly of Rauf Bey, to the Ottoman family and to the caliphate is referred to in Mustafa Kemal's *Nutuk* as well. When he wrote it in 1927, Mustafa Kemal clearly intended the *Nutuk* to be a vindication of the suppression of the PRP in 1925 and of the political trials in the summer of 1926, during which the former PRP leaders were purged and, in some cases, convicted. Depicting the PRP chiefs as closet monarchists with doubtful loyalty to the republic fit this storyline. As reported by Kemal, Rauf had pleaded for a stronger position for the caliph as late as 4 August 1923, when he came to tender his resignation as prime minister, thus implying that Rauf likely was a monarchist in 1924–5 as well.

The third accusation levelled against the opposition party was that the PRP's programme and stance encouraged religious reaction, *irtica*. This was the main argument used by the Independence Tribunal, when it proposed to the cabinet on 5 May 1925 the closure of the PRP. The cabinet followed the tribunal's recommendations and on 3 June decided to close down the party on the grounds that article 6 of its party programme, which advocated respect for religious opinions and beliefs, could be used and in fact had been used by party officials to gain the support of reactionaries and to subvert the existing political order. The term 'religious reaction' (*irtica*) specifically refers to the overthrow of the secular republican order established in 1923–4. In the context of the spring of 1925 it was used to link the PRP to the Kurdish and fundamentalist insurrection of Sheykh Sait of Palu, which had broken out in February 1925 and was suppressed by the army a month later. The restoration of Islamic law and of the caliphate had been among the demands of the rebels.

The political framework erected for the repression of the rebellion was also utilized for closing down the PRP and suppressing its supporters. First, on 25 February, martial law was declared in 14 Eastern provinces and the 1920 High Treason Law (already changed in 1923) was amended to include the political use of religion as a treasonable offence. Then, roughly a week later, the Law on the Maintenance of Order was passed, which gave the executive almost unlimited powers for a period of two years, and established two Independence Tribunals – one for the East, in Diyarbakır and one for the rest of the country, in Ankara. It was the Diyarbakır Independence Tribunal, which first acted against the PRP, closing down all its branch offices in the East, even though there was no evidence of collaboration of the party branches with the rebels. While the PRP had supported the 25 February measures in a show of national solidarity, it opposed the 4 March measures, but not because it was in sympathy with the fundamentalist uprising. The PRP's argument against the passing of the Law on the Maintenance of Order was that it was dangerously elastic and that it was not necessary to take repressive measures throughout the country as the Sheykh Sait rebellion was first and foremost a Kurdish movement, which was unlikely to spread beyond the areas with a Kurdish majority.

As for the conservative credentials of the PRP, monarchism and respect for religion certainly would be typical characteristics of a conservative political movement in a European context. But in the Turkish political climate of the 1920s and 30s favouring restoration of the monarchy and aiding and abetting politics based on religious feeling rendered PRP members dangerous reactionaries, rather than legitimate conservatives. When Recep Peker, the powerful general secretary of the RPP gave his 'Lessons on the reforms' (*İnkılâp Dersleri*) in Ankara's law faculty in 1934–5, he accused conservative parties of harbouring reactionary elements ('In truth the worst reactionaries hide within an outward appearance, which pleases those who are not wide awake'). While he recognized the merits of the British Conservatives, he also stated: 'In new born countries, which have started out on reform, it is necessary to be very watchful of parties that hide their identity under the mask of moderates or conservatives and commit the worst reactionary acts.'[15] Although his statements were made a decade after the closure of the PRP, they seem to be characteristic of the thinking of Ankara's hard-line Kemalists in both periods.

The party manifesto and the political programme

The only way to discern whether these different accusations against the PRP hold water is to look at the PRP's manifesto and the political programme published in November 1924. Together with the speeches and voting patterns of its representatives in the National Assembly, these give the clearest picture of the party's political stance. So let us now look at the political statements of the PRP to see whether these four charges laid at the door of the Progressives are sustainable.

The charge that the PRP founders were motivated by resentment is not entirely without foundation. They saw themselves as the men, who, together with Mustafa Kemal, had started and led the national resistance movement. They had already had difficulty accepting that relative latecomers to the struggle such as İsmet and Fevzi [Çakmak] had become Mustafa Kemal's most trusted aides during the struggle. The fact that they were sidelined even more after the Peace of Lausanne, was still harder to swallow. Nevertheless, the PRP's detailed programme and its manifesto with a clear and closely argued philosophical and political message seem to militate against the idea that it was personal pique alone that motivated its founders. Furthermore, as we shall see, in spite of what Mustafa Kemal said, there were clear differences between the PRP programme and his own 'Nine Principles' in April 1923.[16]

Do we find indications of monarchism and religious reaction in the manifesto and the programme? Let us first look at the manifesto. It starts off with a long paragraph, describing how all sovereignty resides in the nation on principle, but how the exercise of this sovereignty needs to be delegated for practical reasons to representative organs. It argues the case for a separation of powers along the lines of the classic 'trias politica' and then goes on to defend the multi-party system. In these respects it is a classical, liberal political treatise. The manifesto makes reference to the political realities in Turkey as well. The authors state that the nation 'displays the necessary maturity to steer its own destiny', thus refuting the idea (proposed by Mustafa Kemal in his speeches in Trabzon and Samsun in September)[17] that the country was not ripe for political competition. Gradual change, rather than 'exposing the country to shocks' is what the PRP appears to have had in mind. Emphasis is put on the principle of individual liberty (described as a 'social necessity') and on protection of the individual from arbitrary rule.

The liberal and moderate, but in no sense reactionary, tone of the manifesto is repeated in the programme. The party reaffirms that Turkey is a republic based on the sovereignty of the people; that liberalism and democracy form the basis for the party's actions; and that it supports general and individual freedoms. The programme also advocates a reduction in the role of the state, and in a clear reference to the RPP's actions of 1923–4, it states (in article 5) that the constitution will not be changed without a clear mandate from the people.

Article 6 is the famous article, which was used by the Independence Tribunal to argue that the PRP fostered religious reaction. Literally, it runs: 'The party respects religious beliefs and convictions.' Hüseyin Rauf Bey argued at the time that this article was an expression of true secularism (as it speaks of beliefs in the plural) at a time when Islam was still the official state religion. If so, it clearly reflects a different concept of secularism from that used by the Kemalists at the time, which was based on control over rather than respect for religion.

As in the manifesto, so in the programme, too, the separation of executive from legislative and judicial powers received great emphasis. In the chapter on internal affairs, local democracy (with elected officials on all levels) and decentralization were the main themes. The liberal tendencies of the party could also be seen in the articles (17, 18 and 22) that called for an investigation into the working of the bureaucracy, with a view to simplifying its procedures. Neutrality of the state apparatus was sought through a prohibition of membership of political parties for civil servants and soldiers (article 13).

The PRP programme thus was different both from the Nine Principles and from the praxis of the Kemalist majority in important ways: decentralism and separation of powers; individual liberty and a desire for a smaller, depoliticized state against centralism; concentration of powers; and a tendency to strengthen and politicize the state. At the same time, its philosophical basis clearly was to be found in liberalism, not conservatism and there are no traces of monarchism or religious reaction anywhere.

The conclusion has to be that the PRP was not an entirely opportunistic venture, even though personal resentment played a role; that it was not in any way a reactionary or fundamentalist movement; but neither was the party conservative in its philosophy. It saw political legitimacy very much in a 'contractual or semi-contractual agreement' of the rulers with the people, not in 'established usage'.[18]

Instead, it can be characterized as a party with a moderate programme in the late nineteenth-century liberal and secular tradition. In this, the Progressives were out of tune with the political developments and the atmosphere in the Ankara of the mid-1920s. Their behaviour as well as the texts of the manifesto and the programme makes it clear that their basic assumption was that, after the decade of war (1912–22) and the radical changes of 1923–4, the time had now come for a return to normality, with room for political debate and respect for personal liberties. Their manifesto stated that the nation, having attained its independence, had now entered a new era and reached a stage of maturity, in which it would be able to steer its own destiny. In this they were clearly at odds with the hard-line Kemalists, who felt that the country was in the midst of a 'social and cultural revolution', the success of which, the Kemalists believed, could be threatened by allowing political dissent or a separation of powers. We can therefore agree with Frederick Frey's characterization of the PRP as 'post-independence conservatives'.[19] As Frey explains in his general theory on élite politics, after a struggle for independence, there is often a split in the movement, which had before been held together by the desire to maintain or regain independence. One wing of the movement, which Frey labels the 'ardent nationalists', wants to use its new status to embark on far-reaching social and cultural reform, which must make the hard-won independence unassailable in future. To push through this reform programme in the absence of a broad national consensus, these ardent nationalists need to increase and concentrate state power. Opposing the 'ardent nationalists' are the 'post-independence conservatives', who see the achievement of independence as the fulfilment of their ambitions and reject further radical social and cultural change. They see in further upheaval the danger of losing the hard-won gains of the independence struggle and favour evolutionary rather than revolutionary change. They also reject the authoritarian use of concentrated power for a reform programme, which they see as tantamount to the establishment of a dictatorship.

Although clearly inspired by the Turkish case, Frey's model is not tailor-made for Turkey alone. Examples abound in the post-World War II decolonization process (from Indonesia to Algeria and Zimbabwe), but for the Middle East it is perhaps most useful to point to the post-independence regimes in the Arab World (Egypt, Syria, Iraq). These representatives of the last phase of what Albert Hourani has called 'the liberal age' fit the description to a large extent, but within a few years these regimes were toppled by 'Arab socialist' military officers with a radical reformist agenda, who established authoritarian regimes and increased and concentrated the state's power. Although there are many differences between the process in the Arab world and that in Turkey, the almost universal rule that post-independence conservatives lose out to the radicals seems to apply.

While the description 'post-independence conservatives' seems to fit the PRP perfectly, we should bear in mind what 'conservative' means in this context. It is a term denoting the moderate wing of the independence movement, consisting of advocates of evolutionary change and democracy. It has nothing to do with the political philosophy of conservatism as it had been developed in nineteenth-century Europe. As the party's leaders themselves acknowledged, their European example was the French Radical Party of Edouard Herriot[20] and not any of the conservative or religious-conservative political movements of the day.

This was also (belatedly) recognized by İsmet İnönü, who was directly responsible for the suppression of the PRP in 1925. He later seems to have come round to the view that the party represented an acceptable form of moderate politics within the progressive reformist camp. In 1963 he stated in his article '*Siyasî hayatımın 40. yılı ve CHP*' that the PRP had been considered an expression of a 'conservative mentality' (*muhafazakâr bir zihniyet*) at the time, but that the party had never described itself as conservative and that its leaders were in fact 'progressive and reformist people' (*ileri fikirli ve ıslahatçı insanlar*).[21] They were.

18. Institution Building in the Kemalist Republic Compared with Pahlevi Iran: The People's Party*

Imperial heritage

In spite of the striking ideological and programmatic similarities between the regimes of Atatürk and Reza Shah in the 1920s and 1930s, their short-term successes and long-term legacies have been very different. This is undoubtedly caused in part by the very different degrees to which the two leaders were able to institutionalize their personal authoritarian rule and to transfer authority to collective bodies that were able to survive the death, or in the Iranian case, deposition, of the founding father. When discussing the issue of institutionalization in Iran and Turkey, one has to distinguish carefully between state building on the one hand and the underpinning of a particular kind of regime and policies on the other. In terms of state building and the degree to which the characteristics of the modern centralized state had been established, there was a world of difference between the late Ottoman Empire and Qajar Iran. While it is undoubtedly true that there was an old tradition of a state in Iran and a widely shared consciousness of belonging to the realm of the Shah, the indispensable attributes of a modern state, such as efficient taxation, a bureaucratic administration by salaried officials with clear divisions of power and a distinct hierarchy, military conscription and a census enabling both conscription and taxation were all practically non-existent. In the Ottoman Empire, on the other hand, all of these attributes had gradually been developing during a century of reforms, which preceded the coming to power of Mustafa Kemal Pasha.

When looked at from an Ottoman perspective, therefore, the task that faced Reza Khan and his accomplishments resemble those of the reforming Sultan Mahmut II (1808–39) as much as they do Atatürk's. Certainly in his early years his main accomplishments were the building of a unified army and of a degree of centralized control, which contrasted sharply with conditions in the late Qajar Empire, where the ruler had very little effective power outside his own capital. Mustafa Kemal Pasha, on the other hand, could build on a century of achievement in this field. To take just one example: where Reza Khan's main effort in the 1920s was to build a national army out of such disparate elements as the Cossack corps, tribal forces and the Gendarmerie, and then to introduce modern conscription (as opposed to the traditional *bunichah* system),[1] the Ottoman Empire had had military conscription and a unified army since 1844.

Despite the importance of this Ottoman heritage, the Kemalist republic itself had powerful incentives for emphasizing the differences between itself and the empire. First, Mustafa Kemal gradually emerged as the undisputed leader of the post-World War I national resistance movement, a movement that had been started by the leadership of the Committee of Union and Progress (CUP), to which he himself had also belonged, but in whose circles he had played only a minor role. Depicting himself as a *deus ex machina* who created the new Turkey out of nothing, without any reference to the Young Turk heritage, was an important weapon in his elimination of political competitors.[2] Second, as Mustafa Kemal himself remarked at the time, the essential novelty of Kemalist Turkey, and its rejection of the Ottoman past, bolstered Turkey's prestige in Europe. European public opinion had had very little confidence in Ottoman readiness to reform, but Mustafa Kemal's radically new departure gave him a considerable amount of credibility in their eyes.

The essential novelty of the Kemalist republic and its clean break with the Ottoman past was the theme, not only of Kemalist historiography itself, but also of dozens of books published in the West from the 1920s onwards, most of which contrasted the decay of the 'old Turkey' and the dynamism and youthful vigour of the 'new'.[3] From the 1950s onwards (a period and the partial dismantling of the Kemalist state), a different approach has become influential, one associated with political scientist Tarık Zafer Tunaya and sociologists Niyazi Berkes and Şerif Mardin in Turkey, and with Bernard Lewis and Stanford Shaw in the West. This school, if we can call it that, acknowledges the debt of the republic to its immediate predecessors, the *Tanzimat* reformers of the nineteenth century, and particularly the Young Turks of the second constitutional period (1908–18), characterized by Tunaya as the 'laboratory of the republic'.[4]

Both schools, the traditional Kemalist and the 'revisionist' one, have tended to concentrate on questions of policy and ideology – primarily the issues of modernization and national identity. Interesting and complicated though these are, I would like instead to focus on the question of institutional links between empire and republic. Here a picture of almost total continuity emerges. This is true first of all of the army. The success of the nationalist movement in Anatolia was ultimately based on the strength of the remains of the Ottoman army. Although by the end of World War I in October 1918, the army had an effective strength of only some 100,000[5] (down from a peak of around 800,000 in 1916) and was plagued by war weariness and high levels of desertion, it is nevertheless true that it remained intact as an organized, indeed a disciplined, body. It did not disintegrate, nor was there a tendency for leading officers of the regular army to establish themselves as warlords. As Rustow has shown, the main body of officers, those who were now in their thirties and forties, who had been educated in the Western-style military schools and academy and had gained experience and rapid promotion during the years of the Balkan War (1912–13) and the World War (1914–18), supported the national struggle.[6] Once the top officers like Kâzım Karabekir and Ali Fuat accepted Mustafa Kemal's leadership (even after he had been sacked by the Sultan's government) they were in a position to carry out his strategy, because the chain of command remained intact. The army of the national movement continued largely without change under the republic. Until Turkey's entry into NATO in 1952 its doctrines and organization remained much the same, and as late as the 1960s it was still commanded by officers who were the product of the Ottoman Military Academy and had gained their first command experience in World War I (officers like republican presidents Cemal Gürsel and Cevdet Sunay, and the founder of the Justice Party, Ragıp Gümüşpala).

When we turn to the civilian bureaucracy we see almost the same picture. The nationalists early on in the independence struggle weeded out members of the provincial bureaucracy (viz. political appointees like provincial and district governors), who were considered unreliable because of their links to the Istanbul government. Lower levels of provincial administration, though, remained intact. As for the field of finance, the republic inherited two separate bureaucratic structures from the empire: the Ministry of Finance and the administration of the Ottoman public debt, with the latter of the two terminated in 1925.

The means of reproducing these bureaucratic branches also remained virtually unchanged, with the great schools of the empire, which had turned out the officers and civil servants of the *Tanzimat*, Hamidian and Young Turk eras, continuing to fulfil the same function under the republic. Institutions like the Military Academy, the General Staff College and the Civil Service

Academy (*Mülkiye*) continued to provide the state with its governors, diplomats and administrators. In time, these institutions came to serve as centres of Kemalist indoctrination.

As for the composition of the Kemalist bureaucracy, there were no wholesale purges after the nationalists' victory. At the peace conference of Lausanne in 1923, the Turks secured the right to ban 150 undesirable Ottoman Muslims from the country. The number of 150 was completely arbitrary and the names were only filled in (with some difficulty) more than a year after the conclusion of peace. There were a number of army officers and bureaucrats among those banned, but obviously it concerned only a very small number of people. The early years of the republic witnessed political purges within the leadership (notably in the show trials of 1926), but the attempts to purge the state apparatus were rather limited: Law 347 of 25 September 1923 prescribed the expulsion from the armed forces of those officers who had stayed abroad or declined to serve in the 'national forces', while Law 854 of 26 May 1925 did the same for civil servants. The number of people affected seems to have been small, however, and two years later, on 24 May 1928, the passing of Law 1289 gave those officers and civil servants who felt they had been wrongfully sacked the opportunity to appeal.[7] The one major occasion when many civil servants left government service had nothing to do with political purges: when the (then still very small and extremely uncomfortable) town of Ankara was declared the permanent seat of government in October 1923 an important part of the staff of the ministries in Istanbul declined to move with their departments to Ankara.

The one branch of state bureaucracy that did undergo the greatest change was undoubtedly the religious institution. The abolishing of the caliphate and the simultaneous replacement of the office of the *Şeyhülislam*, the highest religious authority, by a directorate under the prime minister; the passing of the law on the unification of education in 1924 and the introduction of a European-style family law in 1926 all increased the power of the state, with the role of the religious establishment contracting accordingly. The reproduction of religious learning also was severely affected by the closure of the *medreses* in 1924, a decline that would only become apparent in the mid-1940s when the older Ottoman-educated generation started to fade. Mustafa Kemal Pasha's ability to push through these reforms almost without opposition from the clergy is testimony to the degree to which the Ottoman religious establishment had already been bureaucratized and brought under state control in the Ottoman Empire.

The People's Party

If the Kemalist republic was the receiver of such a rich institutional inherit-
ance from the empire, what were the Kemalists' own particular contributions to the institutions of the republic? In other words: if the building of a
Kemalist state was no longer a priority, what instruments did the Kemalists
create for the institutionalization of their regime? Here, I think, the answer
can be quite unequivocal: that instrument was the party created by Mustafa
Kemal in 1923, the People's Party (*Halk Fırkası*).

Mustafa Kemal announced his intention to transform the Defence of
Rights Group, the majority faction in the first National Assembly (1920–3),
into a political party on 6 December 1922. At the same time he announced
the new party's name, *Halk Fırkası*, which was remarkable in two respects.
Fırka was the most commonly used term for political party at the time, but
the term had distinctly negative connotations. It recalled the bickering of
factions in the parliaments of the second constitutional period and lacked
the positive connotations associated with *cemiyet* (society), the word used
in the title of the Society for the Defence of the National Rights, in whose
name the independence war had been fought and whose president Mustafa
Kemal still was. Both in this context and in the earlier one of the CUP
(which was often called a *cemiyet-i mukaddes* or 'holy society' by its members, a term also used by Mustafa Kemal for the People's Party in his speech
in Trabzon on 16 September 1924[8]), 'society' seemed a more prestigious as
well as a more inclusive term than 'party'. Had not the delegates to the congress in Sivas (September 1919) sworn, each one of them, to work 'free from
party strife' (*fırkacılık amal-inden münezzeh*)?[9]

The fact that *fırka* was associated with party strife made the choice
of the other word in its name, *halk*, even more remarkable. As Tunçay
has pointed out,[10] this term had gained currency in leftist circles, where
it meant the mass of the population (peasants and workers). In nationalist circles at the time the word *millet* was the word more commonly
used to denote the (Muslim) population as a whole. The name of the new
party therefore aroused the suspicion that it had leftist leanings and might
embrace the idea of class struggle. Mustafa Kemal was quick to dispel any
such thoughts, however. During his tour of the country in early 1923,
in particular during the extensive interviews and speeches he gave in
Eskişehir and Izmit on 15–17 January 1923, he emphatically stated that
large landowners and capitalists were so rare in Turkey that there was
no reason why improving the living standard of the peasants should be
at their expense. Industrial workers, he said, did not number more than

20,000 in all of Turkey, so they could not form the basis of a political party either. The new party would be a party for all sections of society, preaching harmony and not class struggle.[11] Still, the deliberate choice of the word 'halk' indicates the desire on the part of Mustafa Kemal to depict the new party as anti-elitist and working for the masses. In this sense, the use of the term is reminiscent of its use by the *Halka Doğru* (Towards the People) group, founded by Unionists in Izmir in 1917, a group that aimed to spread the message of nationalism and modernism among the masses, but was definitely not socialist.[12]

What Mustafa Kemal had in mind in founding the party was, on the one hand, to create a disciplined and reliable majority in the second National Assembly after the 1923 elections (discipline which had been notably lacking in the first assembly), and on the other, to unite all 'enlightened' elements in the country as a vanguard for the social and cultural revolution he wanted to accomplish. Although Mustafa Kemal himself and the party always claimed to represent the national will and to act in harmony with the wishes of the population at large, his campaign in the spring of 1923 seems to have been aimed rather at uniting the enlightened élite behind him.

The elections in the summer of 1923 took place before the official founding of the new party, but a kind of rudimentary party programme, the Nine Principles (*Dokuz Umde*) was published by Mustafa Kemal, and only candidates who subscribed to them were given the support of the Defence of Rights Group in the elections. The Nine Principles were a concoction of very broad statements on issues like national sovereignty on the one hand, and very specific proposals, designed to win the support of different social groups, on the other.

After the elections, the newly elected members of the Defence of Rights Group in the National Assembly (which comprised all but one of the deputies), reconstituted themselves as the People's Party (PP) on 9 August 1923. Shortly afterwards, they formally declared that the PP was the only heir to the Society for the Defence of the National Rights of Anatolia and Rumelia, and that the PP had taken over all the Society's assets. The local branches of the Defence of Rights organization were not consulted on this move, but neither they nor those politicians who had been equally active in the national resistance movement but who had not been included in Mustafa Kemal's slate for the elections, were in a position to protest. The spurious pedigree of the new party was displayed in particular at the 1927 party congress, when the PP leadership deemed the congress the 'second' PP congress; apparently, the first national conference of the resistance movement, that of Sivas back in September 1919, had been its first!

It is no exaggeration to say that the creation of the PP was one in a chain of events, through which Mustafa Kemal gradually established a power monopoly in 1923–5. Other links in this chain are the change in the High Treason Law in April 1923,[13] the promulgation of the republic with Mustafa Kemal as first president in October, the abolition of the caliphate in March 1924, and the suppression of the liberal and socialist opposition beginning in March 1925. From June 1925 onwards the PP was the only legal party in Turkey, and within this single party, Mustafa Kemal Pasha's position was unassailable. The internal structure of the party, as described by the statutes of 1927, gave him almost unlimited power: he was permanent chairman of the party and he appointed the two other functionaries, the vice-chairman and the secretary-general, who together with him made up the party leadership. As party chairman, he alone was entitled to name candidates for the National Assembly.[14] Since the split in the party in November 1924 (when Mustafa Kemal briefly allowed another party, the Progressive Republican Party to stand alongside the PP) new disciplinary measures were in force, which prevented individual deputies from venting dissident opinions in the National Assembly. All debate was now limited to the closed sessions of the parliamentary party. One could thus be excused for thinking that, with complete control over the only legitimate political party, Kemal would turn it into the main vehicle for enforcing Kemalist policies.

But in March 1925 the parliamentary party agreed to give the government (whose prime minister, İsmet İnönü was appointed by Mustafa Kemal in his other capacity as president of the republic) dictatorial powers under the Law on the Maintenance of Order (*Takrir-i Sükûn Kanunu*), which remained in force for four years. During these years when the enactment of all the most famous Westernizing and secularizing measures that together constitute the Kemalist 'revolution' was done, the party, therefore, played hardly any political role at all. One can therefore say that, having helped to create a secure platform for the president to execute his policies, the party had more or less served its purpose.

The party certainly did not function as an instrument for mass mobilization on the pattern of the socialist or fascist parties that operated in Europe during this era. In the first six years of its existence (1923–9) the party publicly defended the policies of the government, but it made very little effort to actually drum up support for these policies or to encourage grassroots activism. This picture changes from 1930 onwards when the PP began to play a much more active role in these fields. It became much more involved in education and propaganda, and it is certainly no coincidence that the party school for orators was founded in 1931.

The changing role of the PP in the 1930s is directly linked to a change in the nature of the Kemalist regime, which – I would contend – underwent a transition from authoritarian to totalitarian rule, or at least an attempt at it. From the early 1930s onwards, the PP government organized a drive to eliminate all forms of civil society organizations that were not linked to the party. The best-known examples of organizations that were closed down were the Turkish Women's Union, the Freemasons lodges, professional organizations such as the Teachers' Union, the Reserve Officers Society and the Society of Newspaper Journalists, and the cultural and educational clubs of the Turkish Hearths (*Türk Ocakları*), which had survived from the Young Turk era and had been the main meeting place of supporters of cultural Turkish (and Turkic) nationalism since 1912. Nor were education institutions immune; Istanbul University was reformed and purged as well.

These independent organizations were replaced with new ones that were completely under party control: the women's branch of the PP replaced the Women's Union and the People's Houses (*Halkevleri*) were founded in February 1932 as successor to the Turkish Hearths and took over the latter's assets, primarily its buildings. The People's Houses soon became by far the most significant vehicle for mobilization of the party.

The aims of the People's Houses, as articulated by the party leadership were to build national unity through the spread of culture and ideals, to bring villagers and town dwellers closer together, and to explain the principles of the PP to the masses. These aims would be fulfilled by activities in nine different fields: language and literature; fine arts, theatre, sports, welfare, educational courses, libraries and publications, village development, and history. Membership was open to all. It was fully subsidized by the PP and the board of each People's House was appointed by the local party leadership, except for that of Ankara which was appointed by the national leadership. In the first few years after their inception in 1932, the number of houses increased dramatically. In total, 478 People's Houses were founded and from 1940 onwards a total of 4,322 of a rudimentary version of these Houses, called People's Rooms (*Halkodaları*) operated in villages. The People's Houses and the People's Rooms, well aware that over 80 per cent of the population was illiterate, employed various means of communication to spread the message of Kemalist modernization, the most important of which were lectures and speeches. Other forms of communication included films, theatre productions, puppet shows, concerts, expositions and, in the villages, oral instruction and wall posters. For those who were literate, the People's Houses also produced a large number of journals, the most important of which was *Ülkü* (Ideal), the journal of the Ankara People's House.[15]

It may be doubted, however, whether the People's Houses really succeeded in their mission of propagating the Kemalist ideals among the broader strata of the Turkish population. Contemporary accounts seem to indicate that, in spite of all the high-minded ideals, the Houses to a large extent remained a meeting place for intellectuals, teachers, professionals and bureaucrats, and very few peasants or workers ever set foot in them. The People's Houses' greatest success was probably in helping the Kemalists build a dedicated middle class cadre in the towns that would support their policies, rather than in gaining mass support for the reforms. Thus, while the Houses may have helped create a corporate identity for an important section of the 'enlightened' urban middle class, the efforts to encourage a European lifestyle and culture and the Kemalists' lack of interest in, and respect for, expressions of traditional cultures may actually have created resentment among the masses.

One contemporary traveller was Lilo Linke, whose *Allah Dethroned: A Journey through Modern Turkey*, which appeared first in 1937, will figure prominently in the next chapter.[16] She actually made a point of visiting the People's Houses and describes the Samsun *Halk Evi* in some detail.[17] According to her account, one in 40 of Samsun's inhabitants was a member. At the time this would amount to about 800 people. 'Those higher up the social scale' were 'as good as obliged' to take up membership. She copied the week's timetable of activities of the People's House, which looked like this:

Monday:	Women's needlework class
	Football club meeting
	Drama group
	Reading and writing class for adults
	Free legal advice
Tuesday:	Turkish history group
	Choir practice
	Party meeting
	Bookbinding and handicrafts

Wednesday: Committee meetings
Women's dressmaking class
Chamber music class
Turkish language and art group

Thursday: Military band practice
Reading and writing class
Girl's gymnasium group
Museum and exhibition committee

Friday: Orchestra practice
Free medical advice
Village group meeting

Saturday: Sports clubs
Foreign language classes

Sunday: Lectures, concerts, conferences.

Clearly a provincial centre like Samsun had a sizeable core of activists, who devoted quite a bit of spare time to the spreading of Kemalist values. Linke's description of the activities of the House's 'village group' that returned from what was clearly a routine visit to a number of villages, also makes clear why these activities may have created resentment in the countryside. The group (consisting of a student, a dentist, a teacher and the owner of the car in which they travelled) had given literacy classes and medical briefings, but they had also carried out the registration of villagers for the census and enforced the new law on family names. In the eyes of the villagers, the People's House delegation must have looked like just another bunch of state officials making incomprehensible demands.

More than anything else, the development of the People's Houses marks the transformation of the People's Party from a fairly closed cadre party into an instrument for control and mobilization. Three reasons can be discerned for the PP's changing role in the early 1930s. First, the world economic crisis with its attendant dramatic fall in the price of agricultural products severely affected Turkey from 1930 onwards. This in itself created a demand for a more active and interventionist government policy.

Second, Mustafa Kemal's short-lived experiment with a legitimate (but tame) political opposition in 1930 (the Free Republican Party or *Serbest Cumhuriyet Fırkası*) had revealed the widespread discontent in the country

255

and the unpopularity of the PP. When the experiment threatened to run out of control because of the enormous support shown for the opposition party, it was quickly terminated. But for many in the PP, the popularity of the Free Republican Party had come as a rude awakening. Together with a particularly horrifying ritual murder of a junior officer (in Menemen near Izmir on 23 December 1930), which raised the spectre of religious reaction or *irtica*, this led to a realization within the PP that the party's message of social and cultural modernization had not yet gotten across to the mass of the population. This meant that more effort had to be devoted to education and propaganda and that democratization had to be postponed indefinitely.

Third, the seeming inability of the Western democracies to deal with the world economic crisis undermined their credibility as role models. The Soviet Union and Fascist Italy seemed to deal with the crisis much more effectively, with the former continuing its expansionist programme of industrialization and the latter pursuing economic self-sufficiency.[18] While Italy's economic programme ultimately would prove disastrous, this was not so clear at the time. These authoritarian regimes, as well as Hitler's Germany after 1933, undeniably gained many admirers among the leading cadres of the PP. Already in 1932 a group of prominent intellectuals with PP connections had formed the 'Kadro' (Cadre) group, which advocated a much more active role for the party in all sorts of social and cultural spheres. Slightly later, in 1935, the very powerful secretary-general of the party, Recep Peker, proposed that the party take charge of the country's administration. Peker's inspiration was Nazi Germany rather than the Soviet Union, as had been the case with the *Kadro* group.[19] His recommendations were rejected, as Atatürk preferred to put his trust in the state apparatus of army and bureaucracy, but the fact that Turkey was officially declared a one-party state a year later, with state and party functions being merged on all levels, certainly owed a great deal to the authoritarian examples in Europe.

The transition of the PP from a fairly closed, elitist, political organization whose activities were confined almost completely to the National Assembly, to one which attempted to monopolize cultural and social life in an effort to spread Kemalist values to the masses is symbolized by the celebrations of the tenth anniversary of the republic in 1933. Whereas before that date, Mustafa Kemal Pasha usually addressed party caucuses at indoor venues (even for such a momentous occasion as his famous six-day speech of 1927), his speech of 1933 was held in an open-air stadium in Ankara, before a mass audience. The programme of the celebrations, with its parades and gymnastics, clearly resembled similar occasions in Fascist Italy in its imagery and choreography.

Comparing Turkey and Iran

When we compare this development to that in Iran, we see that the examples of Kemalist Turkey and of Fascist Italy and Nazi Germany became increasingly important in Iran in the 1930s. There was a great deal of similarity between the manner in which Reza Shah employed history and linguistics in the service of nation building during the '*Vahdat-e Milli*' campaign and the efforts of the Turkish History Society and the Turkish Language Society. The suppression of the Azeri Turks and the discrimination against Assyrians and Armenians recall the anti-minority polemics of PP stalwarts such as Mahmut Esat Bozkurt and Recep Peker. The denial of a Kurdish identity after 1928 in Iran echoes that in Turkey after 1926. The influence of the Kemalist example seems to have grown after the shah's 1934 state visit to Turkey. Nevertheless, there were important differences between the regimes. Where the PP became more important in the early 1930s as an instrument for mobilization and control, the parties that had been created by Reza Shah and his Minister of Court Taimurtash to replace the ones banned in 1927, first the *Iran-e Now* (New Iran) party, and then its successor, the *Hezb-e Teraqqi* (Progressive Party), although probably modelled on the Kemalist example, never gained a life of their own. The original aim of the *Iran-e Now* party was much the same as that of the PP in Turkey: to 'form a disciplined majority in parliament and ensure that radical, reforming proposals could be passed into law'.[20] But these parties never gained anything like the organizational strength, support or discipline of the PP. Reza Shah dissolved the *Hezb-e Teraqqi* in 1932. He seems to have relied on individuals who were totally dependent on his whim and deeply mistrusted institutions and collective bodies, even those created by himself. Mustafa Kemal, on the other hand, created a party, which, although it was undoubtedly an instrument for authoritarian and later even totalitarian policies, nevertheless formed the training ground where the politicians of the post-war multi-party democracy could learn their trade. It started out as an instrument for control of the National Assembly, but from about 1930 onwards it also began to give a corporate identity to an important section of the urban middle class that saw itself as the 'enlightened' vanguard of a social and cultural revolution. Ervand

Abrahamian sums it up nicely when he says:

> Whereas Mustafa Kemal conscientiously channeled the enthusiastic backing of the intelligentsia into the Republican Party [obviously, the (Republican) People's Party is meant here, EJZ], Reza Shah gradually lost his initial civilian support, and, failing to secure social foundations for his institutions, ruled without the assistance of an organized political party.[21]

19. Touring Anatolia at the End of the Atatürk Era: Kemalist Turkey Observed by Western Visitors*

In the mid-1930s, two people who, after World War II would gain first-rate reputations as scholars in the field of Ottoman studies, decided to travel the length and breadth of Turkey (or as much of it as they could). Their names were Robert Anhegger and Andreas Tietze.

A brief summary of their biographical details may be useful for those who are not intimately familiar with the field of Turkology. Robert Anhegger was born in Vienna in 1911, the son of a German trader. After World War I (much of which he spent in Switzerland), Anhegger moved with his parents to Rotterdam. In 1923 the family moved to Zürich. In Zürich, Anhegger began to study Law, History and Literature at the university, before moving to Vienna in 1932. There he continued his studies, this time in the field of Economic History, Slavonic studies and Islamic studies. He also started to learn Turkish. It was during his studies in Vienna that he befriended Andreas Tietze. They not only shared scholarly interests, but also a passion for left-wing politics. Anhegger made his first trip to Turkey in 1935. In 1939 he received his Ph.D. degree at the University of Zürich and in 1940 he moved (and as it turned out emigrated) to Istanbul. He had several motives for doing so: quite apart from his scholarly interest in Turkey, his background in the Communist movement and the fact that he at that time shared his life with Sura Lisier, a Jewish woman, made him feel unsafe so close to Germany. In Istanbul he worked at the German Archeological Institute until he was dismissed in 1942 for refusing to join up when called to serve in the German army. After his dismissal he worked as a teacher of German language and literature in a number of places, notably Istanbul University. As a German with intimate knowledge of Turkey, who was untainted by any Nazi connections, Anhegger from the early 1950s onwards became the lynchpin of German cultural activities in Istanbul, culminating in his directorship of the Goethe Institute from 1961 to 1968. In 1958 Anhegger married the

Turkish architect Muallâ Eyüboğlu, the sister of the painter Bedri Rahmi. His connections with modern Turkish painters led him to found the first private art gallery in Istanbul in 1957. He later became director of the Goethe Institute in Amsterdam, living alternately in this Dutch city and in Jerusalem. Anhegger died in 2001 in Amsterdam.

Andreas Tietze was born into a Jewish Austrian family in Vienna in 1914. He studied in Vienna and Paris from 1932 to 1937, after which he received his doctorate at the University of Vienna. In 1937 he moved to Istanbul, both to continue his research and, obviously, to escape Nazi persecution, which, as a Jew and Communist, he had every reason to fear. Tietze stayed in Istanbul until 1949. In 1949 he was appointed as assistant professor of Turkish studies at the University of Illinois. After a second stay in Istanbul in 1957–8, he moved to Los Angeles, where he had been appointed at the University of California to teach Turkish and Ottoman language and literature. Tietze, who by now had built a reputation as one of the leading Turkologists of his generation and as an inspiring teacher of the next, eventually became head of department at UCLA, but in the mid-1970s he decided to go back to Vienna as chair of Turkish studies at the university in his native city. There he engaged in a few more fruitful decades of scholarship, until he passed away in 2003.

Anhegger and Tietze undertook their travels in Anatolia in 1936–7. Their 1936 trip lasted from 27 August to 24 September and took them through Central Anatolia. The 1937 journey lasted from 5 September to 3 October and covered West- and Southwest-Anatolia. On both trips they were accompanied by two lady friends, Anhegger's partner Sura and a medical doctor called Erika, whose family name I have been unable to trace. This last-named person is the author of all but a few pages of the travel diaries, which describe the two journeys.

These diaries have come to us in the shape of two typescripts. The first one, 80 pages long (on A-4 format, double-spaced), is entitled *Unsere Anatolienreise 27.8–24.9.1936*. The second, 78 pages long, has the same appearance and is entitled *Die Zweite Anatolienreise 5.9–3.10.1937*. A copy of each of the typescripts was afterwards given to each of the travel companions and Robert Anhegger allowed his to be copied and deposited in the archives of the International Institute of Social History in Amsterdam. I have been unable to trace the whereabouts of the dozens of photographs, which were taken during the trips.

Of course, much of what is being described in these diaries is trivial or of interest to the travellers themselves only. Nevertheless, the text is significant for students of twentieth-century Turkish history. After all, at least two of the travellers were interested and well-qualified observers. They knew the language and were well versed in Turkish, Ottoman and pre-Ottoman history. Added to that is the comparative rarity of this type of source. There is, of course, a sizeable literature on the 'new Turkey' in Western languages, consisting of books which appeared in the 1920s and 30s when the Turkish 'miracle' was still fresh, but hardly any of these books is based on actual first-hand observation in the countryside, outside Istanbul and Ankara.

An exception to this rule is a book published in 1937 by Lilo Linke, called *Allah Dethroned. A Journey through Modern Turkey*.[1] Like Anhegger, Linke was a German. She was born in Berlin in 1906 and worked as a journalist and social worker. Because of her leftist and antimilitarist sympathies, she had had to leave Germany after Hitler's coming to power and settled in London. Beginning her journey in 1935, she travelled northeastern Anatolia (with special permission from the Ministry of Defence) and then central and Western Anatolia. Later, her focus shifted to Latin America. She wrote a book and numerous articles about the Andes countries. After World War II she became UNESCO's consultant on Latin American literature. As far as I have been able to make out, she never returned to Turkey.

Linke came with the express intention to write a book on the changes in Turkey. Hence, her manner of travelling and the way she put her experiences in writing are very different from the Anhegger/Tietze diaries. For one thing, she deliberately sought out officials and members of the governing Kemalist élite to get their views and describe their personalities. The Anhegger/Tietze party, in contrast, had very little contact with these people and depended on their own observations alone. Nevertheless, Linke travelled the same country, and at least partly along the same routes, at almost exactly the same time as Anhegger and Tietze. This, and the fact that she is a sympathetic, but by no means naive, observer of the Kemalist experiment, make it worth our while to compare the data from the Anhegger/Tietze diaries with her findings.

Taken together, these texts afford us a chance to see what had been the effect of the Kemalist modernization programme in the provincial towns and villages of Turkey 12 to 14 years after the establishment of the republic. When trying to measure this effect, it is perhaps useful to make a distinction between the more ideologically inspired measures aimed at the Westernization of Turkey – in other words, what Atatürk himself used to call 'the social and cultural revolution', and the nuts and bolts of modernization: trains, factories and hospitals. I therefore propose to treat the data under the following headings: transport, changing townscapes, health and hygiene, the Kemalist 'revolution', and state control.

Transport

The one thing uppermost in the mind of travellers, who depend on public transport to get anywhere, obviously is the availability and quality of means of transportation. It should come as no surprise, therefore, that the diaries give us a great deal of information on the subject.

Basically, the party travelled by train wherever that was possible, if only for the simple reason that on both trips they had a third class ticket for one month's unlimited travel (bought at 30 liras per person). Judging by their account, the Turkish railway system, consisting of older foreign-owned railways acquired by the republic and newly built extensions, worked rather well. Trains were almost always full, certainly in third class, and most of the time the trains ran on time. Women like Linke, travelling without male companions could still avail themselves of ladies compartments (kadın kompartımanı), although, obviously, these were of no use to the mixed Anhegger/Tietze party. If travelling by train was relatively comfortable, arriving by train created a few problems. This was because in every single Anatolian provincial town the railway station was built at a considerable distance from the town centre. This distance differed from 2 kilometres in the case of Konya (on the old Ottoman line) to as much as 8 kilometres in the case of Malatya.

Railway building had been a top priority among the modernization projects of the Kemalist republic and both the Anhegger/Tietze party and Lilo Linke visited the building site of the most important of the railway projects, that of SIMERYOL (Sivas–Malatya–Erzurum), which aimed to connect the northeast of the country with the rail network and to create a third north–south connection by linking the Sivas–Erzurum line with the Adana–Malatya–Diyarbakır one.

Where trains were unavailable, both the Anhegger/Tietze party and Linke had to travel by road. In the west of the country this meant by bus. The diaries contain lively descriptions of this mode of travel. The busses, mostly American Fords or Chevrolets, were relatively fast. On good roads they averaged up to 70 kilometres an hour. Sometimes they were fully equipped with seats, while at other times the passengers had to sit on carpets, sheepskins and sacks as best they could. Even in the mid-1930s some of routes were quite busy. In Denizli, the travellers saw buses from Muğla, Tavas, Sarayköy, Çal, Uşak and Afyon roll into the *han* they were staying in. For budget travellers the *hans*, with their open courtyards where the busses could unload their passengers, were still the obvious places to stay, hotels being more expensive and not always better. In the east of the country, roughly east of the line Sivas–Kayseri–Adana, busses were rare. Instead, people travelled by truck (*kamyon*). The descriptions of the trucks in the diaries and those by Linke tally exactly with each other. Like the busses, they were strongly built American Fords and Chevrolets. They were privately owned and usually one owner would employ three or four drivers. The trucks could accommodate up to 17 passengers. Luggage was stored on the roof (if there was a roof) and partly on the floor. Passengers sat on and in between the sacks and cases. The average speed of the trucks obviously depended on the state of repair of the road, but lay between 12 and 20 kilometres an hour.

The quality of the roads differed a great deal. In the east in particular they were often very bad indeed and frequent punctures could add hours, indeed days, to the journey. Efforts to improve the roads were underway, but they were still limited to connections between the main towns. Improvements in the road (which had been going on for many years) made it possible for trucks to replace camels on the Iran–Erzurum–Trabzon route, for instance. On the other hand, Alanya could not be reached by motor transport at all. All goods of any size had to be brought in by ship.

Older forms of transport were still very much in evidence. Camel caravans were becoming something of a rarity in east and central Anatolia, but that may also have been due to the fact that there was very little long distance trade. In the southwest, the travellers come across them all the time. Hardly anyone owned a private car and even the trains, busses and trucks were too expensive for many. Those who could not afford this type of modern transport walked or rode a donkey. The diaries state that distances everywhere were still measured in the time it took to walk anywhere (donkeys not being very much quicker).

Changing townscapes

To what extent was life changing in the provincial towns of Anatolia after 15 years of Kemalist rule? When answering this question, it is important to make a distinction between the old towns and the new extensions. The old towns largely were in a very bad state of repair, sometimes even in ruins. The traces of war and ethno-religious conflict between 1912 and 1922 were still much in evidence. A town like Kayseri was full of ruins, among other things of churches, which had been shot to pieces. The town had reputedly deteriorated much since the Greek and Armenian communities, which had once made up one-third of the population, had been 'destroyed'. The travellers hear the same story in Niğde: the town has gone down since the 'slaughter' of the Armenians. When Linke visits the Black Sea towns of Samsun, İnebolu and Giresun, she is told that the economy (notably the trade in hazelnuts and tobacco) has suffered badly because of the departure of the Pontic Greeks, but that Turks have now filled their places and things have improved. Along the railway from Eskişehir to Afyon-Karahisar and İzmir, she sees lots of deserted and ruinous villages and both the diaries and Linke describe how, 13 to 15 years after the great fire, the old Greek and Armenian quarters of İzmir are in ruins, with the debris still being cleared. Some building activity was going on but it was still very patchy.

Outside the old towns it was a different story. There the Kemalists were creating a new Turkey according to their vision of modernity. Three features seem to have been common to all new towns: First, a European-type municipal park (belediye parkı), with flower beds, fountains and tea gardens; second, a statue of the Gazi, the president of the republic; and third, a cinema, which in most towns could still only show silent pictures. Most or all of these features recur in the travellers' descriptions of the towns they visit, be it Konya, Adana, Ödemiş, Isparta, Amasya, Tarsus, Sivas or Malatya.

In those towns which were linked to the rail network, development of this type centred on the (often very long, see above) road linking the station to the old town, which in every case developed into the central axis of the new town. With the exception of Ankara and Adana, this road was also the only one covered with cement or asphalt.

While one could argue that this type of innovation – parks, statues and cinemas – was largely symbolic, serving at best to give the Kemalist élite an opportunity to express a new lifestyle, more substantial improvements were in evidence as well. A crucial element in the development of the country was, of course, electrification. Turkey did not yet have a national grid – that was an achievement of the 1950s and 60s – but a number of towns had local electricity plants. While some towns had built their plants in the 1920s (Malatya had electricity since 1928), electricity was a recent phenomenon in most towns. Sivas, for instance, had electricity since 1934, but the cities to the east, Erzincan, Erzurum, Kars, still had none at the time of Linke and the party's travels. In areas where electricity was introduced, street lighting soon followed. Provision of electricity to private houses often took much longer. In the mid-1930s it was still a rarity outside Istanbul, Ankara, Izmir and Adana. According to the travellers, Amasya acquired electric power shortly before they arrived there in 1936, but there is no street lighting yet and for the time being the power plant only supplies the local cinema.

There are other practical improvements too, but they are fairly small-scale: a new covered market here, a new and hygienic abattoir there. Sometimes a new primary school catches the eye of the travellers, always with its own little school 'museum' where drawings (mostly of the Gazi) and graphs about the development of Turkey are displayed.

Twice the Anhegger/Tietze party come across a major new industrialization project, which was clearly a result of the etatist policies, which had been in place since the early 1930s. In Turhal they visit a new sugar factory. The complex, which is quite separate from the old village, also contains houses for the factory engineers and apartment blocks for the workers. The whole complex is attractively laid out with gardens. A much larger complex of a similar type is visited both by the Anhegger/Tietze party and by Linke. It is a huge new cotton mill, which is being built outside Kayseri with the help of Russian specialists. The complex has extensive sports facilities and living quarters for the staff.

Health and hygiene

By the 1930s, the population of Anatolia was recovering fast from the blows inflicted upon it by the ten years of incessant warfare, ethnic conflict, expulsions, persecutions, hunger and epidemic diseases between 1912 and 1922. According to the 1935 census, the population of Turkey stood at 16.2 million, with an annual net growth of 2.3 per cent – a marked increase when compared with the estimated 13.5 million people who lived in the country in 1927. That the population increased so sharply in the 1920s and 30s was largely due to the disappearance of these Malthusian checks. A number of persistent problems of health and hygiene remained, however.

The overwhelming impression one gets from reading the diaries is that the provincial towns of Turkey before the war were still very dirty (much more so, the travellers say, than the villages). The problem is not limited to the ubiquitous dust. Again and again the travellers describe how the rooms in the *hans* and hotels are infested with all manner of vermin: flees, lice and bedbugs, of which Tietze on one occasion catches over 300 in one night. This in itself must have increased the risk of disease, in particular of typhus, but the only disease which is described in the diaries as endemic and widespread is malaria.

Combating malaria was the highest priority for the medical services of the young republic. A law on the fight against the disease had been passed in 1926. The campaign to eradicate it is described in detail by Linke, who watched health inspectors and doctors at work in the Çukurova in 1935. She describes how, after strong initial resistance, the government campaigns were received much more positively by the village population. Large areas were still infested with malaria, in particular: Izmit, Bursa-Balıkesir, Manisa, Aydın, Eskişehir, Ankara, Konya, Antalya, Mersin and Adana, but, as we know, the anti-malaria campaign would prove one of the most successful centrally organized activities of the republic.

The Kemalist 'revolution'

So far, we have discussed very concrete and tangible signs of development. What about the effect of the famous Kemalist reforms of the mid- to late 1920s, what Kemal himself called his 'social and cultural revolution'? What about the change in dress, alphabet, clock in the countryside?

Actually, the diaries tell us relatively little about these aspects of the Kemalist programme, and what they do tell us leaves a very mixed picture of the degree of change. By and large, the population in the provincial towns now dressed in the European style, but the forced changeover to a new style of dress on the part of an impoverished population had apparently created problems. The lack of good tailors meant that clothes were often ill fitting and the novelty of the dress style meant that people wore combinations, which looked very odd to a European eye. Also, people had to wear their clothes for a very long time, as clothing was expensive. Turkey, although a large cotton producer itself, was still dependent on imports of cloth at this time. The total effect, as both the diaries and Linke confirm, was that the town population looked poor and bedraggled. In the villages many people still wore traditional clothes, but in the towns, traditional clothing had not completely disappeared either: in Malatya many men still wore turbans.

The alphabet reform of 1928 meant that everywhere children were now being taught to read and write in the new alphabet. It also meant that the largest part of school libraries went unused, as the great majority, in fact three quarters, of the books were still in Ottoman script. The Ottoman books in the library of the *Halk Evi* (People's Home) visited by Linke had even been consigned to the basement and could no longer be read. Adults still continued to use the old script in private (as they would do until the 1970s) and even the policeman, who draws up a long report about the travellers in Izmir, does so in Ottoman writing.

The diaries afford an interesting insight into both the achievements and the limits of the alphabet revolution. On a visit to a small village near Konya, the travellers note that the majority of the adult inhabitants are able to read the new script, because a teacher was sent to the village during the campaign to introduce the new alphabet. This means that these villagers can collect out-of-date newspapers and get some idea of what is happening in the world at large. At the same time, though, the village children grow up illiterate because there is no village school.

As for changes in measuring time, the old method (dependent on the numbers of hours of daylight) is still in universal use. When people use the European clock (which had been adopted officially in Turkey in 1926 along with the Christian era) they always mention that they mean 'alafranga' time.

And what about secularization, that cornerstone of Kemalism? The state made its position abundantly clear: the Anhegger/Tietze group notices that in Tire, mosques are now being used as munitions depots. Linke meets with many people, not all of them Kemalist officials, who seem to relish the fact that the power of the clergy has been broken. She also says that she saw hardly any person under 30 years of age perform the prayers. On the other hand, a decade after the banning of the religious orders and the closure of the saint's tombs (*türbe*), the *türbe* she visits in Malatya is still being used as a place of pilgrimage.

What is clear, is that the state had technology on its side in its efforts to spread its message. The committees of the *Halk Evleri* (People's Homes – the cultural and educational centres of the ruling People's Party) conducted their tours of the countryside by car and the radio was becoming a part of everyday life in the towns. Numbers of radio sets were still small (100 in Samsun, and 30 in Malatya, a town of 27,000 inhabitants) but more often than not listening to the radio would have been a communal affair.

State control

One aspect of modern states is that they make unprecedented claims on their citizens and their resources. For these claims to be exerted, effective control over the length and breadth of the country is a precondition. As far as we can tell from the diaries, Kemalist Turkey had been spectacularly successful in this respect by the mid-1930s. The state and its representatives are literally everywhere. This would have been very clear to Turkish citizens, but for our travellers, the all-embracing control of the state manifested itself primarily in the way it kept track of foreigners.

Foreigners not only needed a valid passport and visa to enter the country, but their movements within the country were also strictly controlled. Upon arrival in any locality, they were required to have their residence permits (*ikamet tezkeresi*) checked and registered. Before travelling to their next destination, a permit for that specific place was required. And specific meant precisely that: when the party visited Birgi, but only had a travel permit for Ödemiş, nine kilometres away, they were immediately picked up on their return to Ödemiş by two gendarmes and received a thorough dressing down from the district governor. The gendarmerie, which was responsible for law and order in the countryside, seems to have been especially zealous. Gendarmes were everywhere and their posts were connected to the nearest military exchange in the centre of the *kaza*. In a village near Aksaray, the gendarmes insisted on registering the travellers although they stayed there for less than an hour. In Kayseri they are registered three times, each time when they change trains there. When their bus stops for 20 minutes in a village near Aydın on their second trip, the gendarmerie post is immediately called and the bus has to wait while they are being registered. The police in the towns were much more friendly and polite towards foreigners than the gendarmes. Indeed, they often defended and protected the foreigners, as in Amasya, where the local police officer gave a stern warning to the owner of the hotel where the party stayed, saying '*Bu köylü değil, bu yabancı!*' (This isn't a peasant, but a foreigner!). Nevertheless, they took their task no less seriously for that. When the travellers lose their way in Konya, they are immediately spotted by police officers. They are then handed from *karakol* (police station) to *karakol* until they are back safely in their hotel. In Aksaray, the police accompanied the group to the restaurant where they ate and to the park where they had tea. When they returned to their hotel, the same policeman was waiting for them in their hotel room. When they leave for Nevşehir next morning, the policeman is standing by the bus. In Tarsus they are followed by plain-clothes police and then taken to the *karakol*.

Linke confirms the intensity of state control. In her case, the picture is slightly distorted because she travelled to the northeast of the country, which was a strategically sensitive area. She relates how the truck she is travelling in is halted at Ilıca, 16 kilometres to the west of Erzurum. There all foreigners have to disembark and wait until the garrison in Erzurum has been notified and an officer can come to collect them. Even in the company of an officer she is then stopped twice more, once for a password and once for passport control. Further to the east, she is confronted with a blanket ban on photography in Kars. She is only allowed to travel from Kars to Ardahan in the company of a military officer and once in Ardahan she is forbidden to walk certain streets, to take excursions or to take pictures.

That this type of very tight police control was not limited to foreigners is shown by the passage in the diaries, which describes how the bus from Sivas to Divrik is stopped a number of times at successive police checkpoints before finally clearing the town.

The degree of control over the countryside aimed at, and achieved, by the modernizing state, was not the result of simple policing either. More than once the travellers caught a glimpse of a grimmer reality too. At the train station of Afyon-Karahisar, early into their second journey, they meet Kurds who are being deported. They are dressed in rags and extremely dirty ('much more so than gypsies'). All they carry in the way of possessions is a wooden trunk, which is opened by the police in order to find a letter from the ministry giving a list of names and the route they are to take. They are 'loaded and unloaded like cattle by the officials'. The party comes across a similar scene once more, almost a fortnight later in Aydın. There, in the ruins of a mosque which had been struck by lightning and burnt down the year before, they find figures dressed in rags, who, their guides tell them, are the remains of a large transport of Kurds from Dersim/Tunceli. They 'are simply removed there and distributed over the country. They are then dumped anywhere, without a roof over their head or employment. They do not know a single word of Turkish'.

Linke's travelogue also contains passages, which make clear that the Kurdish problem was still on everybody's minds, although the last large-scale insurrections had been in 1925 and 1929–30. She is told in Malatya that the new governor there 'acted with great firmness' against the 'wild Kurds', hanging the 'most reckless' as an example. She also hears from an incident in the adjoining province to the east, where a whole village was destroyed on the orders of the army commander because two gendarmes had been killed there. According to her source, 'it worked wonders.'

Conclusion

Thus, the diaries, in combination with Linke's book, give us a fairly complicated picture of a country in the midst of change. Clearly, in the provincial towns of Turkey life was being affected by the Kemalist reform programmes. Although people stuck to their old ways in private, and sometimes in public, the appearance of towns, and of the inhabitants, was transformed. The Kemalists spent little effort at improving or restoring the old town centres, but rather built a new Turkey of their own outside them. While many of the changes were of a largely symbolic nature, the quality of life was slowly improving too. Improved roads and railways, the coming of radio and telephone and increasing literacy broadened people's horizons, at least in the towns. Electrification spread year by year. Effective campaigns against endemic diseases like malaria and trachoma were increasing life expectancy even in the villages. The state industries being developed were beginning to give Turkey a measure of self-reliance in some sectors: textiles, sugar, cement. In all of these fields, which together constitute the tangible development of Turkey rather than its ideological reorientation towards the West, the apparently drab İnönü years of the 1930s, rather than the exiting 'revolutionary' phase of the mid-1920s, seem to have made the difference. Underpinning this change was a state apparatus, which had managed to establish full and effective control over the length and breadth of the country to a degree the Ottoman reformers of the nineteenth century could only dream.

Linke, more than the diaries, gives us a picture of the new Kemalist élite, which was shaping the country at this time. She shows them to be optimistic, dynamic, nationalistic and zealous, filled with a sense of hope and pride. But she also refers to their utter disdain for the 'backward' population in the countryside, which, in their eyes, 'needs whipping'. At heart, though, the diaries, and Linke's travelogue, give us a glimpse of the country in transition as it was observed by well-intentioned and well-informed foreigners, who went to see it for themselves, rather than rely on government sources or second-hand information. Therein, rather than in any startling revelations, lies their importance.

20.   Islam in the Service of the Caliphate and the Secular State*

The importance of being secular

Both in political debates on the current state of affairs in Turkey and in the historiography of the country, the dichotomy of religion and secularism is without doubt the dominant paradigm within which analysis takes place. Observers and commentators (both from within Turkey and from abroad) are so preoccupied with the problem of secularism, or to be more exact: with that of laicism, the separation of religion and state, that one's position on the issue has come to be seen as the yardstick whereby any prominent Turkish public figure or intellectual should be judged. Author Orhan Pamuk published his novel *Benim Adım Kırmızı* ('My Name is Red') to such a degree of worldwide critical acclaim that he is now a Nobel laureate, but the debate on this and subsequent novels of the author in Turkey itself was more about his stance on Islam and Westernization than on the literary merits of his work. The candidature of former Islamist Abdullah Gül for the presidency of the republic and in particularly the fact that, if he were to become president, the first lady would be a woman wearing an Islamic headscarf (türban) in public caused an uproar. Militant Kemalists in Turkey, led by the army top brass, hinted darkly that Turkey's secular order was in mortal danger, and declared his candidacy unconstitutional. The campaign for the parliamentary elections that were called to resolve this presidential crisis had as its main issue the threat or otherwise to the secular order and the army's right to interfere in politics to defend that order. The elections ended in a landslide victory for the AKP and Gül was duly elected president by the new assembly.

Historical figures, too, are judged on their stance in the debate on secularism as much as contemporary ones. Indeed, the contemporary debate on secularism is often structured around historical events and figures from the past: For a long time Prime Minister Adnan Menderes, executed by the military in 1961, was hated by Kemalists as the man who allowed

Islam 'back in', but in the 1980s, Izmir international airport was officially named Adnan Menderes Airport, by people who regarded him as the second great architect of modern Turkey (after Atatürk) and who wanted to make a point about their own political stance. The reappraisal of the once despised 'tyrant' Sultan Abdülhamit II by Islamists (who, in this, tend to follow the lead established by right wing Nakshibendi poet/publicist Necip Fazıl Kısakürek in the 1940s and 50s) is as much an illustration of this phenomenon as is the constant reference to figures like Dervish Vahdeti and Kubilay by hardcore Kemalists. The former was an Islamist firebrand, who as one of the leaders of the 'Muhammedan Union' (*Ittihad-i Muhammadi*) and editor of the paper *Volkan* in 1908–9 constantly called for the restoration of religious law. He was accused of instigating the 1909 counterrevolution against the 'secular' Young Turks in Istanbul, and convicted and hanged once the Young Turks had regained control of the capital. The latter was the young teacher and reserve officer, who confronted a group of radical young mystics that came to the Aegean town of Menemen in 1930 and announced that they were the advance guard of an army of Islam that would bring down the 'infidel' republic. Kubilay paid for his courage with his life when his head was sawn off while the populace of Menemen watched in silence. Both of these figures, like Menderes and Abdülhamit, thus serve as markers of the boundary between secularism and (political) Islam in contemporary Kemalist discourse.

The other issue, which has dominated the public debate in – and on – Turkey in recent years, is that of Turkey's possible accession to the European Union (EU). In this debate, too, the question whether Turkey is 'truly secular' is constantly raised and the credentials in this field of leading politicians and other public figures are scrutinized. There is nothing on religion or secularism in the official criteria (the so-called 'Copenhagen criteria') that have to be met by candidate countries; indeed, the issue of religion was never raised in the negotiations with the ten countries that acceded in 2004. In the Turkish case, however, it is raised in the context of concern about the depth and irreversibility of Turkey's secular (*laik*) order. European fears over the stability of Turkey's secular order arose following the 1978–9 revolution in Iran, with governments in the West becoming gravely concerned that Turkey would go the same way. These governments tended to side with the classic Kemalist interpretation of secularism as a protective shield against 'Islamic reaction' (*irtica*). This tendency was strengthened when political Islam was identified as the main threat to the West after the end of the Cold War in the early 1990s and, of course, became even more prominent after the terrorist attacks on New York and Washington of 11 September 2001. Fear of a reversal of the Kemalist laicist order is a constant element in the debate on Turkey's accession to the EU. Does Europe risk the entry of a Trojan horse from that animal's country of origin?

Ironically it has been Europe, which regards itself as secular (although in fact secularism in Europe has never been absolute and in every single European country formal links between state and religion can be demonstrated) that has introduced the religious factor into the membership negotiations. European concerns over Turkish secularism then feed, of course, into the already existing debate on the issue in Turkey, a debate that is exacerbated by the numerous inconsistencies in the European position that stem from fundamentally different views on the nature of secularism.

Side by side with this concern about an Islamic revival, an increasingly fierce critique of the Kemalist interpretation of secularism is also part of the debate both within and outside of Turkey. The dominant Christian-Democrat current in Europe in particular tends to see it as intolerant and unnecessarily restrictive of religious, and religiously inspired, political practice. In taking up this position (which was endorsed by the European Parliament in May 2003), these Europeans seem to side with the interpretation of secularism put forward by Turkish rightwing politicians from Menderes via Demirel and Özal to Erdoğan; an interpretation that sees secularism as an order protecting freedom of conscience *and* religion, and makes a distinction between a lay public arena and religiously inspired individuals who should be allowed to function in it and express their religiosity.

There can thus be little doubt that the nature of the relationship between state and religion in Turkey is an important one, but is also an issue on which misconceptions are widespread. Rather than trying to categorize actors along strict and somewhat artificial lines of secular versus Islamist, it is perhaps enlightening to look at the specific policies of successive late Ottoman and Republican Turkish regimes to get a better picture of the position they have taken with regard to the relationship between state and Islam, and the relationship between nationalism and religion. In this chapter I intend to look in particular at four instances where the state faced acute challenges to its authority and even survival: Sultan Abdülhamit's use of religion to ward of the threats of nationalism and imperialism; the Young Turks' mobilization of Ottoman Muslims against the perceived threat of the Christian minorities; the use of religion by the Turkish nationalists in their struggle against the occupying forces after World War I; and, finally, the attempt of the military rulers of 1980–3 to merge religion and Kemalist nationalism in an effort to break the hold of both socialism and fundamentalism over the

Turkish youth. The article is based on a critical reading of the recent mono-graphic literature on the topic (by authors like Deringil, Toprak, Georgeon, Karpat, Yavuz, Poulton, Seufert, Bora, Davison, Fortna and others).[1]

Abdülhamit II and his new moral order

It is now generally recognized that the long reign of Abdülhamit II (1876–1909) in many ways laid the foundations of what became modern Turkey. This is true in the fields of education, administration (with the expansion of the state bureaucracy and the extension of state control), and communications (telegraph and railways). It can be argued that it is also true where the management of religion is concerned. Abdülhamit was faced first and foremost with the necessity to rebuild a state and society shattered by the disastrous war against Russia of 1877–8. This war, caused ultimately by separatist Serbian and Bulgarian nationalism, had resulted in huge losses of land and income and a very serious refugee problem, as well as a loss of prestige and credibility for the Ottoman ruler. Having lost all confidence in solutions based on a 'Unity of the (Ethnic) Elements' (İttihad-i Anasır) – the remedy that had been so close to the heart of the Young Ottoman con-stitutionalists, Abdülhamit started an ideological counteroffensive, which Poulton has likened to Bismarck's *Kulturkampf*.[2] The policy had two fun-damental aims. One was to create a new basis for solidarity and national unity. The losses of 1878 had decreased the percentage of Christians in the population from 40 to 20 per cent, so it made sense to ground this new basis of solidarity in the shared religious heritage of the Muslim majority. This way, not only could the millions of refugees from the Crimea, the Caucasus and the Balkans, who had been forced to flee their homes because they were Muslims, be integrated more easily on the basis of Muslim solidarity, but the embryonic national movements among the non-Turkish Muslim communi-ties (Albanians, Arabs and Kurds) could also be countered. The other aim of Abdülhamit's policies was to increase his authority and affect a degree of bonding with the population by sacralizing the institution of the monarchy.

In order to increase solidarity and unity on the basis of Islam, a single, standardized and controlled form of 'national' or Ottoman Islam had to be promoted, a process dubbed by Deringil as the 'Ottomanization of the şeriat'.[3] The Hanefi school, which had always been the preferred *mezhep* of the Ottomans, increasingly became the sole recognized authority, even in Arab provinces where the Shafii school had traditionally predominated. The Hanefi interpretation of the religious law was ultimately codified in Ahmed Cevdet Pasha's monumental *Mecelle*, which meant that local judges and *muftis* to a large degree lost their freedom of interpretation and were expected to refer to a written authoritative text.

An officially sanctioned brand of Islam was disseminated through Abdülhamit's fast-growing educational network (Fortna's 'Imperial classrooms'), with textbooks on religion and morality being written for the different levels in primary and secondary education, and through the distribution of popular and simply written publications such as catechisms (*ilmi hal*). The standardized religious message emphasized loyalty to the state and obedience to the authorities. Its central notion, as Georgeon has pointed out, was that of *ahlak* (morality). The order that the Sultan wanted to impose on society was presented as a moral order in which modernization was encouraged but what was seen as the libertarian excesses of the *Tanzimat* era were rejected. This moral order clearly appealed to the Sunni Muslim townspeople of Anatolia, but of course Anatolia was far from uniformly Sunni. In its effort to unify the population, the state undertook campaigns to convert the many dissident Muslim communities of Anatolia and Kurdistan to respectable Sunni Islam. Taking his cue from Western missionaries, the Sultan sent preachers to the Alevi areas and even had mosques and schools built in Alevi villages.

The efforts to increase the authority of the monarchy were based on the sultan's position as caliph. Adülhamit not only used the spurious claim to the caliphate – so brilliantly exploited by the Ottoman negotiating team at the Peace of Kücük Kaynarca in 1774 – to implicitly threaten the imperialist powers of his day; he also used the caliphate to buttress his regime internally. By emphasizing the sacral nature of his office, he could demand not only the loyalty of his subjects, but also the obedience due to successors of the prophet. Loyalty to the throne thus became a religious duty.

The Sultan actively sought the cooperation of religious leaders (primarily dervish sheikhs) as intermediaries, who could connect with the Muslim community and spread the message. Most famous among these was Abdülhamit's long time favourite Ebulhuda from Aleppo, who was considered to be the *eminence grise* of the Yildiz palace at the time, but there were many others.

Abdülhamit was far from unique in his attempts to strengthen his throne by sacralizing it. The emperor Francis-Joseph II of Austria and Tsars Alexander III and Nicolas II also tried to affect a bond with the large majority of their subjects by emphasizing their role as defender of the faith. Even in Queen Victoria's Britain the monarchy projected a far more Christian and virtuous image than it had under the later Georges.

The Young Turks: 'national' means 'Muslim'

In the historiography of Turkey, the rule of the Committee of Union and Progress (CUP) after 1908, and especially after the dethronement of Abdülhamit in 1909, is usually contrasted sharply with the preceding era. There are good reasons for this. The atmosphere of public debate and openness after the revolution was in marked contrast with the suffocating atmosphere of Abdülhamit's final years. Likewise, on the ideological level there was a world of difference between Abdülhamit and the Young Turks. The latter were deeply influenced by a popularized version of positivism as well as by Büchnerian materialism. Their political outlook may have been elitist and authoritarian, but still contrasted sharply with the autocracy of the former sultan.

Nevertheless, the contrast can be overdone. The Young Turks took great pains to juxtapose their own rule with that of Abdülhamit's – the paradigm they touted was that of 'Freedom' (*Hürriyet* – the usual description of the 1908 constitutional revolution) and 'Oppression' (*Istibdad* – Abdülhamit's reign), and the scholarship on this period is in part a reflection of this. It can also be argued that there is an underlying ideological relationship between Abdülhamit's reign and the Young Turk's rule. Abdülhamit consciously tried to shape Ottoman Muslim solidarity into the fulcrum of a reinvigorated Ottoman state and while one can argue whether this constituted the fostering of an Ottoman-Muslim nationalism or rather of a kind of proto-nationalism, there is no doubt that over the years he mobilized Ottoman-Muslim sentiment. In doing so, the Sultan was in tune with underlying developments in society, where, as Keyder has argued, a religiously over-determined division of labour between a fast-growing non-Muslim bourgeoisie and an equally fast-growing Muslim-dominated state bureaucracy created increasing and ultimately unbearable tensions.[4] The roots of the CUP were to be found in the resentment felt by young Muslim bureaucrats and officers at the change in the balance of power between on the one hand the Christian bourgeoisie and the European powers who were perceived as being hand in glove with them and the Ottoman state and its servants on the other. The main grievance of the Young Turks against the Sultan was that his regime weakened the state and failed to protect the Ottoman nation. Their solution, endlessly repeated in their pamphlets and émigré journals, was to create a modern state (with all the trimmings such as a parliament and a constitution) with a rational, 'scientific' system of administration. They were not, however, anti-Islamic, far from it. As Hanioğlu has shown, it was an unquestioning belief in science and education rather than any democratic sentiment that dominated their thinking. Inspired by positivism, they were vehemently anti-clerical, but with the possible exception of Abdullah Cevdet, the 'atheist philosopher' (*dinsiz mutefekkir*) every one of them saw in a 'true' or 'purified' Islam, which was envisioned as a 'rational' religion open to science, a valuable building block of Ottoman reconstruction and a social cement.[5]

In its reconstituted form (from 1906 onwards) the CUP was an organization of Muslim civil servants and army officers, and as we have seen in earlier chapters, in its early days it was not even open to non-Muslims. It was, in other words, a political movement of Ottoman Muslims for Ottoman Muslims. After the period of compromise, inter-party strife and political turmoil between the constitutional revolution of 1908 and the outbreak of the Balkan War in 1912, the policies of the CUP were a – sometimes awkward – compromise between its professed adherence to the ideal of the 'Unity of the (Ethnic) Elements', the underlying principle of the Ottoman constitution and its Ottoman-Muslim nationalism. But from 1912 onwards, and certainly after the Unionist coup d'état of January 1913, Ottoman Muslim nationalism held sway. The Christian communities were now defined as the 'others' and a whole range of 'national' (*millî*) societies, clubs, firms, cooperatives and periodicals was founded in quick succession. Looking at the aims and the membership of these, it is immediately apparent that 'national' now meant 'Ottoman Muslim' only. The identification of the CUP with the Muslim majority produced both the nationalist economic policies of the *Millî İktisat*, through which the committee tried to create a level playing field for Muslim entrepreneurs through state interference in the economy, and to the oppressive and ultimately genocidal ethnic policies of the war years. As in Abdülhamit's days, the politics of Muslim solidarity held a special attraction for the large immigrant communities from the Balkans and the Caucasus, who had themselves been victims of religiously inspired persecution. Shared Muslim identity was a perfect path towards integration and it should thus cause no surprise that immigrants, especially Circassians, were so prominent among the CUP militants (especially in the so-called 'Special Organization', the *Teşkilat-i Mahsusa*).

Of course, the turn to Muslim nationalism was not due solely to the social make-up of the CUP or to the ideological preferences of its leaders. Just as Abdülhamit's 'Islamic turn' had in part been a rational answer to the changed territorial and demographic realities of the empire, so the appeal to Muslim solidarity of the Young Turks was caused in part by the need to mobilize the population in times of war. Most of the empire's soldiers hailed from Anatolia; appealing to the religious worldview of the peasant population of Anatolia made good sense.

Both elements – religious nationalism (with a strong anti-Greek and anti-Armenian bias) and military necessity – continued to play a role in the post-war era, when, during the 'National Struggle' (*Millî Mücadele*) Ottoman Muslim nationalism reached its apogee. From the congresses of Erzurum and Sivas in July and September 1919 to the final sessions of the Ottoman parliament in early 1920; in the rhetoric of Mustafa Kemal Pasha and others in the National Assembly after April 1920: the struggle was always defined as one of Ottoman Muslims for self determination and against the unjust claims of Armenians and Greeks and their European supporters. The definition of 'us' and 'them' in religious terms of course persisted until the exchange of populations agreed upon in Lausanne. It was after all Muslims from Greece who were exchanged with Orthodox from Anatolia, without other factors (for instance, linguistic ones) playing any role at all.[6]

Sacralization

Sultan Abdülhamit had made strong efforts to further sacralize his rule by using religious imagery and most of all through the exaltation of the institution of the caliphate. The Young Turks, minor civil servants and officers, were in a totally different position and any sacralization of their persons was out of the question. They did, however try to sacralize both the committee itself, which was often referred to as a 'Holy Society' (*cemiyeti mukaddes*) and its mission. This came out most clearly with the outbreak of World War I, which was officially declared a *jihad*, but it is also visible in the way the person of the sultan-caliph, Mehmet V Reşat, was presented to the public. Even before the war, during his public visits to Bursa, Edirne and Macedonia in 1910–11, the sultan emphasized the importance of solidarity between the ethnic communities, but he also visited shrines, mosques and dervish convents and surrounded himself with relics.

During the national struggle after war, sacralization was utilized to shore up support for the defence of Anatolia. In Mustafa Kemal's speeches, the earth of Anatolia is not only sacred in the sense that for any nationalist the national territory is sacred but also because Anatolia is the 'heartland of Islam' (*Islamin harîmi ismeti*). What is at stake is the rescuing of the *mukaddesat*, the holy traditions. The flavour of the times and the degree to which the struggle was sacralized is perhaps most visible in the text of the Turkish national anthem, the *İstiklâl Marşı* (Independence March), written in 1921 by Mehmet Akif. If it were not anachronistic to say so, one would be tempted to say that it describes the struggle entirely in terms of a clash of civilizations. Witness verse four:

> Even if a wall of steel surrounds the western horizon
> My heart full of belief is a mighty bulwark.
> You are full of power, don't be afraid! How can the toothless monster
> You call civilization strangle a religion that is so great?

Bureaucratizing Islam

Another important element of continuity between the Hamidian and Young Turk periods is in the efforts to modernize the state apparatus and extend its hold over the country. As in Abdülhamit's days, integrating Sunni Islam into the state bureaucracy (politicizing it in the process) was part of these efforts and a matter of priority for the CUP after the counterrevolution of April 1909 had shown up the vulnerability of the Young Turk regime. First the *Sheihülislam* was given a seat in the cabinet, a move that played an important role in legitimizing the policies of the Committee in particular during the tenure of *Sheihülislam* Musa Kazim. Then, from 1916 onwards, the *Sheihülislam* was removed from the cabinet and subordinated to it, with the jurisdiction over Islamic family law, charitable foundations and religious education being transferred to secular ministries. On the face of it these measures contrast sharply with those of the Hamidian era: where Abdülhamit empowered his preferred Islamic authorities and used them as props to his rule, the Young Turks reduced the status and independence of the Islamic authorities as a whole. The underlying aim, however, remained much the same: to fully control the Islamic establishment and to use it to strengthen the state. Both regimes, Sultan Abdülhamit as much as the CUP, were extremely suspicious of manifestations of Islam that were outside government control.

This tradition of state control of course reached its apogee during the republic. The image of the Kemalist republic, right from the start, was that of a regime that radically broke with the past and introduced a secular, or laicist, order. It is true that the republic took radical measures to limit the influence of Islam on the state within months of its founding. The functions of caliph and of *Sheihülislam* were both abolished by the republic's national assembly in March 1924. At the same time, however, the republic actually *increased* the state's hold over religion. The Presidium for Religious Affairs (*Diyanet İşleri Baskanligi*) that replaced the Sheikhulislamate was given sole responsibility for religious guidance. All imams and muftis were now civil servants. As the central state increased its hold over the country, so did its religious arm: the presidium centrally determined the contents of Friday sermons and instructed muftis on the correct advice to be given to the believers. Over time, the *Diyanet* was turned into a centralized and hierarchical bureaucracy to an extent that had never been achieved by Abdülhamit II. As Davison points out, the state not only restricted religious education – it also fostered it if it could fully control it.[7]

As in the empire, in the republic, too, the state exclusively looked after the religious needs of the Sunni majority, leaving all Muslim dissenters, such as the Alevi, to their own devices. In this respect, the nation state turned out to be as much a Sunni state as the late empire had been.

Morality

If there is one aspect in which there is a clear discontinuity between the late empire on the one hand and the Young Turk and Kemalist eras on the other, it is that of morality. Abdülhamit had sought to base his revived empire on a reinvigorated public morality, the *ahlak* propagated in his school textbooks and in the sermons of the *hatip*s. The Young Turks and Kemalists did nothing of the sort. The Unionist policies after 1913 definitely sought to secularize the social and cultural spheres even when the Unionists were appealing to a sentiment of Muslim nationalism at the same time. The Young Turks and the Kemalists wanted an Islam that was compatible with science and that supported their understanding of the national interest. In the republic this meant that the message was a double one: on the one hand religion was depicted as nothing but the private affair of the believer, on the other the believer was addressed as citizen of the republic with a religious duty to pay taxes and serve in the army.[8] Though there were efforts to strengthen the cohesion of society through the strengthening of a morality based in Islam, these efforts were made by Islamist revivalist movements such as those of Sait Nursi and Süleyman Tunahan. The state only became involved in moral rearmament in the late 1970s.

Kenan Evren: Islam as an antidote

When the Turkish General Staff took power on 12 September 1980, combating the hold of 'foreign' ideologies such as socialism, communism or Islamic fundamentalism over the Turkish youth was at the top of its agenda. Even in their first proclamation after the coup the generals talked about the need to combat 'perverse' (*sapık*) ideologies. Although the military suppressed the leftist and Islamist movements mercilessly, they also realized that an ideological alternative was needed and that traditional secularist Kemalism had too limited an appeal to be able to do the job. Under the personal guidance of coup leader General Kenan Evren (himself the son of an imam), they turned to the ideas of the 'Hearths of the Enlightened' (*Aydınlar Ocakları*). This was an organization of conservative nationalist academics, politicians and businessmen, founded in 1970 to break the hold of left-wing intellectuals over the political debate. The central element in its ideology, which was developed by its first president, İbrahim Kafesoğlu and called the 'Turkish-Islamic Synthesis', was the idea that Islam and the pre-Islamic culture of the Turks displayed a great number of similarities. Turks were therefore naturally attracted to Islam and destined to be its soldiers. As Turkish culture and national identity were shaped by a 2,500-year-old Turkic tradition and a 1,000-year-old religion, Islam was not only compatible with Turkish nationalism, but an integral part of it.

The Hearths of the Enlightened had been gaining influence in government circles since Demirel's 'National Front' coalitions in the late 1970s, but after the 1980 coup they achieved complete control in the fields of culture and education. The organs of the state were given the task of spreading the message of the Turkish–Islamic Synthesis. Poulton has remarked (without further elaborating the theme) that the ideological policies of Kenan Evren bear a certain resemblance to those of Abdülhamit and indeed, the resemblance is striking, both in the medium and in the message.[9]

Religious education was enshrined in the constitution the military had adopted in 1982 (article 24). It proclaimed that the state – and the state alone – was charged with religious education and that instruction in religious culture and moral education was to be compulsory in both primary and secondary education. In school textbooks, Islam was directly linked to values such as nationalism, the unity and indivisibility of the nation, respect for authority and militarism. The *Diyanet* was given a constitutional position as well, and its functions were now more than ever completely subservient to the interests of the state. Yavuz's characterization of Hamidian Islam ('in practice religion was subordinate and acted primarily as a shield for the preservation of the state') is true for the Islam of Evren's *Diyanet* as well. The message put out by the presidium in publications such as its *Cep İlmihali* (Pocket Catechism) is unashamedly nationalist, authoritarian and militarist. National unity was depicted as a religious duty. The *Gazi*-ethos was promoted. A special missionary department was set up in 1981 to combat Kurdish separatist agitation in the southeast. Sunni mosques were built in Alevi villages in considerable numbers. The *Diyanet* benefited enormously from the central role it played in the ideological campaign of the military and of its successors. The number of *Diyanet* employees grew from slightly over 50,000 to nearly 85,000 between 1979 and 1989.

So, all the elements that were prominent in Abdülhamit's era were once again present in the early 1980s: the establishment of state control, the use of the mosque and the school, the emphasis on morality (*ahlak*), missionary activity and mosque-building to combat diversity and unify the nation, and above all the attempt to monopolize religious instruction and use it to support the state. The intermediaries were there as well: Fethullah Gülen, who was to become the most prominent religious figure of the 1990s, owed his meteoric rise in part to his support for the coup d'état of 1980 and his support for the policies of the *Diyanet* afterwards. Throughout the 1980s and the early 1990s Gülen had privileged access to the seat of political power in Ankara. His movement profited from this privileged position and continued to grow. After the fall of the Soviet Union it developed a network of schools in the Balkans, the Caucasus and Central Asia. It was only when the army top brass reversed course and decided to crack down on Islamic organizations from 1997 onwards, that the Fethullahcis came under pressure and their leader was forced to leave the country and settle in the USA.

At the same time, the policies of Kenan Evren also showed up continuities with the Kemalist era in that political activities (or activities that could be interpreted as such) of Islamic movements that were not under state control continued to be regarded as illegal.

Conclusion

What a comparison of these case studies of instances in which the Ottoman/Turkish state instrumentalized Islam to achieve political goals seems to show is an underlying continuity between the late Ottoman Empire and the republic where their 'Islamic' policies are concerned.

Abdülhamit's policies of establishing far-reaching state control over the contents of religious education and instruction, his standardization of the Sharia and his attempts to use the religious message to increase loyalty to the throne in a sense presage the Young Turk measures aimed at a further subjugation of Islam to the state. What the Young Turks did during World War I – removing the *Sheihülislam* from the cabinet and bringing all forms of education, the administration of Islamic law and the charitable foundations (*evkaf*) under the control of secular ministries – was on the face of it different from what the Sultan had done. Where he strengthened the Islamic institutions, the Young Turks weakened them. But both limited the freedom of action of the religious authorities, integrated them further into the state machinery and politicized them. This continued in the Kemalist republic, when all responsibility for religious matters and for the charitable foundations was devolved onto a new Presidium for Religious Affairs, which operated directly under the prime minister and was given extensive powers to centrally determine the message spread in mosques and by muftis.

The early republic clearly broke with the policies of the Hamidian and Young Turk eras in the field of education. Both regimes had put great stock in religious education, centrally determining the curriculum to suit their ideological programme. The Kemalists, by contrast, eliminated religious education altogether. In this area continuity was restored by the neo-Kemalist regime of Kenan Evren after 1980. Determining the content of religious education and using it to buttress loyalty to the state again became a priority for the regime.

If there is a strong continuity between the successive regimes in their quest for control over and instrumentalization of religion, the same is true for the character of the debate surrounding religion. The debate never was one for or against religion. It was, as Andrews has pointed out, about the *interpretation* of religion. The Hamidian regime, the Young Turks, the Kemalists and the neo-Kemalists all employed the means at their disposal to argue the case for *true* Islam: loyal to the Caliph in Abdülhamit's case, open to science in that of the Young Turks, private and non-political in that of the Kemalists, and nationalist with Evren. This Islam was always presented in opposition to an unacceptable Islam that the regimes sought to discredit: liberal in the case of Abdülhamit, obscurantist for the Young Turks, political for the Kemalists and fundamentalist in the eyes of Evren's junta.

What the investigation of these four particular case studies has taught us, I think, is that there are striking similarities in the way successive Ottoman and Turkish republican regimes have handled acute challenges: In times of crisis these regimes recognized that the Muslim component was so central to the identity of the vast majority of their citizenry, that they had no option but to appeal to religion when trying to master the crisis. At the same time we have seen that different types of crises demanded different kinds of appeals to Islam. Abdülhamit II and General Evren were faced by ideological challenges that were felt to be life threatening to their regimes and even to the survival of the state. In the first case, the challenge lay in the centrifugal forces of minority nationalism and in that of political liberalism; in the second case the challenge came from different brands of socialism, from Islamic fundamentalism and – to a lesser extent at the time – from Kurdish separatism. To counter these ideological challenges the rulers had recourse to an appeal to Islamic norms and values, explicitly linked to the political message of dynastic loyalty in the first case and state-centred Turkish nationalism and militarism in the second.

The Young Turks during World War I and the Turkish nationalists of the post-World War I era appealed to religion in a very different manner. Faced with an uphill battle for the survival of their state, they had to mobilize the largest possible majority on the basis of an appeal to a shared identity. What they were concerned with in the years 1912–22 was to find a new 'national' basis on which to build their state. This they found in the Ottoman Muslim identity. Against the backdrop of the rising tensions between Muslims and non-Muslims in the last decades of the nineteenth century and the Balkan Wars of 1912–13 identities had been shaped primarily on the basis of religious affiliation. The loyalty of the Christian minorities was in serious doubt after the Balkan Wars and there was really no other option but to appeal to the core Muslim population of Anatolia, from where most of the Ottoman soldiery was recruited. The same problem presented itself to the resistance movement after World War I. Between 1914 and 1922, sacralization of the struggle, in the shape of *jihad* or a 'holy ideal' and of the national territory (as earth drenched in the blood of martyrs) certainly took place, but, as the policies of the Young Turks during the war and those of the Kemalists after 1922 showed, illumination of state and society was not part of the Young Turk/Kemalist agenda, quite the opposite. The element of 'moral rearmament' was lacking and this makes the policies of the Young Turks and early Kemalists during the large-scale armed struggles of their time very different from those of the preceding Hamidian regime and of the junta of 1980–3, both of which were faced primarily with *ideological* competition. It was the nature of the challenge, which ultimately determined the way in which Islam was instrumentalized, as a basis for a national identity or as a defensive ideology.

21. Turning Points and Missed Opportunities in the Modern History of Turkey: Where Could Things Have Gone Differently?*

For nearly 30 years now I have occupied myself in one way or another with the history of the late Ottoman Empire and the early republic of Turkey, roughly the period between 1880 and 1950. The issues I have touched upon have varied a great deal, from the life in the trenches of Ottoman soldiers in World War I to political purges in 1926; from Sultan Reşat's visit to Kosovo in 1911 to travellers' accounts of Turkey in the late 1930s. Nevertheless, this volume shows that it is possible to discern a thread, a grand narrative, if you like, that connects the different research projects. This thread is the continuity between the late Ottoman Empire, particularly the Young Turk period and the Kemalist republic, politically, ideologically and socially. Within this narrative of continuity I have emphasized the importance of World War I, arguing that the republic of Turkey could only come into existence thanks to the legacy of mobilization, demographic engineering and nationalist economic policies of the war years. I have also emphasized the importance of migration in shaping these processes.

When one studies the transition from the multi-ethnic Ottoman Empire to the secularist (though not secular) Turkish nation state, it is tempting to see the process as one of inevitability. This is still the underlying assumption in many modern studies on Turkey. But, as I have argued in the preceding chapters, the assumption that the Turkish nation was somehow embedded or submerged in the empire, ready to emerge (as I have quoted Bernard Lewis)[1] once the conditions were right, should be questioned. The same is true for the notion that the late Ottoman Empire was a decadent or moribund structure and that the 'national' solution, be it Turkish, Greek, Arab or Armenian, was the only viable one. The emergence of Mustafa Kemal Pasha as the leader of the national resistance movement after World War I was far from inevitable, and Kemalist nationalism and secularism were not the only options open to the ruling élite of the early republic. Freeing ourselves from the teleological mindset, which sees the nation state as the inevitable outcome and relegates the history of the late Ottoman Empire to the status of prehistory of that nation state, is important if we are to gain a realistic insight into the social and political developments of the late Ottoman era and the options open to the people of that era. It is all very well for us to say, with the benefit of hindsight, that they were experiencing the 'imperial twilight', but the time of day may not have been quite as evident to them. Of course, speculation on the collapse of the Ottoman Empire was rife at the turn of the twentieth century, but then again: that had been the situation for nearly a hundred years.

If we try to look at the history of the period afresh, without the benefit of hindsight, we are automatically faced with the question: where could things have gone differently? What were the turning points that shaped Ottoman and Turkish history? This is the question I want to ask here and in doing so I am inspired primarily by Geoffrey Hawthorne's 1991 ground-breaking book *Plausible Worlds: Possibility and Understanding in History and the Social Sciences*.

Of course, a number of them are obvious: the constitutional revolution, the outbreak of World War I, the proclamation of the republic – clearly these are very significant moments. I would like to use this final chapter to review a number of turning points that are not often defined as such in the histo-riography of Turkey and speculate on the possible alternative histories that might have been, had things taken a different turn. These contemplations do not pretend to be based on original research. This is a thought experiment, an exercise in counterfactual history.

Any such discussion, indeed any discussion of late Ottoman history, must begin with the disaster of 1877–8, the great 'War of '93' as it was known to earlier generations who used the *Hijri* calendar. It is difficult to overestimate the importance of this event. To recapitulate the main course of events: in April 1876, in the aftermath of a Christian uprising in Bosnia, Bulgarian nationalists based in Romania and Russia organized a rebellion to the south of the Danube, which was brutally suppressed by the Ottomans with the help of militias (the so-called *Bashibozuks*). Some 15,000 Bulgarian peasants died at the hands of these irregulars, many of whom were Circassians who had themselves been resettled in the area after they had been chased from the Caucasus by the Russians a decade earlier. These events led to war with Serbia and Montenegro, a war which the Ottomans won in three months. They also led to the publication in Britain of William Gladstone's famous pamphlet *The Bulgarian Horrors and the Question of the East*, which after its publication in September 1876 sold over 200,000 copies and turned liberal and Christian opinion in Britain against the Ottomans and left them isolated when Russia intervened on behalf of the Bulgarians. A diplomatic conference in Istanbul in December proposed the creation of two large autonomous Bulgarian provinces under Christian governors, proposals which were rejected by the Ottoman government. As a result, war broke out between Russia and the Ottoman Empire in April 1877. The Russian assault was halted at Kars in the East and famously by *Gazi* Osman Pasha at Plevna in the West, but the fortresses were taken in November–December, after which Ottoman resistance collapsed and the Russian army marched on, ultimately to camp at San Stefano (now Yeşilköy). The Ottoman Empire was forced to sign a peace agreement, which basically ended Ottoman rule in Europe. At the subsequent conference in Berlin the terms were somewhat mitigated, but still the magnitude of the disaster, in terms of loss of territory, income, population and prestige was such that the subsequent decades of Hamidian rule can only be understood meaningfully as a period of slow recovery and adjustment, of finding a new equilibrium administratively, culturally and financially. The extreme caution of the Hamidian regime may have been due in part to the growing paranoia of the sultan himself. It was certainly also caused by a feeling that all had nearly been lost in 1878.

The '93 war' also led to a well-documented human tragedy. Over half a million Muslim refugees permanently left the areas now lost and were resettled elsewhere in the empire. This was to have serious consequences one generation later. The memory of the tragedy was vividly instilled in the minds of the children born in the late 1870s and early 1880s by their refugee parents. The very same people who would become active in the Committee of Union and Progress (CUP) 20 years later came from this generation of children, and the fear of another '93' was part of their mental make up. It is certainly no coincidence that the leading perpetrators of the Armenian massacres counted so many refugees and children of refugees (*muhacirs*) among their number. Dr Bahaettin Şakir's parents had to flee from Bulgaria, Çerkes Mehmet Reşit, the governor of Diyarbakır, was himself a fugitive from the Caucasus and Bulgaria. Celâl Bayar, who organized the expulsion of the Greeks from Western Anatolia in 1914, hailed from Gemlik but he was also the child of refugees from Bulgaria. These people were traumatized by the loss of their homeland in 1878 and determined to prevent a repetition.

But what if the war had not occurred? What if the liberal powers of Western Europe had supported the Ottomans, like they had done in the Crimean War 20 years earlier and thus possibly pre-empted the Russian assault? It is tempting to speculate on the possibility that the parliamentarian and constitutional regime introduced in 1876 could have endured. The constitution was a document that was quite in line with mid-nineteenth century European practice, even if a number of clauses gave it a less liberal character than the Belgian original on which it was based. As Robert Devereux has shown, the elections for parliament can hardly be called democratic in a modern sense but parliament acquitted itself rather well during its two sessions.[2] Without the war it would have been very difficult for Abdülhamit to prorogue parliament indefinitely, as he did, and parliament would have been given the opportunity to mature and gain experience. There would have been a platform where the different ethnic communities could voice their interests, but the divisions between liberals and conservatives would have run across the ethnic divisions (as indeed they did in 1877–8 and even in 1908–13) and might have defused ethnic tension to some degree. It is perhaps not likely that such an arrangement could have stopped the march of separatist nationalism in the long run, but it might have left both the Turks and the other successor states with stronger civic and democratic traditions. The history of the late Ottoman Empire, in other words, could perhaps have been more like that of the Habsburg Empire.

In addition, without the war the *muhacir* problem would not have assumed the importance that it did and the Young Turk generation of 1880 would conceivably not have been poisoned by feelings of resentment and revenge against the Christian communities of the empire.

Of course, much of this argument could be repeated for the Balkan War that broke out in October 1912. The Balkan War in a sense can be seen as the sequel to the 'war of 93', because it was the unresolved questions of 1878 and the unfulfilled ambitions of the Balkan states, particularly in Macedonia, that led them to attack the empire. This war led once again to an influx of refugees on a scale similar to that of 35 years earlier, and among the Young Turks, who predominantly hailed from the Balkans, the Aegean and the capital, there were many who now lost their ancestral home. Their resentment and determination not to let anything similar happen in Anatolia produced in many of them a militancy similar to that of Bahaettin Şakir. Examples are Abdülhalik Renda, the infamous governor of Bitlis and Aleppo in 1915–16 (and a native of Yanina in the Western Balkans) and Şükrü Kaya, the director of resettlement during World War I (a native of Kos). As in 1878, the military disaster of the Balkan War led to the imposition of authoritarian rule, this time through the Unionist coup d'état of January 1913. Parliament was not prorogued this time but it was to all intents and purposes left powerless.

The second turning point that has left a lasting imprint on Turkish history is, I think, the insurrection in Istanbul in April 1909, known as the '31 March incident' (*31 Mart vakası*). The rebellion itself was suppressed with relative ease after 11 days by troops loyal to the CUP. Martial law was declared and a large number of rebels was summarily tried and hanged. Nevertheless it constituted a traumatic experience, which left deep scars on the collective psyche of the Young Turk generation and its successors. The trauma was caused by the fact that the rule of those who saw themselves as the 'heroes of freedom' and as the vanguard of progress had proved to be so fragile, even in their own capital. It was toppled in a morning by a bunch of unruly soldiers and students, without the population of the capital coming to the aid of either the Young Turks or the constitution. Unionist rule could be restored only by intervention of the army. The events of April 1909 installed a deep fear in the Young Turk generation, a fear of the exploitation of the ignorant mass of the population by religious fanatics, resulting in 'religious reaction' (*irtica*), a term that seems to have gained currency in this period. From now on, the Young Turks (Unionists and later, the Kemalists) interpreted events as parts of a master narrative in which the forces of enlightenment were locked in battle with the forces of darkness and in which the illiterate population could not be trusted to make the right choices and could thus easily be manipulated. When in February 1925, an insurrection led by the Nakşibendi dervish Sheikh Sait broke out to the north of Diyarbakır and the rebels demanded the restoration of the caliphate and the Sharia (which even then had not been abolished), Kemalist representatives in the national assembly were quick to point out the parallels with the '31 Mart'. The same happened when a small group of stoned dervishes calling themselves the 'Army of the Caliphate' descended on the Western Anatolian town of Menemen in December 1930 and ritually killed a young teacher who was on duty as a reserve officer at the time. As in the case of the '31 Mart', what particularly shocked the Kemalists about this incident was the fact that the population of the town did not lift a finger to defend either the young officer or the secular republican order.

The legacy of *31 Mart*, Sheikh Sait and Menemen is still very much with us today as the master narrative through which Kemalists see contemporary developments. That Unionist rule was ultimately restored by the armed forces is a lesson that has not been lost on the Kemalists of our day either. Is it going too far to think that without the events of April 1909, the concept of *irtica*, and the attendant Manichean view of society would not have become so dominant in the minds of this generation and the generations educated by them and that the army would not have built quite such a tradition of involvement in politics?

The third turning point of the twentieth century and one that is often overlooked, is, I think, the transformation both of the nature of the Kemalist regime and of the character of Turkish nationalism in the early 1930s. As we know, Mustafa Kemal Pasha himself encouraged his old friend Fethi in 1930 to form an opposition party that shared the fundamental ideals of the governing People's Party (PP) – secularism, nationalism and republicanism – but favoured more economic and political liberalism. When this party, the Free Republican Party (*Serbest Cumhuriyet Fırkası*) proved hugely popular, especially in the developed west of the country, it was closed down after three months. The party establishment of the PP had never been happy with the experiment and it exerted increasing pressure on the president (who had remained party leader) to leave his neutral position and commit himself to his party. In November Mustafa Kemal gave in. An embittered Fethi Okyar felt he had no option but to close down the party rather than having to oppose the president in the political arena.

This, however, was only the beginning of a more far-reaching change in Turkey's political landscape. A month after the closure of the Free Republican Party (FRP), the Menemen incident shocked the Kemalist leadership. Although Mustafa Kemal Pasha's initial plans to deport the population and raze Menemen to the ground were never executed, the incident strengthened the position of the hardliners within the party. They now embarked on a campaign to put an end to all genuine civil society organizations and bring social and cultural life in the country entirely under party control. The first such organization to be suppressed was that of the Turkish Hearths (*Türk Ocakları*). This society, originally founded by the nationalist wing of the Young Turks in 1912, had been revived after the founding of the republic by education minister Hamdullah Suphi Tanrıöver. When it was closed down in 1931, the organization had a network of 267 clubs with over 30,000 members and a programme of activities consisting of lectures, courses, exhibitions and concerts. In 1932 the clubs were replaced with the People's Houses (*Halk Evleri*), which had a very similar programme, but were directly linked to the party.

In the same year, 1931, one of the last remaining newspapers that was critical of government policies, *Yarın* ('Tomorrow'), published by Arif Oruç, an old friend of Mustafa Kemal and Fethi, was closed down after the introduction of a new draconian press law that allowed the government to ban any newspaper that published articles 'contrary to the general policies of the nation'. In 1933, the university in Istanbul, the *Darülfünun*, was formally closed down and reconstituted as the University of Istanbul (*İstanbul Üniversitesi*). The aim of the operation was certainly in part to raise the level of academic education in Turkey, but it was also an ideological purge. When the university was reopened only a third of the former professors were hired.

The attack on independent civil society institutions reached its zenith in 1935, when the Turkish Women's Union, originally founded by women who had been active in the independence war, was pressured into dissolving itself. Already in 1928 the Union had been forced to give up its political demands and had then continued as a social club. But now its activities were halted altogether, ostensibly because its aims (equal rights for women) had now been realized by the government. Also in 1935 the Masonic lodges linked to the Grand Orient of Turkey were told by Interior Minister (and fellow mason) Şükrü Kaya that they would have to extend their summer break indefinitely – which they did for the next 12 years. Even dissident currents within the party, notably the group that had published the journal *Kadro* that favoured a farther-reaching social revolution in 1932–4, had to stop their activities, when İnönü and Atatürk, who had earlier afforded them a degree of protection, gave in to hardliners within the party leadership.

The most interesting aspect of this wave of suppression is that the closed down organizations all shared the basic elements of the Kemalist world view. The people involved were by and large nationalists, secularists and strong believers in education and emancipation. This makes the suppression of these groups very different from that of the derwish orders (*tarikat*) of the mid-1920s. We have to conclude that the suppression of civil society in the 1930s was not primarily about ideology but about an attempt at totalitarian control on the part of the state through the party. The 1930s also witnessed a shift in the content of Kemalist nationalism. Increasingly it was the narrow and xenophobic nationalism of people like Mahmut Esat and Yunus Nadi that dominated the discourse. In their way of thinking the non-Muslim citizens of the republic definitely qualified as 'foreigners' and members of international networks like the masons were branded *kozmopolit*, implying that they could not be loyal citizens of the republic at the same time. This development was, of course, not unique to Turkey. Rather, it reflected the dominant trend all over Central and Eastern Europe.

What if the change in direction of 1930–5 had not taken place? Had Mustafa Kemal Pasha stuck to the course he had himself charted three months earlier and retained his above-party position, it is not unlikely that the FRP could have survived and played a role somewhat similar to that of the Democrat Party (DP) 20 years later. The Kemalist regime was probably not as unpopular in 1930 as it would be in 1950 after the years of economic hardship and repression during World War II, but in free elections the FRP would clearly have been a force to reckon with. If Kemal had supported a degree of pluralism, it is hard to see how the hardliners within the RPP could have developed the totalitarian tendencies I described earlier. In response to the challenge of the FRP, dissident groups within the RPP like *Kadro* could have formulated a new ideological position for the party 30 years before the advent of Bülent Ecevit's 'Left of Center' programme. Civil society organizations like the Women's Union, the Journalists' Association, the Turkish Hearths and the Masonic lodges could have gathered strength over the years. There would have been less opportunity, perhaps, for the extreme nationalists with their xenophobic tendencies like Mahmud Esat Bozkurt to impose their views. Tragedies like the anti-Jewish pogroms in Thrace in 1934 and the discriminatory Wealth Tax (*Varlık Vergisi*), which wiped out the non-Muslim bourgeoisie in 1942, possibly could have been avoided.

Beyond this, if we take our counterfactual exercise even further, a more pluralistic Turkey with a stronger civil society, led perhaps by French-oriented Fethi Okyar with (after Atatürk's death) a man like veteran opposition leader Hüseyin Rauf [Orbay] (a hero of the Balkan War and of the struggle for independence, but also a confirmed Anglophile) by his side, would have fit naturally in the camp of the Allies during World War II. İnönü's Turkey, as we know, concluded a mutual assistance treaty with France and Britain in 1939, but then reneged on it for the next five years, only declaring war on Germany in February 1945. A more liberal Turkey would still have driven a hard bargain, but possibly it would have joined the Allied war effort if not in 1939, then in early 1943 when the Germans had had begun to lose the war. Turkey then would have been among the victors in 1945.

The 1945–7 period is, I think, the final episode that we should consider during this exercise in counterfactual history. The protagonist of this period is without doubt İsmet İnönü. As early as 19 May 1945 he had announced his desire to make Turkey more democratic and on 1 November of that year he declared that Turkey needed an opposition party. As we know, that opposition party came into being in January 1946, when four former RPP members founded the DP. The elections that followed (and which had been brought forward from June 1947 to July 1946) were clearly full of irregularities, but even so the DP was able to show its strength, winning 62 seats in the national assembly. As in 1930, tension between the two parties rose sharply and the hawks within the RPP, led by Prime Minister Recep Peker, did everything they could to delegitimize the opposition, branding them as traitors, communists and even psychopaths. But unlike Mustafa Kemal Pasha in 1930, İsmet stuck to his guns. He conferred with Peker and with opposition leader Celâl Bayar in a manner that is reminiscent of Mustafa Kemal's talks with İsmet and Fethi in 1930. Then, on 12 July 1947 he issued a statement in which he said that political opposition was legitimate and natural and in which he called upon the organs of the state to act impartially. This marked the end of the hardliners. Recep Peker had to resign. From then on until the elections almost three years later, the process of democratization continued to gather pace. The RPP did everything it could to regain popularity by adopting much of the opposition's programme, but with 25 years of authoritarian rule behind it, it lacked credibility in the eyes of the electorate that brought the Democrats to power in May 1950.

Now what would have happened if İsmet had not supported this process, if he had made the same choice that Atatürk made in 1930? This, I think, would not have spoilt Turkey's ability to procure United States support and aid in the context of the start of the Cold War. It may be true that İnönü introduced his reforms partly to carry favour with the West after a war in which Turkey had lost much prestige and was in danger of isolation, but then again: the United States supported, and relied on, regimes as varied and as undemocratic as South Korea, Pakistan and Iran in its global struggle against communism, so it could probably have lived with a dictatorial Turkey as ally. Continued dictatorship, however, would in all probability have blocked Turkey's access to NATO (since even after the introduction of multi-party democracy the Northern European NATO countries still felt very hesitant about Turkish membership of the organization in 1952) and as a corollary its access to the European Economic Community (EEC). After all, in European eyes the main reason why Turkey was seen as a candidate country for the EEC was its value as a NATO partner and the desire to keep the country stable by increasing its prospects for economic growth. It is very unlikely that the association agreement of 1963 would ever have been concluded if Turkey had not been a NATO member.

It is perhaps not too far-fetched to suppose that a continued İnönü dictatorship would have placed Turkey in a position very similar to that of Franco's Spain. Of course, the regimes would have differed a great deal in some respects. İnönü's strict secularism bore no resemblance to Franco's fanatical religiosity and the regime in Spain displayed a violence and brutality that its counterpart in Turkey never had. But still, both countries would have been safely inside the Western bloc, but outside NATO and the EEC/EC, with state-led economic growth; they would have had militarized societies with centralist administrations and strict suppression of dissident (in particular socialist) currents and regional minorities. With the support of the army, such a 1930s political structure could conceivably have lasted until İnönü's death in 1973, much like the old regime in Spain did until the Caudillo's death in 1975. By then, however, such a regime would have been so out of step with the ambitions of the emerging middle classes within the country as well as with developments in Europe, that it would probably collapse.

All in all, Turkey's real history of the post-war period, in spite of all its upheavals, looks much more attractive than this counterfactual scenario. Nevertheless, there is another side to this coin, too. A complete collapse of the regime as in Spain could have paved the way for a radical break with the dictatorial past. In Spain after 1975, Franco's regime had lost all legitimacy outside the circle of hardcore Falangists. That allowed conservatives, liberals and social democrats to battle it out in the political arena without serious outside interference and create a genuine modern democracy. The fact that in Turkey dictatorship made a 'soft landing' after 1945 meant that fundamental structures of the one-party state, as well as part of the ideological legacy have been able to survive within the multi-party environment, a source of much social and political tension in Turkey today.

But this intellectual exercise that I've here engaged in is one of fantasy. The wars of 1877 and 1912 *did* take place. The counterrevolution of April 1909 *did* permanently damage the constitutional period. The embryonic Ottoman parliaments were dissolved and emasculated in 1878 and 1913 respectively. The army *was* given a dominant role in the administration under martial law in 1909 and again in 1913. A decade after he had established a republic based on the concept of national sovereignty (*hakimiyeti milliye*) Mustafa Kemal Pasha *did not* dare to go for multi-party democracy and instead oversaw the establishment of an almost totalitarian grip of state and party over the country. His successor İnönü, however, against the expectation of many, made the opposite choice and opened the way for the development of multi-party democracy in Turkey while preserving much of the legacy of the dictatorial era.

Nevertheless: however unrealistic the alternative scenarios presented in this essay may be, I think it is a very useful exercise for us historians to remind ourselves that the historical developments with which we are all too familiar, should not be seen as inevitable; that from time to time we should deny ourselves the benefit of hindsight. Thinking about what could have been makes us more sensitive to processes and contingencies that we too easily overlook when we already know how the story ends.

Notes

I. Sources and Literature: Introduction

1. Zürcher, Erik Jan, 'The Ottoman Empire and the Turkish republic: an attempt at a new periodisation', *Welt des Islams* 32/2 (1992), pp. 237–53.
2. Davison, Andrew, *Secularism and Revivalism. A Hermeneutic Reconsideration* (New Haven, 1998), p. 177.

1. The Politician as Historian, Historians in Politics: On the *Nutuk* (Speech) of Mustafa Kemal Pasha

* This chapter was published in Dutch in 1992 in modified form: 'De politicus als geschiedschrijver, de historicus in de politiek', in E. de Moor (ed.), *Elf wijzen van interpreteren. Essays over het lezen van teksten uit het islamitisch cultuurgebied* (Nijmegen: Mandara, 1992), pp. 127–37.

1. Şimşir, Bilâl N., *Atatürk'ün Büyük Söylevi Üzerine Belgeler* (Ankara, 1991), is a collection of contemporary reports and documents on the *Nutuk*, mainly from French and British archives.
2. Şehsuvaroğlu, Bedi, *Atatürk'ün Sağlık Hayatı* (Istanbul, 1981), p. 12.
3. Gazi Mustafa Kemal, *Nutuk* (Ankara, 1927).
4. The republic's first reliable census, conducted in 1927, reported that 10.6 per cent of the Turkish population was literate.
5. Kemal Atatürk, *Nutuk 3 Cilt* (Istanbul, 1952–9).
6. Kemal Atatürk, *Söylev/Nutuk* (Ankara, 1973–5).
7. Kemal Atatürk, Nutuk 1919–1927. *Bugünkü Dille Yayına Hazırlayan Prof. Dr. Zeynep Korkmaz* (Ankara, 1991).
8. Cf. Atay, Falih Rıfkı, *Çankaya* (Istanbul, 1968), pp. 31 and 551.
9. Gasi Mustafa Kemal pascha, *Die neue Türkei 1919–1927: Rede gehalten in Angora vom 15–20. Oktober 1927 vor den Abgeordneten und Delegierten der republikanischen Volkspartei* (Leipzig, 1928–9).
10. *A Speech Delivered by Ghazi Mustapha Kemal. President of the Turkish Republic* (Leipzig, 1929) [translator anonymous].

11. See http://www.habertek.net/article.php?article_id=3900.
12. *Nutuk*, 1952 edition (1967 printing), vol. 2, p. 897.
13. Felsefe Kurumu Seminerleri (1974–1975). *Türkiye' de Tarih Eğitimi* (Ankara, 1977), pp. 258, 404–32.
14. Family names were only made compulsory in Turkey in 1934. The family names of leading figures who are best known by their birthname or by the name they were given at an early age are given between square brackets.
15. Zürcher, Erik Jan, *The Unionist factor: The Role of the Committee of Union and Progress in the Turkish National Movement 1905–1926* (Leiden, 1984), p. 162.
16. *Nutuk*, vol. 2, pp. 893–4.
17. This is the main argument of my *Unionist Factor*.

2. Young Turk Memoirs as a Historical Source: Kâzım Karabekir's İstiklâl Harbimiz

*Originally published as: 'Young Turk memoirs as a historical source', *Middle Eastern Studies* 22/4 (1986), pp. 561–70 (translated with additions as: 'Kâzim Karabekir ve *İstiklâl Harbimiz* kitabı', *Tarih ve Toplum* 38 [1986], pp. 339–43).

1. For instance, the collections published by Bilâl N. Şimşir since 1973 (Şimşir, Bilâl N, *İgiliz Belgelerinde Atatürk* [Ankara: Türk Tarih Kurumu, 1973], vol. 1, 1975; vol. 2, 1979; vol. 3), and such Turkish journals as *Belgelerle Türk Tarihi Dergisi* and *Tarih Vesikaları*.
2. Large collections of early Turkish newspapers are to be found both in the *Millî Kütüphane* in Ankara and in the *Atatürk Kitaplığı* in Istanbul.
3. For instance, those of Ali İhsan Sâbis (1943, 1951–2), Ali Fuat [Cebesoy] (1953, 1955, 1960), Kâzım Nami Duru (1957), Kılıç Ali (1955), Hüseyin Rauf [Orbay] (1962–3), Mazhar Müfit Kansu (1966), Mahmut Celâl Bayar (1967), Kâzım Özalp (1971), Halil Kut (1972) and Rıza Nur (1967–8).
4. Halide Edib [Adıvar], *The Turkish Ordeal. Being the Further Memoirs of Halide Edib* (New York/London, 1928).
5. As laid down by him in interviews with the newspapers *Vakit* (in January 1922) and *Milliyet* (in March 1926), and in his speech before the congress of the RPP in 1927, the *Nutuk*.
6. Cf. Zürcher, Erik Jan, *The Unionist Factor. The Role of the Committee of Union and Progress in the Turkish National Movement (1905–1926)* (Leiden: Brill, 1984), pp. 24–30. For a recent example of a widely used history of the Turkish revolution which displays all the characteristics of the 'official' Kemalist tradition, see Kili, Suna, *Türk Devrim Tarihi* (İstanbul: Tekin, 1982).
7. Fethi Okyar, quoted in: Kutay, Cemal (ed.) *Üç Devirde Bir Adam* (İstanbul: Tercüman, 1980).

8. Hüsamettin Ertürk was a leading staff-officer of the *Teşkilât-ı Mahsusa*. He was ordered by Enver Pasha in 1918 to keep the organization intact after the war, as an instrument for the Turkish resistance in the coming struggle. After March, 1920, he served as liaison officer between the General Staff in Ankara and the nationalist underground in Istanbul. His memoirs were published as: Ertürk, Hüsamettin (Samih Nafiz Tansu, ed.), *İki Devrin Perde Arkası* (İstanbul: Nurgök, 1957).

9. Eşref was an important field-officer of the *Teşkilât*. His handwritten memoirs form the basis of several books by Cemal Kutay and are used extensively in Celâl Bayar's memoirs.

10. Cf. Kutay, Cemal, *Birinci Dünya Harbinde Teşkilât-ı Mahsusa* (İstanbul: Tarih, 1962); Stoddard, Philip H., The Ottoman Government and the Arabs, 1911–1918. A Preliminary Study of the Teskilat-i Mahsusa (unpublished Ph.D. thesis, Princeton, 1963, for which Eşref was interviewed) and Zürcher, *The Unionist Factor*, pp. 83–8.

11. There are many editions of the *Nutuk* (cf. the previous chapter). The best-known modern Turkish edition (and the one I used) is Kemal Atatürk, *Nutuk* (İstanbul: Millî Eğitim Bakanlığı, 1967) 3 vols. The English translation published in Istanbul in 1963 (*A Speech Delivered by Mustafa Kemal Atatürk 1927*) is notoriously unreliable.

12. Karabekir, Kâzım, *İstiklâl Harbimiz* (İstanbul: Türkiye, 1960).

13. Cf. Zürcher, *The Unionist Factor*, pp. 38–44. For Karabekir's own role in the CUP see his: *İttihat ve Terakki Cemiyeti 1896–1908* (İstanbul: Faruk Özerengin, 1982), written in 1945.

14. Cf. Dursunoğlu, Cevat, *Millî Mücadelede Erzurum* (Ankara: Ziraat Bankası, 1946) and Tunaya, Tarık Zafer, *Türkiyede Siyasî Partiler* (İstanbul: Doğan Kardeş, 1952), pp. 490–1.

15. In 1919 the strength of Karabekir's Fifteenth Army Corps was 17,860. In the case of total mobilization this strength rose to 30,000 regulars and about 20,000 irregulars (Karabekir, *İstiklâl Harbimiz*, p. 25).

16. Hüseyin Rauf [Orbay] was the son of an Ottoman admiral. He himself became a national hero as commander of the cruiser *Hamidiye* in the Balkan War of 1913. In 1919 he was one of the pioneers of the national resistance movement, sitting on the *Heyet-i Temsiliye* (Representative Committee) of the nationalists and serving in the last Ottoman Parliament. Following his return from exile (the British deported him to Malta in 1920) he served as Minister and Prime Minister in Ankara. His memoirs first appeared in *Yakın Tarihimiz*, a weekly published by Feridun Kandemir for *Türkpetrol* between March 1962 and February 1963.

17. According to a decree of July 1923, army officers could only sit in the assembly after having given up their army command (they were not required to leave the army), but this rule was only enforced in November, 1924.

(Cf. Finefrock, Michael M., From Sultanate to Republic: Mustafa Kemal Atatürk and the Structure of Turkish Politics 1922–1924 (unpublished Ph.D. thesis, Princeton, 1976) p. 227.

18. Cf. Zürcher, Erik Jan, *Political Opposition in the Early Turkish Republic. The Progressive Republican Party (1924–1925)* (Leiden: Brill, 1991), p. 177.

19. Cf. Erman, Azmi Nihat, *İzmir Suikastı ve İstiklâl Mahkemeleri* (İstanbul: Temel, 1971); Kandemir, Feridun, *İzmir Suikastının İçyüzü* (İstanbul: Ekicigil, 1955). Also Zürcher, *The Unionist Factor*, pp. 142–65.

20. Karabekir, Kâzım, *İstiklâl Harbimizin Esasları* (İstanbul: Sinan, 1951).

21. The Independence Tribunals had originally been instituted in 1920 to deal with espionage and desertion. They had been abolished after the Nationalist victory, but two tribunals had been instituted after the passing of the *Takrir-i Sükûn Kanunu* in March 1925, one to deal with the Kurdish insurgency in the east and one to deal with the opposition in the rest of the country.

22. Karabekir, *İstiklâl Harbimizin Esasları*, pp. 190–2.

23. *Atatürk'ün hâtırasına alenen hakaret eden veya söven kimse bir yıldan üç yıla kadar hapis cezasıyla cezalandırılır* (Anyone attacking or insulting the memory of Ataturk shall be punished with one to three years imprisonment) (Article 1).

24. The whole story of the trial of Tahsin Demiray is given in Demiray, Tahsin, *İstiklâl Harbimizin Müdafaası* (İstanbul: Türkiye, 1969).

25. *Bundan sonraki ahval herkesçe görülmüş ve görülmektedir* (Karabekir, *İstiklâl Harbimiz*, p. l).

26. For instance, those of Rauf Orbay in *Yakın Tarihimiz*, vol. 3, pp. 50–2. Cf. also Talât Hasırcıoğlu, 'Kâzım Karabekir Mustafa Kemal Paşayı Tutuklamayı reddediyor', *Belgelerle Türk Tarihi Dergisi* 4 (1968), pp. 10–14.

27. Zürcher, Erik Jan, 'Ataturk and the start of the national resistance movement', *Anatolica* 8 (1981), pp. 99–113.

28. Rauf [Orbay] in *Yakın Tarihimiz*, vol. 3, p. 48; Ali Fuat [Cebesoy], *Milli Mücadele Hatıraları*, (İstanbul: Vatan, 1953), p. 72.

29. Atatürk, *Nutuk*, vol. 2, pp. 596–601.

30. Tunaya, *Türkiyede Siyasî Partiler*, pp. 537–9; Frey, Frederick W., *The Turkish Political Elite* (Cambridge, MA: MIT, 1965), pp. 306–23; Tunçay, Mete, *Türkiye Cumhuriyetinde Tek Parti Yönetiminin Kurulması (1923–1931)* (Ankara: Yurt, 1981), pp. 42–7.

31. Cf. Karaman, Sami Sabit, *Trabzon ve Kars Hatıraları: İstiklâl Mücadelesi ve Enver Paşa* (İstanbul, 1949). Also Dumont, Paul, 'La fascination du bolchévisme. Enver Pacha et le parti des soviets populaires. 1919–1922', *Cahiers du Monde Russe et Soviétique* 16/2 (1975), pp. 141–66.

32. Cf. Dumont, 'La fascination du bolchévisme', and Dumont, Paul, 'Bolchévisme et Orient. Le parti communiste Turc de Mustafa Suphi. 1918–21', *Cahiers du Monde Russe et Soviétique* 18/4 (1977), pp. 377–409.

Also Yerasimos, Stefanos, *Türk-Sovyet İlişkileri. Ekim Devriminden Milli Mücadeleye* (İstanbul: Gözlem, 1979).

3. The Historiography of the Constitutional Revolution: Broad Consensus, Some Disagreement and a Missed Opportunity

*This text was presented as a paper at the Conference *Ivresse de la Liberté*, held in Paris in 2008, and has not been published before.

1. Ramsaur, Ernest Edmonton, *The Young Turks: Prelude to the Revolution of 1908* (Princeton, 1957); Kuran, Ahmed Bedevi, *İnkılap Tarihimiz ve Jön Türkler* (Istanbul, 1945), and *İnkılap Tarihimiz ve İttihad ve Terakki* (Istanbul, 1948); Bayur, Yusuf Hikmet, *Türk İnkılabı Tarihi 10 Cilt* (Istanbul, 1940–67); Ahmad, Feroz, *The Young Turks. The Committee of Union and Progress in Turkish Politics 1908–1914* (Oxford, 1969); Akşin, Sina, *Jön Türkler ve İttihat ve Terakki* (Istanbul, 1980); Kansu, Aykut, *The Revolution of 1908 in Turkey* (Leiden, 1997); Hanioğlu, M. Şükrü, *The Young Turks in Opposition* (Oxford, 1995), and *Preparation for a Revolution. The Young Turks 1902–1908* (Oxford, 2002); Gawrych, George, *The Crescent and the Eagle. Ottoman Rule and the Albanians, 1874–1923* (London, 2006).

2. Roden Buxton, Charles, *Turkey in Revolution* (London, 1909); Knight, E.F., *The Awakening of Turkey. The Turkish Revolution of 1908* (Boston and Tokyo, 1910).

3. Niyazi, Ahmet, *Hatırat-ı Niyazi yahud Tarihçe-yi İnkılab-ı Kebir-i Osmaniden bir Sahife* (Istanbul, 1910).

4. Külçe, Süleyman, *Firzovik Toplantısı ve Meşrutiyet* (Izmir, 1944).

5. Knight, *Awakening*, pp. 135ff.

6. Uzunçarşılı, İsmail Hakkı '1908 Yılında ikinci meşrutiyetin ne suretle ilan edildiğine dair vesikalar', *Belleten* 20 (1956), pp. 103–74.

7. Pasinler, Galip, 'Galip Paşa' nın hatıraları', *Hayat Tarih Mecmuası* 2/6–9 (July–October 1966).

8. Actually the main Young Turk organization led by Ahmed Rıza was called the Committee of Progress and Union (*Terakki ve İttihad Cemiyeti*) after the second congress of Ottoman liberals in 1907 and it was under this name that it merged with the Salonika-based Ottoman Freedom Society (*Osmanlı Hürriyet Cemiyeti*). At the time of the revolution, therefore, this was the name of the organization, but soon after the revolution the older and better known name Committee of Union and Progress (*İttihad ve Terakki Cemiyeti*) was adopted once more. In this chapter I have therefore used the more common abbreviation CUP instead of the historically correct CPU.

9. Gawrych incorrectly identifies this area as near Resne (see Gawrych, *The Crescent and the Eagle*, p. 150). Also, Ahmad incorrectly states that

Enver – in setting up this band – was following Niyazi's example (see Ahmad, *The Young Turks*, p. 7). Enver in fact moved a week earlier than Niyazi.

10. There certainly were not the 200 mentioned by Ahmad in *The Young Turks*, p. 7.

11. The 800 waiting for him in the hills mentioned by Kansu (*The Revolution of 1908 in Turkey*, p. 90) are not supported by any evidence.

12. Aydın belonged to the same Third Army military region as did Macedonia – a point not made clear by any of the works mentioned here.

13. *Enver Paşa'nın Anıları* (Istanbul: İletişim Yayınları, 1991).

4. The Rise and Fall of 'Modern' Turkey: Bernard Lewis's Emergence Fifty Years On

*This chapter was originally published as *Opkomst en Ondergang van het 'Moderne' Turkije* (Leiden, CNWS, 1998).

1. Lewis, Bernard, *The Emergence of Modern Turkey* (London: Oxford University Press, 1961. Revised edition: 1968).

2. Ahmad, Feroz, *The Making of Modern Turkey* (London: Routledge, 1993), p. ix.

3. Lewis, *Emergence*, p. 1.

4. Lewis, *Emergence*, p. 473.

5. Berkes, Niyazi, *The Development of Secularism in Turkey* (Montreal: McGill University Press, 1964).

6. Tunaya, Tarık Zafer, *Türkiye'de Siyasi Partiler 1859–1952* (Istanbul, n.p., 1952).

7. Lewis, *Emergence*, p. 2.

8. Faroqhi, Suraiya, 'Crisis and change', in İnalcık, Halil, with Quataert, Donald, *An Economic and Social History of the Ottoman Empire* (Cambridge: Cambridge University Press, 1994), p. 413 and Abou-el-Haj, Rifaat, *The Formation of the Modern State: The Ottoman Empire, Sixteenth to Eighteenth Centuries* (Albany: SUNY Press, 1991). The pioneers of this critique were Owen, Roger, 'The Middle East in the eighteenth century. An "Islamic" society in decline: A critique of Gibb and Bowen' s *Islamic Society and the West,*' in *Review of Middle Eastern Studies* 1 (1975), pp. 101–12, and İslamoğlu, Huri and Keyder, Çağlar, 'Osmanlı tarihi nasıl yazılmalı?' in *Toplum ve Bilim* 1/1 (1977), pp. 49–80.

9. Findley, Carter Vaughn, *Bureaucratic Reform in the Ottoman Empire. The Sublime Porte, 1789–1922* (Princeton: Princeton University Press, 1980) and *Ottoman Civil Officialdom. A Social History* (Princeton: Princeton University Press, 1989).

10. Lewis, *Emergence*, pp. 155–6.

11. Lewis, *Emergence*, p. 156.

12. Lewis, *Emergence*, p. 264.

13. Thobie, Jacques, *Intérêts et Imperialisme Français dans l' Empire Ottoman* (Paris: Sorbonne, 1977).

14. Quataert, Donald, *Ottoman Manufacturing in the Age of the Industrial Revolution* (Cambridge: Cambridge University Press, 1993), pp. 161ff.

15. Kasaba, Reşat, *The Ottoman Empire and the World Economy. The Nineteenth Century* (Albany: SUNY Press, 1988), pp. 87–106.

16. Quataert, Donald, *Social Disintegration and Popular Resistance in the Ottoman Empire 1881–1908. Reactions to European Economic Penetration* (New York: NYU Press, 1983).

17. Toledano, Ehud, *Osmanlı Köle Ticareti 1840–1890* (Istanbul: Yurt, 1994). Translation of his unpublished Ph.D. thesis (Princeton, 1980).

18. Karpat, Kemal, *Ottoman Population 1830–1914. Demographic and Social Characteristic* (Madison: University of Wisconsin Press, 1985).

19. McCarthy, Justin, *The Arab World, Turkey and the Balkans (1878–1914). A Handbook of Historical Statistics* (Boston: G.K. Hall, 1982).

20. Duben, Allen, and Behar, Cem, *Istanbul Households. Marriage, Family and Fertility* (Cambridge: Cambridge University Press, 1991).

21. A good example is: Georgeon, François and Dumont, Paul (ed.), *Vivre dans l' Empire Ottoman. Sociabilités et relations intercommunautaires (xviiie – xxe siècles)* (Paris: l'Harmattan, 1997).

22. *Archivum Ottomanicum 5* (1973), pp. 97–128.

23. For instance in Quataert, Donald and Zürcher, Erik Jan, *Workers and Working Class in the Ottoman Empire and the Turkish Republic* (London: I.B.Tauris, 1995), pp. 127–46.

24. Brockett, Gavin, 'Collective action and the Turkish revolution: towards a framework for the social history of the Atatürk era, 1923–38', *Middle Eastern Studies* 34/4 (October 1998), pp. 44–66.

25. Zürcher, Erik Jan, *The Unionist Factor. The Role of the Committee of Union and Progress in the Turkish National Movement (1905–1926)* (Leiden: Brill, 1984) and; by the same author,'The Ottoman Empire and the Turkish republic. An attempt at a new periodization', *Welt des Islams* 32/2 (1992), pp. 237–53.

26. Lewis, *Emergence*, p. 242.

27. See primarily Berber, Engin, *Sancılı Yıllar: İzmir 1918–1922. Mütareke ve Yunan İşgali Döneminde İzmir Sancağı* (Ankara: Ayraç, 1997); Criss, Nur Bilge, *Istanbul under Allied Occupation 1918–1923* (Leiden: Brill, 1999); Demirel, Ahmet, *Birinci Meclis' te Muhalefet. İkinci Grup* (Istanbul: İletişim, 1994) and Tanör, Bülent, *Türkiye'de Yerel Kongre İktidarları (1918–1920)* (Istanbul: AFA, 1992).

28. Lewis, *Emergence*, p. 233.

29. Toprak, Zafer, *Türkiye'de 'Milli İktisat' (1908–1918)* (Ankara: Yurt, 1982). A revised and expanded edition was published by Tarih Vakfı/Yurt in Istanbul in 1995.

30. Lewis, *Emergence*, p. 350.

31. Akçam, Taner, *A Shameful Act. The Armenian Genocide and the Question of Turkish Responsibility* (New York: Metropolitan, 2006).
32. Bloxham, Donald, *The Great Game of Genocide. Imperialism, Nationalism, and the Destruction of the Ottoman Armenians* (Oxford: Oxford University Press, 2005).
33. Arı, Kemal, *Büyük Mübadele. Türkiye'ye Zorunlu Göç 1923–1925* (Istanbul: Tarih Vakfı/Yurt, 1999).
34. Prätor, Sabine, *Der Arabische Faktor in der Jungtürkischen Politik* (Berlin: Klaus Schwarz, 1993); Kayalı, Hasan, *Arabs and Young Turks* (Berkeley: University of California Press, 1997).
35. McCarthy, Justin, *Muslims and Minorities. The Population of Ottoman Anatolia and the End of Empire* (New York: NYU Press, 1983).
36. Zürcher, Erik Jan, 'Between death and desertion. The experience of the Ottoman soldier in World War I', *Turcica* 28 (1996), pp. 236–57.
37. Lewis, *Emergence*, p. 257.
38. Lewis, *Emergence*, p. 479.
39. Lewis, *Emergence*, p. 480.
40. Lewis, *Emergence*, p. 286.
41. Andrews, Peter, *Ethnic Groups in the Republic of Turkey*, TAVO Reihe B Nr. 60 (Wiesbaden: Harrassowitz, 1989); Van Bruinessen, Martin, *Agha, Sheikh and State. The Social and Political Structures of Kurdistan* (London: ZED, 1992) (and many subsequent articles) and Bozarslan, Hamit, *La Question Kurde: Etats et Minorities au Moyen-Orient*, (Paris: Presses de Sciences-Po, 1997) (and many articles).
42. Cf. especially: Mardin, Şerif, *Religion and Social Change in Modern Turkey. The Case of Bediüzzaman Said Nursi* (Albany: SUNY Press, 1989) and Göle, Nilüfer, *The Forbidden Modern* [a mistranslation of ' Modern Mahrem', which should be rendered something like ' The Modern Taboo'], (Ann Arbor: University of Michigan Press, 1996).
43. Lewis, *Emergence*, p. 63.

5. The Ottoman Empire 1850–1922: Unavoidable Failure?

*This chapter has not been published before. It was presented in 2004 as a paper at the conference *Empires in Modern Times* in Geneva.

1. Brown, Carl L., *Imperial Legacy. The Ottoman Imprint on the Balkans and the Middle East* (New York: Columbia University Press, 1996).
2. The expression 'Eastern Question' entered into diplomatic parlance at the time of the Congress of Verona in 1822. For a detailed survey of the problem see Anderson, Matthew A., *The Eastern Question 1774–1923 A Study in International Relations* (London: Macmillan, 1972) (first edition 1966). For an excellent brief summary, see: Phillips, Walter Alison, 'Eastern Question,

the' in *Encyclopaedia Britannica* (Chicago/London, 1962, vol. 7), pp. 861–8, based on the same author's contributions to the *Cambridge Modern History*.

3. The most influential of these critics was Mehmet Ziya Gökalp (1876–1924), often regarded as the 'father of Turkish nationalism'. See: Heyd, Uriel, *Foundations of Turkish Nationalism. The Life and Teachings of Ziya Gökalp* (London, 1950), pp. 74ff.

4. Zürcher, Erik Jan, 'Young Turks, Ottoman Muslims and Turkish nationalists: identity politics 1908–1938', in Karpat, Kemal H. (ed.), *Ottoman Past and Today's Turkey* (Leiden: Brill, 2000), pp. 150–79.

5. Hanioğlu, M. Şükrü, *Preparing for a Revolution. The Young Turks 1902–1908* (Oxford: Oxford University Press, 2001), p. 292.

6. Zürcher, Erik Jan, 'The Ottoman conscription system in theory and practice, 1844–1918', *International Review of Social History* 43/3 (1998), pp. 437–49.

7. Shaw, Stanford and Shaw, Ezel, *History of the Ottoman Empire and Modern Turkey. Vol. 2. Reform, Revolution and Republic* (Cambridge: Cambridge University Press, 1977), pp. 106–13.

8. See: Findley, Carter Vaughn, *Bureaucratic Reform in the Ottoman Empire. The Sublime Porte 1792–1922* (Princeton, 1980).

9. Stephanie Cronin makes this clear in 'Conscription and popular resistance in Iran (1925–1941)' in Zürcher, Erik Jan (ed.), *Arming the State. Military Conscription in the Middle East and Central Asia 1775–1925* (London: I.B.Tauris, 1999), pp. 145–68. For further comparisons between the two countries, see: Atabaki, Touraj and Zürcher, Erik Jan (ed.), *Men of Order. Authoritarian Modernisation in Turkey and Iran* (London: I.B.Tauris, 2003).

10. 'Malikane', *Encyclopaedia of Islam. New edition*, vol. 6 (Leiden: Brill, 1991), pp. 277–8; 'Mültezim', *Encyclopaedia of Islam. New edition*, vol. 7 (Leiden: Brill, 1993), pp. 550–1.

11. For these macro-economic trends, see: Pamuk, Şevket, *The Ottoman Empire and European capitalism, 1820–1913. Trade, Investment and Production* (Cambridge: Cambridge University Press, 1987).

12. Clay, Christopher, *Gold for the Sultan. Western Bankers and Ottoman Finance 1865–1881* (London: I.B.Tauris, 2000), pp. 503ff.

13. Ahmed Emin [Yalman], *Turkey in the World War* (New Haven: Yale, 1930), p. 157.

14. Mitchell, Brian, *International Historical Statistics. Europe 1750–1988* (third edition) (New York: Stockton, 1992).

15. Posthumus, Nicolaas W., *Goederenprijzen op de beurs van Amsterdam 1585–1914. Wisselkoersen te Amsterdam 1609–1914* (Leiden: Brill, 1943).

16. For a useful summary, based on recent research, of the problems involved in estimating the population, see: Quataert, Donald, 'The age of reforms, 1812–1914', in İnalcık, Halil with Quataert, Donald (ed.), *An Economic and Social History of the Ottoman Empire 1300–1914* (Cambridge: Cambridge

University Press, 1994), in particular, pp. 777–98. The main problem is uncertainty about the average size of the households. Adding one person per household adds five million people to the total.

17. Ahmed Emin [Yalman], *Turkey in the World War*, pp. 78–80.

18. Larcher, Maurice, *La guerre turque dans la guerre mondiale* (Paris: Chiron, 1926), pp. 589–90.

19. Quataert, Donald, *Social Disintegration and Popular Resistance in the Ottoman Empire, 1881–1908. Reactions to European Economic Penetration* (New York: New York University Press, 1983), pp. 48–9.

20. Ahmed Emin [Yalman], *Turkey in the World War*, p. 89.

21. See: Van den Boogert, Maurits H., Ottoman Dragomans and European Consuls. The Protection System in Eighteenth-Century Aleppo, unpublished Ph.D. thesis (Leiden University, 2002).

22. Mardin, Şerif, *The Genesis of Young Ottoman Thought. A Study in the Modernization of Turkish Political Ideas* (Princeton: Princeton University Press, 1962).

23. Gorgeon, François, *Abdulhamid II le Sultan Caliphe* (Paris: Fayard, 2003), pp. 192ff; Deringil, Selim, *The Well-protected Domains. Ideology and the Legitimation of Power in the Ottoman Empire 1876–1909* (London: I.B.Tauris, 1998). On p. 17 Deringil explicitly compares Abdülhamit's policies with those of the Tsars.

24. See Keyder, Çağlar, *State and Class in Turkey. A Study in Capitalist Development* (London: Verso, 1987), pp. 49–90.

25. Zürcher, Erik Jan, 'Young Turks, Ottoman Muslims and Turkish nationalists: identity politics 1908–1938' in Karpat, Kemal H. (ed.), *Ottoman Past and Today's Turkey* (Leiden, 2000), pp. 150–79.

26. Zürcher, Erik Jan, 'The Ottoman conscription system in theory and practice, 1844–1918', *International Review of Social History* 43/3 (1998), pp. 437–49. The information is based on British consular reports.

27. Toprak, Zafer, *Türkiye'de Millî İktisat* (Ankara: Yurt, 1982) was the groundbreaking work on this subject. Since then, Toprak has published several works on the same subject but with the emphasis on different aspects of the national economy programme. The latest is: *İttihat ve Terakki ve Cihan Harbi. Savaş Ekonomisi ve Türkiye'de Devletçilik* (İstanbul: Homer, 2003).

6. The Ides of April: A Fundamentalist Uprising in Istanbul in 1909?

*Originally published as: 'The Ides of April. A fundamentalist uprising in Istanbul in 1909?' in Van Dijk, C. and De Groot, A.H., *State and Islam* (Leiden, 1996), pp. 64–76.

1. Berkes, Niyazi, *The Development of Secularism in Turkey* (Montreal: McGill, 1964).

2. Davison, Roderic H., *Reform in the Ottoman Empire 1856–1876* (New York: Gordian, 1973); Lewis, Bernard, *The Emergence of Modern Turkey* (London: Oxford University Press, 1961).

3. Findley, Carter Vaughn, *Bureaucratic Reform in the Ottoman Empire. The Sublime Porte 1789–1922* (Princeton: Princeton University, 1980).

4. Yapp, Malcolm E., *The Making of the Modern Middle East 1792–1923* [A History of the Middle East, vol. 5] (London/New York: Longman, 1987), pp. 36–45.

5. Pamuk, Şevket, *The Ottoman Empire and European Capitalism, 1820–1913. Trade, Investment and Production* (Cambridge: Cambridge University, 1987); Keyder, Çağlar, *State and Class in Turkey. A Study in Capitalist Development* (London/New York: Verso, 1987), pp. 27–48; Kasaba, Reşat, *The Ottoman Empire and the World Economy. The Nineteenth Century* (Binghamton: State University of New York, 1988).

6. Davison, *Reform*, pp. 100–2; Yapp, *The Making of the Modern Middle East*, pp. 112–14.

7. Mardin, Şerif, *The Genesis of Young Ottoman Thought. A Study in the Modernization of Turkish Political Ideas* (Princeton: Princeton University, 1962).

8. Devereux, Robert, *The First Ottoman Constitutional Period. A Study of the Mithat Constitution and Parliament* (Baltimore: Johns Hopkins, 1963), pp. 21–94; Davison, *Reform*, pp. 358–408.

9. Lewis, *Emergence*, pp. 174–82. Shaw, Stanford, *History of the Ottoman Empire and Modern Turkey Vol. 2* (Cambridge: Cambridge University Press, 1977), pp. 172–272.

10. Shaw, *History*, pp. 112–13.

11. Hanioğlu, M. Şükrü, *Bir Siyasal Örgüt Olarak 'Osmanlı İttihad ve Terakki Cemiyeti' ve 'Jön Türklük', Cilt 1: (1889–1902)* (İstanbul: İletişim, 1986); Ramsaur, Ernest Edmondson, *The Young Turks. Prelude to the Revolution of 1908* (New York: Russel and Russel, Second printing [First printing: Princeton: Princeton University, 1957], 1970).

12. Zürcher, Erik Jan, *The Unionist Factor. The Role of the Committee of Union and Progress in the Turkish National Movement* (Leiden: Brill, 1984), pp. 19–44.

13. Ahmad, Feroz, *The Young Turks. The Committee of Union and Progress in Turkish Politics 1908–1914* (Oxford: Clarendon, 1969), pp. 15–21.

14. Akşin, Sina, *Jön Türkler ve İttihat ve Terakki* (İstanbul: Remzi, 1987), pp. 107–8.

15. Tunaya, Tarık Zafer, *Türkiye'de Siyasî Partiler 1859–1952* (Istanbul: n.p., 1952), pp. 239–47.

16. Akşin, *Jön Türkler*, pp. 110–16.

17. Akşin, *Jön Türkler*, pp. 122–3.

18. Güven, Gül Çağalı, '80 Yılında 31 Mart', *Cumhuriyet*, 13 April 1989, p. 13.
19. Tunaya, *Siyasî Partiler,* pp. 261–75.
20. The most important scholarly literature is: Bayur, Yusuf Hikmet, *Türk İnkılâbî Tarihi. Cilt: I-Kısım: 2* (Ankara: Türk Tarih Kurumu, 1983), pp. 182–217; and Akşin, Sina, *Jön Türkler ve İttihat ve Terakki*, pp. 121–40. For popular literature based on memoirs see: Danişmend, İsmail Hami, *Sadr-ı-a'zam Tevfik Paşa'nın' Dosyasındaki Resmi ve Hususi Vesikalara Göre: 31 Mart Vak'ası* (İstanbul: İstanbul, Third printing, 1986); Adıvar, Halide Edib, *Memoirs of Halide Edib* (London/New York: Century, 1926) and Yalçın, Hüseyin Cahit, *Siyasal Anılar* (Istanbul: İş Bankası, 1976).
21. Algemeen Rijksarchief's Gravenhage, Tweede Afdeling, Kabinetsarchief van het Ministerie van Buitenlandse Zaken betrefffende politieke rapportage door Nederlandse diplomatieke vertegenwoordigers in het buitenland 1871–1940 [hereafter referred to as *ARA*], 471/162 (1 April 1909); *ARA,* 506/175 (6 April 1909).
22. *ARA* 543/191 (14 April 1909).
23. *ARA* 546/192 (15 April 1909).
24. Adıvar, *Memoirs*, p. 279; Akşin, *Jön Türkler,* p. 127.
25. *ARA* 550/194 (16 April 1909).
26. *ARA,* 553/196 (17 April 1909).
27. Danişmend, *Sadr-ı-a'zam*, pp. 40–97.
28. *ARA,* 553/196 (17 April 1909).
29. *ARA,* 578/200 (20 April 1909).
30. Akşin, *Jön Türkler,* p. 133.
31. *ARA,* 601/206 (25 April 1909).
32. *ARA,* 624/214 (27 April 1909), *ARA* 636/219 (29 April 1909).
33. Güven, '80 Yılında 31 Mart', Akşin, *Jön Türkler,* p. 121.
34. Güven, '80 Yılında 31 Mart', p. 11.
35. *ARA* 490/172 (5 April 1909).
36. Güven, '80 Yılında 31 Mart'.
37. *ARA* 553/196 (17 April 1909).
38. Akşin, *Jön Türkler,* p. 127; Bayur , *Türk İnkılâbı Tarihi*, pp. 186–7; Danişmend, *Sadr-ı-a'zam*, pp. 21–3.
39. Güven, '80 Yılında 31 Mart'.
40. Akşin, *Jön Türkler,* pp. 128–30; Bayur, *Türk İnkılâbı Tarihi*, pp. 184–5.
41. *ARA,* 540/190 (13 April 1909).
42. *ARA,* 562/199 (19 April 1909).
43. Olson, Robert, *The Emergence of Kurdish Nationalism and the Sheikh Said Rebellion, 1880–1925* (Austin: University of Texas, 1989), pp. 91–127.
44. *TCBMM Zabit Ceridesi*, vol. 14, pp. 306–11.

7. Sultan Mehmet V's Visit to Kosovo in June 1911

* Originally published as: 'Kosovo revisited: Sultan Reshad's Macedonian journey in 1911', *Middle Eastern Studies* 35/4 (1999), pp. 26–39.

1. It is perhaps useful to point out that Macedonia was not an Ottoman administrative unit. The area so described comprised the provinces (*vilâyets*) of Salonica, Kosovo (capital: Üsküp) and Monastir.

2. This is evident from Karabekir, Kâzım, *İttihat ve Terakki Cemiyeti 1896–1909* (İstanbul: private, 1982 [written in 1945]), p. 176.

3. Zürcher, Erik Jan, 'Niyâzî Bey, Ahmed' in *Encyclopaedia of Islam. New Edition*, vol. 8 (Leiden: Brill, 1995), pp. 67–8.

4. In November 1908 a so-called Pan-Albanian conference in Monastir (Bitola) endorsed a plan to use a modified Latin alphabet for the Albanian language and to introduce it in schools in Albania.

5. Şevket Turgut Pasha was an officer of Circassian descent, who commanded the Kosovo army corps during the 1908 revolution and after. He also was the Commander of the Thracian army corps in the Balkan War. After World War I he held the position of Minister of Supplies and of War under Damat Ferit Pasha, but had to resign because of his nationalist sympathies. After his retirement from the army in 1919 he worked as a trader until his death in 1924.

6. Malcolm, Noel, *Kosovo. A Short History* (London: Macmillan, 1998), pp. 239–43. Malcolm gives the number of Albanians who blocked the railway at Kaçanik as 9,000.

7. Malcolm gives the total number of Ottoman troops involved in the campaign as 40,000 (Malcolm, *Kosovo*), p. 242.

8. Bartl, Ernst, *Die albanische Muslime zur Zeit der nationalen Unabhängigkeitsbewegung 1878 – 1912* (Wiesbaden, 1968), pp. 167ff. For a more recent study of Albanian nationalism and the Ottoman reaction in this period, see Gawrych, George, *The Crescent and the Eagle. Ottoman Rule, Islam and the Albanians 1874–1913* (London: I.B.Tauris, 2006).

9. On the Macedonian question see Adanır, Fikret, *Makedonya Sorunu* (Istanbul, 1996).

10. In 1911, the newspapers stated that Mehmet Reşat's earlier visit to Salonica with his father had taken place in 1863, but that must be a mistake since his father died in 1861.

11. Georgeon, François, 'Le Sultan caché. Réclusion du souverain et mise en scène du pouvoir à l'époque d'Abdülhamid II (1876–1909)', *Turcica* 29 (1997), pp. 93–124.

12. Deringil, Selim, *The Well-protected Domains. Ideology and the Legitimation of Power in the Ottoman Empire, 1876–1909* (London, 1998).

13. Prince Reşat was born as son of Sultan Abdülmecit in the Çirağan Palace in Istanbul on 16 November 1844. He succeeded his brother Abdülhamit as Sultan on 27 April 1909 and reigned until his death on 3 July 1918.

For a biography see Karal, Enver Ziya, 'Mehmed V' in *İslam Ansiklopedisi*, vol. 7 (İstanbul: Millî Eğitim Matbaası, no date), pp. 557–62.

14. That Prince Reşat took the official name of Mehmet V on his accession was also an act of historic symbolism. The name Mehmet had not been used by rulers since the late seventeenth century and its revival on this occasion was meant to evoke memories of Mehmet II, the conqueror of Istanbul in 1453. Reşat was portrayed as a second conqueror because his accession was the result of the taking of the city by the Action Army which suppressed the counterrevolution known as the 31 March incident (*31 Mart vakası*).

15. The Sultan's private secretary at the time, Halit Ziya Uşaklıgil, describes the preparations in detail in *Saray ve Ötesi. Son Hatıralar* (İstanbul: İnkılâp ve Aka, 1965) (second edition, two volumes in one binding), pp. 238–9, 260–1.

16. The *Turgut Reis* and the *Barbaros Hayrettin* were the largest capital ships in the Ottoman navy in 1911. They had been built in Germany in 1890–1 as the *Weissenburg* and the *Kurfürst Friedrich Wilhelm* of the imperial German navy. By 1910 these pre-dreadnought battleships were obsolete and sold to the Ottoman navy. The *Barbaros Hayrettin* was sunk by a British submarine in 1915, while the *Turgut Reis* went on to serve as a stationary training ship in Gölcük and was finally broken up in 1950 (Bernd Langensiepen and Ahmet Güleryüz, *The Ottoman Steam Navy 1828–1923* [London, 1995]).

17. Uşaklıgil, *Saray ve Ötesi*, p. 245.

18. Unless otherwise stated, the facts are given as reported in *Senin* (the temporary name of the newspaper *Tanin* when the latter was banned by the government). Many of the reports are by Hakkı Tarik (Us). Us is his family name, but family names were introduced only in 1934, so at this time he was still only H.T. The reporting in the newspaper is detailed, but it should be kept in mind that it was the unofficial organ of the CUP and strongly biased in favour of that organization. In the references the Mali date generally used in the Ottoman Empire at the time is followed by the date in the Gregorian calendar (e.g. 1/14 June).

19. Halit Ziya (1869–1945) was a scion of a prominent trading family from Izmir, the Uşakizadeler, to which Atatürk's wife, Latife Hanım, also belonged. He first worked in the tobacco monopoly and then served Sultan Reşat as secretary for four years. Thereafter his career was an academic one. Halit Ziya is known as Turkey's first successful novelist in the European manner.

20. PRO/FO 195/2381/54. Consulate in Salonica (Lamb) to Embassy in Istanbul. Report of 11 June 1911.

21. Ibid.

22. Gazi Evrenos Bey (d. 1417), a Greek convert to Islam, was an Ottoman military commander under both Sultan Murat I and Sultan Bayezit I. His son and grandsons also served with distinction in the Ottoman army.

23. Among these was Şemsi Efendi, the founder (in 1870) of the first private primary school for Muslims in the empire. His was the primary school

attended by Mustafa Kemal (Atatürk). In 1879 the school was renamed *Terakki Mektebi* (Progress School) when it received *Rüşdiye* (middle school) status. In 1919 the school was moved to Şişli in Istanbul. It continues to exist today. Since 1994 it has been located in Levent.

24. *Lloyd Ottoman* 134 (10 June 1911), p. 4.
25. *Lloyd Ottoman* 131 (7 June 1911), p. 4. Whether this report (based on rumours circulating before the arrival of the sultan) is actually correct, is unclear.
26. *Senin* of 28 May/11 June 1911; PRO/FO 195/2381/54.
27. On this interesting society see Özçelik, Selahittin, *Donanma-yı Osmani Muavenet-i Milliye Cemiyeti* (Ankara, 2000).
28. *Lloyd Ottoman* 136 (13 June 1911), p. 4.
29. PRO/FO 195/2381/25. Report from consul Üsküp (Hugh) to consul Salonica (Lamb), 19 June 1911.
30. Ibid.
31. PRO/FO 195/2381/26. Report from consul Üsküp (Hugh) to consul Salonica (Lamb), 22 June 1911.
32. PRO/FO 195/2381/27. Report from consul Üsküp (Hugh) to consul Salonica (Lamb), 19 June 1911.
33. *Senin*, 2/15 June 1911 (report of 1/14 June); *Lloyd Ottoman* 137 (14 June 1911), report of the Agence Ottomane.
34. Malcolm, *Kosovo*, p. 244. Malcolm bases his work on the memoirs of Serbian vice-consul Rakic.
35. Pears, Sir Edwin, *Forty Years in Constantinople. The Recollections of Sir Edwin Pears 1873–1915* (London: Herbert Jenkins, 1916), p. 308.
36. Uşaklıgil, p. 266.
37. PRO/FO 195/2381/27. Report from consul Üsküp (Hugh) to consul Salonica (Lamb), 26 June 1911.
38. *Lloyd Ottoman* 139 (16 June 1911).
39. PRO/FO 294/47 (political correspondence Monastir)/38 Report by Arthur Geary (consul) to Sir C.M. Marling, Chargé d'Affaires, Constantinople, 27 June 1911.
40. *Lloyd Ottoman* 145 (23 June 1911).
41. Quotation from *Senin* in *Osmanische Lloyd* 148 (27 June 1911), 1 'Pressestimmen'.
42. Zürcher, Erik Jan, 'Muslim nationalism: the missing link in the genesis of modern Turkey', *Hamizrah Hehadash (The New East)* 39 (Jerusalem: Magnes Press, 1998), pp. 67–83.

8.   Who Were the Young Turks?

* This chapter was newly written, based on several earlier publications: 'Yıkımın ve yenilenmenin mimarları: Kemalist jenerasyona ve Jön Türklere dair bir grup

biyografisi denemesi', in Alkan, Mehmet Ö, Bora, Tanıl and Koraltürk, Murat, (ed.), *Mete Tunçay'a Armağan* (Istanbul: İletişim, 2007), pp. 539–72; 'How Europeans adopted Anatolia and discovered Turkey', *European Review* 13/3 (2005), pp. 379–94, and 'The Young Turks – Children of the borderlands?', *International Journal of Turkish Studies* 9/1-2 (2003), pp. 275–86. The latter was translated into Italian as 'I "Giovanni Turchi": Figli delle terre di frontiera?', *Rivista Storica Italiana* 115/2 (2003), pp. 543–55.

1. Ahmad, Feroz, *The Young Turks. The Committee of Union and Progress in Turkish Politics 1908–14* (Oxford: Clarendon, 1969); Allen, Henry Elisha, *The Turkish Transformation. A Study in Social and Religious Development* (Chicago: University of Chicago, 1935) [reprinted, New York: Greenwood Press, 1968]; Lewis, Geoffrey, *Modern Turkey* (London & Tonbridge: Ernest Benn Limited, 1974); Lewis, Bernard, *The Emergence of Modern Turkey* (Oxford: Oxford University Press, 1961); Shaw, Stanford and Shaw, Ezel, *History of the Ottoman Empire and Modern Turkey*. Vol. II: Reform, Revolution and Republic: The Rise of Modern Turkey, 1808–1975 (Cambridge: Cambridge University Press, 1977); Robinson, Richard D., *The First Turkish Republic. A Case Study in National Development* (Cambridge, MA: Harvard University Press, 1963) and Akşin, Sina, *Jön Türkler ve İttihat ve Terakki* (Istanbul: Remzi, 1987).

2. Following the usage established in my *Unionist Factor* and later in *Turkey A Modern History* (1993) I use the term 'Young Turk' for the whole group that was involved in the constitutionalist agitation before 1908, the CUP and its off-shoots between 1908 and 1918, the leadership of the national resistance movement after World War I and the leadership of the early republic (until 1950).

3. Gövsa, İbrahim Alâettin, *Türk Meşhurları Ansiklopedisi* (Istanbul: Yedigün Nesriyati, 1946).

4. Notable exceptions are Camilla Dawletschin-Linder's biography of Celâl Bayar: *Diener seines Staates. Celâl Bayar (1883–1986) und die Entwicklung der modernen Türkei* (Wiesbaden: Harassowitz, 2003); Şükrü Hanioğlu's study of Abdullah Cevdet: *Bir Siyasal Düşünür olarak Doktor Abdullah Cevdet ve Dönemi* (Istanbul, 1981); Ada Holly Shissler's *Between Two Worlds. Ahmet Ağaoğlu and the New Turkey* (London: I.B.Tauris, 2003) or Andrew Mango's *Atatürk* (London: John Murray, 1999).

5. I have chosen the following 14 representative activists of the first generation:
   Ishak Sükuti (Diyarbakır, 1868)
   Abdullah Cevdet (Arapkır, 1869)
   İbrahim Temo (Struga near Ohrid, 1865)
   Hüseyinzade Ali (Selyan, Azerbaijan, 1864)
   Ahmet Rıza (Istanbul, 1859)
   Mizancı Murat (Dargi (Caucasus), 1854)
   Bahaettin Şakır (Sliven, 1870)

Nazım (Salonica/Thessaloniki, 1870)
Ağaoğlu Ahmet (Shusa, Azerbaijan, 1869)
Ahmet Ferit (Bursa, 1877)
Ahmet Saip (Lezgi, Caucasus, 1859)
Yusuf Akçura (Simbirsk, 1874)
Tunalı Hilmi (Turgovishte, 1871)
Çerkes Mehmet Reşit (Bjedno, Caucasus, 1873)

6. Those ten leaders were:
Mehmet Talât (Edirne, 1874)
Mithat Şükrü [Bleda] (Salonica/Thessaloniki, 1874)
Evranoszade Rahmi [Arslan] (Salonica/Thessaloniki, 1874)
Mehmet Tahir (Bursa, 1861)
Nakiyüddin [Yücekök] (Nasliç/Neapolis, 1866)
Edip Servet [Tör] (Adapazarı, 1880)
Kâzım Nami [Duru] (Istanbul, 1877)
Ömer Naci (Istanbul, 1878),
İsmail Canbolat (Istanbul, 1880)
Hakkı Baha [Pars] (Bursa, ?)

7. Enver, hero of the 1908 revolution and of the wars in Tripolitania and the Balkans, of course later became the Ottoman Minister of War and Vice-commander in Chief. His is an interesting example of the complications involved in tracing the geographical background of the Young Turks. He was born in Istanbul, where his father and mother had also been born, but the family, originally Christian Gagauz Turks, hailed from the Crimea. After the Russian occupation of the Crimea, they had moved to Kilia on the Danube. When the Russians occupied that area in 1877, the family fled to Abana in the province of Kastamonu, whence they moved to Istanbul. Although Enver was born there in 1881, he grew up mostly in Monastir, where his father got a job as a technician for the Ministry of Public Works before he was eight years old (Şevket Süreyya Aydemir, *Makedonya' dan Orta Asya' ya Enver Paşa Cilt. 1 (1860–1908)* (Istanbul: Remzi, 1972), pp. 177ff.).

8. As representatives of the group of politically active officers, I have chosen:
Enver (Istanbul, 1880)
Ali Fethi [Okyar] (Pirlepe/Prilep, 1880)
Sadık (Istanbul, 1860)
İsmail Hakkı (Monastir/Bitola, 1879)
Fahrettin [Altay] (İşkodra/Skhoder, 1880)
Ali İhsan (Sabis) (Istanbul, 1882)
Mustafa Kemal [Atatürk] (Salonica/Thessaloniki, 1881)
Ali Fuat [Cebesoy] (Istanbul, 1883, but born in a Circassian family that had been settled in Crete)
Halil [Kut] (Istanbul, 1881)

Kâzım Karabekir (Istanbul, 1882)
Kâzım [Özalp] (Köprülü/Velesh, 1880)
Süleyman Askeri (?, 1884)
İsmet [İnönü] (Izmir, 1884, but born in a Kurdish family from Malatya)
Ali [Çetinkaya] (Afyon, 1878)
Seyfi [Düzgören] (Istanbul, 1880)
Cafer Tayyar [Eğilmez] (Priştine/Prishtina, 1879)
Niyazi (Resne/Resen, 1874)
Eyüp Sabri (Ohri/Ohrid, 1876)
Hüsrev Sami [Kızıldoğan] (Gümülcine/Dimetoka, 1884)
Aziz Ali (Cairo, 1879)
Ahmet Cemal (Istanbul, 1872)

9. The one striking exception was Colonel Sadık, the commander of the cavalry regiment in Monastir, who protected the Unionist officers there. He was born in Istanbul in 1860. But Sadık was exceptional in other ways as well. A deeply religious man, he fell out with the committee after the revolution and ultimately was forced to leave the country after the Unionist coup d'état of 1913.

10. Vagyan, Arsen, *Osmanlı İmparatorluğu ve Kemalist Türkiyenin Devlet-İktidar Sisteminde Çerkesler* (İstanbul: Belge, 2004), p. 280.

11. I have studied the following members of the Central Committee:
Hüseyin Kadri (?, 1870)
Mehmet Talât (Edirne, 1874)
Midhat Şükrü [Bleda] (Salonica/Thessaloniki, 1874)
Hayri Efendi (Ürgüp, 1867)
Ahmet Rıza (Istanbul, 1859)
Enver (Istanbul, 1880)
Habib
İpekli Hafız İbrahim (İpek/Pec, ?)
Nâzım (Salonica/Thessaloniki, 1870)
Ömer Naci (Istanbul, 1878),
İhsan Namık
Haci Adil [Arda] (Edirne, 1869)
Eyüp Sabri [Akgöl] (Ohri/Ohrid, 1876)
Ziya
Ahmet Nesimi [Sayman] (Crete, ?)
Hüseyinzade Ali [Turan] (Selyan, Azerbaijan, 1864)
Ali Fethi [Okyar] (Pirlepe/Prilep, 1880)
Halil [Menteşe] (Milas, 1874)
Sait Halim (Cairo, 1863)
Bahaettin Şakir (İslimiye/Sliven, 1870)
Ziya Gökalp (Diyarbakır, 1875)

Rüsuhi
Emrullah Ef. (Lüleburgaz, 1858)
Küçük Talat [Muşkara]
Kara Kemal (Istanbul, 1868)
Hilmi (Şavşat, 1885)

12. For the leadership of the national resistance I have looked at:
Mustafa Kemal [Atatürk] (Salonica/Thessaloniki, 1881)
Mahmut Celâl [Bayar] (Gemlik, 1884 in a family of refugees from Bulgaria)
Kavaklı Fevzi [Çakmak] (Istanbul, 1876)
İsmet [İnönü] (Izmir, 1884, in a Kurdish family from Malatya)
Cami [Aykut] (Istanbul, 1877)
Celalettin Arif (Erzurum, 1875)
İsmail Fazıl (Kandiye/Iraklion, 1856, from an immigrant Circassian family)
Bekir Sami [Kunduh] (Sambay (Caucasus), 1867, Ossetian)
Adnan [Adıvar] (Gallipoli/Gelibolu, 1882)
Yusuf Kemal (Tengirşenk) (Boyabat, 1878)
Hakkı Behiç [Bayiç] (Istanbul, 1886, in a Circassian immigrant family)
Rıza Nur (Sinop, 1878)
Ahmet Ferit [Tek] (Bursa, 1879, in an Istanbul-based family)
Ahmet Muhtar (Çanakkale, 1870)
Abdülkadır Kemali [Öğütçü] (Adana, 1881)
Zekai [Apaydın] (Graveshka (Bosnia), 1877)
Hamdullah Suphi [Tanrıöver] (Istanbul, 1886)

13. This list consists of the following persons:
Ismet Inönü (Izmir, 1884)
Fevzi Çakmak (Istanbul, 1876)
Kâzım Özalp (Köprülü/Veles, 1880)
Mustafa Abdülhalik Renda (Yanya/Janina, 1881)
Refik Saydam (Istanbul, 1882)
Şükrü Kaya (Istanköy/Kos, 1883)
Şükrü Saraçoglu (Ödemiş, 1887)
Recep Peker (Istanbul, 1888)
Ali Çetinkaya (Afyonkarahisar, 1878)
Mahmut Celâl Bayar (Gemlik, 1884)
Fuat Ağrali (Midilli/Lesbos, 1878)
Tevfik Rüştü Aras (Çanakkale, 1883)
Ali Rana Tarhan (Istanbul, 1883)
Muhlis Erkmen (Bursa, 1891)
Hulusi Alatas (Beyşehir, 1882)
Saffet Arikan (Erzincan, 1887)

Şakir Kesebir (Köprülü/Velesh, 1889)
Süleyman Sırrı (Salonica/Thessaloniki, 1874)
Hasan Ali Yücel (Istanbul, 1897)
Reşit Galip (Rodos, 1893)
Hasan Hüsnü Saka (Trabzon, 1885)
Zekai Apaydın (Bosna/Bosnia, 1877)
Mahmut Esat Bozkurt (Kuşadası, 1892)
Esat Sagay (Salonica/Thessaloniki, 1874)
Hilmi Uran (Bodrum, 1884)
Naci Tınaz (Serfice/Servia, 1882)

14. The president and his circle consists of the following persons:
Mustafa Kemal Atatürk (Salonica/Thessaloniki, 1881)
Kılıç Ali (Emrullahzade Asaf) (Istanbul, 1889)
Nuri Conker (Salonica/Thessaloniki, 1881)
Salih Bozok (Salonica/Thessaloniki, 1881)
İsmail Müştak Mayakon (Yenişehir/Larissa, 1882)
Müfit Özdeş (Kırsehir, 1874)
Falih Rıfkı Atay (Istanbul, 1893)
Hasan Cavit Betül (?)
Cevat Abbas Gürer (Niş/Nish, 1887)
Tahsin Uzer (Salonica/Thessaloniki, 1879)
Edip Servet Tör (Adapazarı, 1880).

9. The Young Turk Mindset

*This chapter is based on: 'Yıkımın ve yenilenmenin mimarları: Kemalist jenerasyona ve Jön Türklere dair bir grup biyografisi denemesi', in Alkan, Mehmet Ö, Bora, Tanıl and Koraltürk, Murat (ed.), *Mete Tunçay'a Armağan* (Istanbul: İletişim, 2007), pp. 539–72.

1. Pamuk, Şevket, *The Ottoman Empire and European Capitalism 1820–1913: Trade, Investment and Production* (Cambridge, 1987).

2. Reşat Kasaba has argued against the 'compradore' character of the Christian bourgeoisie in his *The Ottoman Empire and the World Economy: The Nineteenth Century* (Albany, 1988); Hilmar Kaiser has criticized the idea that the Christians enriched themselves at the expense of the Ottoman Empire in his *Imperialism, Racism, and Development Theories. The Construction of a Dominant Paradigm on Ottoman Armenians* (Ann Arbor, 1997).

3. The process is described very well in: Schmitt, Oliver Jens, *Levantiner. Lebenswelten und Identitäten einer ethnokonfessionellen Gruppe im osmanischen Reich im 'langen 19. Jahrhundert'(Habil.-Schr.)* (München, 2005).

4. Göçek, Fatma Müge, *Rise of the Bourgeoisie, Demise of Empire: Ottoman Westernization and Social Change* (Oxford, 1996); Fawaz, Laila, *Merchants and in Nineteenth-century Beirut* (Cambridge, MA, 1983); Anastassiadou,

Meropi, *Salonique 1830–1912: une ville ottomane à l'age des Réformes* (Leiden, 1997); Mazower, Mark, *Salonica, City of Ghosts: Christians, Muslims and Jews, 1430–1950* (London, 2004).

5. Karabekir, Kâzım, *İttihat ve Terakki Cemiyeti 1896–1909.* [written in 1945] (İstanbul, 1982), p. 138.

6. See, for instance, Enver's speech to the villagers of the Tikvesh region in *Enver Paşa' nın Anıları 1881–1908 (Yayına Hazırlayan Halil Erdoşan Cengiz)* (İstanbul, 1991), pp. 105ff.

7. M. Şükrü Hanioğlu, *The Young Turks in Opposition* (New York/Oxford, 1995).

8. In his speech at the opening of the tenth anniversary celebrations of the republic in Ankara on 29 October 1933.

9. Tunaya, Tarık Zafer, *Türkiye' de Siyasal Partiler III İttihat ve Terakki* (İstanbul, 1989), p. 22. Many of the popular works of French romantic novelists were also available in Ottoman Turkish. *The Count of Monte Cristo* by Dumas Père, a very topical novel for Young Turk conspirators, had been available in translation since 1871, for instance.

10. Tunaya, *Siyasal Partiler*, p. 214.

11. 'O child of the Turkish future! Look: Even in these circumstances your duty is to save the Turkish independence and republic! The strength you need is present in the pure blood in your veins! (*Ey Türk istikbalinin evladı! İşte bu ahval ve şerait içinde dahi vazifen Türk istiklal ve cumhuriyetini kurtarmaktır! Muhtacolduğun kudret, damarlarındaki asıl kanda mevcuttur!*).

12. In a sense the Young Turk criticisms of Sultan Abdülhamit were paradoxical. On the one hand they described his regime as over-powerful and even a tyranny, but on the other they accused him of weakness vis-à-vis the European powers.

13. The Mürzsteg agreement between Russia and Austria was concluded in October 1903 as a reaction to the Ilinden uprising of August 1903, which had been repressed with great brutality by the Ottoman army. It foresaw the establishment of an international gendarmerie force in Macedonia.

14. Duru, Kâzım, *'İttihat ve Terakki' Hatıralarım* (İstanbul, 1957), p. 14.

15. The only exception were the Romanian-speaking Vlahs, who as a small minority were as much under threat of Serbian and Greek irredentism as the Turks. This explains the fact that some Vlahs, like the famous Batzaria Efendi, would enter the CUP before the revolution.

16. Hanioğlu, M. Şükrü, *Preparation for a Revolution. The Young Turks 1902–1908* (Oxford, 2001), p. 267.

17. The formation of special volunteer units, composed of members who were ready to offer their lives for the 'sacred cause' was foreseen in articles 49 and 50 of the CUP Regulations. See, for instance, Bayar, Celâl, *Ben de Yazdım. Milli Mücadele'ye Gidiş, Vol. 1* (İstanbul, 1965), p. 128. The formal

founding of the *Teşkilat-i Mahsusa* seems to have occurred only in 1914 (Bıyıklıoğlu, Tevfik, *Trakya' da Milli Mücadele I* (Ankara, 1955), pp. 88–90) but it seems to have existed as an informal grouping before that date.

18. Zürcher, Erik Jan, *The Unionist Factor. The Role of the Committee of Union and Progress in the Turkish National Movement (1905–1926)* (Leiden, 1984), pp. 83ff.

19. The initiation ritual is described by Enver (*Enver Paşa' nın Anıları*, pp. 60–1) and Kâzım Karabekir (*İttihat ve Terakki Cemiyeti*, pp. 166ff.).

20. Tunaya, *Siyasal Partiler*; Bayar, *Ben de Yazdım*, p. 128.

21. See also the chapters 'Ides of April' and 'Turning Points and Missed Opportunities in the Modern History of Turkey' in this volume.

22. Nezir-Akmeşe, Handan, *The Birth of Modern Turkey: The Ottoman Military and the March to World War I* (London, 2005).

23. For a groundbreaking analysis of militarist nationalism in contemporary Turkey, see: Altınay, Ayşegül, *The Myth of the Military-Nation: Militarism, Gender, and Education in Turkey* (New York, 2005).

24. Balkan şehirlerinde geçerken çocukluğum
    Her lahzâ bir alev gibi hasretti duyduğum
    Kalbimde vardı Byron'u bedbaht eden melâl
    Gezdim o yaşta dağları hülyâm içinde lâl
    Aldım Rakofça kırlarının hür havasını
    Duydum akıncı cedlerinin ihtirasını
    Her yaz şimâle doğru asırlarca bir koşu
    Bağrımda bir akis gibi kalmış uğultulu
    Malüpken ordu, yaslı dururken bütün vatan
    Rüyama girdi her gece bir fatihâne zan
    Hicretlerin bakıyyesi, hicrânlı duygular;

25. Köroğlu, Erol, *Türk Edebiyatı ve Birinci Dünya Savaşı (1914–1918). Propagandadan Milli Kimlik İnşasına* (İstanbul, 2004), p. 121.

26. Birdoğan, Nejat, *İttihat-Terakki'nin Alevilik Bektaşilik Araştırması (Baha Sait Bey)* (İstanbul, 1994).

27. Birdoğan, *İttihat*, p. 7.

28. Yoldaşlar, nasip olmazsa görmek o günü, Ölürsem kurtuluştan once yani, Alıp götürün Anadolu' da bir köy mezarlığına gömün beni.

10. Atatürk as a Unionist

*Annual lecture of the LSE chair of Turkish Studies, at SOAS, London, February 2009.

1. Mango, Andrew, *Atatürk* (London: John Murray, 1999); McFie, A.L., *Atatürk* (London: Longman, 1994), Kreiser, Klaus, *Atatürk Eine Biographie* (München: Beck, 2008).

2. Erickson, Edward J., *Defeat in Detail. The Ottoman Army in the Balkans 1912–1913* (Westport: Praeger, 2003); Erickson, Edward J., *Ordered to Die. A History of the Ottoman Army in the First World War* (Westport: Greenwood, 2001); Handan Nezir-Akmese, *The Birth of Modern Turkey. The Ottoman Military and the March to World War I* (London: I.B.Tauris, 2005).

3. Karabekir, Kâzım, *İttihat ve Terakki Cemiyeti 1896–1909* (İstanbul: n.p, 1982), p. 179.

4. Cengiz, Halil Erdoğan, *Enver Paşa'nın Anıları 1881–1908* (İstanbul: İletişim, 1991), pp. 107–8.

5. Mango, *Atatürk,* p. 84.

6. Mango, *Atatürk,* p. 87 (on the basis of Atatürk's own recollections).

7. Aktepe, Münir, 'Atatürk'ün Sofya ataşeliğine kadar İttihat ve Terakki ile olan münasebetleri', *Belleten* 38 (1974), p. 285.

8. Erickson, *Defeat in Detail,* pp. 259–72.

9. Aktepe, 'Atatürkün Münasebetleri', pp. 284–5.

10. Sertoğlu, Mithat, 'Balkan savaşı sonlarında Edirne'nin kurtarılması hususunda hemen teşebbüse geçilmesi için Atatürk'ün harbiye nezaretine uyarışına dair bilinmeyen bir belge', *Belleten* 32 (1968), pp. 459–68.

11. Tufan, Naim M., *Rise of the Young Turks. Politics, the Military and Ottoman Collapse* (London: I.B.Tauris, 2000), p. 290.

12. Ali Fethi [Okyar], *Bolayır Muharebesinde Adem-Muvaffakiyetin Esbabı. 'Askeri Mağlubiyetlerimizin Esbabı' Muharririne Cevap* (İstanbul: Tüccarzade İbrahim Hilmi, 1330/1914–15).

13. According to Atatürk's recollection in 1926. See: Borak, Sadi and Kocatürk, Utkan (eds), *Atatürk'ün Söylev ve Demeçleri* (Ankara: TİTE, 1972), pp. 108–10.

14. For the story of the coup see Esath, Mustafa Ragip, *İttihat ve Terakki Tarihinde Esrar Perdesi ve Yakup Cemil Niçin Öldürüldü* (İstanbul: Hürriyet, 1975).

15. Deny, Jean, 'Les souvenirs du Gazi Moustapha Kemal. Version française d'après l'original turc', *Revue des études islamiques* 1 (1927), pp. 117–222, specifically 132–3 and 207–17.

16. *Atatürk'ün Tamim, Telgraf ve Beyannameleri IV (1917–1938)* (Ankara: TİTE, 1964), pp. 1–8.

17. Hüseyin Rauf [Orbay] in *Yakın Tarihimiz,* vol. 2, pp. 337, 368.

18. Zürcher, Erik Jan, *The Unionist Factor* (Leiden: Brill, 1984), p. 65.

11.   The Ottoman Legacy of the Kemalist Republic

* Originally published as: 'The Ottoman legacy of the Kemalist republic', in Atabaki, Touraj (ed.), *The State and the Subaltern. Modernization, Society and the State in Turkey and Iran* (London: I.B.Tauris, 2007), pp. 95–110.

1. Zürcher, Erik Jan, 'Young Turks, Ottoman Muslims and Turkish nationalists: identity politics 1908–1938', in Karpat, Kemal H. (ed.), *Ottoman Past and Today's Turkey* (Leiden: Brill, 2000), p. 170.
2. Zürcher, 'Identity politics', p. 169.
3. Zürcher, Erik Jan, 'The Ottoman Empire and the armistice of Mudros' in Cecil, Hugh and Liddle, Peter H. (ed.), *At the Eleventh Hour. Reflections, Hopes and Anxieties at the Closing of the Great War, 1918* (London: Leo Cooper), pp. 266–75. This was still true as late as 1923. See Unan, Nimet (ed.), *Atatürk'ün Söylev ve Demeçleri II (19-6-1938)* (Ankara: Türk Tarih Kurumu, 1959), p. 60.
4. Zürcher, Erik Jan, 'The borders of the republic reconsidered', *Bilanço 1923/1998. International Conference on History of the Turkish Republic a Reassessment. Volume I: Politics – Culture – International Relations* (Ankara: TUBA, 1999), pp. 53–9.
5. Zürcher, Erik Jan, 'Between death and desertion. The experience of the Ottoman soldier in World War I', *Turcica* 28 (1996), pp. 235–58.
6. This data has been taken from McCarthy, Justin, *Muslims and Minorities. The Population of Ottoman Anatolia and the End of the Empire* (New York: NY University Press, 1983), and in particular from chapter 7, 'The end of Ottoman Anatolia'. Although McCarthy has often been criticized for his interpretation of the Armenian massacres, I am not aware of a better analysis of population statistics than his.
7. Cf. Hartmann, Richard, *Im neuen Anatolien* (Leipzig: Hinrichs, 1928), p. 86; Linke, Lilo, *Allah Dethroned. A Journey through Modern Turkey* (London: Constable, 1937), p. 278; and Zürcher, Erik Jan, 'Two young Ottomanists discover Kemalist Turkey: the travel diaries of Robert Anhegger and Andreas Tietze', *Journal of Turkish Studies* 26/2 (2002), pp. 359–69.
8. The population movements are described in Berber, Engin, *Sancılı Yıllar: İzmir 1918–1922 Mütareke ve Yunan İşgali Döneminde İzmir Sancağı* (Ankara: Ayraç, 1997), pp. 57–70 and 317–30 (for the Sancak of Izmir only), and by Şenşekerci, Erkan, *Türk Devriminde Celâl Bayar (1918–1960)* (İstanbul: Alfa Yayınları, 2000), pp. 35–8. The latter work is based in part on the memoirs of Bayar, who together with the military commanders Pertev (Demirhan) and Cafer Tayyar (Eğilmez) was in charge of the deportations.
9. See McCarthy, *Muslims and Minorities,* chapter 7.
10. Kemal [Atatürk], *Nutuk* (Vol. 2) (İstanbul: Millî Eğitim Basımevi, 1967), p. 684.
11. For a comprehensive discussion of the problem, see Akın, Rıdvan, *TBMM Devleti (1920–1923). Birinci Meclis Döneminde Devlet Erkleri ve İdare* (İstanbul: İletişim, 2001), pp. 197–217.
12. Tarık Zafer Tunaya describes the legal aspects of the transition to a new state in 'Türkiye Büyük Millet Meclisisi hükümetinin kuruluşu ve hukukî karakteri', *İstanbul Hukuk Fakültesi Mecmuası* 23 (1957), pp. 227–47.

13. Unan, Nimet (ed.), *Atatürk'ün Söylev ve Demeçleri II (19–6-1938)* (Ankara: Türk Tarih Kurumu, 1959), pp. 70, 92.
14. Zürcher, Erik Jan, *Political Opposition in the Early Turkish Republic. The Progressive Republican Party (1924–1925)* (Leiden: Brill, 1991); Tunçay, Mete, *T.C.'nde Tek Parti Yönetimi'nin Kurulması (1923–1931)* (reprint of 1981 edition) (İstanbul: Cem, 1989).
15. Jaeschke, Gotthard, *Türk İnkılabı Tarihi Kronolojisi,* vol. 2 (İstanbul: İstanbul Üniversitesi, 1941), p. 73 (translated by Niyazi Recep Aksu).
16. Zürcher, 'Two young Ottomanists', pp. 359–69.
17. Soysal, İlhami, *Yüzellilikler* (İstanbul: Gür, 1985).
18. Tunçay, *T.C.'nde Tek Parti Yönetimi'nin Kurulması (1923–1931),* p. 178.
19. Çavdar, Tevfik, 'Halkevleri', in Belge, Murat (ed.), *Cumhuriyet Dönemi Türkiye Ansiklopedisi* (İstanbul: İletişim, 1984), p. 878.
20. Cf. Dumont, Paul, 'The origins of Kemalist ideology', in Landau, Jacob (ed.), *Atatürk and the Modernization of Turkey* (Boulder: Westview, 1984), pp. 25–44.
21. Hanioğlu, M. Şükrü, *The Young Turks in Opposition* (Oxford: Oxford University Press, 1995), pp. 7–18.
22. Nye, Robert A., *The Origins of Crowd Psychology. Gustave Le Bon and the Crisis of Mass Democracy in the Third Republic* (London: Sage, 1975). Le Bon was extremely popular and influential, not only among the Young Turks, but also among contemporary intellectuals in the Balkans and the Arab world.
23. Zürcher, Erik Jan, 'Ottoman sources of Kemalist thought', in: Özdalga, Elisabeth (ed.), *Late Ottoman Society. The Intellectual Legacy* (London: Routledge/Curzon, 2005), pp. 14–27.
24. Karabekir, Kâzım, *İttihat ve Terakki Cemiyeti 1896–1909* (İstanbul: private publication, 1982), pp. 176. The text dates from 1945.
25. Among the most important studies are: Mardin, Şerif, *Jön Türklerin Siyasi Fikirleri 1898–1908* (Ankara: İş Bankası, 1964); Hanioğlu, M. Şükrü, *The Young Turks in Opposition* (Oxford: Oxford University Press, 1995); Heyd, Uriel *Foundations of Turkish Nationalism. The Life and Teachings of Ziya Gökalp* (London: Luzac, 1950); Parla, Taha, *The Social and Political Thought of Ziya Gökalp 1871–1924* (Leiden: Brill, 1985); Shissler, A. Holly, *Turkish Identity between two Empires. Ahmet Ağaoğlu 1869–1919* (London: I.B.Tauris, 2002); Georgeon, François, *Türk Milliyetçiliğinin Kökenleri. Yusuf Akçura (1876–1935)* (Ankara, 1986); Hanioğlu, M. Şükrü, *Bir Siyasal Düşünür olarak Doctor Abdullah Cevdet ve Dönemi* (Ankara: Üçdal, 1981); Üstel, Füsun, *Türk Ocakları (1912–1931)* (İstanbul: İlestişim, 1997); Arai, Masami, *Turkish Nationalism in the Young Turk Era* (Leiden: Brill, 1992) and Debus, Esther, *Sebilürreşad: Eine Vergleichende Untersuchung zur Islamischen Opposition der vor- und nachkemalistischen Ära* (Frankfurt: Peter Lang, 1991).

26. Zürcher, Erik Jan, 'The vocabulary of Muslim nationalism', *International Journal of the Sociology of Language* 137 (1999), pp. 81–92.
27. Hanioğlu, M. Şükrü ,'Garbcılar: their attitudes toward religion and their impact on the official ideology of the Turkish Republic', *Studia Islamica* 86 (1997/2), pp. 134–58.
28. Heyd, *Foundations of Turkish Nationalism*, pp. 63 ff.
29. Toprak, Zafer, *Türkiye' de Milli İktisat 1908–1918* (İstanbul: Yurt, 1982) and later editions.
30. Georgeon, *Türk Milliyetçiliğinin Kökenleri*, p. 109.
31. For detailed discussions of Turkish populism, see Toprak, Zafer, 'İkinci meşrutiyette solidarist düşünce: halkçılık', *Toplum ve Bilim* 1 (1977), pp. 92–123; Tekeli, İlhan and Şaylan, Gencay, 'Türkiye' de halkçılık ideolojisinin evrimi', *Toplum ve Bilim* 6–7 (1978), pp. 44–110.

12. The Ottoman Conscription System in Theory and Practice, 1844–1918

* This chapter was previously published, though in slightly different form, as 'The Ottoman conscription system in theory and practice, 1844–1918', *International Review of Social History* 43/3 (1998), pp. 437–49.

1. On the reign of Selim III: Shaw, Stanford J, *Between Old and New. The Ottoman Empire under Selim III, 1789–1807* (Cambridge, MA, 1971); On Selim's fall: *Between Old and New*, pp. 345ff.; On the *Nizam-i Cedid* army: Shaw, Stanford J. 'The origins of Ottoman military reform: the Nizam-i Cedid army of Sultan Selim III', *Journal of Modern History* 37 (1965), pp. 291–306.
2. See Cronin, Stephanie, 'Conscription and popular resistance in Iran, 1925–1941', *International Review of Social History* 43/3 (1998), pp. 451–71.
3. See Fahmy, Khaled, 'The Nation and its deserters: conscription in Mehmed Ali's Egypt', *International Review of Social History* 43/3 (1998), pp. 421–36.
4. The army reforms of Sultan Mahmut II are described in Shaw, Stanford and Shaw, Ezel, *History of the Ottoman Empire and Modern Turkey. Volume II: Reform, Revolution and Republic. The Rise of Modern Turkey 1808–1975* (Cambridge, 1977), pp. 41–5 and in Çoker, Fahri, 'Tanzimat ve ordudaki yenilikler', in Murat Belge (ed.), *Tanzimattan Cumhuriyete Türkiye Ansiklopedisi*, vol. 5 (İstanbul, 1985), pp. 1260–6.
5. Deny, Jean, 'Redif' in: *Encyclopaedia of Islam. New Edition*, Vol. VIII (Leiden, 1995), pp. 370–1.
6. There are several editions of the Edict of Gülhane. I relied on Petermann (mit Ramis Efendi), *Beiträge zu einer Geschichte der neuesten Reformen des Osmanischen Reiches, enthaltend den Hattischerif von Gülhane, den Ferman von 21 November 1839 und das neueste Strafgesetzbuch* (Berlin, 1842). The quote is taken from pp. 11–12.

7. 'Redif' in *Islâm Ansiklopedisi* 9 (Istanbul, 1971), pp. 666–8.

8. Deny, Jean, 'Redif' in *Encyclopaedia of Islam* gives 31 August 1912 as the date of the decision to abolish the *Redif*, on the authority of the official collection of Ottoman legislation known as *Düstur*, vol. IV, p. 615.

9. Belge, Murat (ed.), *Tanzimattan Cumhuriyete Türkiye Ansiklopedisi*, vol. 5 (İstanbul, 1985), p. 1263.

10. *Qur`a qânûnnâme-i humâyûnu* (Istanbul, 1286/1870–1), parts 1 and 4.

11. *Mükellefiyet-i askeriye qânûn-u muvaqqatası* (İstanbul, 1332/1916), articles 14 and 21.

12. PRO/FO 195/2323, report of 20 June 1909 by military attaché, Constantinople (H. Conyers Surtees).

13. PRO/FO 195/2323, report of 28 May 1909 by military attaché, Constantinople.

14. Karpat, Kemal H., *Ottoman Population 1830–1914. Demographic and Social Characteristics* (Madison, 1985); McCarthy, Justin, *The Arab World, Turkey and the Balkans: A Handbook of Historical Statistics* (Boston, 1982); Akbayar, Nuri,'Tanzimat'tan sonra Osmanlı devleti nüfusu', in Belge, Murat (ed.), *Tanzimattan Cumhuriyete Türkiye Ansiklopedisi*, vol. 5 (İstanbul, 1985), pp. 1238–46.

15. Shaw, Stanford J., 'The Ottoman census system and population', *International Journal of Middle East Studies* 9 (1978), pp. 325–38.

16. Ahmed Emin [Yalman], *Turkey in the World War* (New Haven, 1930), p. 79.

17. See for instance the biography of Atatürk's bodyguard: Coşar, Ömer Sami , *Atatürk'ün Muhafızı Topal Osman* (n.p., n.d.), p. 5, describing recruitment in Giresun. However, when the British consuls reported on the reactions to mobilization in their stations at the request of the Committee of Imperial Defence (request by Sir Maurice Hankey, secretary to the CID, dated 25 October 1912), they described a very patchy response: Salonica: 'prompt'; Gallipoli: 'sullen'; Izmit: 'willing'; Adana: 'unwilling'; Adalia (Antalya): 'reluctant'; Alexandretta (Iskenderun): 'prompt and willing' (PRO/FO 195/2445, pp. 260–322).

18. PRO/FO 195/2346, report of 10 April 1910 by military attaché, Constantinople (Tyrrell). The same general picture emerges from many eyewitness reports.

19. Reports by the British consuls in Damascus and Antalya are illustrative. The consul in Damascus, in his report of 7 December 1912 says that in the first weeks of October there was much enthusiasm to go to the war. As many as 60–70 per cent of Muslims presented themselves, but after reverses and because of bad treatment, enthusiasm dropped and by the end of October only 30 per cent of Muslims responded. People started to flee and hide. Of a company of 130 regulars sent from Damascus to Aleppo, 40 deserted on the way (PRO/FO 195/2445, pp. 291, 311).

20. PRO/FO 195/2323. Report from embassy Constantinople containing a summary of the new recruitment law in translation.

21. *Mükellefiyet-i Askeriye Qânûn-u Muvaqqatisi* (1916 conscription law), articles 91, 92.

22. Ahmet İzzet [Furgaç], *Denkwürdigkeiten des Marschalls Izzet Pascha* (Leipzig, 1927), p. 169.

23. PRO/FO 195/2323, report of 26 September 1909.

24. *Qur`a qânûnnâme-i humâyûnu*, (Istanbul: Matba`a-i Âmire, (1286/1870–1)), article 70.

25. Bowen, H., 'Bedel' in *Encyclopaedia of Islam. New Edition*, vol. I (Leiden, 1960), p. 855.

26. Davison, Roderic H, *Reform in the Ottoman Empire 1856–1876* (New York, 1973) (reprint of 1963 edition), pp. 94–5.

27. PRO/FO 195/2323, report of 20 June 1909.

28. Heinzelmann, Tobias, *Heiliger Kampf oder Landesverteidigung? Die Diskussion um die Einführung der allgemeinen Militärpflicht im Osmanischen Reich 1826 – 1856* (Frankfurt am Main, 2004).

29. At this time, the measure may well have been largely symbolic. In 1912 only 5 per cent of those liable to serve seem to have answered the call (PRO/FO 195/2445, p. 291) and according to one report (PRO/FO 195/2456, p. 60 yearly military report, Constantinople), no Christians were called up in 1914.

30. PRO/FO 195/2323, report of 20 June 1909.

31. According to reports from Gallipoli and Rhodes in 1912 (PRO/FO 195/2445, pp. 275, 363).

32. Larcher, Maurice, *La guerre turque dans la guerre mondiale* (Paris, 1926), pp. 589–90.

33. PRO/FO 195/2346 (report of 17 January 1910), p. 126; PRO/FO 195/2456, p. 60 (report of 1914); Larcher, *La guerre turque*, p. 590.

34. Schrader, F., et al, *Atlas de la géographie moderne* (Paris, 1914), maps 28 and 33.

35. There are quite a few eyewitness reports from the Turkish side of the front in the Balkan War. Among the best are: Ashmead-Bartlett, Ellis, *With the Turks in Thrace* (London, 1913); and James, Lionel, *With the Conquered Turk. The Story of a Latter-Day Adventurer* (London, [1913]).

13. The Ottoman Soldier in World War I

*This chapter is a combination of three published works: 'Ottoman labour battalions in World War I', in Kieser, Hans-Lukas, and Schaller, Dominik J. (ed.), *Der Völkermord an den Armeniern und die Shoah. The Armenian Genocide and the Shoah,* (Zürich: Chronos, 2002), pp. 187–96; 'Between death and desertion. The experience of Ottoman soldier in World War I', *Turcica* 28 (1996), pp. 235–58 and 'Hizmet etmeyi başka biçimlerle reddetmek: Osmanlı imparatorluğunun son dönemlerinde asker kaçaklığı', in Heval Çınar, Özgür and Üsterci Coşkun (eds), *Çarklardaki Kum: Vicdani Red* (Istanbul: İletişim, 2008), pp. 59–68. Prior to that, parts of 'Between death and desertion' were presented as papers at the conference *The war experienced* in Leeds, September 1994 and at the 7th conference on the social and economic history of the Ottoman Empire in Heidelberg in July 1995. These papers benefited from the critical remarks made by colleagues at these conferences, in particular those of Peter Liddell, Yigal Sheffy, Justin McCarthy and Ercüment Kuran.

1. There are many testimonies to this effect. See, for example, Kress von Kressenstein, Friedrich Freiherr, *Mit den Türken zum Suezkanal* (Berlin: Otto Schlegel, 1938), p. 39.

2. Tütengil, Cavit Orhan, '1927 yılında Türkiye' in *Atatürk'ün Büyük Söylevi'nin 50. Yılı Semineri. Bildiriler ve tartışmalar* (Ankara: Türk Tarih Kurumu, 1980), p. 56. Because the numbers quoted refer to 1927, the villagers concerned are almost exclusively Muslim, the Armenians and Greeks, who had a much higher rate of literacy, having left or having been killed.

3. Kannengiesser, Hans, *The Campaign in Gallipoli* (London: Hutchinson, 1927), p. 157.

4. A complete collection of the journal is to be found in the library of the Oriental Institute of the University of Bonn, while the university library of Tübingen has a collection of the yearbooks *(Zwischen Kaukasus and Sinai. Jahrbuch des Bundes der Asienkämpfer* (Berlin-Tempelhof: Deutsche Buchhandlung Mulzer und Cleeman), vols 1 (1921), 2 (1922), 3 (1923).

5. Apart from Wallach, Jehuda L., *Anatomie einer Militärhilfe. Die Preussisch-deutschen Militärmissionen in der Türkei 1835 – 1919* (Düsseldorf: Droste, 1976), which does concentrate on military matters, the other leading studies are: Trumpener, Ulrich, *Germany and the Ottoman Empire 1914–1918* (Princeton, 1966) and Weber, F.G., *Eagles on the Crescent. Germany, Austria and the Diplomacy of the Turkish Alliance, 1914–1918* (Ithaca, 1970). The pre-war German–Ottoman rapprochement is studied in Sullivan, Charles D., *Stamboul Crossings. German Diplomacy in Turkey 1908–1914,* Ph.D. thesis (Nashville: Vanderbilt University, 1977).

6. Belen, Fahri, *Birinci Cihan Harbinde Türk Harbi,* 5 vols (Ankara: Genelkurmay Harb Tarihi ve Stratejik Etüt Başkanlığı, 1963–7).

7. Stoddard, Phillip, in his unpublished Ph. D. thesis, The Ottoman Government and the Arabs 1911–1918: A Preliminary Study of the Teşkilat-i Mahsusa (Princeton, 1963), p. 231.

8. Such as Schilling, Dr Victor, 'Kriegshygienische Erfahrungen in der Türkei', *Zwischen Kaukasus und Sinai* 2 (1922), pp. 71–89. A detailed study of the German medical service in the Ottoman Empire is: Becker, Helmut, *Aeskulap zwischen Reichsadler und Halbmond. Sanitätswesen und Seuchenbekämpfung im türkischen Reich während des Ersten Weltkrieges* (Herzogenrath: Murken-Altrogge, 1990).

9. The existence of this source was kindly pointed out to me by Dr Yigal Sheffy of the Dayan Center, Tel-Aviv. It can be found in the monthly intelligence summaries, ref. PRO/WO 157/687ff. (Egyptian front) and PRO/WO 157/776ff. (Mesopotamian front).

10. Kress, *Mit den Türken zum Suezkanal*, p. 36.

11. Kress, *Mit den Türken zum Suezkanal*, p. 39.

12. Ahmed Emin [Yalman], *Turkey in the World War* (New Haven: Yale University Press, 1930) p. 79.

13. PRO/WO 157/735, 25 May 1918.

14. Pomiankowski, Joseph, *Der Zusammenbruch des Ottomanischen Reiches* (Graz: Akademische Druck und Verlagsanstalt, 1969) (reprint of the 1928 edition), p. 103.

15. The lower number is arrived at on the basis of the enumeration given by Erol Çatma in his *Asker İşçiler* (İstanbul: Ceylan, 1998, pp. 40ff.) The higher number is given by Austrian ambassador Pomiankowski in his *Zusammenbruch des Osmanischen Reiches*, p. 93.

16. During the war most Ottoman units were seriously undermanned. One of the witnesses, whose testimony is given by Raymond H. Kevorkian in his 'Receuil de témoignages sur l'estermination des amele tabouri ou bataillons de soldats-ouvriers Arméniens de l'armée Ottomane pendant la première guerre mondiale', *Revue d'histoire arménienne contemporaine*, 1 (1995), pp. 289–303, says there were 350 men in the battalion to start with. Another says that 280 were killed in the battalion he was a part of.

17. Çatma, *Asker İşçiler*, pp. 41–2.

18. Toprak, Zafer, *Türkiye'de 'Milli İktisat'(1908–1918)* (Ankara: Yurt, 1982), p. 318.

19. Document 33 (no. 6738) in *Documents* (Ankara: Directorate General of Press and Information, n. d.), pp. 91–2, kindly provided by Hilmar Kaiser.

20. Document 33 (no. 6738), where the communication commander asks for more armed troops to watch the workers and also a telegram of 25 July 1915 from the Chief of Staff in Istanbul asking for special watchfulness. *Askeri Tarih Belgeleri Dergisi*, special issue 1, p. 92, kindly provided by Hilmar Kaiser.

21. Morgenthau, Harry, *Secrets of the Bosphorus* (London: Hutchinson, 1918), p. 199.

22. Zürcher, 'Between death and desertion', pp. 249–50.

23. Nogales, Rafael de, *Four Years beneath the Crescent* (London: Scribner's, 1926), p. 45. The author describes wholesale desertion of Armenian troops as a very serious threat to the Ottomans.

24. Kevorkian, 'Receuil de témoignages', p. 290 (testimony of the Swiss Zurlinden). The same method is described by the German Künzler in Urfa and (on the authority of others) by Morgenthau in his memoirs. (Cf. Akçam, *İnsan Hakları*, p. 243).

25. Kevorkian, 'Receuil de témoignages', p. 295.
26. Akçam, *İnsan Hakları*, p. 244.
27. Kaiser, Hilmar, 'The Baghdad Railway and the Armenian genocide, 1915–1916' in Hovannisian, Richard G. (ed.), *Remembrance and Denial: The Case of the Armenian Genocide* (Detroit: Wayne State University Press, 1999), pp. 67–112.
28. Sarafian, Ara, 'The absorption of Armenian women and children into Muslim households as a structural component of the Armenian genocide' in Bartov, Omer and Mack, Phyllis (ed.), *In God's Name: Genocide and Religion in the Twentieth Century* (Oxford/New York: Berghahn, 2001), p. 211.
29. Report by a Dr Krieger, discovered by Hilmar Kaiser in the Central Zionist Archives in Jerusalem in Z 3 (Zionistischer Zentralbüro Berlin 1911–20), file 66 (Konstantinopel 1913–18) and used with his kind permission.
30. PRO/WO 157/700, 12 January 1916.
31. Kut, Halil, *Bitmeyen Savaş. Kütulamare Kahramanı Halil Paşa'nın Anıları*, ed. by M. Taylan Sorgun (İstanbul: Yedigün, 1972), p. 191. This is confirmed on the British side by Aubrey Herbert in *Mons, Anzac and Kut* (London: Hutchinson, 1919), p. 253.
32. Liman von Sanders, *Fünf Jahre Türkei* [Five years in Turkey] (Berlin: Scherl, 1920), p. 242.
33. Kress, *Mit den Türken zum Suezkanal*, p. 39.
34. According to one German witness, the Kurdish troops were totally unreliable and it was impossible to form more regular units out of them because they refused to obey other Kurds, taking their orders only from the Turkish commander-in-chief (Hans-Joachim von Loeschebrand-Horn, 'Der Feldzug der Süleimanije-Gruppe in Kurdistan im Sommer 1916', *Zwischen Kaukasus und Sinai* 3 (1923), p. 121.
35. According to Dr Georg Mayer, who was charged with reforming the Ottoman army medical service in December 1913, syphilis was so widespread that it did not count as a ground for rejection. Instead, the syphilitics were formed into labour battalions (report by Mayer cited in Becker, *Aeskulap*, p. 42).
36. Larcher, Maurice, *La guerre turque dans la guerre mondiale*, appendices 44 and 50. Larcher bases himself on the official statistics released by the Ottoman War Ministry in 1919. The number of 800,000 refers to the number of armed and trained regulars. A much higher number (around 2 million) is also mentioned, but this is impossibly high: Indeed, the number given by Ahmed Emin Yalman for the maximum reservists of all types. This is also true for the total number of men called up, which Larcher puts at 2.85 million. All numbers are in fact rough estimates. The British estimates varied a great deal from time to time and from place to place, but the average was 600,000–700,000.

37. Larcher, *La guerre turque,* appendix 45, 48.
38. PRO/WO 157/703, 1 April 1916 and PRO/WO 157/704, 12 May 1916. Also: PRO/WO 157/717, 26 July 1917.
39. Pomiankowski, *Zusammenbruch,* pp. 242–3.
40. Kress, *Mit den Türken zum Suezkanal,* p. 24.
41. Cf. Pomiankowski, *Zusammenbruch,* p. 57.
42. Figures given in Rhodes James, Robert, *Gallipoli* (London: Pan, 1974), p. 348. Rhodes James estimates the actual number of casualties at about 300,000. Liman gives the rather optimistic estimates of 66,000 dead and 152,000 wounded (Liman, *Fünf Jahre Türkei,* p. 135).
43. Pomiankowski, *Zusammenbruch,* p. 225.
44. Liman, *Fünf Jahre Türkei,* p. 240.
45. Larcher, *La guerre turque,* appendix 50.
46. Cf. Yalman, *Turkey in the World War,* p. 81.
47. Schilling, *Kriegshygiënische Erfahrungen,* pp. 75–6; PRO/WO 157/735, 26 April 1918.
48. Schilling, *Kriegshygiënische Erfahrungen,* p. 88.
49. PRO/WO 157/735, 1 March 1918.
50. Larcher, *La guerre turque,* appendix 51, p. 602.
51. PRO/WO 157/713, 8 March 1917.
52. Liman, *Fünf Jahre Türkei,* p. 241.
53. Liman, *Fünf Jahre Türkei,* p. 241.
54. Guse, Felix, *Die Kaukasusfront im Weltkrieg bis zum Frieden von Brest* (Leipzig: Koehler und Amelang, 1940), p. 92.
55. Zürcher, Erik Jan, 'Welingelichte kringen? De politieke berichtgeving van de Nederlandse ambassade in Istanbul in de eerste wereldoorlog', *Sharqiyyat* 1/1 (1988), p. 78. This is confirmed by Pomiankowski, who says that one stroke equalled two days of arrest or one day of incarceration (Pomiankowski, *Zusammenbruch,* p. 243).
56. PRO/WO 157/724, 15 February 1918.
57. PRO/WO 157/714, 3 March 1917.
58. For instance: PRO/WO 157/700, 4 January 1916; 157/723, 10 January 1918; 157/735, 25 April 1918.
59. PRO/WO 157/700, 4 January 1916.
60. Ibid.
61. Cf. Sâbis, Ali Ihsan, *Hatıralarım. Birinci Dünya Harbi,* vol. 3 (Istanbul: Nehir, 1991), p. 331.
62. Ölçen, Mehmet Arif, *Vetluga Irmağı* (Ankara: Ümit, 1994), p. 38.
63. I am indebted to my colleague Dr Dick Douwes for this observation.
64. PRO/WO, 157/725, 10 March 1918.
65. PRO/WO 157/724, 17 February 1918.
66. PRO/WO 157/735, 29 May 1918.

67. Atay, Falih Rıfkı, *Zeytindağı* (İstanbul: Varlık, 1964) (5th impression), p. 191.
68. Cf. the report by General von Seeckt in Wallach, Jehuda L., *Anatomie einer Militärhilfe*, p. 263.
69. PRO/WO, 157/735, 29 May 1918.
70. Ibid.
71. These data come from several different reports: PRO/WO 157/700, 16 January 1916; 157/724, 9 February 1918; 157/725, 14 March 1918; 157/735, 25 April 1918.
72. Becker, *Aeskulap*, pp. 126, 167.
73. 60, PRO/WO 175/715, 10 May 1917.
74. Pomiankowski, *Zusammenbruch*, p. 165.
75. A report by Mayer in Becker, *Aeskulap*, p. 59.
76. WO/PRO 157/753, passim.
77. Yalman, *Turkey in the World War*, p. 85.
78. Kress, *Mit den Türken zum Suezkanal*, p. 30.
79. PRO/WO 157/700, Appendix III, January 1916.
80. Becker, *Aeskulap*, p. 66; PRO/WO 157/703, 12–18 April 1916.
81. Becker, *Aeskulap*, p. 63. The *Yıldırım* operations (code-named 'Pasha II' by the Germans) was a plan for the concentration of a Turkish-German force the size of an army group in Northern Syria for an attack on Baghdad. When the situation on the Syrian front became very threatening later in 1917, the project was abandoned and the force was directed south, to the Palestinian front instead.
82. PRO/WO 157/701, 19 February 1916.
83. Kress, *Mit den Türken zum Suezkanal*, p. 170. Pomiankowski (*Zusammenbruch*) also mentions this fact.
84. PRO/WO 157/725, 3 March 1918.
85. PRO/WO 157/700, 7 January 1916.
86. Yalman, *Turkey in the World War*, p. 86.
87. Yalman, *Turkey in the World War*, p. 88.
88. PRO/WO 157/700, 20 January 1916.
89. Kress, *Mit den Türken zum Suezkanal*, p. 42.
90. PRO/WO 157/701, 3 February 1916.
91. PRO/WO 157/700, 20 January 1916.
92. PRO/WO 157/713, 2 March 1917. A deserter's statement of 5 March that over 80 per cent of the camels at the front had died does not seem credible.
93. See for a discussion of the problems with the food supply and the attendant corruption: 'Osmanlı İmparatorluğu'nun 1. dünya savaşındaki ekonomik düzenlemeleri içinde iaşe nezareti ve Kara Kemal Bey'in yeri', in İlkin, Selim and Tekeli, İlhan (ed.), *Cumhuriyetin Harcı, Cilt 2, Köktenci Modernitenin Ekonomik Politikasının Gelişimi içinde Yeri* (İstanbul, 2004), pp. 1–44.
94. Von Seeckt, in Wallach, *Anatomie einer Militärhilfe*, p. 263.

95. PRO/WO 157/701, 25 February 1916.

96. Sâbis, *Hatıralarım*, p. 332.

97. PRO/WO 157/703, 20 April 1916.

98. These data are taken from: Baldry, John, 'Al-Yaman and the Turkish occupation 1849–1914', *Arabica* XXIII, 1976, pp. 156–96.

99. 'Yemen songs' are published in a number of collections of folk songs, for instance in: Özbek, Mehmet, *Folklor ve Türkülerimiz* (İstanbul: Ötüken, 1975).

100. That this was the prevailing sentiment is attested by Guse, *Der Kaukaususfront,* p. 92.

101. Larcher in *La guerre turque* gives the following numbers: killed 325,000; wounded 400,000; missing, deserted, prisoner: 1.5 million. Becker (*Aeskulap,* p. 441) gives several different estimates, of which one has the same numbers for total strength, killed and wounded, but an unrealistically low 250,000 for missing/prisoner. This apparently does not count deserters among the missing. Another estimate (by Wicker) cited by Becker gives a total of 1.6 million for the number of soldiers the empire put into the field. This must refer to the number effectively serving rather than the number of those called up. Wicker gives the number of persons killed as 300,000 and that of the wounded as 600,000. The official Turkish data, cited by Ahmet Emin Yalman (*Turkey in the World War,* p. 252), give the numbers for sick (over 3 million, of whom over 400,000 died) and wounded (nearly 712,000, of whom nearly 60,000 died) but these numbers are hardly exact.

102. The political and military leadership in Ankara was faced both with the problem of desertion it inherited from the world war, which had resulted in a countryside infested with armed bands, and with the continuing problem of desertion in its own forces. As early as July 1920 the assembly debated a proposal to introduce 'independence tribunals' (*İstiklal Mahkemeleri*) to combat desertion. Over the summer of 1920 the number of desertions kept on growing and by September 1920 the assembly was ready to take action. At the insistence of the government and Chief of Staff Fevzi Pasha a Law on Deserters (*Firari Kanunu*) was enacted on 11 September, and the Independence Tribunals were instituted and given unrestricted authority to enforce the law. Two weeks later the tribunals were also given jurisdiction over cases brought under the 'High Treason Law' (*Hıyaneti Vataniye Kanunu*).

14. The Ottoman Empire and the Armistice of Moudhros

* Originally published as: 'The Ottoman Empire and the armistice of Mudros', in Cecil, Hugh and Liddle, Peter H. (ed.), *At the Eleventh Hour. Reflections, Hopes and Anxieties at the Closing of the Great War* (London: Leo Cooper, 1998), pp. 266–75.

1. Belen, Fahri, *Birinci Cihan Harbinde Türk Harbi. 1918 Yıl Hareketleri. Beşinci Cilt* (Ankara: Genelkurmay, 1967), p. 205.
2. Belen, *Türk Harbi*, p. 204.
3. Toprak, Zafer, *Türkiye'de Millî İktisat (1908–1918)* (Ankara: Yurt, 1982), pp. 313–44.
4. Ahmed Emin [Yalman], *Turkey in the World War* (New Haven: Yale University Press, 1930), p. 265.
5. Belen, *Türk Harbi*, p. 209.
6. The Turkish source on the negotiations is the serialized version of Rauf [Orbay]'s memoirs, published in *Yakın Tarihimiz* [Our Recent History], vol. 1, pp. 112, 144, 177, 208, 239, 272, 304, 336; vol. 2, pp. 16–18; 48–50; 80–82 (Ankara: Türkpetrol, n. d.).
7. Text in *Yakın Tarihimiz*, vol. 2, p. 49.
8. Cf. Einstein, Lewis, *Inside Constantinople. A Diplomatist's Diary during the Dardanelles Expedition* (London: John Murray, 1917).
9. *Yakın Tarihimiz*, vol. 2, pp. 82, 144–6.
10. Belen, *Türk Harbi*, p. 215.
11. Tunaya, Tarık Zafer, *Türkiye'de Siyasî Partiler. Cilt 2: Mütareke Dönemi* (İstanbul: Hürriyet Vakfı, 1986), pp. 245–63, 472–92.
12. Zürcher, Erik Jan, *Opposition in the Early Turkish Republic. The Progressive Republican Party (1924–1925)* (Leiden: Brill, 1991).
13. See, for instance, Mustafa Kemal Pasha's speech on his arrival in Ankara in December 1919, in Unan, Nimet (ed.), *Atatürk' ün Söylev ve Demeçleri 2 (1906–1938)* (Ankara: Türk Tarih Kurumu, 1959), pp. 4–15.
14. See, for instance, Halide Edib [Adıvar], *The Turkish Ordeal* (London: The Century, 1928); Atay, Falih Rıfkı, *Çankaya* (Istanbul: Bateş, 1980) and Karaosmanoğlu, Yakup Kadri, *Sodom ve Gomore* (İstanbul: Bilgi, 1966) [original edition: 1928].

15. Renewal and Silence: Post-war Unionist and Kemalist Rhetoric on the Armenian Genocide

*Paper presented in 2007 at the W.A.T.S-conference at Stanford University, Palo Alto. To be published in: Suny, Ronald and Göçek, Fatma Müge (ed.), *A Question of Genocide, 1915, Armenians and Turks at the End of the Ottoman Empire* (Oxford University Press, forthcoming).

1. Zürcher, Erik Jan, *The Unionist Factor. The Role of the Committee of Union and Progress in the Turkish National Movement (1905–1926)* (Leiden: Brill, 1984).
2. Lewis, Bernard, *The Emergence of Modern Turkey* (London: Oxford University Press, 1961), p. 350.
3. Zürcher, Erik Jan, 'Young Turks, Ottoman Muslims and Turkish nationalists: identity politics 1908–1938' in: Karpat, Kemal H. (ed.), *Ottoman Past and Today's Turkey* (Leiden: Brill, 2000), pp. 150–79.

4. Deringil, Selim, *The Well-protected Domains. Ideology and the Legitimation of Power in the Ottoman Empire (1876–1909)* (London: I.B.Tauris, 1998) and Yavuz, Hakan, *Islamic Political Identity in Turkey* (London: Oxford University Press, 2003).
5. Zürcher, Erik Jan, 'How Europeans adopted Anatolia and created Turkey', *European Review* 13/3 (2005), pp. 379–94.
6. Cf. Gawrych, George, 'The culture and politics of violence in Turkish society 1903–1914', *Middle Eastern Studies* 3 (1986), pp. 307–30.
7. Zürcher, Erik Jan, 'The vocabulary of Muslim nationalism', *International Journal of the Sociology of Language* 137 (1999), pp. 81–92.
8. Underground networks trying to prepare for the post-war situation became active as soon as the armistice had been concluded. Members of Enver Pasha's 'Special Organization' (*Teşkilat-i Mahsusa*), especially those of Circassian origin, seem to have formed the backbone of these networks. The most important of the networks was *Karakol* (The Guard), founded in October 1918 at the behest of Enver and Talât Pashas. This network smuggled quite significant amounts of weaponry and equipment as well as a large number of people to Anatolia in the period between November 1918 and March 1920. Many of those smuggled to Anatolia were people who not only brought vital skills to the emerging resistance movement but who could also be expected to arrested for alleged war crimes. In 1919–20 *Karakol* also nursed political ambitions, trying to determine the course of the national resistance in Anatolia and establishing independent relations with the Bolsheviks.
9. Tunaya, Tarık Zafer, *Türkiye'de Siyasal Partiler. Cilt II Mütareke Dönemi* (İstanbul: Hürriyet, 1986), pp. 92–137.
10. Tunaya, *Siyasal Partiler,* pp. 71–84.
11. Mango, Andrew, *Atatürk* (London: John Murray, 1999), p. 199.
12. İğdemir, Uluğ, *Sivas Kongresi Tutanakları* (Ankara: Türk Tarih Kurumu, 1969), p. 113.
13. İğdemir, *Sivas Kongresi Tutanakları,* pp. 2–22.
14. İğdemir, *Sivas Kongresi Tutanakları,* p. 107.
15. Unan, Nimet (ed.), *Atatürk'ün Söylev ve Demeçleri, vol. 2 (1906–1938)* (Ankara: Türk Tarih Kurumu, 1959), p. 12.
16. Akçam, Taner, 'Sevr ve Lozan'ın başka tarihi' in Zürcher, Erik Jan (ed.), *Türkiye' de Etnik Çatışma. İmparatorluktan Cumhuriyete* (İstanbul: İletişim, 2005), pp. 51–89.
17. Ilıkan, Selma and Ilıkan, Faruk, *Ankara İstiklâl Mahkemesi* (İstanbul: Simurg, 2005) [a transcript of the court records].
18. The reasons to doubt the authenticity of the text are internal as well as external. The provenance is unclear as, to the best of my knowledge, no one has been able to trace this supposed Swiss journalist, not even under the more usual spelling of Emil Hildebrandt or any other permutation. There is no mention

of the interview in contemporary Turkish sources either. The text itself seems to be strangely at odds with the actual proceedings of the tribunals (which did not mention the massacres). There are slips, which may have been due to the reporter, but are otherwise hard to explain. Surely, someone as intimately familiar with the CUP. as Mustafa Kemal would not talk about the 'Committee of the Union of the Young Turks'? The 'interview' could easily have been made up, as it contains no actual facts beyond those that were common knowledge in Turkey by July 1926 and were widely published in the Turkish press.

19. Akçam, Taner, *A Shameful Act. The Armenian Question and the Question of Turkish Responsibility* (New York: Metropolitan, 2006), p. 11.
20. Yalçın, Hüseyin Cahit, *Tanıdıklarım* (İstanbul: YKY, 2001), pp. 81–3.
21. I gratefully acknowledge the contribution of Müge Göçek here, who has pointed out to me the importance of the existence of this coalition in explaining the silence of the early republic on the Armenian.

IV. Towards the Nation State: Introduction

1. Meeker, Michael E, *A Nation of Empire. The Ottoman Legacy of Turkish Modernity* (Berkeley, 2001).
2. See for a good example: Brockett, Gavin, 'Collective action and the Turkish revolution: towards a framework for the social history of the Atatürk era, 1923–38' in Kedourie, Sylvia (ed.), *Turkey before and after Atatürk: Internal and External Affairs* (London: Frank Cass, 1999), pp. 44–66. See also: Atabaki, Touraj (ed.), *The State and the Subaltern. Modernization, Society and the State in Turkey and Iran* (London, 2007).
3. For a discussion of the problems involved, see *History and Theory*, 40/1 (2002), pp. 135–48.

16. Young Turks, Ottoman Muslims and Turkish Nationalists: Identity Politics 1908–38

*This text was originally submitted as a paper for a conference in Madison, Wisconsin in June 1996. I could not be present at the conference in Madison because of (very happy) personal circumstances at the time, but I did submit my draft paper and I also presented preliminary versions at workshops in Vienna in 1996 and in Princeton in 1997. I would like to thank the conveners of the conference (Kemal Karpat) and of the workshops (Gabriele Paleczek and Şükrü Hanioğlu) for the opportunity to raise these issues and the colleagues who commented on the papers, notably Mete Tunçay, Andrew Mango and Çağlar Keyder in Vienna and Martin van Bruinessen and Halil Berktay in Princeton, for sharpening my focus.

1. The best concise description of this process can be found in Anderson, Matthew, *The Eastern Question, 1774–1923: A Study in International Relations* (London, 1972).

2. Hanioğlu, M. Şükrü, *The Young Turks in Opposition* (Oxford, 1995), pp. 205–6.
3. Zürcher, Erik Jan, 'The Ottoman Empire and the Turkish republic: an attempt at a new periodization', *Welt des Islams* 32 (1992), pp. 237–53.
4. There are a number of excellent studies on the Young Turk movement: Ramsaur, Ernest, *The Young Turks: Prelude to the Revolution of 1908* (New York, 1957); Hanioğlu, M. Şükrü, *The Young Turks in Opposition*; Ahmad, Feroz, *The Young Turks: The Committee of Union and Progress in Turkish Politics 1908–1914* (Oxford, 1969); Akşin, Şina, *Jön Türkler ve İttihat ve Terakki* (Istanbul, 1987).
5. Hanioğlu, *Young Turks in Opposition*, p. 208.
6. Cf. Lewis, Bernard, *The Emergence of Modern Turkey* (Oxford, 1961), p. 208.
7. Lewis, *The Emergence of Modern Turkey*, p. 229.
8. Georgeon, François, *Aux origines du nationalisme turc: Yusuf Akçura (1876–1935)* (Paris, 1980).
9. Devereux, Robert, *The First Ottoman Constitutional Period: A Study of the Midhat Constitution and Parliament* (Baltimore, 1964), p. 74.
10. Hanioğlu, *Young Turks in Opposition*, pp. 200–3.
11. Cf. Akşin, Şina, *31 Mart Olayı* (Ankara, 1970).
12. For the Pan-Islamist current, see: Landau, Jacob, *The Politics of Pan-Islam: Ideology and Organization* (Oxford, 1990), esp. pp. 73–142.
13. Cf. Landau, Jacob, *Panturkism in Turkey: A Study in Irredentism* (London, 1981), pp. 28–71.
14. Cf. Kushner, David, *The Rise of Turkish Nationalism, 1876–1908* (London, 1977) and Ami, Masami, *Turkish Nationalism in the Young Turk Era* (Leiden, 1992).
15. Berkes, Niyazi, *The Development of Secularism in Turkey* (Montreal, 1964), pp. 337–66.
16. See for example Debus, Esther, *Sebilürreşat. Eine vergleichende Untersuchung zur islamischen Opposition der vor- und nachkemalistischen Ära* (Frankfurt, 1991).
17. See for instance, Shaw, Stanford and Shaw, Ezel, *A History of The Ottoman Empire and the Turkish Republic*, vol. 2, *The Rise of Modern Turkey 1808–1975* (Cambridge, 1977), pp. 301–10 and Lewis, Geoffrey, *Modern Turkey* (London, 1974), pp. 55–6.
18. Hanioğlu, *Young Turks in Opposition*, p. 211.
19. Cf. Zürcher, Erik Jan, *The Unionist Factor: The Role of the Committee of Union and Progress in the Turkish National Movement 1905–1926* (Leiden, 1984), pp. 34–43.
20. That the CUP did create the national resistance movement after World War I is the main thesis of my *Unionist Factor*.

21. The most authoritative study of the 'National Economy' programme is Toprak, Zafer, *Türkiye'de 'Milli İktisat' (1908–1918)* (Ankara, 1982).

22. Obviously, we are not talking here about the Marxist concept of a 'progressive national bourgeoisie' as the opposite of a 'compradore bourgeoisie' (Cf. Gordon, Alec, 'The theory of the "progressive" national bourgeoisie', *Journal of Contemporary Asia*, 3 (1973), pp. 192–303. Our use of the concept reflects that of the Unionists themselves.

23. Cf. Stoddard, Philip, The Ottoman Government and the Arabs, 1911 to 1918: A Preliminary Study of the Teskilat-i Mahsusa (Unpublished Ph.D. dissertation, Princeton University, 1963) a pioneering study of the organization. But Stoddard concentrates on the organization's activities in the Arab lands and hardly mentions either the economic programme or the persecution of the Armenians.

24. Mahmut Celâl Bayar (1884–1987), trained as a banker, joined the CUP in 1907. From 1908 to 1918 he headed the party organization in Izmir. He helped to organize the national resistance against the Greeks in Izmir in 1919, was Economic Affairs Minister, 1932–7; Prime Minister, 1937–9; and third President of the Turkish Republic, 1950–60.

25. Celâl Bayar, *Ben de Yazdım. Millî Mücadeleye Giriş*, vol. 5 (İstanbul, 1967), pp. 1572–82.

26. The Armenian scholar Vahakn Dadrian has published both on the 1919 court martial ('The Documentation of the World War I Armenian massacres in the proceedings of the Turkish military tribunal', *International Journal of Middle East Studies* 23 (1991), pp. 549–76) and on the German and Austrian witnesses ('Documentation of the Armenian genocide in German and Austrian sources' in Charny, Israel (ed.), *The Widening Circle of Genocide* (New Brunswick, 1994), pp. 77–125. For an interesting study by a Turkish scholar who accepts the reality of the genocide, see Akçam, Taner, *Türk Ulusal Kimliği ve Ermeni Sorunu* (İstanbul, 1992).

27. Tanör, Bülent, *Türkiye'de Yerel Kongre İktidarları (1918–1920)* (İstanbul, 1992), pp. 21–2. A number of these congresses have been described in detail, partly by their organizers themselves. The best known works of this type are Dursunoğlu, Cevat, *Millî Mücadelede Erzurum* (Ankara, 1946); Çarıklı, Hacim Muhittin, *Balıkesir ve Alaşehir Kongreleri* (Ankara, 1967) and Bıyıklıoğlu, Tevfik, *Trakya'da Millî Mücadele* (Ankara, 1956). Recently, an excellent study on the genesis of the resistance movement of the Aegean Coast, on the basis of the papers of one of its leaders, has been published: İlkin, Selim and Tekeli, İlhan, *Ege'de Sivil Direnişten Kurtuluş Savaşına Geçerken Uşak Heyet-i Merkeziyesi ve İbrahim (Tahtakılıç) Bey* (Ankara, 1991).

28. Jäschke, Gotthard, 'Nationalismus und Religion im türkischen Befreiungskriege', *Welt des Islams* 18 (1936), pp. 54–69.

29. Rustow, Dankwart A., *Politics and Islam*.

30. Karpat, Kemal H., *Turkey's Politics: The Transition to a Multi-party System* (Princeton, 1959), p. 254.
31. Toprak, Türkiye'de 'Millî İktisat', pp. 63–6.
32. Toprak, Türkiye'de 'Millî İktisat', p. 63.
33. Ahmad, *Young Turks*, p. 6.
34. This is shown by the use of the plural, as in *islâmlara yapılan mezâlim* (atrocities committed on the Muslims) (Arslanoğlu, Cem-Ender, *Kars Millî İslâm Şûrâsî (5.11.1918–17.1.1919)* ve Cenubigarbî Kafkas Hükûmeti Muvakkata-i Milliyesi (18 Ocak-13 Nisan 1919) (Ankara, 1986 [?]), p. 149.
35. Arslanoğlu, *Kars Millî*, pp. 149–50.
36. The twelfth of Wilson's Fourteen Points guarantees the Turkish parts of the Ottoman Empire 'a secure sovereignty'. See Helmreich, Paul C., *From Paris to Sèvres. The Partition of the Ottoman Empire at the Peace Conference of 1919–1920* (Columbus, 1974), p. 8.
37. Trabzon, Erzurum, Sivas, Diyarbekir, Mamuerelaziz, Van, Bitlis and the sancak (district) of Canik.
38. Dursunoğlu, *Millî Mücadelede Erzurum*, p. 143.
39. Dursunoğlu, *Millî Mücadelede Erzurum*, p. 51.
40. Dursunoğlu, *Millî Mücadelede Erzurum*, p.152.
41. Dursunoğlu, *Millî Mücadelede Erzurum*, p.160.
42. Dursunoğlu, *Millî Mücadelede Erzurum*, p. 63.
43. Dursunoğlu, *Millî Mücadelede Erzurum*, p. 147. See: Heyd, Uriel, *Foundations of Turkish Nationalism: The Life and Teachings of Ziya Gökalp* (London, 1950), pp. 63ff. Gökalp derived this part of his ideas from the German sociologist Ferdinand Tönnies.
44. It is interesting to note that the 1921 edition of the famous Redhouse dictionary does not list 'race' among the meanings of *ırk* (p. 1295).
45. Dursunoğlu, *Millî Mücadelede Erzurum*, p. 158.
46. Çarıklı, *Kongreleri*, p. 211; Rustow has pointed out that Cilicia seems to have been the only area where the local resistance movement claimed to speak for the Turks. The society claimed that over 90 per cent of the population in the area was Turkish. The explanation of this attitude may be that in Cilicia the danger of incorporation into a larger Armenia was secondary to that of being made a part of French Syria. Basing the argument on Muslim identity would not have set apart the population of Cilicia from that of Syria (see Rustow, Dankwart A., 'Politics and Islam in Turkey 1920–1955' in Frye, Richard N. *Frye, Islam and the West* [The Hague, 1957], p. 71).
47. In fact the representative character of this congress is even more doubtful than that of the regional ones. The number of participants is uncertain, but it was definitely small: between 21 and 25 at the start of the conference and between 29 and 38 by the end, when a number of members of Mustafa Kemal's

staff had been appointed representatives of different provinces which had not sent any. (Tanör, Bülent, 'Millî Mücadele'de kongreler' in Belge, Murat (ed.), *Tanzimat'tan Cumhuriyet'e Türkiye Ansiklopedisi*, vol. 4 (İstanbul, 1985), pp. 1146–7.

48. İğdemir, Uluğ, *Sivas Kongre Tutanakları* (Ankara, 1969), p. 113.
49. Arsan, Nimet (ed.), *Atatürk'ün Söylev ve Demeçleri*, vol. 3 (1918–37) (Ankara, 1961), p. 12.
50. İğdemir, *Sivas Kongre Tutanakları*, pp. 113–14.
51. İğdemir, *Sivas Kongre Tutanakları*, p. 114.
52. Rustow, 'Politics and Islam', p. 72.
53. Ahmad, Feroz, 'Politics and Islam in modern Turkey', *Middle Eastern Studies* 19, pp. 3–21.
54. İğdemir, *Sivas Kongre Tutanakları*, pp. 107–11.
55. Unan, Nimet (ed.), *Atatürk'ün Söylev ve Demeçleri*, vol. 2 (1906–38) (Ankara, 1959), p. 12. This speech of 28 December 1919 is incorrectly dated 28 December 1920.
56. Unan, *Söylev,* vol. 2, p. 14.
57. Unan, *Söylev,* vol. 2, p. 9.
58. Unan, *Söylev,* vol. 2, p. 12.
59. Mustafa Kemal Atatürk, *Nutuk*, vol. 1 (İstanbul, 1967), pp. 12–16.
60. Unan, *Söylev,* vol. 2, p. 9.
61. Unan, *Söylev,* vol. 2, p. 12.
62. Unan, *Söylev,* vol. 2, p. 15.
63. A very clear example of this is Falih Rıfkı Atay' s *Zeytindağı* (1938), which contain his memoirs of his days as a young officer attached to Cemal Pasha's headquarters in Jerusalem and Damascus.
64. An English translation of the text may be found in Smith, Elaine Diana, *Turkey. The Origins of the Kemalist Movement (1919–1923)* (Washington, 1959), pp. 153–4. The translation, taken from Ahmet Emin [Yalman], contains mistakes, however.
65. Curiously, some versions of this text (for instance: Smith on the authority of Ahmed Emin [Yalman], but also Goloğlu, Mahmut, *Millî Mücadele Tarihi 3: Üçüncü Meşrutiyet. 1920* [Ankara, 1970], p. 80) read 'inside or outside the lines of the armistice'. This is also the version given in Grinnell Mears, Eliot, *Modern Turkey* (New York, 1929), who relies on Toynbee and two other sources of 1922. Mears claims that his text is a 'close translation from the Turkish' (p. 630).
66. This passage presents another interesting textual problem: the text as presented by Smith speaks of 'Ottoman Muslims, united in religion, in race and in aim'. This is also the version we find in Ateş, Toktamış, *Türk Devrim Tarihi* (İstanbul, 1980), p. 155 ('*dini, soyu, istekleri bir olan*'); in Goloğlu, *Millî Mücadele Tarihi*, p. 3 and Stanford Shaw, *History of the Ottoman Empire and Modern Turkey*, p. 2 ('United in religion, in race and

in aspirations'). This textual tradition goes back to the 1920s when we find this formula in Arnold Toynbee and Kenneth Kirkwood's *Turkey* (p. 85) and in Mears' *Modern Turkey* (p. 630). But there is another textual tradition in which 'origin' takes the place of 'aim'. This is the one we find in modern texts such as Kili, Suna, *Türk Devrim Tarihi* (İstanbul, 1982), p. 48 ('*dince, soyca ve asılca*') and Aydemir, Şevket Süreyya, *Tek Adam. Mustafa Kemal* (İstanbul, 1975), vol. 2, p. 226 ('*dinen, ırkan ve aslen*'). This tradition goes back at least to the 1930s, because in the school textbook *Tarih IV* (İstanbul, 1931) we find on p. 46 the same expression. The confusion seems to be between 'emelen' (in aspiration), which is what we find in the *İnönü/ Türk Ansiklopedisi*, and 'aslen' (in origin). If this is indeed the case, the confusion must be a very old one, because this is an easy mistake to make with a manuscript text, but it is hardly conceivable with a printed one.

67. Aydemir, *Tek Adam,* p. 226.
68. Parla, Reha, *Belgelerle Türkiye Cumhuriyetinin Uluslararası Temelleri* (Lefkoşa, private publication, 1985), p. 72.
69. The population exchange or *mübadele* recently has begun to receive attention in Turkey, but it still awaits serious research.
70. Beşikçi, İsmail, *Cumhuriyet Halk Fırkasının Tüzüğü (1927) ve Kürt Sorunu* (İstanbul, 1978), p. 83.
71. Sami N. Özerdim, *Atatürk Devrimi Kronolojisi* (Ankara, 1974), p. 75.
72. Beşikçi, *Cumhuriyet Halk Fırkasının Tüzüğü,* p. 94.
73. *Tarih IV Türkiye Cumhuriyeti* (İstanbul, 1931), p. 182.
74. See, for example. Karal, Enver Ziya, 'The principles of Kemalism', in Kazancıgil, Ali and Özbudun, Ergun (ed.), *Atatürk Founder of a Modern State* (London, 1991), p. 18.
75. Quoted in Dumont, Paul, 'Origins of Kemalist ideology' in Landau, Jacob (ed.)., *Atatürk and the Modernization of Turkey* (Boulder, 1984), p. 29.
76. Alp, Tekin, *Le Kémalisme* (Paris, 1937), pp. 251ff.
77. See Heyd, *Foundations,* pp. 63ff. Gökalp also derived this part of his ideas from the German sociologist Ferdinand Tönnies.
78. Alp, Tekin, *Kémalisme,* p. 264.

17. Were the Progressives Conservative?

*This chapter was previously published in Turkish as: 'Terakkiperver cumhuriyet fırkası ve siyasal muhafazakârlık', in Çigdem, Ahmet (ed.), *Modern Türkiye'de Siyasî Düşünce: Muhafazakârlık, Vol. 5* (Istanbul: İletişim, 2003), pp. 40–53.

1. Burke, Edmund, *Reflections on the Revolution in France* (London, 1790).
2. Lord Hailsham [Quintin Hogg], *The Case for Conservatism* (London: Penguin, 1947).
3. Scruton, Roger, *The Meaning of Conservatism* (London: Macmillan, 1980).

4. Cecil, Lord Hugh, *Conservatism* (London: Williams & Northgate, 1912), p. 48.

5. Scruton, *The Meaning of Conservatism*, p. 55.

6. Scruton, *The Meaning of Conservatism*, pp. 53ff.

7. Mannheim, Karl, *Konservatismus. Ein Beitrag zur Soziologie des Wissens* (Frankfurt: Suhrkamp, 1984) [orig. *Habilitation*, Heidelberg, 1925], p. 124.

8. Friedrich Karl Christian Ludwig Büchner (29 March 1824–1 May 1889), author of *Kraft und Stoff: Empirisch-naturphilosophische Studien* (Force and Matter: Empiricophilosophical Studies, 1855), the ' bible' of nineteenth-century materialism.

9. Nye, Robert, *The Origins of Crowd Psychology. Guave LeBon and the Crisis of Mass Democracy in the Third Republic* (London: Sage, 1975), p. 39. LeBon was an important source of inspiration to the Action Française in France and the Fascists in Italy.

10. Cf. Zürcher, Erik Jan, *Millî Mücadelede İttihatçılık* (Istanbul, 1987), chapters 3 and 4.

11. İrem, Nazım, 'Turkish conservative modernism: birth of a national quest for cultural renewal', *International Journal of Middle East Studies* 34 (2002), pp. 87–112 is a very interesting account of one such intellectual group, the followers of Bergson. Although the author clearly shows that there existed in Turkey intellectuals who rejected the dominant positivist and rationalist paradigm, I do not think he succeeds in showing that they had any real political influence. The author incorrectly identifies the PRP as an attempt by the Kemalist state to organize a 'loyal opposition' (p. 87).

12. Mustafa Kemal [Atatürk], *Nutuk* (Ankara: Milli Eğitim Bakanlığı, 1967), p. 729; Hüseyin Rauf [Orbay], Hatıraları, *Yakın Tarihimiz*, p. 167; *Zabıt Ceridesi*, vol. 10, p. 133.

13. Mustafa Kemal [Atatürk,] *Nutuk*, II, pp. 852–61.

14. Though *The Times* never published the interview, Mustafa Kemal's statements were included in Macartney's report on the interview to the British ambassador in Istanbul. Interestingly, a Turkish version of the interview published in *Hakimiyeti Milliye* on 11 December 1924, but it had a completely different and conciliatory tone towards the opposition, almost diametrically opposed to Macartney's unpublished rendering of Kemal's statements. Cf. Zürcher, Erik Jan, *Political Opposition in the Early Turkish Republic. The Progressive Republican Party 1924–1925* (Brill: Leiden, 1991), pp. 60–2.

15. Peker, Recep, *İnkılab Dersleri Notları* (Ankara, 1935), p. 74.

16. As the RPP did not yet have a full programme, the Nine Principles are the only point of reference for a comparison between the programmes of two parties.

17. Zürcher, *Political Opposition*, pp. 125–6.

18. Scruton, *The Meaning of Conservatism*, p. 55.
19. Frey, Frederick W., *The Turkish Political Elite* (Cambridge: MIT Press, 1965), pp. 327–30.
20. Zürcher, *Political Opposition*, p. 106.
21. Tevetoğlu, Fetih, 'Terakkiperver cumhuriyet partisi', *Türk Kültürü*, 264 (1985), p. 286.

18. Institution Building in the Kemalist Republic Compared with Pahlevi Iran: The People's Party

*Originally published in: Atabaki, Touraj and Zürcher, Erik Jan (ed.), *Men of Order: Authoritarian Modernization under Atatürk and Reza Shah* (London: I.B. Tauris, 2004), pp. 98–112.

1. Cronin, Stephanie, 'Conscription and popular resistance in Iran (1925–1941)' in Zürcher, Erik Jan (ed.), *Arming the State. Military Conscription in the Middle East and Asia 1775–1925* (London: I.B.Tauris, 1999), pp. 145–68.
2. This issue is debated in my *The Unionist Factor. The Role of the Committee of Union and Progress in the Turkish National Movement 1905–1926* (Leiden: Brill, 1984).
3. Even as late as 1993, leading scholar Feroz Ahmad in his *The Making of Modern Turkey* (London: Routledge, 1993), writes: 'The destruction of the Ottoman Empire proved to be a blessing, for the Turks were now free to rediscover themselves and to make a fresh start by abandoning a *decadent* past' (p. 77 [italics added for emphasis, EJZ]).
4. Tunaya, Tarık Zafer, *Türkiye'de Siyasal Partiler. Cilt 1, İkinci Meşrutiyet Dönemi* (İstanbul: Hürriyet, 1984), p. XXI.
5. Larcher, Maurice, *La guerre turque dans la guerre mondiale* (Paris: Chiron, 1926), appendices 44 and 50.
6. Rustow, Dankwart A., 'The army and the founding of the Turkish republic', *World Politics* 11 (1959), pp. 513–52.
7. Jäschke, Gotthard, *Türk İnkılâbı Tarihi Kronolojisi* (Istanbul: Millî Mecmua, 1939), vol. 1, p. 156; vol. 2, pp. 50, 73.
8. *Hakimiyet-i Milliye*, 18 September 1924.
9. İğdemir, Uluğ, *Sivas Kongresi Tutankları* (Ankara: TTK, 1969), p. 3.
10. Tunçay, Mete, *T.C.'nde Tek Parti Yönetimi'nin Kurulması* (1923–31) (Istanbul: Cem, 1989 (1981)), p. 48.
11. İnan, Arı, *Gazi Mustafa Kemal Atatürk'ün 1923 Eskişehir – İzmit Konuşmaları* (Ankara: TTK, 1982), pp. 118ff.
12. Tunaya, *Siyasal Partiler*, p. 417.
13. Finefrock, Michael M., From Sultanate to Republic. Mustafa Kemal and the Structure of Turkish Politics 1922–24, unpublished Ph.D. thesis (Princeton University, 1976).

14. Tunçay, *T. C.'nde Tek Parti*, p. 384.
15. Çavdar, Tevfik, 'Halkevleri' in Belge, Murat Belge (ed.), *Cumhuriyet Dönemi Türkiye Ansiklopedisi,* vol. 4, (Istanbul: İletişim, n. d. [1984]), p. 878 gives all the essential information on the People's Houses' aims and organization.
16. Linke, Lilo, *Allah Dethroned. A Journey through Modern Turkey* (London: Constable, 1937).
17. Linke, *Allah Dethroned,* pp. 169ff.
18. Cassels, Alan, *Fascist Italy. Second Edition* (Arlington Heights: Harlan Davidson, 1985), pp. 60–2.
19. Mango, Andrew, *Atatürk* (London: John Murray, 1999), p. 501.
20. Elliot, Matthew, 'New Iran and the dissolution of party politics under Reza Shah', in: Atabaki, Touraj and Zürcher, Erik Jan (ed.), *Men of Order: Authoritarian Modernization under Ataturk and Reza Shah* (London: I.B.Tauris, 2004), pp. 65–97.
21. Abrahamian, Ervand, *Iran between Two Revolutions* (Princeton: Princeton University Press, 1982), p. 149.

19. Touring Anatolia at the End of the Atatürk Era: Kemalist Turkey Observed by Western Visitors

* Formerly published as 'Two young Ottomanists discover Kemalist Turkey. The travel diaries of Robert Anhegger and Andreas Tietze', *Journal of Turkish Studies* 26/1 (2006), pp. 359–69.

1. Linke, Lilo, *Allah Dethroned. A Journey through Modern Turkey* (London: Constable, 1937).

20. Islam in the Service of the Caliphate and the Secular State

* Paper presented in 2005 at St Anthony's College, Oxford.

1. Deringil, Selim, *The Well-protected Domains. Ideology and the Legitimation of Power in the Ottoman Empire 1876–1909* (London, 1998); Toprak, Binnaz, *Islam and Political Development in Turkey* (Leiden, 1981); Georgeon, François, *Abdulhamit II. Le sultan calife* (Paris, 2003); Karpat, Kemal H. (ed.), *Ottoman Past and Today's Turkey* (Leiden, 2000); Yavuz, Hakan, *Islamic Political Identity in Turkey* (Oxford, 2003); Poulton, Hugh, *Top Hat, Grey Wolf and Crescent. Turkish Nationalism and the Turkish Republic* (London, 1997); Seufert, Günter, *Politischer Islam in der Türkei. Islamismus als symbolische Repräsentation einer sich moderniesirenden muslimischen Gesellschaft* (Stuttgart, 1997); Bora, Tanıl, *Türk Sağının Üç Hali* (Istanbul, 1999); Shankland, David, *Islam and Society in Turkey* (Beverley, 1999); Davison, Andrew, *Secularism and Revivalism. A Hermeneutic Reconsideration* (New

Haven, 1998); Fortna, Benjamin, *Imperial Classroom. Islam, the State and Education in the Late Ottoman Empire* (Oxford, 2002).

2. Poulton, *Top Hat, Grey Wolf and Crescent*, p. 59.

3. Whether we can actually say, as Yavuz does, that the state promoted Muslim *nationalism* is debatable, because the Hamidian regime promoted loyalty to the state and to the sovereign, not to any nation (cf. Yavuz, *Islamic Political Identity*, p. 44).

4. Keyder, Çağlar, *State and Class in Turkey. A Study in Capitalist Development* (London, 1987), chapters 2–3.

5. Hanioğlu, M. Şükrü, *The Young Turks in Opposition* (Oxford, 1995), chapter 9.

6. Kitromilidis, Paschalis, 'The Greek–Turkish population exchange', in: Zürcher, Erik Jan (ed.), *Philologiae et Historiae Turcicae Fundamenta IV. History of Turkey in the Twentieth Century* (Berlin, 2008); Ladas, Stephen, *The Exchange of Minorities: Bulgaria, Greece and Turkey* (New York, 1932).

7. Davison, *Secularism*, p. 139. In Davison' s view the interpretations that emphasize the control element, such as those offered by Binnaz Toprak, Çağlar Keyder and Şerif Mardin, are one-sided and should be balanced with an appreciation of the degree to which separation of the religious and the political was achieved.

8. See: Soymen, M., *Cep İlmihali* (Ankara, 2000), pp. 115–17.

9. Poulton, *Top Hat, Grey Wolf and Crescent*, p. 184.

21. Turning Points and Missed Opportunities in the Modern History of Turkey: Where Could Things Have Gone Differently?

* This is the text of a lecture given to history students of Middle East Technical University at the Netherlands Institute for Higher Education in Ankara in November 2007.

1. Cf. Part I of this collection.

2. Devereux, Robert, *The First Ottoman Constitutional Period: A Study of the Midhat Constitution and Parliament* (Baltimore: The Johns Hopkins University Press, 1964).

Bibliography of Erik J. Zürcher

'Het buurtcafé', *Hollands Maandblad* 338 (1976), pp. 25–28. [Translation of: Abasıyanık, Sait Faik, *Mahalle Kahvesi*].

'Atatürk and the start of the national resistance movement', *Anatolica* 8 (1981), pp. 99–113.

The Unionist Factor. The Role of the Committee of Union and Progress in the Turkish National Movement (1905–1926) (Leiden: Brill, 1984), 201 p. [Translated as: *Millî Mücadelede İttihatçılık*, (Istanbul: Bağlam, 1987), 336 p.; second Turkish edition 1995, third edition (at İletişim, Istanbul) 2003].

'La théorie du "langage-soleil" et sa place dans la reforme du langue turque,' in Auroux, Sylvain (ed.), *La linguistique fantastique* (Paris: Denoel, 1984), pp. 83–91. (Translated as 'Güneş-dil teorisi ve Türk dil reformundaki yeri,' *Birikim*, 2 (1989), pp. 52–55.

Een Lange Zomer in Istanbul (Amsterdam: Meulenhoff, 1984), 179 p. [Translation of: Gürsel, Nedim, *Uzun Sürmüş bir Yaz*].

Review of: Landau, Jacob, 'Panturkism in Turkey', *Tijdschrift voor Geschiedenis* 97/4 (1984), pp. 643–4.

'Bepalende factoren in de positie van de Christenen in Turkije', *Christendemokratische Verkenningen* 6 (1985), pp. 255–9.

De Huwelijksfirma (Weesp: Het Wereldvenster, 1985), 81 p. [Translation of Yıldız, Bekir, *Evlilik Şirketi*].

Review of: Quataert, Donald, *Social Disintegration and Popular Resistance in the Ottoman Empire 1881–1908*, *Bibliotheca Orientalis* 42/3–4 (1985), pp. 440–1.

Reviews of: Hale, William, *The Political and Economic Development of Modern Turkey* and of Kazancıgil, Alil and Özbudun, Ergun (ed.), *Atatürk Founder of a Modern State*, *Anatolica* 12 (1985), 174–5.

De Moderne Geschiedenis van Turkije, Den Haag: Turks Publicatie- en Informatiecentrum, 1986, 33 p.

De Konijnen van de Commandant, (Amsterdam: Meulenhoff, 1986), 175 p. [Translation of: Gürsel, Nedim, *Komutanın Tavşanları*].

'Achttien gedichten van Orhan Veli Kanık', *Hollands Maandblad* 466 (1986), pp. 24–30 [Translation of 18 poems by Orhan Veli Kanık].

'Young Turk Memoirs as a Historical Source', *Middle Eastern Studies* 22/4 (1986), pp. 561–70 [translated with additions as: 'Kâzim Karabekir ve İstiklâl Harbimiz kitabı', *Tarih ve Toplum* 38 (1986), 339–43].

Review of: Oehrig, Ottmar, *Die Türkei im Spannungsfeld extremer Ideologien*, *Welt des Islams* 26, pp. 227–9.

'Turkije na de Eerste Wereldoorlog. De demografische en economische aspecten,' *Verleden Tijdschrift*, 1/2 (1987), pp. 16–18.

Review of: Landau, Jacob, *Tekin Alp, Turkish Patriot*, *Middle Eastern Studies* 23/1 (1987), pp. 126–7.

'Atatürk ve Muhalefet. 1924'teki Çok Partili Demokrasi', *Tarih ve Toplum*, 8/1 (1988), pp. 16–19 [translated as: 'Atatürk and Multi-party Democracy in 1924', in: *1. Uluslararası Atatürk Sempozyumu (21–23 Eylül 1987)* (Ankara: Atatürk Kültür, Dil ve Tarih Yüksek Kurumu, 1994), pp. 729–36].

'Het huis van de oorlog. Europa in de ogen der Turken', *Fibula*, 29/1 (1988), pp. 22–30.

'Welingelichte kringen? De berichtgeving van de Nederlandse Ambassade in Istanbul tijdens de Eerste Wereldoorlog', *Sharqiyyât* 1/1 (1988), pp. 61–79.

'De tunnel' in: *Denderende Verhalen. Per Trein Door de Wereldliteratuur* (Amsterdam: Meulenhoff, 1988), pp. 145–54 [translation of Nedim Gürsel, *Tünel*].

Ik Luister Naar Istanbul. Zes moderne Turkse dichters (Amsterdam: Meulenhoff/ Poetry International, 1988), 75 p.

Niks Politie Asjeblief (Baarn: Ambo, 1988), 106 p. [translation of: Ören, Aras, *Bitte Nix Polizei*].

Review of: McCarthy, Justin, *Muslims and Minorities. The Population of Ottoman Anatolia at the End of the Empire*, *Bibliotheca Orientalis* 15/5–6 (1988), pp. 748–50.

'The characteristics and significance of the Progressive Republican Party (1924–1925)', in *Acts of the Second International Meeting on Modern Ottoman Studies and the Turkish Republic* (Leiden: NINO, 1989), pp. 97–106.

De Eerste Vrouw (Amsterdam: Meulenhoff, 1989), 118 p. [translation of:Gürsel, Nedim, *İlk Kadın*].

Review of: Keyder, Cağlar, *State and Class in Turkey. A Study in Capitalist Development*, *Sharqiyyat* 1/3 (1989), pp. 253–7.

'Terakkiperver Cumhuriyet Fırkası', *Sosyalizm ve Toplumsal Mücadeleler Ansiklopedisi*, vol. 6 (Istanbul: İletişim, 1990), pp. 1890–1.

'The influence of the French Radical Party on Young Turk political thinking', in Turan, İlter and Bacqué-Grammont, Jean-Jacques (ed.), *De la révolution française à la Turquie d'Atatürk* (Istanbul: Isis, 1990), pp. 197–203.

Political Opposition in the Early Turkish Republic. The Progressive Republican Party (1924–1925) (Leiden: Brill, 1991), 177 p. [translated as: *Terakkiperver Cumhuriyet Fırkası*, (Istanbul: Bağlam, 1991), 205 p.].

'The last phase in the history of the committee of union and progress (1923–1924)', in: *Actes de la première rencontre internationale sur l'Empire Ottoman et la Turquie moderne* (Istanbul: Isis, 1991), pp. 369–77.

'The Ottoman Empire and the Turkish Republic: an attempt at a new periodisation', *Welt des Islams* 32/2 (1992), pp. 237–53.

'Murat V,' *Encyclopaedia of Islam. New Edition*, vol. 7 (Leiden: Brill, 1992), p. 599.

'De politicus als geschiedschrijver, de historicus in de politiek', in De Moor, Ed (ed.), *Elf Wijzen van Interpreteren. Essays Over Het Lezen van Teksten Uit Het Islamitisch Cultuurgebied* (Nijmegen: Mandara, 1992), pp. 127–37.

Review of: Olson, Robert, *The Emergence of Kurdish Nationalism and the Sheikh Sait Rebellion 1880–1925, Welt des Islams* 32/1 (1992), pp. 154–7.

Review of: Frutiger, Uarda, *Ärtztin im Orient auch wenn's dem Sultan nicht gefällt. Josephina Th. Zürcher (1866–1932), Bibiotheca Orientalis* 49/1-2 (1992), pp. 280–1.

Review of: Landau, Jacob, *The Politics of Panislam. Ideology and Organization, Middle Eastern Studies* 27/4 (1992), pp. 699–700.

Turkey: a Modern History (London: I.B.Tauris, 1993, second revised edition: London, 1997, 1998; third fully revised and annotated edition: London, 2003), 385 p. [translated into Dutch as: *Een Geschiedenis van Het Moderne Turkije* (Nijmegen: SUN, 1995), 446 p.; second revised and annotated Dutch edition: Amsterdam, 2006, 507 p.; translated into Turkish as *Modernleşen Turkiye'nin Tarihi* (Istanbul: Iletisim, 1995), 523 p. (22 editions 1997–2008); Translated into Greek as *Synchroni Historia tis Tourkias* (Athens: Alexandreia, 2004), 508 p.; translated into Ivrit as *Turkia Historia Modernit* (Tel-Aviv: Tel-Aviv University Press, 2005), 456 p.; translated into Bahasa Indonesia as *Sejarah modern Turki* (Jakarta: Gramedia, 2006), 499 p.; translated into Italian as *Storia della Turchia dalla fine dell'Impero Ottomano ai giorni nostri* (Rome: Donzelli, 2007), 458 p.].

'De erfenis van Atatürk', *Geografie Educatief* 2/1 (1993), pp. 29–32.

'Turkije', *Europa Periodiek* 10/3 (1993), p. 12.

'Turkije en Europa na de Koude Oorlog', *Internationale Spectator* 47/9 (1993), pp. 497–501.

Review of: Schmidt, Jan, *Through the Legation Window, Wiener Zeitschrift für die Kunde des Morgenlandes* 83 (1993), pp. 376–9.

'Gelukkig is Hij Die Zich "Turk" noemt.'. Nationale Identiteit en Persoonlijkheidscultus in Turkije* (Amsterdam: IISG, 1994), 38 p.

Ed. with Tunçay, Mete, *Socialism and Nationalism in the Ottoman Empire 1876–1923* (London: I.B.Tauris, 1994), 222 p. [translated as: *Osmanli Imparatorluğunda Sosyalizm ve Milliyetçilik (1876–1923)* (Istanbul: Iletisim, 1995), 264 p.].

'Niyâzî Bey, Ahmed', *Encyclopaedia of Islam. New Edition*, vol. 8 (Leiden: Brill, 1994), pp. 65–6.

'Reshîd Pasha, Mustafâ', *Encyclopaedia of Islam. New Edition*, vol. 8 (Leiden: Brill, 1994), pp. 484–6.

'Sabâh al-Dîn', *Encyclopaedia of Islam. New Edition*, vol. 8 (Leiden: Brill, 1994), p. 669.

'Sâdik Rif'ât Pasha', *Encyclopaedia of Islam. New Edition*, vol. 8 (Leiden: Brill, 1994), p. 726.

Review of: Arai, Masami, *Turkish Nationalism in the Young Turk Era, Bibliotheca Orientalis*, 51/1-2 (1994), pp. 208–10.

Review of: Clayer, Nathalie et al., *Presse turque et presse de Turquie, Wiener Zeitschrift für die Kunde des Morgenlandes* 84 (1994), pp. 338–40.

Review of: Debus, Esther, *Sebilürreşad. Eine vergleichende Untersuchung zur isla-mischen Opposition der vor- und nach-kemalistischen Ära, Welt des Islams* 34 (1994), pp. 108–10.

Review of: Quataert, Donald, *Ottoman Manufacturing in the Age of the Industrial Revolution, British Journal of Middle Eastern Studies* 21/2 (1994), pp. 260–1.

Ed. with Quataert, Donald, *Workers and Working Class in the Ottoman Empire 1840–1950* (London, I.B.Tauris, 1995), 208 p. [translated as: *Osmanlıdan Cumhuriyet Türkiyesine Kadar İşçiler* (Istanbul: İletişim, 1998), 242 p.].

'De identiteitscrisis van Turkije', *Soera* 3/2 (1995), pp. 4–7.

'Osmaanse Joden, Joodse Turken', in Cohen, Julie Marthe and Zwiep, Irene (ed.), *Joden in de Wereld van de Islam* (Amsterdam: Bulaaq, 1995), pp. 129–46.

Review of: Macfie, A.L., *Atatürk, Tijdschrift voor Geschiedenis*, 108 (1995), pp. 455–6.

Review of: Prätor, Sabine, *Der arabische Faktor in der Jungtürkischen Politik, Wiener Zeitschrift für die Kunde des Morgenlandes* 85 (1995), pp. 386–7.

Review of: Shaw, Stanford J., *Turkey and the Holocaust, The Middle East Journal* 49/4 (1995), pp. 681–2.

'Little Mehmet in the desert: the war experience of the Ottoman soldier', in Liddle, Peter H. and Cecil Hugh (ed.), *Facing Armageddon. The First World War Experienced* (London: Leo Cooper/Pen and Sword, 1996), pp. 230–41.

'Sheref, `Abd al–Rahmân', *Encyclopaedia of Islam. New Edition*, vol. 9, (Leiden: Brill, 1996), p. 417

'Shükrü Bey', *Encyclopaedia of Islam. New Edition*, vol. 9, (Leiden: Brill), p. 499.

'Between death and desertion. The experience of the Ottoman soldier in World War I,' *Turcica* 28 (1996), pp. 235–58.

'De ongetemde staat', *Wordt Vervolgd* 29/10 (1996), pp. 12–14.

'Turkey's policy towards central Asia: pragmatism versus ideology', in *1er Colloque Universitaire Amsterdam/Tunis* (Amsterdam: Universiteit van Amsterdam, 1995/6), pp. 39–45.

'The Ides of April. A fundamentalist uprising in Istanbul in 1909?' in Van Dijk, C. and De Groot, A.H. (ed.), *State and Islam* (Leiden: CNWS, 1996), pp. 64–76.

Review of: Ahmad, Feroz, *The Making of Modern Turkey, Bibliotheca Orientalis*, LIII, 1–2, pp. 290–2.

Reviews of: Kafadar, Cemal, *Between Two Worlds*, Faroqhi, Suraya, *Kultur und Alltag im Osmanischen Reich* and İslamoğlu-İnan, Huri, *State and Peasant in the Ottoman Empire, Tijdschrift voor Geschiedenis*, 109, pp. 531–3.

'Islam en politiek: Turkije', in Driessen, Henk (ed.), *Het Huis Van de Islam* (Nijmegen: SUN, 1997), pp. 361–9.

Review of: Brown, L. Carl (ed.), *Imperial Legacy. The Ottoman Imprint on the Balkans and the Middle East, British Journal of Middle Eastern Studies* 24/2 (1997), pp. 274–5.

'Muslim nationalism: the missing link in the genesis of modern Turkey', *Hamizrah Hehadash. The New East* 39 (1998), pp. 67–83 [in Hebrew].

'Turkije: ouwe vrijster of begeerlijke bruid?' *Internationale Spectator* 52/5 (1998), pp. 273–6.

'Turkije – een erfenis van nomadisme, vlucht en migratie', in Heins, J.J. and Kox. H.L.M. (ed.), *Mensen op Drift. Migratie en Ontwikkeling* (Amsterdam: VU, 1998), pp. 37–45.

With Lucassen, Jan, 'Conscription and resistance: the historical context', *International Review of Social History* 43/3 (1998), pp. 405–19.

'The Ottoman conscription system in theory and practice, 1844–1918', *International Review of Social History* 43/3 (1998), pp. 437–49.

Opkomst en Ondergang van Het 'Moderne' Turkije (Leiden: CNWS, 1998), 23 p.

'The Ottoman Empire and the armistice of Mudros', in Cecil, Hugh Cecil and Liddle, Peter H. (ed.), *At the Eleventh Hour. Reflections, Hopes and Anxieties at the Closing of the Great War, 1918* (London: Leo Cooper, 1998), pp. 266–75.

Review of: Neumann, Christoph, *Das indirekte Argument: ein Plädoyer für die Tanzimat Vermittels der Historie: die geschichtliche Bedeutung von Ahmed Cevdet Pashas Ta`rih, Bibliotheca Orientalis* LV 1–2 (1998), pp. 308–10.

Review of: Landau, Jacob, *Pan-Turkism. From Irredentism to Coopera- tion, British Journal of Middle Eastern Studies*, 25/1 (1998), pp. 173–4.

Ed., *Arming the State: Military Conscription in the Middle East and Central Asia* (London: I.B.Tauris, 1999), 168 p. [translated as: *Devletin silâhlanması. Ortadoğu'da ve Orta Asya'da Zorunlu Askerlik (1775–1925)* (Istanbul: Bilgi, 2003), 200 p].

'The vocabulary of Muslim nationalism', *International Journal of the Sociology of Language*, 137 (1999), pp. 81–92.

'Kosovo revisited. Sultan Reshad's Macedonian journey in 1911,' *Middle Eastern Studies* 35/4 (1999), pp. 26–39.

'The borders of the republic reconsidered', *Bilanço 1923/1998. International Conference on History of the Turkish Republic a Reassessment. Volume I: Politics – Culture – International Relations* (Ankara: TUBA, 1999), pp. 53–9.

'Terakkiperver Djumhuriyyet Firkasi', *Encyclopaedia of Islam. New Edition,* vol. 10 (Leiden: Brill, 2000), pp. 417–18.

'Turkey, Republic of,' *Encyclopaedia of Islam. New Edition,* vol. 10 (Leiden: Brill, 2000), pp. 693–7.

'Young Turks, Ottoman Muslims and Turkish nationalists: identity politics 1908–1938', in Karpat, Kemal H. (ed.), *Ottoman Past and Today's Turkey* (Leiden: Brill, 2000), pp. 150–79.

'The core terminology of Kemalism: *mefkure, millî, muasir, medenî*', in Georgeon, François (ed.), *Les mots de politique de l'Empire Ottoman a la Turquie kemal- iste* (Paris: EHESS/ESA 8032 (CNRS), 2000), pp. 55–64.

Review of: Mango, Andrew, *Atatürk, Middle Eastern Studies* 36/3 (2000), pp. 253–7.

Review article: 'The Ottoman Twilight', reviews of: Kleinert, Claudia, *Die Revision der Historiographie des Osmanischen Reiches am Beispiel von Abdülhamid* II; Deringil, Selim, *The Well-protected Domains*, Özcan, Azmi, *Indian Muslims, the Ottomans and Britain (1877–1924)*; Kayalı, Hasan, *Arabs and Young Turks*; Poulton, Hugh, *Top Hat, Grey Wolf and Crescent*; Macfie, A.L., *The End of the Ottoman Empire, British Journal of Middle East Studies* 27/2 (2000), pp. 201–7.

Ed. with Van Schendel, Willem, *Identity Politics in Central Asia and the Muslim world: Nationalism, Ethnicity and Labour in the 20th Century* (London: I.B. Tauris, 2001), 235 p. [translated as: *Orta Asya ve İslam Dünyasında Kimlik Politikaları. 20. Yüzyılda Milliyetçilik, Etnisite ve Emek* (Istanbul: İletişim, 2004), 296 p.].

With Willem van Schendel, 'Introduction: opting out, opting in, exclusion and assimilation: States and nations in the twentieth century', in Van Schendel, Willem and Zürcher, Erik Jan (ed.), *Identity Politics in Central Asia and the Muslim World: Nationalism, Ethnicity and Labour in the 20th Century* (London: I.B.Tauris, 2001), pp. 1–12.

'"Fundamentalism" as an exclusionary device in Kemalist Turkish nationalism', in Van Schendel, Willem and Zürcher, Erik Jan (ed.), *Identity Politics in Central Asia and the Muslim World: Nationalism, Ethnicity and Labour in the 20th Century* (London: I.B.Tauris, 2001), pp. 209–22.

'Yeni Othmanlilar', *Encyclopaedia of Islam. New Edition*, vol. 11 (Leiden: Brill, 2002), pp. 331–2.

'Two young Ottomanists discover Kemalist Turkey. The travel diaries of Robert Anhegger and Andreas Tietze', *Journal of Turkish Studies*, 26/1 (2002), pp. 359–69.

'Ottoman labour battalions in World War I', in Kieser, Hans-Lukas and Schaller, Dominik J. (ed.), *Der Völkermord an den Armeniern und die Shoah. The Armenian Genocide and the Shoah* (Zürich: Chronos, 2002), pp. 187–96.

'Kemalist düşüncenin Osmanlı kaynakları', in Bora, T. (ed.), *Modern Türkiyede Siyasi Düşünce: 2. Kemalizm* (Istanbul: Iletişim), pp. 44–55 [also published as: 'Ottoman sources of Kemalist thought', in Özdalga, Elisabeth (ed.), *Late Ottoman Society. The Intellectual Legacy* (London: Routledge, 2005), pp. 14–27].

Review of: Criss, Nur Bilge, *Istanbul under Allied Occupation, 1918–1923* in *Die Welt des Islams/International Journal for the Study of Modern Islam*, 42 (2002), pp. 124–6.

'Yüzellilikler (the 150 Undesirables)', *Encyclopaedia of Islam. New Edition*, vol. 11 (Leiden: Brill, 2002), p. 363.

'Terakkiperver Cumhuriyet Fırkası ve siyasal muhafazakârlık', in Çiğdem, Ahmet (ed.), *Muhafazakarlık* [= *Modern Türkiye'de siyasi düşünce* vol. 5] (Istanbul: İletişim, 2003), pp. 40–53.

'Enver Pascha, Ismail', in Hirschfeld, Gerhard et al. (ed.), *Enzyklopädie Erster Weltkrieg* (Paderborn-München-Wenen-Zürich: Ferdinand Schöningh, 2003), pp. 458–9.

'Talât Pascha, Mehmed', in Hirschfeld, Gerhard et al. (ed.), *Enzyklopädie Erster Weltkrieg*, (Paderborn-München-Wenen-Zürich: Ferdinand Schöningh, 2003), p. 917.

'Sykes-Picot Abkommen', in Hirschfeld, Gerhard et al. (ed.), *Enzyklopädie Erster Weltkrieg*, (Paderborn-München-Wenen-Zürich: Ferdinand Schöningh, 2003), p. 916.

'Osmanisches Reich', in Hirschfeld, Gerhard et al. (ed.), *Enzyklopädie Erster Weltkrieg*, (Paderborn-München-Wenen-Zürich: Ferdinand Schöningh, 2003), pp. 758–62.

'The Young Turks – Children of the borderlands?' *International Journal of Turkish Studies* 9/1–2 (2003), pp. 275–86 [translated as: 'I "Giovanni Turchi": Figli delle terre di frontiera?', *Rivista Storica Italiana* 115/2 (2003), pp. 543–55.

'Het Britse leger onderdrukte Irakese opstand met gifgas', *Historisch Nieuwsblad* 3/2003, pp. 40–1.

'Testland Turkije', *Vrij Nederland* 9/2003, pp. 47–9.

'Ver van huis: gedichten van Roni Margulies', in Sayed-Gohrab, Ashgar and Ter Haar, Johan (ed.), *'De band met. U, mijn vriend, verbreek ik niet'. Liber amicorum voor Kamil Banak* (Leiden: TCIMO, 2003), pp. 133–8 [translation of poems by Roni Margulies].

'Op de bazaar van de kennisverkopers', *Transfer* 10/9 (2003), p. 11.

Review of: Jung, Dietrich and Piccolo, Wolfgango, *Turkey at the Crossroads. Ottoman Legacies and a Greater Middle East, International Journal of Turkish Studies* 9/1–2 (2003), pp. 328–30.

'Zoeken naar de breuklijn. Een verkenning naar de rol van de Turkse Islam in de toetreding van Turkije tot de Europese Unie in het licht van de "botsing der beschavingen"' in WRR, *De Europese Unie, Turkije en de Islam* (Amsterdam: Amsterdam University Press, 2004), pp.79–170 [translated as 'Searching for the Fault Line', in WRR, *The European Union, Turkey and Islam* (Amsterdam University Press, 2004), pp. 83–174).

With Atabaki, Touraj, 'Introduction', in Atabaki, Touraj and Zürcher, Erik Jan (ed.), *Men of Order. Authoritarian Modernization under Atatürk and Reza Shah* (London: I.B.Tauris, 2004), pp. 1–12.

'Institution building in the Kemalist republic: the role of the People's Party', in Atabaki, Touraj and Zürcher, Erik Jan (ed.), *Men of Order. Authoritarian Modernization under Atatürk and Reza Shah* (London: I.B.Tauris, 2004), pp. 98–112.

Ed. with Atabaki, Touraj, *Men of Order. Authoritarian Modernization under Atatürk and Reza Shah* (London: I.B.Tauris, 2004), 286 p.

'Turkije en de EU: kansen en risico's', *Atlantisch Perspectief* 28/3 (2004), pp. 4–8.

Ed., *İmparatorluktan Cumhuriyete Türkiye'de Etnik Çatışma* (Istanbul: İletişim, 2005), 175 p. [second edition 2005, third edition 2006].

'Giriş: demografi mühendisliği ve modern Türkiye'nin doğuşu', in: Zürcher, Erik Jan (ed.), *İmparatorluktan Cumhuriyete Türkiye'de Etnik Çatışma* (Istanbul: İletişim, 2005), pp. 9–17.

Savaş, Devrim ve Uluslaşma. Türkiye Tarihinde Geçiş Dönemi (1908–1928) (Istanbul Bilgi Universitesi, 2005), 331 p.

Ed., 'Focus on Turkey', *European Review* 13/3 (2005), pp. 374–494.

'Introduction to the "Focus on Turkey"', *European Review* 13/3 (2005), pp. 377–8.

'How Europeans adopted Anatolia and discovered Turkey', *European Review* 13/3 (2005), pp. 379–94.

'De Turkse paradox. Religie in dienst van de seculiere staat', in Ten Hooven, Marcel and De Wit, Theo (ed.), *Ongewenste Goden. De Publieke Rol van Religie in Nederland* (Amsterdam: SUN, 2006), pp. 162–73.

'The Ottoman legacy of the Kemalist republic', in Atabaki, Touraj (ed.), *The State and the Subaltern. Modernization, Society and the State in Turkey and Iran* (London: I.B.Tauris, 2007), pp. 95–110.

'Region or discipline? The debate about area studies', in In 't Groen, Adriaan et al. (ed.), *Knowledge in Ferment. Dilemmas in Science, Scholarship and Society* (Leiden: Leiden University Press, 2007), pp. 243–56.

'Griechisch-orthodoxe und muslimische Flüchtlinge und Deportierte in Griechenland und der Türkei seit 1912', in Bade, Klaus J. et al. (ed.), *Enzyklopädie Migration in Europa vom 17. Jahrhundert bis zur Gegenwart* (Paderborn/ München: Ferdinand Schöningh/Wilhelm Fink, 2007), pp. 623–7.

'Yıkımın ve yenilenmenin mimarları: Kemalist jenerasyona ve Jön Türklere dair bir grup biyografisi denemesi', in Alkan, Mehmet Ö., Bora, Tanıl and Koraltürk, Murat (ed.), *Mete Tunçay'a Armağan* (Istanbul: İletişim, 2007), pp. 539–72.

'Turkije' s visie op Europa: voorbeeld en vijand', *Leidraad:* 8/2007, pp. 10–15.

'Turkish secularism in a European context', in Goren, Nimrod and Nachmani, Amikam (ed.), *The Importance of Being European. Turkey, the EU and the Middle East* (Jerusalem: The Hebrew University, 2007), pp. 131–40.

'Hizmet etmeyi başka biçimlerle reddetmek: Osmanlı İmparatorluğunun son dönemlerinde asker kaçaklığı', in Heval Çınar, Özgün and Üsterci, Coşkun (ed.), *Çarklardaki Kum: Vicdani Red* (Istanbul: İletişim, 2008), pp. 59–68.

'Drie gedichten van Roni Margulies', in *Poetry International 2008. Poezie van dichters uit de hele wereld* (Amsterdam: De Arbeiderspers, 2008), pp. 67–70 [translation of three poems by Roni Margulies].

'A tentativa de liderança fracassada da Turquia através da integração regional', in Wieseborn, Marianne and Griffiths, Richard T. (eds), *Progressos de Integração Regional e Cooperação Intercontinental desde 1989* (Rio Grande do Sul: UFRGS, 2008), pp. 131–42.

'The Turkish perception of Europe. Example and enemy', in Wintle, Michael (ed.), *Imagining Europe. Europe and European Civilisation as Seen from Its Margins and by the Rest of the World in the Nineteenth and Twentieth Centuries* (Bruxelles e.a: Peter Lang, 2008), pp. 93–104.

Ed., *Turkey in the Twentieth Century. La Turquie au vingtième siècle* (Berlin: Klaus Schwarz, 2008), 688 p. [= *Philologiae at Historiae Turcicae Fundamenta II*].

'From empire to republic – Problems of transition, continuity and change', in Zürcher, Erik Jan (ed.), *Turkey in the Twentieth Century. La Turquie au vingtième siècle* (Berlin: Klaus Schwarz, 2008), pp. 15–30.

'Refusing to serve by other means: desertion in the late OttomanEmpire', in: Özgür Heval Çınar and Coşkun Üsterci (ed.), *Conscientious Objection. Resisting Militarized Society* (London: Zed, 2009), pp. 45–52.

'The late Ottoman Empire as a laboratory of demographic engineering', *Il Mestiere di Storico* 1 (2009), 7–18 [published by Viella (Rome) for SISSCO].

Review of: Geoff R. Berridge, *Gerald Fitzmaurice (1865–1939). Chief Dragoman of the British Embassy in Constantinople.* Leiden: Martinus Nijhoff, 2007, in: *International Journal of Turkish Studies* 15/1–2 (2009), pp. 165–8.

Index